Django 2 Web Development Cookbook
Third Edition

100 practical recipes on building scalable Python web apps
with Django 2

Jake Kronika
Aidas Bendoraitis

BIRMINGHAM - MUMBAI

Django 2 Web Development Cookbook
Third Edition

Commissioning Editor: Kunal Chaudhari
Acquisition Editor: Trusha Shriyan
Content Development Editor: Flavian Vaz
Technical Editor: Leena Patil
Copy Editor: Safis Editing
Project Coordinator: Sheejal Shah
Proofreader: Safis Editing
Indexer: Aishwarya Gangawane
Graphics: Alishon Mendonsa
Production Coordinator: Shantanu Zagade

First published: October 2014
Second edition: January 2016
Third edition: October 2018

Production reference: 1301018

Published by Packt Publishing Ltd.
Livery Place
35 Livery Street
Birmingham
B3 2PB, UK.

ISBN 978-1-78883-768-2

www.packtpub.com

To my loving wife, Veronica, for being everything our family needs and more.

To my parents, Dianne and Jim, and my siblings, Jessica and David, for always pushing me to be better than I thought I could be.

– Jake Kronika

`mapt.io`

Mapt is an online digital library that gives you full access to over 5,000 books and videos, as well as industry leading tools to help you plan your personal development and advance your career. For more information, please visit our website.

Why subscribe?

- Spend less time learning and more time coding with practical eBooks and Videos from over 4,000 industry professionals

- Improve your learning with Skill Plans built especially for you

- Get a free eBook or video every month

- Mapt is fully searchable

- Copy and paste, print, and bookmark content

Packt.com

Did you know that Packt offers eBook versions of every book published, with PDF and ePub files available? You can upgrade to the eBook version at `www.packt.com` and as a print book customer, you are entitled to a discount on the eBook copy. Get in touch with us at `customercare@packtpub.com` for more details.

At `www.packt.com`, you can also read a collection of free technical articles, sign up for a range of free newsletters, and receive exclusive discounts and offers on Packt books and eBooks.

Contributors

About the authors

Jake Kronika, a senior software engineer with nearly 25 years' experience, has been working with Python since 2005, and Django since 2007. Evolving alongside the web development space, his skillset encompasses HTML5, CSS3, and ECMAScript 6 on the frontend, plus Python, Django, Ruby on Rails, Node.js, and much more besides on the server side.

Currently a senior software engineer and development team lead, he collaborates with skilled designers, business stakeholders, and developers around the world to architect robust web applications. In his spare time, he also provides full-spectrum web services as sole proprietor of Gridline Design and Development.

Prior to this book, he has acted as a technical reviewer for several other Packt titles.

Aidas Bendoraitis has been professionally working with web technologies for over a decade. Over the last 10 years at a Berlin-based company, studio 38 pure communication GmbH, together with a creative team, he has developed a number of small and large-scale Django projects, mostly in the cultural area. At the moment he is also working as software architect at a London-based mobile startup, Hype.

Aidas regularly attends the meetups of the Django User Group in Berlin, occasionally visits Django and Python conferences, and writes a blog about Django.

I would like to thank my wife, Sofja, for her support and patience while writing this book during late evenings and weekends. Also I would like to thank studio 38 pure communication GmbH and namely Reinhard Knobelspies for introducing Django to me 10 years ago. Finally, I would like to thank Vilnius University in Lithuania for teaching the main programming concepts, without which I wouldn't be working in the positions I currently have.

About the reviewer

Joe Jasinski has acquired over 15 years' experience in the IT industry, and has bachelor's and master's degrees in computer science from Illinois Wesleyan University and DePaul University respectively.

He led a team of talented programmers at Imaginary Landscape, where he spent 8 years developing web applications in Python, Django, and related technologies. In his free time, he is one of the organizers of the Chicago Python User Group (ChiPy). He currently works at one of the leading data and measurement companies, and is helping to build a data science platform established on Python, Spark, and Kubernetes.

Packt is searching for authors like you

If you're interested in becoming an author for Packt, please visit `authors.packtpub.com` and apply today. We have worked with thousands of developers and tech professionals, just like you, to help them share their insight with the global tech community. You can make a general application, apply for a specific hot topic that we are recruiting an author for, or submit your own idea.

Table of Contents

Preface

The Django framework was specifically engineered to help developers construct robust, powerful web applications quickly and efficiently. It takes much of the drudgery and repetition out of the process, solving questions such as project structure, database object-relational mapping, templating, form validation, sessions, authentication, security, cookie management, internationalization, basic administration, and an interface to access data from scripts. Django is built upon the Python programming language, which itself enforces clear and easy-to-read code. Besides the core framework, Django has been designed to enable developers to create third-party modules that can be used in conjunction with your own apps. Django has an established and vibrant community, where you can find source code, get help, and contribute.

Web Development with Django Cookbook, Third Edition, will guide you through every stage of the web development process with the Django 2.1 framework. We start with configuration and structuring of the project, either under a virtual environment or in Docker. Then, you will learn how to define the database structure with reusable components, and to manage it throughout the lifetime of your project. The book will move on to the forms and views used to enter and list the data. We proceed with responsive templates and JavaScript to augment the user experience. After this, you will customize the administration interface in order to streamline the workflow of website editors. From there, we shift focus to the stability and robustness of your project, helping to secure and optimize your apps. You will also learn how to integrate your own functionality into Django CMS. Next, we examine how to efficiently store and manipulate hierarchical structures. Then dawns the realization that collecting data from different sources and providing your own data to others in a range of formats is simpler than you might think. We will then introduce you to some tricks for programming and debugging your Django project code. Finally, you will see just a few of the available options for testing your code, and deploying your project to a remote dedicated server.

In contrast to many other Django books, which are concerned only with the framework itself, this book covers several important third-party modules that will equip you with the tools necessary for complete web development. Additionally, we provide examples using the Bootstrap frontend framework and the jQuery JavaScript library, both of which simplify the creation of advanced and complex user interfaces.

Who this book is for

If you have experience with Django, and are looking to enhance your skills, this book is for you. We have designed the content for intermediate and professional Django developers who are aiming to build robust projects that are multilingual, secure, responsive, and can scale over time.

What this book covers

Chapter 1, *Getting Started with Django 2.1*, illustrates the fundamental setup and configuration steps necessary for any Django project. We cover virtual environments and Docker, project settings across environments, and multiple version control systems.

Chapter 2, *Database Structure and Modeling*, explains how you can write reusable code for use in construction of your models. The first thing to define with new apps are the data models, which form the backbone of any project. Also, you will learn how to manage database schema changes and data manipulations using Django migrations.

Chapter 3, *Forms and Views*, looks first at common forms and ways to construct their markup effectively, and then the views to present dynamic forms, lists, and details of your data to users.

Chapter 4, *Templates and JavaScript*, covers practical examples of using templates and JavaScript together. We combine these facets, rendered templates present information to the user, and JavaScript provides crucial enhancements in modern websites for a rich user experience.

Chapter 5, *Customizing Template Filters and Tags*, reviews how to create and use your own template filters and tags. As you will see, the default Django template system can be extended to meet template developers' needs.

Chapter 6, *Model Administration*, explores the default Django administration interface, and guides you through extending it with your own functionality.

Chapter 7, *Security and Performance*, delves into several ways, both inherent to and external from Django, to secure and optimize your projects.

Chapter 8, *Django CMS*, deals with the best practices of using Django CMS, the most popular open source content management system made with and for Django, and then adapting it to your project's specific requirements.

Chapter 9, *Hierarchical Structures*, examines tree-like structure creation and manipulation in Django, and the benefits of incorporating the `django-mptt` or `treebeard` libraries into such workflows. This chapter shows you how to use both for the display and administration of hierarchies.

Chapter 10, *Importing and Exporting Data*, demonstrates the transfer of data from and to different formats, as well as its provision between various sources. Within this chapter, custom management commands are used for data import, and we utilize REST APIs for data export.

Chapter 11, *Bells and Whistles*, shows some additional snippets and tricks that are useful in everyday web development and debugging.

Chapter 12, *Testing and Deployment*, provides a few examples of how to test your project code, and gives options for automating repetitive tasks and deployment on a remote server.

To get the most out of this book

To develop with Django 2.1 using the examples in these pages, you will need the following:

- Python 3.6 or higher
- The Pillow library for image manipulation
- Either the MySQL database and the MySQLdb bindings, or the PostgreSQL database
- Docker Desktop or Docker Toolbox for complete system virtualization, or virtualenv to keep each project's Python modules separated
- Git or Subversion for version control

All other specific requirements are separately mentioned in each recipe.

Download the example code files

You can download the example code files for this book from your account at `www.packt.com`. If you purchased this book elsewhere, you can visit `www.packt.com/support` and register to have the files emailed directly to you.

You can download the code files by following these steps:

1. Log in or register at www.packt.com.
2. Select the **SUPPORT** tab.
3. Click on **Code Downloads & Errata**.
4. Enter the name of the book in the **Search** box and follow the onscreen instructions.

Once the file is downloaded, please make sure that you unzip or extract the folder using the latest version of:

- WinRAR/7-Zip for Windows
- Zipeg/iZip/UnRarX for Mac
- 7-Zip/PeaZip for Linux

The code bundle for the book is also hosted on GitHub at https://github.com/PacktPublishing/Django-2-Web-Development-Cookbook-Third-Edition. In case there's an update to the code, it will be updated on the existing GitHub repository.

We also have other code bundles from our rich catalog of books and videos available at https://github.com/PacktPublishing/. Check them out!

Download the color images

We also provide a PDF file that has color images of the screenshots/diagrams used in this book. You can download it here: https://www.packtpub.com/sites/default/files/downloads/9781788837682_ColorImages.pdf.

Conventions used

There are a number of text conventions used throughout this book.

CodeInText: Indicates code words in text, database table names, folder names, filenames, file extensions, pathnames, dummy URLs, user input, and Twitter handles. Here is an example: "For this recipe to work, you will need to have the contenttypes app installed."

A block of code is set as follows:

```
# settings.py or config/base.py
INSTALLED_APPS = (
    # ...
    'django.contrib.contenttypes',
)
```

When we wish to draw your attention to a particular part of a code block, the relevant lines or items are set in bold:

```
{% block meta_tags %}
    {{ block.super }}
    {{ idea.get_meta_tags }}
{% endblock %}
```

Any command-line input or output is written as follows:

```
(myproject_env)$ pip3 install "Django~=2.1.0"
```

Bold: Indicates a new term, an important word, or words that you see on screen. For example, words in menus or dialog boxes appear in the text like this. Here is an example: "We can see here that the upload-related action buttons are also replaced with a **Remove** button."

Warnings or important notes appear like this.

Tips and tricks appear like this.

Sections

In this book, you will find several headings that appear frequently (*Getting ready*, *How to do it...*, *How it works...*, *There's more...*, and *See also*).

To give clear instructions on how to complete a recipe, use these sections as follows:

Getting ready

This section tells you what to expect in the recipe and describes how to set up any software or any preliminary settings required for the recipe.

How to do it...

This section contains the steps required to follow the recipe.

How it works...

This section usually consists of a detailed explanation of what happened in the previous section.

There's more...

This section consists of additional information about the recipe in order to increase your knowledge of it.

See also

This section provides helpful links to other useful information for the recipe.

Get in touch

Feedback from our readers is always welcome.

General feedback: If you have questions about any aspect of this book, mention the book title in the subject of your message and email us at `customercare@packtpub.com`.

Errata: Although we have taken every care to ensure the accuracy of our content, mistakes do happen. If you have found a mistake in this book, we would be grateful if you would report this to us. Please visit `www.packt.com/submit-errata`, selecting your book, clicking on the Errata Submission Form link, and entering the details.

Piracy: If you come across any illegal copies of our works in any form on the internet, we would be grateful if you would provide us with the location address or website name. Please contact us at copyright@packt.com with a link to the material.

If you are interested in becoming an author: If there is a topic that you have expertise in and you are interested in either writing or contributing to a book, please visit authors.packtpub.com.

Reviews

Please leave a review. Once you have read and used this book, why not leave a review on the site that you purchased it from? Potential readers can then see and use your unbiased opinion to make purchase decisions, we at Packt can understand what you think about our products, and our authors can see your feedback on their book. Thank you!

For more information about Packt, please visit packt.com.

Getting Started with Django 2.1 **1**

In this chapter, we will cover the following topics:

- Working with a virtual environment
- Creating a virtual environment project file structure
- Working with Docker
- Creating a Docker project file structure
- Handling project dependencies with pip
- Including external dependencies in your project
- Configuring settings for development, testing, staging, and production environments
- Defining relative paths in the settings
- Creating and including local settings
- Setting up STATIC_URL dynamically for Subversion users
- Setting up STATIC_URL dynamically for Git users
- Setting UTF-8 as the default encoding for MySQL configuration
- Setting the Subversion ignore property
- Creating a Git ignore file
- Deleting Python-compiled files
- Respecting the import order in Python files
- Creating app configuration
- Defining overwritable app settings

Introduction

In this chapter, we will see a few good practices when starting a new project with Django 2.1 on Python 3. Some of the tricks introduced here are the best ways to deal with the project layout, settings, and configurations, whether using virtualenv or Docker to manage your project. However, for some tricks, you might want to find some alternatives online or in other books about Django. Feel free to evaluate and choose the best bits and pieces for yourself while digging deep into the Django world.

We are assuming that you are already familiar with the basics of Django, Subversion and Git version control, MySQL and PostgreSQL databases, and command-line usage. Also, we assume that you are using a Unix-based operating system, such as macOS X or Linux. It makes more sense to develop with Django on Unix-based platforms as the websites will most likely be published on a similar server, therefore, you can establish routines that work the same while developing as well as deploying. If you are locally working with Django on Windows, the routines are similar; however, they are not always the same.

Using Docker for your development environment, regardless of your local platform, can improve the portability of your applications through deployment, since the environment within the Docker container can be matched precisely to that of your deployment server. Finally, whether developing with Docker or not, we assume that you have the appropriate version control system and database server already installed to your local machine.

 You can download the example code files for all Packt books that you have purchased from your account at http://www.packtpub.com. If you purchased this book elsewhere, you can visit http://www.packtpub.com/support and register in order to have the files emailed directly to you.

Working with a virtual environment

It is very likely that you will develop multiple Django projects on your computer. Some modules, such as Python Imaging Library (or Pillow) and MySQLdb, can be installed once and then shared for all projects. Other modules, such as Django, third-party Python libraries, and Django apps, will need to be kept isolated from each other. The virtualenv tool is a utility that separates all of the Python projects in their own realms. In this recipe, we will see how to use it.

Getting ready

To manage Python packages, you will need **pip**. It is included in your Python installation if you are using Python 3.4+. If you are using another version of Python, install pip by executing the installation instructions at http://pip.readthedocs.org/en/stable/ installing/. Let's install the shared Python modules, **Pillow** and **MySQLdb**, and the **virtualenv** utility, using the following commands:

```
$ sudo pip3 install Pillow~=5.2.0
$ sudo pip3 install mysqlclient~=1.3.0
$ sudo pip3 install virtualenv~=16.0.0
```

How to do it...

Once you have your prerequisites installed, create a directory where all your Django projects will be stored, for example, virtualenvs under your home directory. Perform the following steps after creating the directory:

1. Go to the newly created directory and create a virtual environment that uses the shared system site packages:

    ```
    $ cd ~/virtualenvs
    $ mkdir myproject_env
    $ cd myproject_env
    $ virtualenv --system-site-packages .
    Using base prefix '/usr/local'
    New python executable in ./bin/python3.6
    Also creating executable in ./bin/python
    Installing setuptools, pip, wheel...done.
    ```

2. To use your newly created virtual environment, you need to execute the activation script in your current shell. This can be done with the following command:

    ```
    $ source bin/activate
    ```

3. Depending on the shell you are using, the source command may not be available. Another way to source a file is with the following command, which has the same result (note the space between the dot and bin):

    ```
    $ . bin/activate
    ```

4. You will see that the prompt of the command-line tool gets a prefix of the project name, as follows:

```
(myproject_env)$
```

5. To get out of the virtual environment, type the following command:

```
(myproject_env)$ deactivate
```

How it works...

When you create a virtual environment, a few specific directories (bin, include, and lib) are created in order to store a copy of the Python installation and some shared Python paths are defined. When the virtual environment is activated, whatever you have installed with pip or easy_install will be put in and used by the site packages of the virtual environment, and not the global site packages of your Python installation.

To install the latest Django 2.1.x in your virtual environment, type the following command:

```
(myproject_env)$ pip3 install "Django~=2.1.0"
```

See also

- The *Creating a virtual environment project file structure* recipe
- The *Working with Docker* recipe
- The *Deploying on Apache with mod_wsgi* recipe in Chapter 12, *Testing and Deployment*

Creating a virtual environment project file structure

A consistent file structure for your projects makes you well organized and more productive. When you have the basic workflow defined, you can get in the business logic more quickly and create awesome projects.

Getting ready

If you haven't done this yet, create a `virtualenvs` directory, where you will keep all your virtual environments (read about this in the *Working with a virtual environment* recipe). This can be created under your home directory.

Then, create a directory for your project's environment, for example, `myproject_env`. Start the virtual environment in it. We would suggest adding a `commands` directory for local shell scripts that are related to the project, a `db_backups` directory for database dumps, and a `project` directory for your Django project. Also, install Django in your virtual environment if you haven't already done so.

How to do it...

Follow these steps in order to create a file structure for your project:

1. With the virtual environment activated, go to the `project` directory and start a new Django project as follows:

    (myproject_env)$ django-admin.py startproject myproject

    For clarity, we will rename the newly created directory `django-myproject`. This is the directory that you will put under version control, therefore, it will have `.git`, `.svn`, or similar subdirectories.

2. In the `django-myproject` directory, create a `README.md` file to describe your project to the new developers. You can also put the pip requirements with the Django version and include other external dependencies (read about this in the *Handling project dependencies with pip* recipe).

3. The `django-myproject` directory will also contain the following:
    *   Your project's Python package, named `myproject`
    *   Django apps (we recommend having an app called `utils` for different functionalities that are shared throughout the project)
    *   A `locale` directory for your project translations if it is multilingual
    *   The `externals` directory for external dependencies that are included in this project if you decide not to use pip requirements

4. In your project's root, `django-myproject`. Create the following:
    - A `media` directory for project uploads
    - A `site_static` directory for project-specific static files
    - A `static` directory for collected static files
    - A `tmp` directory for the upload procedure
    - A `templates` directory for project templates

5. The `myproject` directory should contain your project settings in `settings.py` and a `config` directory (read about this in the *Configuring settings for development, testing, staging, and production environments* recipe), as well as the `urls.py` URL configuration.

6. In your `site_static` directory, create the `site` directory as a namespace for site-specific static files. Then, we will divide the static files between categorized subdirectories in it. For instance, see the following:
    - `scss` for Sass files (optional)
    - `css` for the generated minified Cascading Style Sheets (CSS)
    - `img` for styling images and logos
    - `js` for JavaScript and any third-party module combining all types of files, such as the TinyMCE rich-text editor

7. Besides the `site` directory, the `site_static` directory might also contain overwritten static directories of third-party apps, for example, `cms` overwriting static files from Django CMS. To generate the CSS files from Sass and minify the JavaScript files, you can use the CodeKit or Prepros applications with a graphical user interface.

8. Put your templates that are separated by the apps in your `templates` directory. If a template file represents a page (for example, `change_item.html` or `item_list.html`), then put it directly in the app's template directory. If the template is included in another template (for example, `similar_items.html`), put it in the `includes` subdirectory. Also, your `templates` directory can contain a directory called `utils` for globally reusable snippets, such as pagination and language chooser.

How it works...

The whole file structure for a complete project in a virtual environment will look similar to the following:

```
myproject_env/
├──── bin/
├──── commands/
├──── db_backups/
├──── include/
├──── lib/
└──── project/
      └──── django-myproject/
            ├──── externals/
            │     ├──── apps/
            │     └──── libs/
            ├──── locale/
            ├──── media/
            ├──── myapp1/
            ├──── myapp2/
            ├──── myproject/
            │     ├──── config/
            │     │     ├──── __init__.py
            │     │     ├──── base.py
            │     │     ├──── dev.py
            │     │     ├──── prod.py
            │     │     ├──── staging.py
            │     │     └──── test.py
            │     ├──── tmp/
            │     ├──── __init__.py
            │     ├──── settings.py
            │     ├──── settings.py.example
            │     ├──── urls.py
            │     └──── wsgi.py
            ├──── requirements/
            │     ├──── dev.txt
            │     ├──── prod.txt
            │     ├──── staging.txt
            │     └──── test.txt
            ├──── site_static/
            │     └──── site/
            │           ├──── css/
            │           ├──── img/
            │           └──── js/
            ├──── static/
            ├──── templates/
            │     ├──── admin/
            │     ├──── myapp1/
```

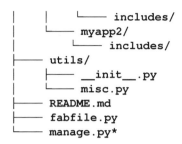

```
│       │        └──── includes/
│       └──── myapp2/
│                └──── includes/
├──── utils/
│       ├──── __init__.py
│       └──── misc.py
├──── README.md
├──── fabfile.py
└──── manage.py*
```

See also

- The *Handling project dependencies with pip* recipe
- The *Including external dependencies in your project* recipe
- The *Configuring settings for development, testing, staging, and production environments* recipe
- The *Deploying on Apache with mod_wsgi* recipe in `Chapter 12`, *Testing and Deployment*

Working with Docker

Sometimes more flexibility is needed across projects than simply to differentiate Python package versions. For example, it might be necessary to support an application on an existing version of Python itself, or perhaps MySQL, while simultaneously developing an update that relies upon a newer version of the software. Docker is capable of that level of isolation.

Docker is a system for creating configured, customized virtual machines called containers. It allows duplicating the setup of any production server precisely. In some cases, it is even possible to deploy pre-built containers directly to remote servers as well.

Getting ready

First, you will need to install the Docker Engine, following the instructions to be found at `https://www.docker.com/get-started`. This usually includes the Compose tool, which makes it simple to manage systems that require multiple containers, ideal for a fully isolated Django project. If needed, installation details for Compose are available at `https://docs.docker.com/compose/install/`.

How to do it...

With Docker and Compose installed, we will start by creating a
myproject_docker directory. Within this, create subdirectories named apps, config,
media, project, static, and templates. Then, we will create three configuration files:

- A requirements.txt file defining Python dependencies, under the config
  directory
- Dockerfile for the Django application container, in the myproject_docker
  root
- A docker-compose.yml file identifying all of the services making up the
  application environment, also in the myproject_docker root

The requirements.txt, which lives under the config subdirectory, is much the same as
if using a virtual environment (see the *Working with a virtual environment* recipe), though we
will include all dependencies here, not just those that differ from other projects. Because we
are likely trying to match our Docker environment to that of the production server, we will
generally require very specific versions of each module. In this case, we limit to the latest
patch within a minor version range. For example, here, we would prefer mysqlclient
1.3.13 over mysqlclient 1.3.3, but we would not yet upgrade to mysqlclient
1.4.0:

```
# config/requirements.txt
Pillow~=5.2.0
mysqlclient~=1.3.0
Django~=2.1.0
```

Dockerfile will define how to build the environment within the container:

```
# Dockerfile
FROM python:3
RUN apt-get update \
    && apt-get install -y --no-install-recommends \
        mysql-client libmysqlclient-dev
WORKDIR /usr/src/app
ADD config/requirements.txt ./
RUN pip3 install --upgrade pip; \
    pip3 install -r requirements.txt
RUN django-admin startproject myproject .; \
    mv ./myproject ./origproject
```

We start with the official image for Python 3, install some dependencies for MySQL, set our working directory, add and install Python requirements, and then start a Django project.

Finally, `docker-compose.yml` puts together the Django application container with other services, such as a MySQL database, so that we can run them together with ease:

```
# docker-compose.yml
version: '3'
services:
  db:
    image: 'mysql:5.7'
  app:
    build: .
    command: python3 manage.py runserver 0.0.0.0:8000
    volumes:
      - './project:/usr/src/app/myproject'
      - './media:/usr/src/app/media'
      - './static:/usr/src/app/static'
      - './templates:/usr/src/app/templates'
      - './apps/external:/usr/src/app/external'
      - './apps/myapp1:/usr/src/app/myapp1'
      - './apps/myapp2:/usr/src/app/myapp2'
    ports:
      - '8000:8000'
    links:
      - db
```

As we can see in the `volumes` section, we will also need to add subdirectories within `myproject_docker` named `project`, `media`, `static`, and `templates`, plus each of the `apps` for the project. These directories will house the code, configuration, and other resources that are exposed within the container.

How it works...

With our basic configuration in place, we can now issue commands to Docker to build and start up our services. If the system we built was using only `Dockerfile`, this could be done without Compose, using direct `docker` engine commands. However, in a Compose setup there is a special `docker-compose` wrapper command that makes it easier to coordinate multiple interconnected containers.

The first step is to build our containers, as defined by the `docker-compose.yml` file. The first time that you build, any images used as starting points need to be loaded locally, and then each instruction in the `Dockerfile` is performed sequentially within the resultant machine:

```
myproject_docker/$ docker-compose build
db uses an image, skipping
Building app
Step 1/6 : FROM python:3
3: Pulling from library/python
f49cf87b52c1: Pull complete
7b491c575b06: Pull complete
b313b08bab3b: Pull complete
51d6678c3f0e: Pull complete
09f35bd58db2: Pull complete
0f9de702e222: Pull complete
73911d37fcde: Pull complete
99a87e214c92: Pull complete
Digest:
sha256:98149ed5f37f48ea3fad26ae6c0042dd2b08228d58edc95ef0fce35f1b3d9e9f
Status: Downloaded newer image for python:3
 ---> c1e459c00dc3
Step 2/6 : RUN apt-get update && apt-get install -y --no-install-recommends
mysql-client libmysqlclient-dev
 ---> Running in 385946c3002f
Get:1 http://security.debian.org jessie/updates InRelease [63.1 kB]
Ign http://deb.debian.org jessie InRelease
Get:2 http://deb.debian.org jessie-updates InRelease [145 kB]
Get:3 http://deb.debian.org jessie Release.gpg [2434 B]
Get:4 http://deb.debian.org jessie Release [148 kB]
Get:5 http://security.debian.org jessie/updates/main amd64 Packages [607
kB]
Get:6 http://deb.debian.org jessie-updates/main amd64 Packages [23.1 kB]
Get:7 http://deb.debian.org jessie/main amd64 Packages [9064 kB]
Fetched 10.1 MB in 10s (962 kB/s)
Reading package lists...
Reading package lists...
Building dependency tree...
Reading state information...
The following extra packages will be installed:
  libdbd-mysql-perl libdbi-perl libmysqlclient18 libterm-readkey-perl
  mysql-client-5.5 mysql-common
Suggested packages:
  libclone-perl libmldbm-perl libnet-daemon-perl libsql-statement-perl
The following NEW packages will be installed:
  libdbd-mysql-perl libdbi-perl libterm-readkey-perl mysql-client
  mysql-client-5.5
```

```
The following packages will be upgraded:
  libmysqlclient-dev libmysqlclient18 mysql-common
3 upgraded, 5 newly installed, 0 to remove and 8 not upgraded.
Need to get 4406 kB of archives.
After this operation, 39.8 MB of additional disk space will be used.
Get:1 http://security.debian.org/ jessie/updates/main libmysqlclient-dev
amd64 5.5.59-0+deb8u1 [952 kB]
Get:2 http://deb.debian.org/debian/ jessie/main libdbi-perl amd64
1.631-3+b1 [816 kB]
Get:3 http://security.debian.org/ jessie/updates/main mysql-common all
5.5.59-0+deb8u1 [80.2 kB]
Get:4 http://deb.debian.org/debian/ jessie/main libdbd-mysql-perl amd64
4.028-2+deb8u2 [119 kB]
Get:5 http://security.debian.org/ jessie/updates/main libmysqlclient18
amd64 5.5.59-0+deb8u1 [674 kB]
Get:6 http://deb.debian.org/debian/ jessie/main libterm-readkey-perl amd64
2.32-1+b1 [28.0 kB]
Get:7 http://security.debian.org/ jessie/updates/main mysql-client-5.5
amd64 5.5.59-0+deb8u1 [1659 kB]
Get:8 http://security.debian.org/ jessie/updates/main mysql-client all
5.5.59-0+deb8u1 [78.4 kB]
debconf: delaying package configuration, since apt-utils is not installed
Fetched 4406 kB in 5s (768 kB/s)
(Reading database ... 21636 files and directories currently installed.)
Preparing to unpack .../libmysqlclient-dev_5.5.59-0+deb8u1_amd64.deb ...
Unpacking libmysqlclient-dev (5.5.59-0+deb8u1) over (5.5.58-0+deb8u1) ...
Preparing to unpack .../mysql-common_5.5.59-0+deb8u1_all.deb ...
Unpacking mysql-common (5.5.59-0+deb8u1) over (5.5.58-0+deb8u1) ...
Preparing to unpack .../libmysqlclient18_5.5.59-0+deb8u1_amd64.deb ...
Unpacking libmysqlclient18:amd64 (5.5.59-0+deb8u1) over (5.5.58-0+deb8u1)
...
Selecting previously unselected package libdbi-perl.
Preparing to unpack .../libdbi-perl_1.631-3+b1_amd64.deb ...
Unpacking libdbi-perl (1.631-3+b1) ...
Selecting previously unselected package libdbd-mysql-perl.
Preparing to unpack .../libdbd-mysql-perl_4.028-2+deb8u2_amd64.deb ...
Unpacking libdbd-mysql-perl (4.028-2+deb8u2) ...
Selecting previously unselected package libterm-readkey-perl.
Preparing to unpack .../libterm-readkey-perl_2.32-1+b1_amd64.deb ...
Unpacking libterm-readkey-perl (2.32-1+b1) ...
Selecting previously unselected package mysql-client-5.5.
Preparing to unpack .../mysql-client-5.5_5.5.59-0+deb8u1_amd64.deb ...
Unpacking mysql-client-5.5 (5.5.59-0+deb8u1) ...
Selecting previously unselected package mysql-client.
Preparing to unpack .../mysql-client_5.5.59-0+deb8u1_all.deb ...
Unpacking mysql-client (5.5.59-0+deb8u1) ...
Setting up mysql-common (5.5.59-0+deb8u1) ...
Setting up libmysqlclient18:amd64 (5.5.59-0+deb8u1) ...
```

```
Setting up libmysqlclient-dev (5.5.59-0+deb8u1) ...
Setting up libdbi-perl (1.631-3+b1) ...
Setting up libdbd-mysql-perl (4.028-2+deb8u2) ...
Setting up libterm-readkey-perl (2.32-1+b1) ...
Setting up mysql-client-5.5 (5.5.59-0+deb8u1) ...
Setting up mysql-client (5.5.59-0+deb8u1) ...
Processing triggers for libc-bin (2.19-18+deb8u10) ...
Removing intermediate container 385946c3002f
 ---> 6bca605a6e41
Step 3/6 : WORKDIR /usr/src/app
Removing intermediate container 3b23729581ef
 ---> 75bf10f0bee4
Step 4/6 : ADD config/requirements.txt ./
 ---> 31a62236f4b9
Step 5/6 : RUN pip3 install --upgrade pip; pip3 install -r requirements.txt
 ---> Running in 755a1b397b5d
Requirement already up-to-date: pip in /usr/local/lib/python3.6/site-
packages
Collecting Pillow~=5.2.0 (from -r requirements.txt (line 2))
  Downloading Pillow-5.2.0-cp36-cp36m-manylinux1_x86_64.whl (5.9MB)
Collecting mysqlclient~=1.3.0 (from -r requirements.txt (line 3))
  Downloading mysqlclient-1.3.0.tar.gz (76kB)
Collecting Django~=2.1.0 (from -r requirements.txt (line 4))
  Downloading Django-2.1.1-py3-none-any.whl (7.1MB)
Collecting pytz (from Django~=2.1.0->-r requirements.txt (line 4))
  Downloading pytz-2017.3-py2.py3-none-any.whl (511kB)
Building wheels for collected packages: mysqlclient
  Running setup.py bdist_wheel for mysqlclient: started
  Running setup.py bdist_wheel for mysqlclient: finished with status 'done'
  Stored in directory:
/root/.cache/pip/wheels/0e/11/a1/e81644c707456461f470c777f13fbd11a1af8eff0c
a71aaca0
Successfully built mysqlclient
Installing collected packages: Pillow, mysqlclient, pytz, Django
Successfully installed Django-2.1.1 Pillow-5.2.0 mysqlclient-1.3.0
pytz-2017.3
Removing intermediate container 755a1b397b5d
 ---> 12308a188504
Step 6/6 : RUN django-admin startproject myproject .; mv ./myproject
./origproject
 ---> Running in 746969588bd3
Removing intermediate container 746969588bd3
 ---> 8bc2b0beb674
Successfully built 8bc2b0beb674
Successfully tagged myprojectdocker_app:latest
```

This will create a local image based on the code in the `myproject_docker` directory. We can see a list of the built images available, as follows:

```
myproject_docker/$ docker images
REPOSITORY            TAG      IMAGE ID       CREATED          SIZE
myprojectdocker_app   latest   6a5c66f22a02   39 seconds ago   814MB
python                3        c1e459c00dc3   4 weeks ago      692MB
```

The state of the machine, after each step, is cached so that future build commands do as little work as possible, based only on the steps after which a change was made. For example, if we build again right away, then everything should come from the cache:

```
myproject_docker/$ docker-compose build
db uses an image, skipping
Building app
Step 1/6 : FROM python:3
 ---> c1e459c00dc3
Step 2/6 : RUN apt-get update && apt-get install -y --no-install-recommends
mysql-client libmysqlclient-dev
 ---> Using cache
 ---> f2007264e96d
Step 3/6 : WORKDIR /usr/src/app
 ---> Using cache
 ---> 9621b97ef4ec
Step 4/6 : ADD config/requirements.txt ./
 ---> Using cache
 ---> 6a87941c7876
Step 5/6 : RUN pip3 install --upgrade pip; pip3 install -r requirements.txt
 ---> Using cache
 ---> 64a268b8cba6
Step 6/6 : RUN django-admin startproject myproject .; mv ./myproject
./origproject
 ---> Using cache
 ---> 8bc2b0beb674
Successfully built 8bc2b0beb674
Successfully tagged myprojectdocker_app:latest
```

Although we added a project to the container via the `Dockerfile`, the `project` volume set up for the app would mask some files when the container is running. To get around this, we moved the project files within the container aside to an `origproject` directory. Compose allows us to easily `run` commands against our services, so we can copy those project files so they are accessible in the volume by executing the following command:

```
myproject_docker/$ docker-compose run app cp \
> origproject/__init__.py \
> origproject/settings.py \
> origproject/urls.py \
```

```
> origproject/wsgi.py \
> myproject/
```

We can see that the previously masked project files are now exposed for us to easily edit outside of the container, too:

```
myproject_docker/$ ls project
__init__.py   settings.py   urls.py   wsgi.py
```

Once our services are built and the Django project is created, we can use `docker-compose` to bring `up` the environment, passing an optional `-d` flag to detach the process from our terminal. Detaching runs the containers in exactly the same way, except we can use the terminal to invoke other commands in the meantime. With the containers attached, we are only able to view logs that are exposed by the container (generally what is output to `stdout` or `stderr`). The first time we start our Compose environment, any pure image-based services will also need to be pulled down. For example, we might see something like this:

```
myproject_docker/$ docker-compose up -d
Creating network "myprojectdocker_default" with the default driver
Pulling db (mysql:5.7)...
5.7: Pulling from library/mysql
f49cf87b52c1: Already exists
78032de49d65: Pull complete
837546b20bc4: Pull complete
9b8316af6cc6: Pull complete
1056cf29b9f1: Pull complete
86f3913b029a: Pull complete
f98eea8321ca: Pull complete
3a8e3ebdeaf5: Pull complete
4be06ac1c51e: Pull complete
920c7ffb7747: Pull complete
Digest:
sha256:7cdb08f30a54d109ddded59525937592cb6852ff635a546626a8960d9ec34c30
Creating myprojectdocker_db_1 ... done
Creating myprojectdocker_app_1 ... done
```

At this point, Django is now accessible, just as it would be when run directly on your machine and accessing `http://localhost:8000/`:

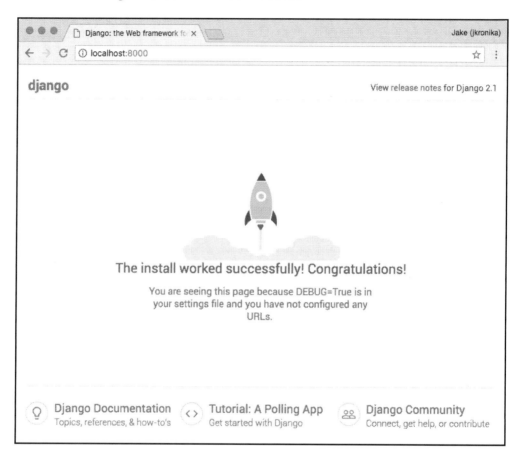

It is often necessary to execute commands within an already up-and-running container, and Docker provides a simple way to do this, as well. As an example, we can connect to the machine at a command-line prompt, similarly to how we might access a remote machine over SSH, as follows:

```
myproject_docker/$ docker exec -it myproject_docker_app_1 /bin/bash
root@042bf38a407f:/usr/src/app# ls
db.sqlite3   external      manage.py        media     myapp1     myapp2
myproject    origproject   requirements.txt static    templates
root@042bf38a407f:/usr/src/app# ls myproject
__init__.py  __pycache__  settings.py  urls.py  wsgi.py
root@042bf38a407f:/usr/src/app# exit
myproject_docker/$
```

The preceding code instructs Docker to execute `/bin/bash` on the `myprojectdocker_app_1` container. The `-i` flag makes the connection interactive, and `-t` allocates a TTY shell. Shutting down is just as easy. If the container is running in attached mode, simply issue a *Ctrl-C* keyboard command to end the process. When using the `-d` flag to start the container, however, we instead issue a command to shut it down:

```
myproject_docker/$ docker-compose down
Stopping myprojectdocker_app_1 ... done
Removing myprojectdocker_app_1 ... done
Removing myprojectdocker_db_1 ... done
Removing network myprojectdocker_default
```

There's more...

Read more from the extensive documentation of Docker at `https://docs.docker.com/`, and specifically about using Compose with Django at `https://docs.docker.com/compose/django/`. In the *Creating a Docker project file structure* recipe, we also go into greater depth around the organization of files and configuration to replicate a production environment.

See also

- The *Working with a virtual environment* recipe
- The *Creating a Docker project file structure* recipe

Creating a Docker project file structure

Although Docker provides an isolated environment within which to configure and run your project, development code and certain configurations can still be stored outside the container. This enables such files to be added to version control, and persists the files when a container is shut down. In addition, Docker adds flexibility that allows us to directly recreate an environment that might be used in production, helping to ensure that the conditions in development will much more closely match the real world.

Getting ready

Before you begin, set up a Docker environment as described in the *Working with Docker* recipe.

How to do it...

The basic structure already created separates aspects of our project into logical groups:

- All applications to be used in the project are stored under the `apps` directory, which allows them to be pulled in individually either from version control or other source locations.
- `project` and `templates` are also distinct, which makes sense since the settings and templates for one project switch be shared, whereas applications are commonly intended to be reusable.
- The `static` and `media` files are separated as well, allowing them to be deployed to separate static content containers (and servers) easily.

To make full use of these features, let's update the `docker-compose.yml` file with some enhancements:

```yaml
# docker-compose.yml
version: '3'
services:
  proxy:
    image: 'jwilder/nginx-proxy:latest'
    ports:
      - '80:80'
    volumes:
      - '/var/run/docker.sock:/tmp/docker.sock:ro'
  db:
    image: 'mysql:5.7'
    ports:
      - '3306'
    volumes:
      - './config/my.cnf:/etc/mysql/conf.d/my.cnf'
      - './mysql:/var/lib/mysql'
      - './data:/usr/local/share/data'
    environment:
      - 'MYSQL_ROOT_PASSWORD'
      - 'MYSQL_USER'
      - 'MYSQL_PASSWORD'
      - 'MYSQL_DATABASE'
  app:
    build: .
    command: python3 manage.py runserver 0.0.0.0:8000
    volumes:
      - './project:/usr/src/app/myproject'
      - './media:/usr/src/app/media'
      - './static:/usr/src/app/static'
      - './templates:/usr/src/app/templates'
```

```
      - './apps/external:/usr/src/app/external'
      - './apps/myapp1:/usr/src/app/myapp1'
      - './apps/myapp2:/usr/src/app/myapp2'
    ports:
      - '8000'
    links:
      - db
    environment:
      - 'SITE_HOST'
      - 'MEDIA_HOST'
      - 'STATIC_HOST'
      - 'VIRTUAL_HOST=${SITE_HOST}'
      - 'VIRTUAL_PORT=8000'
      - 'MYSQL_HOST=db'
      - 'MYSQL_USER'
      - 'MYSQL_PASSWORD'
      - 'MYSQL_DATABASE'
  media:
    image: 'httpd:latest'
    volumes:
      - './media:/usr/local/apache2/htdocs'
    ports:
      - '80'
    environment:
      - 'VIRTUAL_HOST=${MEDIA_HOST}'
  static:
    image: 'httpd:latest'
    volumes:
      - './static:/usr/local/apache2/htdocs'
    ports:
      - '80'
    environment:
      - 'VIRTUAL_HOST=${STATIC_HOST}'
```

With these changes, there are some corresponding updates needed in the Django project settings as well. The end result should look similar to the following:

```
# project/settings.py
# ...

ALLOWED_HOSTS = []
if os.environ.get('SITE_HOST'):
    ALLOWED_HOSTS.append(os.environ.get('SITE_HOST'))

# ...

DATABASES = {
    'default': {
```

```
        'ENGINE': 'django.db.backends.sqlite3',
        'NAME': os.path.join(BASE_DIR, 'db.sqlite3'),
    }
}

if os.environ.get('MYSQL_HOST'):
    DATABASES['default'] = {
        'ENGINE': 'django.db.backends.mysql',
        'HOST': os.environ.get('MYSQL_HOST'),
        'NAME': os.environ.get('MYSQL_DATABASE'),
        'USER': os.environ.get('MYSQL_USER'),
        'PASSWORD': os.environ.get('MYSQL_PASSWORD'),
    }

# ...

# Logging
# https://docs.djangoproject.com/en/dev/topics/logging/
LOGGING = {
    'version': 1,
    'formatters': {
        'verbose': {
            'format': '%(levelname)s %(asctime)s %(module)s %(process)d
%(thread)d %(message)s'
        },
        'simple': {
            'format': '%(levelname)s %(message)s'
        },
    },
    'handlers': {
        'console': {
            'level': 'DEBUG',
            'class': 'logging.StreamHandler',
            'formatter': 'simple'
        },
        'file': {
            'level': 'DEBUG',
            'class': 'logging.FileHandler',
            'filename': '/var/log/app.log',
            'formatter': 'simple'
        },
    },
    'loggers': {
        'django': {
            'handlers': ['file'],
            'level': 'DEBUG',
            'propagate': True,
        },
```

```
    }
}

if DEBUG:
    # make all loggers use the console.
    for logger in LOGGING['loggers']:
        LOGGING['loggers'][logger]['handlers'] = ['console']

# ...

# Static files (CSS, JavaScript, Images)
# https://docs.djangoproject.com/en/2.1/howto/static-files/

STATIC_URL = '/static/'
STATIC_ROOT = os.path.join(BASE_DIR, 'static')
if os.environ.get('STATIC_HOST'):
    STATIC_DOMAIN = os.environ.get('STATIC_HOST')
    STATIC_URL = 'http://%s/' % STATIC_DOMAIN

MEDIA_URL = '/media/'
MEDIA_ROOT = os.path.join(BASE_DIR, 'media')
if os.environ.get('MEDIA_HOST'):
    MEDIA_DOMAIN = os.environ.get('MEDIA_HOST')
    MEDIA_URL = 'http://%s/' % MEDIA_DOMAIN
```

Furthermore, the `my.cnf` file is referenced in `docker-compose.yml` as a volume attached to the `db` service. Although there would be no error, specifically, if it were left out; a directory would be automatically created to satisfy the volume requirement. At a minimum, we can add an empty file under the `config` folder, or we might add options to MySQL right away, such as the following:

```
# config/my.cnf
[mysqld]
sql_mode=STRICT_TRANS_TABLES
```

Then, add a `bin` subdirectory in `myproject_docker`, inside of which we will add a `dev` script (or `dev.sh`, if the extension is preferred):

```
#!/usr/bin/env bash
# bin/dev
# environment variables to be defined externally for security
# - MYSQL_USER
# - MYSQL_PASSWORD
# - MYSQL_ROOT_PASSWORD
DOMAIN=myproject.local

DJANGO_USE_DEBUG=1 \
```

```
DJANGO_USE_DEBUG_TOOLBAR=1 \
SITE_HOST="$DOMAIN" \
MEDIA_HOST="media.$DOMAIN" \
STATIC_HOST="static.$DOMAIN" \
MYSQL_HOST="localhost" \
MYSQL_DATABASE="myproject_db" \
  docker-compose $*
```

Make sure the script is executable by modifying the permissions, as in the following:

```
myproject_docker/$ chmod +x bin/dev
```

Finally, the development hosts need to be mapped to a local IP address, such as via /etc/hosts on macOS or Linux. Such a mapping for our project would look something like this:

```
127.0.0.1    myproject.local media.myproject.local static.myproject.local
```

How it works...

In docker-compose.yml, we have added more services and defined some environment variables. These make our system more robust and allow us to replicate the multi-host paradigm for serving static files that is preferred in production.

The first new service is a proxy, based on the jwilder/nginx-proxy image. This service attaches to port 80 in the host machine and passes requests through to port 80 in the container. The purpose of the proxy is to allow use of friendly hostnames rather than relying on everything running on localhost.

Two other new services are defined toward the end of the file, one for serving media and another for static files:

- These both run the Apache httpd static server and map the associated directory to the default htdocs folder from which Apache serves files.
- We can also see that they each define a VIRTUAL_HOST environment variable, whose value is drawn from corresponding host variables MEDIA_HOST and STATIC_HOST, and which is read automatically by the proxy service.
- The services listen on port 80 in the container, so requests made for resources under that hostname can be forwarded by the proxy to the associated service dynamically.

The db service has been augmented in a few ways:

- First, we ensure that it is listening on the expected port 3306 in the container network.
- We also set up a few volumes so that content can be shared outside the container—a my.cnf file allows changes to the basic running configuration of the database server; the database content is exposed as a mysql directory, in case there is a desire to back up the database itself; and we add a data directory for SQL scripts, so we can connect to the database container and execute them directly if desired.
- Lastly, there are four environment variables that the mysql image makes use of—MYSQL_ROOT_PASSWORD, MYSQL_HOST, MYSQL_USER, and MYSQL_PASSWORD. These are declared, but no value is given, so that the value will be taken from the host environment itself when we run docker-compose up.

The final set of changes in docker-compose.yml are for the app service itself, the nature of which are similar to those noted previously:

- The port definition is changed so that port 8000 is only connected to within the container network, rather than binding to that port on the host, since we will now access Django via the proxy.
- More than simply depending on the db service, our app now links directly to it over the internal network, which makes it possible to refer to the service by its name rather than an externally accessible hostname.
- As with the database, several environment variables are indicated to supply external data to the container from the host. There are pass-through variables for MEDIA_HOST and STATIC_HOST, plus SITE_HOST and a mapping of it to VIRTUAL_HOST used by the proxy.
- While the proxy connects to virtual hosts via port 80 by default, we are running Django on port 8000, so the proxy is instructed to use that port instead via the VIRTUAL_PORT variable.
- Last but not least, the MySQL MYSQL_HOST, MYSQL_USER, MYSQL_PASSWORD and MYSQL_DATABASE variables are passed into the app for use in the project settings.

This brings us to the updates to `settings.py`, which are largely centered around connectivity and security:

- To ensure that access to the application is limited to expected connections, we add `SITE_HOST` to `ALLOWED_HOSTS` if one is given for the environment.
- For `DATABASES`, the original `sqlite3` settings are left in place, but we replace that default with a configuration for MySQL if we find the `MYSQL_HOST` environment variable has been set, making use of the MySQL variables passed into the `app` service.
- As noted in the *Working with Docker* recipe, we can only view logs that are exposed by the container. By default, the Django `runserver` command does not output logging to the console, so no logs are technically exposed. The next change to `settings.py` sets up `LOGGING` configurations so that a simple format will always be logged to the console when `DEBUG=true`.
- Finally, instead of relying upon Django to serve static and media files, we check for the corresponding `STATIC_HOST` and `MEDIA_HOST` environment variables and, when those exist, set the `STATIC_URL` and `MEDIA_URL` settings accordingly.

With all of the configurations updated, we need to have an easy way to run the container so that the appropriate environment variables are supplied. Although it might be possible to export the variables, that would negate much of the benefit of isolation we gain from using Docker otherwise. Instead, it is possible to run `docker-compose` with inline variables, so a single execution thread will have those variables set in a specific way. This is, ultimately, what the `dev` script does.

Now we can run `docker-compose` commands for our development environment—which includes a MySQL database, separate Apache servers for media and static files, and the Django server itself—with a single, simplified form:

```
myproject_docker/$ MYSQL_USER=myproject_user \
> MYSQL_PASSWORD=pass1234 \
> ./bin/dev up -d
Creating myprojectdocker_media_1 ... done
Creating myprojectdocker_db_1 ... done
Creating myprojectdocker_app_1 ... done
Creating myprojectdocker_static_1 ... done
```

In the `dev` script, the appropriate variables are all defined for the command automatically, and `docker-compose` is invoked at once. The script mentions in comments three other, more sensitive variables that should be provided externally, and two of those are included here. If you are less concerned about the security of a development database, these could just as easily be included in the `dev` script itself. A more secure, but also more convenient way of providing the variables across runs would be to `export` them, after which they become global environment variables, as in the following example:

```
myproject_docker/$ export MYSQL_USER=myproject_user
myproject_docker/$ export MYSQL_PASSWORD=pass1234
myproject_docker/$ ./bin/dev build
myproject_docker/$ ./bin/dev up -d
```

Any commands or options passed into `dev`, such as `up -d` in this case, are forwarded along to `docker-compose` via the `$*` wildcard variable included at the end of the script. With the host mapping complete, and our container up and running, we should be able to access the system by `SITE_HOST`, as in `http://myproject.local/`.

The resultant file structure for a complete Docker project might look something like this:

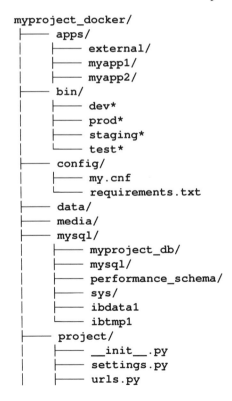

```
myproject_docker/
├── apps/
│   ├── external/
│   ├── myapp1/
│   └── myapp2/
├── bin/
│   ├── dev*
│   ├── prod*
│   ├── staging*
│   └── test*
├── config/
│   ├── my.cnf
│   └── requirements.txt
├── data/
├── media/
├── mysql/
│   ├── myproject_db/
│   ├── mysql/
│   ├── performance_schema/
│   ├── sys/
│   ├── ibdata1
│   └── ibtmp1
├── project/
│   ├── __init__.py
│   ├── settings.py
│   ├── urls.py
```

```
|           └──── wsgi.py
├──── static/
├──── templates/
├──── Dockerfile
├──── README.md
└──── docker-compose.yml
```

There's more...

You can find additional details about the configuration that might be specified in `my.cnf`; see *MySQL documentation for Using Options Files*, found at `https://dev.mysql.com/doc/refman/5.7/en/option-files.html`.

See also

- The *Creating a virtual environment project file structure* recipe
- The *Working with Docker* recipe
- The *Handling project dependencies with pip* recipe
- The *Including external dependencies in your project* recipe
- The *Configuring settings for development, testing, staging, and production environments* recipe
- The *Setting UTF-8 as the default encoding for MySQL configuration* recipe
- The *Deploying on Apache with mod_wsgi* recipe in `Chapter 12`, *Testing and Deployment*

Handling project dependencies with pip

The most convenient tool to install and manage Python packages is pip. Rather than installing the packages one by one, it is possible to define a list of packages that you want to install as the contents of a text file. We can pass the text file into the pip tool, which will then handle installation of all packages in the list automatically. An added benefit to this approach is that the package list can be stored in version control. If you have gone through the *Working with Docker* recipe, then you have already seen this.

Generally speaking, it is ideal and often sufficient to have a single requirements file that directly matches your production environment. When changing versions or adding and removing dependencies, this can be done on a development machine and then managed through version control. It can then be as simple as switching branches to go from one set of dependencies (and associated code changes) to another.

In some cases, environments differ enough that you will need to have at least two different instances of your project: the development environment, where you create new features, and the public website environment that is usually called the production environment, in a hosted server. There might be development environments for other developers, or special tools that are needed during development but are unnecessary in production. Also, you may have a testing and staging environment in order to test the project locally and in a public website-like situation.

For good maintainability, you should be able to install the required Python modules for development, testing, staging, and production environments. Some of the modules will be shared and some of them will be specific to a subset of the environments. In this recipe, we will see how to organize the project dependencies for multiple environments and manage them with pip.

Getting ready

Before using this recipe, you need to have a Django project ready, either with pip installed and a virtual environment activated, or via Docker. For more information on how to do this, read the *Working with a virtual environment* recipe, or the *Working with Docker* recipe, respectively.

How to do it...

Execute the following steps one by one to prepare pip requirements for your virtual environment Django project:

1. Let's go to your Django project that you have under version control and create a requirements directory with these text files, if you haven't already done so:
   - base.txt for shared modules
   - dev.txt for the development environment
   - test.txt for the testing environment
   - staging.txt for the staging environment
   - prod.txt for production

2. Edit `base.txt` and add the Python modules that are shared in all environments, line by line. For example, we might migrate our original `requirements.txt` as `base.txt`, which would give us this in our virtual environment project:

```
# base.txt
Django~=2.1.0
djangorestframework
-e git://github.com/omab/python-social-
auth.git@6b1e301c79#egg=python-social-auth
```

3. If the requirements of a specific environment are the same as in `base.txt`, add the line including `base.txt` in the requirements file of that environment, as in the following example:

```
# prod.txt
-r base.txt
```

4. If there are specific requirements for an environment, add them after the `base.txt` inclusion, as shown in the following:

```
# dev.txt
-r base.txt
django-debug-toolbar
selenium
```

5. You can run the following command in a virtual environment in order to install all of the required dependencies for the development environment (or analogous command for other environments), as follows:

```
(myproject_env)$ pip3 install -r requirements/dev.txt
```

With a Docker setup, we follow steps 1-4 in almost precisely the same manner, except the `requirements` directory would live underneath the `config` directory. From there, a few additional steps are needed to install the correct requirements by environment:

1. The `Dockerfile` file will need to be updated to select the appropriate requirements file based on a build argument, which here defaults to `prod`:

```
# Dockerfile
FROM python:3
RUN apt-get update \
    && apt-get install -y --no-install-recommends \
        less mysql-client libmysqlclient-dev
WORKDIR /usr/src/app
ARG BUILD_ENV=prod
ADD config/requirements ./requirements
```

```
RUN pip3 install --upgrade pip; \
    pip3 install -r requirements/$BUILD_ENV.txt
RUN django-admin startproject myproject .; \
    mv ./myproject ./origproject
```

2. The `docker-compose.yml` file needs to pass through this argument using the current environment variable, as in the following:

```
# docker-compose.yml
version: '3'
services:
  db:
    image: "mysql:5.7"
  app:
    build:
      context: .
      args:
        BUILD_ENV: $BUILD_ENV
    command: "python3 manage.py runserver 0.0.0.0:8000"
    volumes:
      - "./project:/usr/src/app/myproject"
      - "./media:/usr/src/app/media"
      - "./static:/usr/src/app/static"
      - "./templates:/usr/src/app/templates"
      - "./apps/external:/usr/src/app/external"
      - "./apps/myapp1:/usr/src/app/myapp1"
      - "./apps/myapp2:/usr/src/app/myapp2"
    ports:
      - "8000:8000"
    depends_on:
      - db
```

3. Scripts under `bin` for each environment are then updated to set the appropriate value for the BUILD_ENV variable. For example, we would update the `dev` script as follows:

```
#!/usr/bin/env bash
# bin/dev
# ...

BUILD_ENV="dev" \adds
#...
  docker-compose $*
```

4. We simply use the environment-specific script when building the container, and the argument passes through automatically, causing the correct requirements file to be added to the container:

```
myproject_docker/$ MYSQL_USER=myproject_user \
> MYSQL_PASSWORD=pass1234 \
> ./bin/dev build
```

How it works...

The preceding `pip3 install` command, whether it is executed explicitly in a virtual environment or during the build process for a Docker container, downloads and installs all of your project dependencies from `requirements/base.txt` and `requirements/dev.txt`. As you can see, you can specify a version of the module that you need for the Django framework and even directly install from a specific commit at the Git repository, as done for `social-app-django` in our example.

> In practice, installing from a specific commit would rarely be useful, for instance, only when having third-party dependencies in your project, with specific functionality, that are not supported in any other versions.

When you have many dependencies in your project, it is good practice to stick to a narrow range of release versions for Python module release versions. Then you can have greater confidence that the project integrity will not be broken due to updates in your dependencies, which might contain conflicts or backward incompatibility. This is particularly important when deploying your project or handing it off to a new developer.

If you have already manually installed the project requirements with pip one by one, you can generate the `requirements/base.txt` file using the following command within your virtual environment:

```
(myproject_env)$ pip3 freeze > requirements/base.txt
```

The same can be executed within the Docker app container, as in the following:

```
myproject_docker/$ docker exec -it myproject_docker_app_1 \
> /bin/bash
root:/usr/src/app# pip3 freeze > requirements/base.txt
```

There's more...

If you want to keep things simple and are sure that, for all environments, you will be using the same dependencies, you can use just one file for your requirements named `requirements.txt`, generated by definition, as in the following:

```
(myproject_env)$ pip3 freeze > requirements.txt
```

To install the modules in a new virtual environment, simply call the following command:

```
(myproject_env)$ pip3 install -r requirements.txt
```

 If you need to install a Python library from other version control system, or at a local path, you can learn more about pip from the official documentation at `http://pip.readthedocs.org/en/latest/reference/pip_install.html`.

See also

- The *Working with a virtual environment* recipe
- The *Working with Docker* recipe
- The *Including external dependencies in your project* recipe
- The *Configuring settings for development, testing, staging, and production environments* recipe

Including external dependencies in your project

Sometimes, it is better to include external dependencies directly within your project. This ensures that whenever a developer upgrades third-party modules, all of the other developers will receive the upgraded version in the next update from the version control system (Git, Subversion, or others).

Also, it is better to have external dependencies included in your project when the libraries are taken from unofficial sources, that is, somewhere other than the **Python Package Index (PyPI)** or different version control systems.

Getting ready

Start with a virtual environment with a Django project in it.

How to do it...

Execute the following steps one by one for a virtual environment project:

1. If you haven't done so already, create an `externals` directory under your Django project `django-myproject` directory. Then, create the `libs` and `apps` directories under it. The `libs` directory is for the Python modules that are required by your project, for example, Boto, Requests, Twython, and Whoosh. The `apps` directory is for third-party Django apps, for example, Django CMS, Django Haystack, and django-storages.

    We highly recommend that you create `README.md` files in the `libs` and `apps` directories, where you mention what each module is for, what the used version or revision is, and where it is taken from.

2. The directory structure should look something similar to the following:

```
externals/
├─── apps/
│    ├─── cms/
│    ├─── haystack/
│    ├─── storages/
│    └─── README.md
└─── libs/
     ├─── boto/
     ├─── requests/
     ├─── twython/
     └─── README.md
```

3. The next step is to put the external libraries and apps under the Python path so that they are recognized as if they were installed. This can be done by adding the following code in the settings:

```python
# settings.py
import os, sys
BASE_DIR = os.path.dirname(os.path.dirname(
    os.path.abspath(__file__)))

EXTERNAL_BASE = os.path.join(BASE_DIR, "externals")
```

```
EXTERNAL_LIBS_PATH = os.path.join(EXTERNAL_BASE, "libs")
EXTERNAL_APPS_PATH = os.path.join(EXTERNAL_BASE, "apps")
sys.path = ["", EXTERNAL_LIBS_PATH, EXTERNAL_APPS_PATH] + sys.path
```

How it works...

A module is meant to be under the Python path if you can run Python and import that module. One of the ways to put a module under the Python path is to modify the `sys.path` variable before importing a module that is in an unusual location. The value of `sys.path`, as specified by the `settings.py` file, is a list of directories starting with an empty string for the current directory, followed by the directories in the project, and finally the globally shared directories of the Python installation. You can see the value of `sys.path` in the Python shell, as follows:

```
(myproject)$ ./manage.py shell
>>> import sys
>>> sys.path
```

The same could be done for a Docker project, assuming the container name were `django_myproject_app_1`, as follows:

```
myproject_docker/$ docker exec -it django_myproject_app_1 \
> python3 manage.py shell
>>> import sys
>>> sys.path
```

When trying to import a module, Python searches for the module in this list and returns the first result that is found.

Therefore, we first define the `BASE_DIR` variable, which is the absolute path to one level higher than the `settings.py` file. Then, we define the `EXTERNAL_LIBS_PATH` and `EXTERNAL_APPS_PATH` variables, which are relative to `BASE_DIR`. Lastly, we modify the `sys.path` property, adding new paths to the beginning of the list. Note that we also add an empty string as the first path to search, which means that the current directory of any module should always be checked first before checking other Python paths.

This way of including external libraries doesn't work cross-platform with the Python packages that have C language bindings, for example, `lxml`. For such dependencies, we would recommend using the pip requirements that were introduced in the *Handling project dependencies with pip* recipe.

There's more...

With a Docker project, there is significantly more control of the libraries and apps that are installed within the container:

- For Python libraries needed for the project, we can use version specifications in the `requirements.txt` file to require a version known to be compatible. Furthermore, it was demonstrated in the *Handling project dependencies with pip* recipe that we can differentiate these requirements by environment, as well as being so precise as to require an exact repository version using the `-e` flag.
- All Django applications are stored under the `apps` directory. Here would reside not only the code for ones specifically under development, but also any external apps that are not made available globally via the `requirements.txt` dependency list.

See also

- The *Creating a virtual environment project file structure* recipe
- The *Creating a Docker project file structure* recipe
- The *Handling project dependencies with pip* recipe
- The *Defining relative paths in the settings* recipe
- The *Using the Django shell* recipe in `Chapter 11`, *Bells and Whistles*

Configuring settings for development, testing, staging, and production environments

As noted earlier, you will be creating new features in the development environment, testing them in the testing environment, then putting the website onto a staging server to let other people try the new features, and lastly, the website will be deployed to the production server for public access. Each of these environments can have specific settings and you will see how to organize them in this recipe.

Getting ready

In a Django project, we'll create settings for each environment: development, testing, staging, and production.

How to do it...

Follow these steps to configure project settings:

1. In the `myproject` directory, create a `config` Python module with the following files:
   - `__init__.py`
   - `base.py` for shared settings
   - `dev.py` for development settings
   - `test.py` for testing settings
   - `staging.py` for staging settings
   - `prod.py` for production settings

2. Put all of your shared settings in `config/base.py`.

3. If the settings of an environment are the same as the shared settings, then just import everything from `base.py` there, as follows:

   ```
   # myproject/config/prod.py
   from .base import *
   ```

4. Apply the settings that you want to attach or overwrite for your specific environment in the other files, for example, the development environment settings should go to `dev.py`, as shown in the following:

   ```
   # myproject/config/dev.py
   from .base import *
   EMAIL_BACKEND = 'django.core.mail.backends.console.EmailBackend'
   ```

5. At the beginning of `myproject/settings.py`, import the configurations from one of the environment settings and then additionally attach specific or sensitive configurations, such as `DATABASES` or `API` keys that shouldn't be under version control, as follows:

   ```
   # myproject/settings.py
   from .config.dev import *

   DATABASES = {
   ```

```
        "default": {
            "ENGINE": "django.db.backends.mysql",
            "NAME": "myproject",
            "USER": "root",
            "PASSWORD": "root",
        }
    }
```

6. Create a `settings.py.example` file that should contain all the sensitive settings that are necessary for a project to run, however, with empty values set.

How it works...

By default, the Django management commands use the settings from `myproject/settings.py`. Using the method that is defined in this recipe, we can keep all of the required non-sensitive settings for all environments under version control in the `config` directory. On the other hand, the `settings.py` file itself would be ignored by version control and will only contain the settings that are necessary for the current development, testing, staging, or production environments.

There's more...

In the *Creating a Docker project file structure* recipe, we introduced an alternative approach using environment variables to store sensitive or environment-specific settings. We go into greater depth into this method of differentiating settings in the *Creating and including local settings* recipe as well.

See also

- The *Creating a Docker project file structure* recipe
- The *Creating and including local settings* recipe
- The *Defining relative paths in the settings* recipe
- The *Setting the Subversion ignore property* recipe
- The *Creating a Git ignore file* recipe

Defining relative paths in the settings

Django requires you to define different file paths in the settings, such as the root of your media, the root of your static files, the path to templates, and the path to translation files. For each developer of your project, the paths may differ as the virtual environment can be set up anywhere and the user might be working on macOS, Linux, or Windows. Even when your project is wrapped in a Docker container, it reduces maintainability and portability to define absolute paths. In any case, there is a way to define these paths dynamically so that they are relative to your Django project directory.

Getting ready

Have a Django project started, and open `settings.py`.

How to do it...

Modify your path-related settings accordingly, instead of hardcoding the paths to your local directories, as follows:

```python
# settings.py
import os
BASE_DIR = os.path.dirname(os.path.dirname(os.path.abspath(__file__)))

# ...

TEMPLATES = [{
    # ...
    DIRS: [
        os.path.join(BASE_DIR, 'templates'),
    ],
    # ...
}]

# ...

LOCALE_PATHS = [
    os.path.join(BASE_DIR, 'locale'),
]

# ...

MEDIA_ROOT = os.path.join(BASE_DIR, 'media')
STATIC_ROOT = os.path.join(BASE_DIR, 'static')
```

```
STATICFILES_DIRS = [
    os.path.join(BASE_DIR, 'site_static'),
]

FILE_UPLOAD_TEMP_DIR = os.path.join(BASE_DIR, 'tmp'
```

How it works...

By default, Django settings include a BASE_DIR value, which is an absolute path to the directory containing manage.py (usually one level higher than the settings.py file). Then, we set all of the paths relative to BASE_DIR using the os.path.join function.

Based on the directory layout we set down in the *Creating a virtual environment project file structure* recipe, we would insert 'myproject' as an intermediary path segment for each of the previous examples, since the associated folders were created within that one. For Docker projects, as shown in the *Creating a Docker project file structure* recipe, we set the volumes for media, static, and so forth to be alongside manage.py in BASE_DIR itself.

See also

- The *Creating a virtual environment project file structure* recipe
- The *Creating a Docker project file structure* recipe
- The *Including external dependencies in your project* recipe

Creating and including local settings

Configuration doesn't necessarily need to be complex. If you want to keep things simple, you can work with a single settings.py file for common configuration and use environment variables for settings that should be kept private and not in version control.

Getting ready

Most of the settings for a project will be shared across all environments and saved in version control. These can be defined directly within the settings.py file. However, there will be some settings that are specific to the environment of the project instance, or sensitive and require additional security such as database or email settings. We will expose these using environment variables.

How to do it...

To use local settings in your project, first we must draw values from environment variables for any configurations in settings.py that will differ across environments or that would be a security risk if stored in version control. It is a good practice to be very clear and unique when naming these variables, but also take into account those that already exist in the environment. Some examples follow:

1. Whether or not to use DEBUG mode will generally differ per environment, where debugging would be on in development, but not by default:

```python
# settings.py
DEBUG = False
if os.environ.get('DJANGO_USE_DEBUG'):
    DEBUG = True
```

2. Similarly, we might want the debug_toolbar to be active in development, or perhaps only in certain situations even then, so we could add it only when necessary:

```python
# settings.py
INSTALLED_APPS = [
    # ...
]
if os.environ.get('DJANGO_USE_DEBUG_TOOLBAR'):
    INSTALLED_APPS += ('debug_toolbar',)

MIDDLEWARE = [
    # ...
]
if os.environ.get('DJANGO_USE_DEBUG_TOOLBAR'):
    MIDDLEWARE += (
        'debug_toolbar.middleware.DebugToolbarMiddleware',)
```

3. Perhaps we use a SQLite3 database in testing, but a MySQL database in development, staging, and production. Also, in development, the MySQL database might be on localhost, but have its own separate domain in staging and production. Finally, storing the credentials for the connection in any environment is a security risk. We can handle all of these scenarios just as easily with the following updates to settings.py:

```python
# settings.py
DATABASES = {
    'default': {
        'ENGINE': 'django.db.backends.sqlite3',
        'NAME': os.path.join(BASE_DIR, 'db.sqlite3'),
```

```
        }
    }
if os.environ.get('MYSQL_HOST'):
    DATABASES['default'] = {
        'ENGINE': 'django.db.backends.mysql',
        'HOST': os.environ.get('MYSQL_HOST'),
        'NAME': os.environ.get('MYSQL_DATABASE'),
        'USER': os.environ.get('MYSQL_USER'),
        'PASSWORD': os.environ.get('MYSQL_PASSWORD'),
    }
```

How it works...

As you can see, the local settings are not directly stored in settings.py, they are rather included via externally defined environment variables and evaluated in the settings.py file itself. This allows you to not only create or overwrite the existing settings, but also adjust the tuples or lists from the settings.py file. For example, we add debug_toolbar to INSTALLED_APPS here, plus its associated MIDDLEWARE, in order to be able to debug the SQL queries, template context variables, and so on.

Defining the values of these variables can be done in one of two ways. In development, we can declare them within runtime commands, as in the following:

```
$ DJANGO_USE_DEBUG=1 python3 manage.py runserver 8000
```

This sets the DJANGO_USE_DEBUG variable for this particular process, resulting in DEBUG=True in settings.py as per the examples listed earlier. If there are many variables to define, or the same values will be set every time the server starts, it may be handy to create a reusable script to do so. For example, in the development environment, we can create a dev shell script, such as the following:

```
#!/usr/bin/env bash
# bin/dev
# environment variables to be defined externally for security
# - MYSQL_USER
# - MYSQL_PASSWORD
# - MYSQL_ROOT_PASSWORD

DJANGO_USE_DEBUG=1 \
DJANGO_USE_DEBUG_TOOLBAR=1 \
MYSQL_HOST=localhost \
MYSQL_DATABASE=myproject_db \
  python3 manage.py runserver 8000
```

Store the above in a `bin` directory alongside `manage.py` in your project, and make sure it is executable, as follows:

```
$ chmod +x bin/dev
```

Then, in a terminal, we can now start our development server, with all of the appropriate settings, as in the following:

```
$ MYSQL_USER=username MYSQL_PASSWORD=pass1234 bin/dev
```

The resultant `runserver` command will receive values not only for the MySQL username and password given here, but also all of the variables set in the `dev` script itself.

See also

- The *Creating a virtual environment project file structure* recipe
- The *Creating a Docker project file structure* recipe
- The *Toggling the Debug Toolbar* recipe in `Chapter 11`, *Bells and Whistles*

Setting up STATIC_URL dynamically for Subversion users

If you set `STATIC_URL` to a static value, then each time you update a CSS file, a JavaScript file, or an image, you will need to clear the browser cache in order to see the changes. There is a trick to work around clearing the browser's cache. It is to have the revision number of the version control system shown in `STATIC_URL`. Whenever the code is updated, the visitor's browser will force the loading of all-new static files.

This recipe shows how to put a revision number in `STATIC_URL` for Subversion users.

Getting ready

Make sure that your project is under the Subversion version control and you have `BASE_DIR` defined in your settings, as shown in the *Defining relative paths in the settings* recipe.

Then, create the `utils` module in your Django project, and also create a file called `misc.py` there.

How to do it...

The procedure to put the revision number in the STATIC_URL settings consists of the following two steps:

1. Insert the following content:

```
# utils/misc.py
import subprocess


def get_media_svn_revision(absolute_path):
    repo_dir = absolute_path
    svn_revision = subprocess.Popen(
        "svn info | grep 'Revision' | awk '{print $2}'",
        stdout=subprocess.PIPE,
        stderr=subprocess.PIPE,
        shell=True,
        cwd=repo_dir,
        universal_newlines=True)
    rev = svn_revision.communicate()[0].partition('\n')[0]
    return rev
```

2. Modify the settings.py file and add the following lines:

```
# settings.py
# ... somewhere after BASE_DIR definition ...
from utils.misc import get_media_svn_revision
STATIC_URL = f'/static/{get_media_svn_revision(BASE_DIR)}/'
```

How it works...

The get_media_svn_revision() function takes the absolute_path directory as a parameter and calls the svn information shell command in that directory to find out the current revision. We pass BASE_DIR to the function, as we are sure that it is under version control. Then, the revision is parsed, returned, and included in the STATIC_URL definition.

See also

- The *Setting up STATIC_URL dynamically for Git users* recipe
- The *Setting the Subversion ignore property* recipe

Setting up STATIC_URL dynamically for Git users

If you don't want to refresh the browser cache each time you change your CSS and JavaScript files, or while styling images, you need to set STATIC_URL dynamically with a varying path component. With the dynamically changing URL, whenever the code is updated, the visitor's browser will force loading of all-new uncached static files. In this recipe, we will set a dynamic path for STATIC_URL when you use the Git version control system.

Getting ready

Make sure that your project is under the Git version control and you have BASE_DIR defined in your settings, as shown in the *Defining relative paths in the settings* recipe.

If you haven't done so yet, create the utils module in your Django project. Also, create a misc.py file there.

How to do it...

The procedure to put the Git timestamp in the STATIC_URL setting consists of the following two steps:

1. Add the following content to the misc.py file placed in utils/:

```python
# utils/misc.py
import subprocess
from datetime import datetime

def get_git_changeset(absolute_path):
    repo_dir = absolute_path
    git_show = subprocess.Popen(
        "git show --pretty=format:%ct --quiet HEAD",
        stdout=subprocess.PIPE,
        stderr=subprocess.PIPE,
        shell=True,
        cwd=repo_dir,
        universal_newlines=True)
    timestamp = git_show.communicate()[0].partition('\n')[0]
    try:
        timestamp = datetime.utcfromtimestamp(int(timestamp))
```

```
except ValueError:
    return ""
changeset = timestamp.strftime('%Y%m%d%H%M%S')
return changeset
```

2. Import the newly created `get_git_changeset()` function in the settings and use it for the `STATIC_URL` path, as follows:

```
# settings.py
# ... somewhere after BASE_DIR definition ...
from utils.misc import get_git_changeset
STATIC_URL = f'/static/{get_git_changeset(BASE_DIR)}/'
```

How it works...

The `get_git_changeset()` function takes the `absolute_path` directory as a parameter and calls the `git` show shell command with the parameters to show the Unix timestamp of the `HEAD` revision in the directory. As stated in the previous recipe, we pass `BASE_DIR` to the function, as we are sure that it is under version control. The timestamp is parsed, converted to a string consisting of year, month, day, hour, minutes, and seconds, returned; and included in the definition of `STATIC_URL`.

See also

- The *Setting up STATIC_URL dynamically for Subversion users* recipe
- The *Creating the Git ignore file* recipe

Setting UTF-8 as the default encoding for MySQL configuration

MySQL proclaims itself as *the most popular open source database*. In this recipe, we will tell you how to set UTF-8 as the default encoding for it. Note that if you don't set this encoding in the database configuration, you might get into a situation where LATIN1 is used by default with your UTF-8-encoded data. This will lead to database errors whenever symbols such as € are used. Also, this recipe will save you from the difficulties of converting the database data from LATIN1 to UTF-8, especially when you have some tables encoded in LATIN1 and others in UTF-8.

Getting ready

Make sure that the MySQL database management system and the MySQLdb Python module are installed and you are using the MySQL engine in your project's settings.

How to do it...

Open the /etc/mysql/my.cnf MySQL configuration file in your favorite editor and ensure that the following settings are set in the [client], [mysql], and [mysqld] sections, as follows:

```
# /etc/mysql/my.cnf
[client]
default-character-set = utf8

[mysql]
default-character-set = utf8

[mysqld]
collation-server = utf8_unicode_ci
init-connect = 'SET NAMES utf8'
character-set-server = utf8
```

If any of the sections don't exist, create them in the file. If the sections do already exist, add these settings to the existing configurations. Then, restart MySQL in your command-line tool, as follows:

```
$ /etc/init.d/mysql restart
```

How it works...

Now, whenever you create a new MySQL database, the databases and all of their tables will be set in UTF-8 encoding by default. Don't forget to set this on all computers on which your project is developed or published.

There's more...

For a Docker project, these settings can be added to the config/my.cnf file and saved to version control. This file will automatically be added as /etc/mysql/my.cnf within the container at build time. Furthermore, any developer that pulls down the code will automatically gain the configuration.

See also

- The *Creating a virtual environment project file structure* recipe
- The *Creating a Docker project file structure* recipe

Setting the Subversion ignore property

Make sure that your Django project is under the Subversion version control.

How to do it...

1. Open your command-line tool and set your default editor as nano, vi, vim, or any other that you prefer, as follows:

    ```
    $ export EDITOR=nano
    ```

    If you don't have a preference, we would recommend using nano, which is very intuitive and a simple text editor for the terminal.

2. Then, go to your project directory and type the following command:

    ```
    $ svn propedit svn:ignore myproject
    ```

3. This will open a temporary file in the editor, where you need to put the following file and directory patterns for Subversion to ignore:

    ```
    # Project files and directories
    static
    media
    tmp
    # Byte-compiled / optimized / DLL files
    __pycache__
    *.py[cod]
    *$py.class
    # C extensions
    *.so
    # PyInstaller
    *.manifest
    *.spec
    # Installer logs
    ```

```
pip-log.txt
pip-delete-this-directory.txt
# Unit test / coverage reports
htmlcov
.tox
.coverage
.coverage.*
.cache
nosetests.xml
coverage.xml
*.cover
# Translations
*.pot
# Django stuff:
*.log
# PyBuilder
target
```

4. Save the file and exit the editor. For every other Python package in your project, you will need to ignore several files and directories too. Just go to a directory and type the following command:

```
$ svn propedit svn:ignore .
```

5. Then, put this in the temporary file, save it, and close the editor:

```
# Byte-compiled / optimized / DLL files
__pycache__
*.py[cod]
*$py.class
# C extensions
*.so
# PyInstaller
*.manifest
*.spec
# Installer logs
pip-log.txt
pip-delete-this-directory.txt
# Unit test / coverage reports
htmlcov
.tox
.coverage
.coverage.*
.cache
nosetests.xml
coverage.xml
*.cover
# Translations
```

```
*.pot
# Django stuff:
*.log
# PyBuilder
target
```

How it works...

In Subversion, you need to define the ignore properties for each directory of your project. Mainly, we don't want to track the Python-compiled files, for instance, `*.pyc`. We also want to ignore the `static` directory, where static files from different apps are collected, `media`, which contains uploaded files and changes together with the database, and `tmp`, which is temporarily used for file uploads.

 If you keep all your settings in a `config` Python package, as described in the *Configuring settings for development, testing, staging, and production environments* recipe, add `settings.py` to the ignored files too.

See also

- The *Creating and including local settings* recipe
- The *Creating the Git ignore file* recipe

Creating the Git ignore file

If you are using Git—the most popular distributed version control system—ignoring some files and folders from version control is much easier than with Subversion.

Getting ready

Make sure that your Django project is under the Git version control.

How to do it...

Using your favorite text editor, create a .gitignore file at the root of your Django project, and put the following files and directories there:

```
# .gitignore
# Project files and directories
/myproject/static/
/myproject/tmp/
/myproject/media/
# Byte-compiled / optimized / DLL files
__pycache__/
*.py[cod]
*$py.class
# C extensions
*.so
# PyInstaller
*.manifest
*.spec
# Installer logs
pip-log.txt
pip-delete-this-directory.txt
# Unit test / coverage reports
htmlcov/
.tox/
.coverage
.coverage.*
.cache
nosetests.xml
coverage.xml
*.cover
# Translations
*.pot
# Django stuff:
*.log
# Sphinx documentation
docs/_build/
# PyBuilder
target/
```

How it works...

The .gitignore file specifies patterns that should intentionally be untracked by the Git version control system. The .gitignore file that we created in this recipe will ignore the Python-compiled files, local settings, collected static files, temporary directory for uploads, and media directory with the uploaded files.

 If you keep all of your settings in a config Python package, as described in the *Configuring settings for development, testing, staging, and production environments* recipe, add settings.py to the ignored files too.

There's more...

With Git ignore files, we have the ability to follow a whitelist pattern rather than a blacklist, which means we can indicate what files we want to *include* rather than those we should omit. In addition, the patterns given in .gitignore are honored for all levels of the tree below where the file resides, making them extremely powerful. For example, the file could be written in this manner for a Docker project:

```
# .gitignore
# ignore everything in the root by default
/*
# allow this file of course
!.gitignore
# allowed root directories
!/apps/
!/bin/
!/config/
!/data/
!/project/
!/static/
!/templates/
# allowed root files
!/Dockerfile
!/docker-compose.yml
# files allowed anywhere
!README.md
# specifically ignore certain deeper items
__pycache__/
```

See also

- The *Creating a virtual environment project file structure* recipe
- The *Creating a Docker project file structure* recipe
- The *Setting the Subversion ignore property* recipe

Deleting Python-compiled files

When you run your project for the first time, Python compiles all of your *.py code in bytecode-compiled files, *.pyc, which are used later for execution.

Normally, when you change the *.py files, *.pyc is recompiled; however, sometimes when switching branches or moving the directories, you need to clean up the compiled files manually.

Getting ready

Use your favorite editor and edit or create a .bash_profile file in your home directory.

How to do it...

1. Add this alias at the end of .bash_profile, as follows:

```
# ~/.bash_profile
alias delpyc='find . -name "*.pyc" -delete'
```

2. Now, to clean the Python-compiled files, go to your project directory and type the following command on the command line:

```
$ delpyc
```

How it works...

At first, we create a Unix alias that searches for the *.pyc files and deletes them in the current directory and its children. The .bash_profile file is executed when you start a new session in the command-line tool.

See also

- The *Setting the Subversion ignore property* recipe
- The *Creating the Git ignore file* recipe

Respecting the import order in Python files

When you create the Python modules, it is good practice to stay consistent with the structure in the files. This makes it easier for other developers and yourself to read the code. This recipe will show you how to structure your imports.

Getting ready

Create a virtual environment and create a Django project in it.

How to do it...

Use the following structure in a Python file that you create. Starting with the first line in the file, put the imports categorized in sections, as follows:

```python
# System libraries
import os
import re
from datetime import datetime

# Third-party libraries
import boto
from PIL import Image

# Django modules
from django.db import models
from django.conf import settings

# Django apps
from cms.models import Page

# Current-app modules
from . import app_settings
```

How it works...

We have five main categories for the imports, as follows:

- System libraries for packages in the default installation of Python
- Third-party libraries for the additionally installed Python packages
- Django modules for different modules from the Django framework
- Django apps for third-party and local apps
- Current-app modules for relative imports from the current app

There's more...

When coding in Python and Django, use the official style guide for Python code, PEP 8. You can find it at `https://www.python.org/dev/peps/pep-0008/`.

See also

- The *Handling project dependencies with pip* recipe
- The *Including external dependencies in your project* recipe

Creating app configuration

When developing a website with Django, you create one module for the project itself, and then multiple Python modules called applications (or, more commonly, apps) that combine the different modular functionalities and usually consist of models, views, forms, URL configurations, management commands, migrations, signals, tests, and so on. The Django framework has application registry, where all apps and models are collected and later used for configuration and introspection. Since Django 1.7, meta information about apps can be saved in the `AppConfig` instance for each used app. Let's create a sample `magazine` app to take a look at how to use the app configuration there.

Getting ready

You can create a Django app in one of three ways:

- Generate all of the files manually, which can be an excellent tool for learning, but is far from the most efficient approach.
- Use the `startapp` command in your virtual environment, as follows:

```
(myproject_env)$ django-admin.py startapp magazine
```

Learn how to use virtual environments in the *Working with a virtual environment* and *Creating a virtual environment project file structure* recipes.

- Use the `startapp` command in a Docker project, as follows:

```
myproject_django/$ docker-compose run app django-admin.py startapp
magazine
```

 Learn how to use Docker in the *Working with Docker* and *Creating a Docker project file structure* recipes.

With your `magazine` app created, add a `NewsArticle` model to `models.py`, create administration for the model in `admin.py`, and put `"magazine"` in `INSTALLED_APPS` in the `settings.py`. If you are not yet familiar with these tasks, study the official Django tutorial at:

`https://docs.djangoproject.com/en/2.1/intro/tutorial01/`.

How to do it...

Follow these steps to create and use the app configuration:

1. Create the `apps.py` file and put the following content in it, as follows:

```python
# magazine/apps.py
from django.apps import AppConfig
from django.utils.translation import ugettext_lazy as _


class MagazineAppConfig(AppConfig):
    name = "magazine"
    verbose_name = _("Magazine")
```

```
def ready(self):
    from . import signals
```

2. Edit the __init__.py file in the magazine module to contain the following content:

```
# magazine/__init__.py
default_app_config = "magazine.apps.MagazineAppConfig"
```

3. Let's create a signals.py file and add some signal handlers there:

```
# magazine/signals.py
from django.db.models.signals import post_save, post_delete
from django.dispatch import receiver
from django.conf import settings

from .models import NewsArticle


@receiver(post_save, sender=NewsArticle)
def news_save_handler(sender, **kwargs):
    if settings.DEBUG:
        print(f"{kwargs['instance']} saved.")


@receiver(post_delete, sender=NewsArticle)
def news_delete_handler(sender, **kwargs):
    if settings.DEBUG:
        print(f"{kwargs['instance']} deleted.")
```

How it works...

When you run an HTTP server or invoke a management command, django.setup() is called. It loads the settings, sets up logging, and prepares the app registry. This registry is initialized in three steps, as follows:

- Django imports the configurations for each item from INSTALLED_APPS in the settings. These items can point to app names or configuration directly, for example, "magazine" or "magazine.apps.NewsAppConfig".
- Django tries to import models.py from each app in INSTALLED_APPS and collect all of the models.
- Finally, Django runs the ready() method for each app configuration. This method is a correct place to register signal handlers, if you have any. The ready() method is optional.

- In our example, the MagazineAppConfig class sets the configuration for the magazine app. The name parameter defines the name of the current app. The verbose_name parameter is used in the Django model administration, where models are presented and grouped by apps. The ready() method imports and activates the signal handlers that, when in DEBUG mode, print in the terminal that a NewsArticle object was saved or deleted.

There is more...

After calling django.setup(), you can load the app configurations and models from the registry as follows:

```
>>> from django.apps import apps as django_apps
>>> magazine_app_config = django_apps.get_app_config("magazine")
>>> magazine_app_config
<MagazineAppConfig: magazine>
>>> magazine_app_config.models_module
<module 'magazine.models' from '/usr/src/app/magazine/models.py'>
>>> NewsArticle = django_apps.get_model("magazine", "NewsArticle")
>>> NewsArticle
<class 'magazine.models.NewsArticle'>
```

You can read more about app configuration in the official Django documentation at https://docs.djangoproject.com/en/2.1/ref/applications/.

See also

- The *Working with a virtual environment* recipe
- The *Working with Docker* recipe
- The *Defining overwritable app settings* recipe
- Chapter 6, *Model Administration*

Defining overwritable app settings

This recipe will show you how to define settings for your app that can be then overwritten in your project's settings.py file. This is useful especially for reusable apps.

Getting ready

Follow the steps for *Getting ready* in the *Creating app configuration* recipe to create your Django app.

How to do it...

1. If you just have one or two settings, you can use the following pattern in your models.py file. If the settings are extensive and you want to have them organized better, create an app_settings.py file in the app and put the settings in the following way:

```python
# magazine/models.py or magazine/app_settings.py
from django.conf import settings
from django.utils.translation import ugettext_lazy as _

SETTING1 = getattr(settings, "MAGAZINE_SETTING1", "default value")
MEANING_OF_LIFE = getattr(settings, "MAGAZINE_MEANING_OF_LIFE", 42)
STATUS_CHOICES = getattr(settings, "MAGAZINE_STATUS_CHOICES", (
    ("draft", _("Draft")),
    ("published", _("Published")),
    ("not_listed", _("Not Listed")),
))
```

2. If the settings were defined in an app_settings.py file, then you can import and use them in models.py, as follows:

```python
# magazine/models.py
from django.db import models
from django.utils.translation import ugettext_lazy as _

from .app_settings import STATUS_CHOICES


class NewsArticle(models.Model):
    # ...
    status = models.CharField(_("Status"),
                              max_length=20,
                              choices=STATUS_CHOICES)
```

3. If you want to overwrite the STATUS_CHOICES setting for a given project, you simply open settings.py for that project and add the following:

```
# settings.py
from django.utils.translation import ugettext_lazy as _

# ...

MAGAZINE_STATUS_CHOICES = (
    ("imported", _("Imported")),
    ("draft", _("Draft")),
    ("published", _("Published")),
    ("not_listed", _("Not Listed")),
    ("expired", _("Expired")),
)
```

How it works...

The getattr(object, attribute_name[, default_value]) Python function tries to get the attribute_name attribute from object and returns default_value if it is not found. In this case, different settings are tried in order to be taken from the Django project settings.py module or, if they are not found, the default values are assigned.

2
Database Structure and Modeling

In this chapter, we will cover the following topics:

- Using model mixins
- Creating a model mixin with URL-related methods
- Creating a model mixin to handle creation and modification dates
- Creating a model mixin to take care of meta tags
- Creating a model mixin to handle generic relations
- Handling multilingual fields
- Enabling schema microdata enhancements
- Using migrations
- Switching from South migrations to Django migrations
- Changing a foreign key to the many-to-many field

Introduction

When you start a new app, the first thing that you do is create the models that represent your database structure. We are assuming that you have already created Django apps, or, at the very least, have read and understood the official Django tutorial. In this chapter, you will see a few interesting techniques that will make your database structure consistent throughout the different apps in your project. Then, you will see how to create custom model fields, in order to handle the internationalization of the data in your database. At the end of the chapter, you will see how to use migrations to change your database structure during the process of development.

Using model mixins

In object-oriented languages, such as Python, a **mixin** class can be viewed as an interface with implemented features. When a model extends a mixin, it implements the interface and includes all of its fields, properties, and methods. The mixins in Django models can be used when you want to reuse the generic functionalities in different models multiple times.

Getting ready

First, you will need to create reusable mixins. A good place to keep your model mixins is in a utils module, such as the one that we will create later in the chapter (along with some typical examples of mixins). If you create a reusable app that you will share with others, keep the model mixins in the reusable app, instead—possibly in a base.py file.

How to do it...

Open the models.py file of any Django app that you want to use mixins with, and type the following code:

```
# demo_app/models.py
from django.db import models
from django.utils.translation import ugettext_lazy as _

from utils.models import (CreationModificationDateMixin,
                          MetaTagsMixin,
                          UrlMixin)


class Idea(UrlMixin, CreationModificationDateMixin, MetaTagsMixin):
    class Meta:
        verbose_name = _("Idea")
        verbose_name_plural = _("Ideas")

    title = models.CharField(_("Title"), max_length=200)
    content = models.TextField(_("Content"))

    def __str__(self):
        return self.title
```

How it works...

Django model inheritance supports three types of inheritance: abstract base classes, multi-table inheritance, and proxy models. Model mixins are abstract model classes, in that we define them by using an abstract `Meta` class, with specified fields, properties, and methods. When you create a model such as `Idea`, as shown in the preceding example, it inherits all of the features from `UrlMixin`, `CreationModificationDateMixin`, and `MetaTagsMixin`. All of the fields of these abstract classes are saved in the same database table as the fields of the extending model. In the following recipes, you will learn how to define your model mixins.

There's more...

To learn more about the different types of model inheritance, refer to the official Django documentation, available at
`https://docs.djangoproject.com/en/2.1/topics/db/models/#model-inheritance`.

See also

- The *Creating a model mixin with URL-related methods* recipe
- The *Creating a model mixin to handle creation and modification dates* recipe
- The *Creating a model mixin to take care of meta tags* recipe

Creating a model mixin with URL-related methods

For every model that is appropriate to detail on its own distinct page, it is a good practice to define the `get_absolute_url()` method. This method can be used in templates, and also in the Django admin site, to preview the saved object. However, `get_absolute_url()` is ambiguous, as it returns the URL path instead of the full URL.

In this recipe, we will look at how to create a model mixin that provides simplified support for model-specific URLs. This mixin will:

- Allow you to define either the URL path or the full URL in your model
- Generate the other of these automatically based on the one you define
- Define the `get_absolute_url()` method behind the scenes

Getting ready

If you haven't yet done so, create a `utils` package to save your mixins under. Then, create a `models.py` file in the `utils` package (alternatively, if you create a reusable app, put the mixins in a `base.py` file in your app).

How to do it...

Execute the following steps, one by one:

1. Add the following content to the `models.py` file of your `utils` package:

```python
# utils/models.py
from urllib.parse import urlparse, urlunparse

from django.conf import settings
from django.db import models


class UrlMixin(models.Model):
    """
    A replacement for get_absolute_url()
    Models extending this mixin should have
    either get_url or get_url_path implemented.
    """
    class Meta:
        abstract = True

    def get_url(self):
        if hasattr(self.get_url_path, "dont_recurse"):
            raise NotImplementedError
        try:
            path = self.get_url_path()
        except NotImplementedError:
            raise
        website_host = getattr(settings,
```

```
                            "SITE_HOST",
                            "localhost:8000")
        return f"http://{website_host}/{path}"
    get_url.dont_recurse = True

    def get_url_path(self):
        if hasattr(self.get_url, "dont_recurse"):
            raise NotImplementedError
        try:
            url = self.get_url()
        except NotImplementedError:
            raise
        bits = urlparse(url)
        return urlunparse(("", "") + bits[2:])
    get_url_path.dont_recurse = True

    def get_absolute_url(self):
        return self.get_url_path()
```

2. To use the mixin in your app, import the mixin from the utils package, inherit the mixin in your model class, and define the get_url_path() method, as follows:

```
# demo_app/models.py
from django.db import models
from django.urls import reverse
from django.utils.translation import ugettext_lazy as _

from utils.models import UrlMixin


class Idea(UrlMixin):
    # ...

    def get_url_path(self):
        return reverse("idea-detail", kwargs={
            "pk": str(self.pk),
        })
```

3. If you check this code in the staging or production environment, or run a local server with a different IP or port than the defaults, set the SITE_HOST in the local settings. You might do so by using environment variables, as discussed in the *Creating and including local settings* recipe in Chapter 1, *Getting Started with Django 2.1*. Alternatively, you can use a multi-file approach, like the one detailed in the *Configuring settings for development, testing, staging, and production environments* recipe, also in Chapter 1, *Getting Started with Django 2.1*. The latter would be set up as follows:

```
# settings.py or config/prod.py
# ...
SITE_HOST = 'www.example.com'
```

How it works...

The UrlMixin class is an abstract model that has three methods, as follows:

- get_url() retrieves the full URL of the object.
- get_url_path() retrieves the absolute path of the object.
- get_absolute_url() mimics the get_url_path() method.

The get_url() and get_url_path() methods are expected to be overwritten in the extended model class; for example, Idea. You can define get_url(), and get_url_path() will strip it to the path. Alternately, you can define get_url_path(), and get_url() will prepend the website URL to the beginning of the path.

 The rule of thumb is to always overwrite the get_url_path() method.

In the templates, use get_url_path() when you need a link to an object on the same website, as follows:

```
<a href="{{ idea.get_url_path }}">{{ idea.title }}</a>
```

Use `get_url()` for links to be surfaced outside of the websites, such as in emails, RSS feeds, or APIs; an example is as follows:

```
<a href="{{ idea.get_url }}">{{ idea.title }}</a>
```

The default `get_absolute_url()` method will be used in the Django model administration for the **View on site** functionality, and might also be used by some third-party Django apps.

See also

- The *Using model mixins* recipe
- The *Creating a model mixin to handle creation and modification dates* recipe
- The *Creating a model mixin to take care of meta tags* recipe
- The *Creating a model mixin to handle generic relations* recipe
- The *Configuring settings for development, testing, staging, and production environments* recipe, in Chapter 1, *Getting Started with Django 2.1*
- The *Creating and including local settings* recipe in Chapter 1, *Getting Started with Django 2.1*

Creating a model mixin to handle creation and modification dates

It is common to include timestamps in your models, for the creation and modification of your model instances. In this recipe, you will learn how to create a simple model mixin that saves the creation and modification dates and times for your model. Using such a mixin will ensure that all of the models use the same field names for the timestamps, and have the same behaviors.

Getting ready

If you haven't yet done so, create the `utils` package to save your mixins. Then, create the `models.py` file in the `utils` package.

How to do it...

Open the `models.py` file of your `utils` package, and insert the following content there:

```
# utils/models.py
from django.db import models
from django.utils.translation import ugettext_lazy as _

class CreationModificationDateMixin(models.Model):
    """
    Abstract base class with a creation
    and modification date and time
    """
    class Meta:
        abstract = True

    created = models.DateTimeField(
        _("creation date and time"),
        auto_now_add=True)
    updated = models.DateTimeField(
        _("modification date and time"),
        auto_now=True)
```

How it works...

The `CreationModificationDateMixin` class is an abstract model, which means that extending model classes will create all of the fields in the same database table—that is, there will be no one-to-one relationships that make the table difficult to handle. This mixin has two date-time fields, each set to receive the date and time when the object is saved. For the `created` field, the current date-time is only set on the initial save, when the related item is added, by setting the `auto_now_add` flag to `True`. Similarly, the `modified` field is set on every save, via `auto_now=True`. Because these field values are handled automatically, Django marks them as read-only for us, so that we don't have to specify the `editable=False` flag ourselves.

To make use of this mixin, we just have to import it and extend our model, as follows:

```
# demo_app/models.py
# ...
from utils.models import (CreationModificationDateMixin, UrlMixin)


class Idea(CreationModificationDateMixin, UrlMixin):
    # ...
```

See also

- The *Using model mixins* recipe
- The *Creating a model mixin to take care of meta tags* recipe
- The *Creating a model mixin to take care of schema microdata* recipe
- The *Creating a model mixin to handle generic relations* recipe

Creating a model mixin to take care of meta tags

When you optimize your site for search engines, you not only have to use semantic markup for each page, but you also have to include appropriate meta tags. For maximum flexibility, it helps to have a way to define content for common meta tags, specific to objects that have their own detail pages on your website. In this recipe, we will look at how to create a model mixin for the fields and methods related to keyword, description, author, and copyright meta tags.

Getting ready

As detailed in the previous recipes, make sure that you have the utils package for your mixins. Also, create a directory structure, templates/utils, under the package, and inside of that, create a meta.html file to store the basic meta tag markup.

How to do it...

1. Add the following basic meta tag markup to meta.html:

   ```
   {# templates/utils/meta.html #}
   <meta name="{{ name }}" content="{{ content }}">
   ```

2. Open the models.py file from this package in your favorite editor, and add the following content:

   ```
   # utils/models.py
   from django.db import models
   from django.template import loader
   from django.utils.safestring import mark_safe
   ```

```python
from django.utils.translation import ugettext_lazy as _

class MetaTagsMixin(models.Model):
    """
    Abstract base class for generating meta tags
    """
    class Meta:
        abstract = True

    meta_keywords = models.CharField(
        _("Keywords"),
        max_length=255,
        blank=True,
        help_text=_("Separate keywords by comma."))
    meta_description = models.CharField(
        _("Description"),
        max_length=255,
        blank=True)
    meta_author = models.CharField(
        _("Author"),
        max_length=255,
        blank=True)
    meta_copyright = models.CharField(
        _("Copyright"),
        max_length=255,
        blank=True)

    def get_meta(self, name, content):
        tag = ""
        if name and content:
            tag = loader.render_to_string('utils/meta.html', {
                'name': name,
                'content': content,
            })
        return mark_safe(tag)

    def get_meta_keywords(self):
        return self.get_meta('keywords', self.meta_keywords)

    def get_meta_description(self):
        return self.get_meta('description', self.meta_description)

    def get_meta_author(self):
        return self.get_meta('author', self.meta_author)

    def get_meta_copyright(self):
        return self.get_meta('copyright', self.meta_copyright)
```

```
def get_meta_tags(self):
    return mark_safe("\n".join((
        self.get_meta_keywords(),
        self.get_meta_description(),
        self.get_meta_author(),
        self.get_meta_copyright(),
    )))
```

How it works...

This mixin adds four fields to the model that extends from it: `meta_keywords`, `meta_description`, `meta_author`, and `meta_copyright`. Corresponding `get_*` methods, used to render the associated meta tags, are also added. Each of these passes the `name` and appropriate field `content` to the core `get_meta` method, which uses this input to return rendered markup, based on the `meta.html` template. Finally, a shortcut `get_meta_tags` method is provided to generate the combined markup for all of the available metadata at once.

If you use this mixin in a model, such as `Idea`, which is shown in the *Using model mixins* recipe at the start of this chapter, you can put the following in the HEAD section of your detail page template to render all of the meta tags at once, as follows:

```
{% block meta_tags %}
    {{ block.super }}
    {{ idea.get_meta_tags }}
{% endblock %}
```

Here, a `meta_tags` block has been defined in a parent template, and this snippet shows how the child template redefines the block, including the content from the parent first as `block.super`, and extending it with our additional tags from the `idea` object. You could also render only a specific meta tag by using something like the following:

```
{{ idea.get_meta_description }}
```

As you may have noticed from the `models.py` code, the rendered meta tags are marked as safe – that is, they are not escaped, and we don't need to use the safe template filter. Only the values that come from the database are escaped, in order to guarantee that the final HTML is well formed. The database data in the `meta_keywords` and other fields will automatically be escaped when we `render_to_string` for the `meta.html` template, because that template does not specify `{% autoescape off %}` in its content.

See also

- The *Using model mixins* recipe
- The *Creating a model mixin to handle creation and modification dates* recipe
- The *Creating a model mixin to take care of schema microdata* recipe
- The *Creating a model mixin to handle generic relations* recipe
- The *Arranging the base.html template* recipe in `Chapter 4`, *Templates and JavaScript*

Creating a model mixin to handle generic relations

Aside from normal database relationships, such as a foreign-key relationship or a many-to-many relationship, Django has a mechanism to relate a model to an instance of any other model. This concept is called **generic relations**. For each generic relation, there is a content type of the related model that is saved, as well as the ID of the instance of that model.

In this recipe, we will look at how to abstract the creation of generic relations in the model mixins.

Getting ready

For this recipe to work, you will need to have the `contenttypes` app installed. It should be in the `INSTALLED_APPS` directory, by default, as shown in the following code:

```python
# settings.py or config/base.py
INSTALLED_APPS = (
    # ...
    'django.contrib.contenttypes',
)
```

Again, make sure that you have already created the `utils` package for your model mixins.

How to do it...

1. Open the `models.py` file in the `utils` package in a text editor, and insert the following content there:

```python
# utils/models.py
from django.contrib.contenttypes.fields import GenericForeignKey
from django.contrib.contenttypes.models import ContentType
from django.core.exceptions import FieldError
from django.db import models
from django.utils.translation import ugettext_lazy as _


def object_relation_mixin_factory(
        prefix=None,
        prefix_verbose=None,
        add_related_name=False,
        limit_content_type_choices_to=None,
        limit_object_choices_to=None,
        is_required=False):
    """
    returns a mixin class for generic foreign keys using
    "Content type - object Id" with dynamic field names.
    This function is just a class generator

    Parameters:
    prefix: a prefix, which is added in front of
                        the fields
    prefix_verbose: a verbose name of the prefix, used to
                        generate a title for the field column
                        of the content object in the Admin
    add_related_name: a boolean value indicating, that a
                        related name for the generated content
                        type foreign key should be added. This
                        value should be true, if you use more
                        than one ObjectRelationMixin in your
                        model.

    The model fields are created like this:
        <<prefix>>_content_type: Field name for the "content type"
        <<prefix>>_object_id: Field name for the "object id"
        <<prefix>>_content_object: Field name for the "content
object"
    """
    p = ""
    if prefix:
        p = f"{prefix}_"
```

```
        prefix_verbose = prefix_verbose or _("Related object")
        limit_content_type_choices_to = (limit_content_type_choices_to
                                         or {})
        limit_object_choices_to = limit_object_choices_to or {}

        content_type_field = f"{p}content_type"
        object_id_field = f"{p}object_id"
        content_object_field = f"{p}content_object"



        class TheClass(models.Model):
            class Meta:
                abstract = True



        if add_related_name:
            if not prefix:
                raise FieldError("if add_related_name is set to "
                                 "True, a prefix must be given")
            related_name = prefix
        else:
            related_name = None

        optional = not is_required

        ct_verbose_name = _(f"{prefix_verbose}'s type (model)")

        content_type = models.ForeignKey(
            ContentType,
            verbose_name=ct_verbose_name,
            related_name=related_name,
            blank=optional,
            null=optional,
            help_text=_("Please select the type (model) "
                        "for the relation, you want to build."),
            limit_choices_to=limit_content_type_choices_to,
            on_delete=models.CASCADE)

        fk_verbose_name = prefix_verbose

        object_id = models.CharField(
            fk_verbose_name,
            blank=optional,
            null=False,
            help_text=_("Please enter the ID of the related object."),
            max_length=255,
            default="") # for migrations
        object_id.limit_choices_to = limit_object_choices_to
```

```
# can be retrieved by
# MyModel._meta.get_field("object_id").limit_choices_to

content_object = generic.GenericForeignKey(
    ct_field=content_type_field,
    fk_field=object_id_field)

TheClass.add_to_class(content_type_field, content_type)
TheClass.add_to_class(object_id_field, object_id)
TheClass.add_to_class(content_object_field,
                      content_object)

return TheClass
```

2. The following code snippet is an example of how to use two generic relationships in your app (put this code in demo_app/models.py):

```
# demo_app/models.py
from django.db import models

from utils.models import (
    object_relation_mixin_factory as generic_relation)

FavoriteObjectMixin = generic_relation(is_required=True)

OwnerMixin = generic_relation(
    prefix="owner",
    prefix_verbose=_("Owner"),
    is_required=True,
    add_related_name=True,
    limit_content_type_choices_to={
        'model__in': ('user', 'institution')
    })

class Like(FavoriteObjectMixin, OwnerMixin):
    class Meta:
        verbose_name = _("Like")
        verbose_name_plural = _("Likes")

    def __str__(self):
        return _("%(owner)s likes %(obj)s") % {
            "owner": self.owner_content_object,
            "obj": self.content_object,
        }
```

How it works...

As you can see, this snippet is more complex than the previous ones. The `object_relation_mixin_factory`, which we have aliased to `generic_relation`, for short, in our import, is not a mixin itself; it is a function that generates a model mixin – that is, an abstract model class to extend from. The dynamically created mixin adds the `content_type` and `object_id` fields, and the `content_object` generic foreign key that points to the related instance.

Why can't we just define a simple model mixin with these three attributes? A dynamically generated abstract class allows us to have prefixes for each field name; therefore, we can have more than one generic relation in the same model. For example, the `Like` model, which was shown previously, will have the `content_type`, `object_id`, and `content_object` fields for the favorite object, and `owner_content_type`, `owner_object_id`, and `owner_content_object` for the one (user or institution) that liked the object.

The `object_relation_mixin_factory` function, which we have aliased to `generic_relation`, for short, adds the possibility to limit the content type choices by the `limit_content_type_choices_to` parameter. The preceding example limits the choices for `owner_content_type` to only the content types of the `User` and `Institution` models. Also, there is the `limit_object_choices_to` parameter, which can be used by custom form validation to limit the generic relations to only specific objects. For example, we might want to allow favorites for only the objects with a published status.

See also

- The *Creating a model mixin with URL-related methods* recipe
- The *Creating a model mixin to handle creation and modification dates* recipe
- The *Creating a model mixin to take care of meta tags* recipe
- The *Creating a model mixin to take care of schema microdata* recipe
- The *Implementing the Like widget* recipe in `Chapter 4`, *Templates and JavaScript*

Handling multilingual fields

Django uses the internationalization mechanism to translate verbose strings in the code and templates. However, it's up to the developer to decide how to implement the multilingual content in the models. There are several third-party modules that handle translatable model fields; however, I prefer the simple solution that will be introduced to you in this recipe.

The advantages of the approach that you will learn about are as follows:

- It is straightforward to define multilingual fields in the database.
- It is simple to use the multilingual fields in database queries.
- You can use contributed administration to edit models with the multilingual fields, without additional modifications.
- If you need it, you can easily show all of the translations of an object in the same template.
- You can use database migrations to add or remove languages.

Getting ready

Have you created the `utils` package, as has been used in the preceding recipes of this chapter? You will now need a new `fields.py` file within the `utils` app, for the custom model fields.

How to do it...

Execute the following steps to define the multilingual character field and multilingual text field:

1. Open the `fields.py` file and create the base multilingual field, as follows:

```
# utils/fields.py
from django.conf import settings
from django.db import models
from django.utils.translation import get_language


class MultilingualField(models.Field):
    SUPPORTED_FIELD_TYPES = [models.CharField, models.TextField]

    def __init__(self, verbose_name=None, **kwargs):
        self.localized_field_model = None
```

```
        for model in MultilingualField.SUPPORTED_FIELD_TYPES:
            if issubclass(self.__class__, model):
                self.localized_field_model = model
        self._blank = kwargs.get("blank", False)
        self._editable = kwargs.get("editable", True)
        super().__init__(verbose_name, **kwargs)

    @staticmethod
    def localized_field_name(name, lang_code):
        lang_code_safe = lang_code.replace("-", "_")
        return f"{name}_{lang_code_safe}"

    def get_localized_field(self, lang_code, lang_name):
        _blank = (self._blank
                    if lang_code == settings.LANGUAGE_CODE
                    else True)
        localized_field = self.localized_field_model(
            f"{self.verbose_name} ({lang_name})",
            name=self.name,
            primary_key=self.primary_key,
            max_length=self.max_length,
            unique=self.unique,
            blank=_blank,
            null=False, # we ignore the null argument!
            db_index=self.db_index,
            default=self.default or "",
            editable=self._editable,
            serialize=self.serialize,
            choices=self.choices,
            help_text=self.help_text,
            db_column=None,
            db_tablespace=self.db_tablespace)
        return localized_field

    def contribute_to_class(self, cls, name,
                            private_only=False,
                            virtual_only=False):
        def translated_value():
            language = get_language()
            val = self.__dict__.get(
                MultilingualField.localized_field_name(
                        name, language))
            if not val:
                val = self.__dict__.get(
                    MultilingualField.localized_field_name(
                            name, settings.LANGUAGE_CODE))
            return val
```

```
# generate language-specific fields dynamically
if not cls._meta.abstract:
    if self.localized_field_model:
        for lang_code, lang_name in settings.LANGUAGES:
            localized_field = self.get_localized_field(
                lang_code, lang_name)
            localized_field.contribute_to_class(
                    cls,
                    MultilingualField.localized_field_name(
                            name, lang_code))
        setattr(cls, name, property(translated_value))
    else:
        super().contribute_to_class(
            cls, name, private_only, virtual_only)
```

2. In the same file, subclass the base field for character and text field forms, as follows:

```
class MultilingualCharField(models.CharField, MultilingualField):
    pass


class MultilingualTextField(models.TextField, MultilingualField):
    pass
```

Now, we'll consider an example of how to use the multilingual fields in your app, as follows:

1. First, set multiple languages in the settings for your project:

```
# settings.py or config/base.py
LANGUAGE_CODE = "en-us"

LANGUAGES = (
    ("en-us", "US English"),
    ("en-gb", "British English"),
    ("de", "Deutsch"),
    ("fr", "Français"),
    ("lt", "Lietuvių kalba"),
)
```

2. Then, open the models.py file from the demo_app and create the multilingual fields for the Idea model, as follows:

```
# demo_app/models.py
from django.db import models
from django.utils.translation import ugettext_lazy as _
```

```
    from utils.fields import (
        MultilingualCharField,
        MultilingualTextField)

class Idea(models.Model):
    class Meta:
        verbose_name = _("Idea")
        verbose_name_plural = _("Ideas")

    title = MultilingualCharField(_("Title"),
                                   max_length=200)
    description = MultilingualTextField(_("Description"),
                                         blank=True)
    content = models.MultilingualTextField(_("Content"))

    def __str__(self):
        return self.title
```

How it works...

The example of `Idea` will generate a model that is similar to the following:

```
class Idea(models.Model):
    title_en_us = models.CharField(
        _("Title (US English)"),
        max_length=200)
    title_en_gb = models.CharField(
        _("Title (British English)"),
        max_length=200,
        blank=True)
    title_de = models.CharField(
        _("Title (Deutch)"),
        max_length=200,
        blank=True)
    title_fr = models.CharField(
        _("Title (Français)"),
        max_length=200,
        blank=True)
    title_lt = models.CharField(
        _("Title (Lietuvi kalba)"),
        max_length=200,
        blank=True)

    description_en_us = models.TextField(
        _("Description (US English)"),
        blank=True)
```

```
description_en_gb = models.TextField(
    _("Description (British English)"),
    blank=True)
description_de = models.TextField(
    _("Description (Deutch)"),
    blank=True)
description_fr = models.TextField(
    _("Description (Français)"),
    blank=True)
description_lt = models.TextField(
    _("Description (Lietuvi kalba)"),
    blank=True)

content_en_us = models.TextField(
    _("Content (US English)"))
content_en_gb = models.TextField(
    _("Content (British English)"))
content_de = models.TextField(
    _("Content (Deutch)"))
content_fr = models.TextField(
    _("Content (Français)"))
content_lt = models.TextField(
    _("Content (Lietuvi kalba)"))
```

In addition to this, there will be three properties – title, description, and content – that will return the corresponding field in the currently active language. These will fall back to the default language if no localized field content is available. For instance, if the default language were en-us and the active language were de, but the description_de were empty, then the description would fall back to description_en_us, instead.

The MultilingualCharField and MultilingualTextField fields will juggle the model fields dynamically, depending on your LANGUAGES setting. They will overwrite the contribute_to_class() method that is used when the Django framework creates the model classes. The multilingual fields dynamically add character or text fields for each language of the project, and a simple migration to add the appropriate fields in the database. Also, the properties are created in order to return the translated value of the currently active language or the main language, by default.

For example, you can have the following code in the template:

```
<h1>{{ idea.title }}</h1>
<div>{{ idea.description|urlize|linebreaks }}</div>
```

This will show the text in American or British English, German, French, or Lithuanian, depending on the currently selected language. However, it will fall back to US English if the translation doesn't exist.

Here is another example. If you want to have your `QuerySet` ordered by the translated titles in the view, you can define it as follows:

```
qs = Idea.objects.order_by(f"title_{request.LANGUAGE_CODE}")
```

See also

- The *Using migrations* recipe

Enabling schema microdata enhancements

The content delivered in a web application is generally very rich, but there are often important details embedded within plain human-readable text, and search engines cannot easily understand them. When such additional information becomes available, though, search result entries for the content can be similarly enriched, increasing SEO rankings and making it easier for users to find what they are looking for.

Part of this is the data that we exposed in the *Creating a model mixin to take care of meta tags* recipe, earlier in the chapter; however, for certain types of objects, you can build something even more structured. To make this possible, you can identify schema microdata, as per the `https://schema.org` specification, for objects that are represented in the application. In this recipe, we will approach the creation of a model mixin for fields and methods related to the microdata about item types and properties.

Getting ready

As noted in the previous recipes, make sure that you have the `utils` package, containing a `models.py` file for your mixins.

How to do it...

1. Open the `models.py` file from this package in your favorite editor, and add the following content:

   ```
   # utils/models.py
   from enum import Enum
   from functools import reduce
   from django.db import models
   ```

```python
from django.utils.translation import ugettext_lazy as _


class ChoiceEnum(Enum):
    @classmethod
    def choices(cls):
        return tuple((x.name, x.value) for x in cls)


class ItemPropChoiceEnum(ChoiceEnum):
    @classmethod
    def choices(cls, scope=None):
        sources = [cls] + cls.parents()
        choices = reduce((lambda x, y: tuple(set(x) | set(y))),
                         sources)
        if scope:
            choices = tuple(set(choices) & set(scope.choices()))
        return choices

    @classmethod
    def parents(cls):
        return []


class ItemType(ChoiceEnum):
    THING = "Thing"
    CREATIVE_WORK = "CreativeWork"
    BOOK = "Book"


class BooleanFieldItemProp(ItemPropChoiceEnum):
    ABRIDGED = "abridged"


class CharFieldItemProp(ItemPropChoiceEnum):
    ACCESS_MODE = "accessMode"
    ALTERNATE_NAME = "alternateName"
    BOOK_EDITION = "bookEdition"
    DESCRIPTION = "description"
    HEADLINE = "headline"


class TextFieldItemProp(ItemPropChoiceEnum):
    @classmethod
    def parents(cls):
        return [CharFieldItemProp]
```

```python
class ForeignKeyItemProp(ItemPropChoiceEnum):
    ABOUT = "about"
    SUBJECT_OF = "subjectOf"
    WORK_EXAMPLE = "workExample"
    WORK_TRANSLATION = "workTranslation"


class ManyToManyFieldItemProp(ItemPropChoiceEnum):
    @classmethod
    def parents(cls):
        return [ForeignKeyItemProp]


class OneToOneFieldItemProp(ItemPropChoiceEnum):
    def parents(self):
        return [ForeignKeyItemProp]


class UrlFieldItemProp(ItemPropChoiceEnum):
    ADDITIONAL_TYPE = "additionalType"
    SAME_AS = "sameAs"
    URL = "url"


class SchemaMicrodata(models.Model):
    class Meta:
        abstract = True

    @classmethod
    def itemprop_fields(cls):
        return []

    itemtype = models.CharField(_("Microdata item type"),
                                max_length=100,
                                blank=True,
                                choices=ItemType.choices())

    def itemtype_attribute(self):
        attr = loader.render_to_string(
            "utils/itemtype.attr.html",
            {"itemtype": self.get_itemtype_display()})
        return mark_safe(attr)
```

2. Then, add a `signals.py` file to the demo_app, with the following content:

```python
# demo_app/signals.py
from django.db.models import CharField
from django.db.models.signals import class_prepared
from django.dispatch import receiver
from django.template import loader
from django.utils.safestring import mark_safe

from utils import models


@receiver(class_prepared)
def augment_with_itemprops_microdata(sender, **kwargs):
    if issubclass(sender, models.SchemaMicrodata):
        for field_name in sender.itemprop_fields():
            field = None
            for fld in sender._meta.fields:
                if fld.get_attname() == field_name:
                    field = fld
            type = field.__class__.__name__ if field else "None"
            enum = getattr(models, f"{type}ItemProp", None)
            if enum:
                display_name = field.verbose_name or field.name
                itemprop_field_name = f"{field.name}_itemprop"
                itemprop_field = CharField(
                    f"{display_name} microdata item property",
                    name=itemprop_field_name,
                    max_length=200,
                    unique=False,
                    blank=True,
                    null=False,
                    default="",
                    editable=True,
                    choices=enum.choices(),
                    db_tablespace=field.db_tablespace)
                itemprop_field.auto_created = True
                itemprop_field.contribute_to_class(
                    sender,
                    itemprop_field_name)

                def itemprop_attr(sender_instance):
                    prop_key = getattr(sender_instance,
                                       itemprop_field_name,
                                       None)
                    prop_val = field.choices
                    attr = loader.render_to_string(
                        "utils/itemprop.attr.html",
```

```
                              {"itemprop": getattr(sender_instance,
                                           itemprop_field_name,
                                           None)})
                  return mark_safe(attr)

              setattr(sender,
                  f"{itemprop_field_name}_attribute",
                  property(itemprop_attr))
```

3. To load the signals at the right time, we have to provide a custom app configuration. We build the config in demo_app/apps.py, as follows:

```
# demo_app/apps.py
from django.apps import AppConfig
from django.utils.translation import ugettext_lazy as _


class DemoAppConfig(AppConfig):
    name = "demo_app"
    verbose_name = _("Demo App")

    def ready(self):
        from . import signals
```

This configuration is enabled by setting it as the app's default, as follows:

```
# demo_app/__init__.py
default_app_config = "demo_app.apps.DemoAppConfig"
```

4. In the templates/utils directory, add an itemtype.attr.html file, as follows:

```
{# utils/itemtype.attr.html #}
{% if itemtype %}
    itemscope itemtype="//schema.org/{{ itemtype }}"{% endif %}
```

Also, create an itemprop.attr.html file, as follows:

```
{# utils/itemprop.attr.html #}
{% if itemprop %}
    itemprop="{{ itemprop }}"{% endif %}
```

5. Finally, we just need to make use of the mixin in the demo_app/models.py:

```python
# demo_app/models.py
# ...
from utils.models import SchemaMicrodata


class Idea(SchemaMicrodata):
    # ...
    @classmethod
    def itemprop_fields(cls):
        return ["title", "content"] + super().itemprop_fields()
```

How it works...

In Python 3.4, a new Enum class was introduced, filling a gap in the core functionality, as compared to other languages. Enumerations, which are fixed sets of key-value pairs, are perfect for use when generating model field choices. Since there is a specific taxonomy for https://schema.org microdata itemtype and itemprop names, we can enumerate those available options. However, we can't simply use an Enum itself as the choices value, since that field must contain an iterable (list or tuple) where each element is itself an iterable of exactly two items. Instead, we create a ChoiceEnum subclass of Enum, with a choices() method that generates the tuple of 2-tuples needed by Django.

Another strength of the https://schema.org microdata is a rich taxonomy tree, where nested types inherit properties from their more generic parent types. Unfortunately, it is not inherently possible to have the same type of inheritance with Enum objects, which cannot be extended once they define properties. To add this functionality, we create another ItemPropChoiceEnum. This richer version of the ChoiceEnum supports a way to define parents() for the enumeration. The choices() logic is augmented to use this hierarchy to compose a union of all of the available choices for a given enumeration and its parents.

Now that we have the starting points, we will create a single list of values for use in itemtype attributes, and then several field-type-specific lists for itemprop attributes. There is some unavoidable duplication across the item property enumerations, because certain properties allow for very particular types, and others are less strict.

 Note that the item type and item property enumerations shown here are far from exhaustive. The complete hierarchy of schema types can be found at https://schema.org/docs/full.html.

The last piece that we will add to our `util` is the `SchemaMicrodata` model mixin, which provides an `itemtype` field to any models that use it, similar to the metadata fields added in the *Creating a model mixin to take care of meta tags* recipe, earlier in this chapter. A convenient method is also provided, in order to generate a safe HTML snippet for the `itemtype` attribute, to be used in templates as follows:

```
<section {{ thing.itemtype_attribute }}>...</section>
```

Next, we will set up a receiver that acts on the `class_prepared` signal, which is triggered whenever a model is loaded and ready for use, and we will wire it up to be loaded when the application configuration is ready. The receiver checks the `sender` (a model) to see if it subclasses the `SchemaMicrodata` mixin that we just created, and finds the set of fields to be augmented with `itemprop`. If choices are available for the field's type (for example, `CharFieldItemProp` for a `CharField`), it is then paired with an autogenerated `itemprop` field, using those choices. The result might be something like the following:

```python
class Idea(SchemaMicrodata):
    title = models.CharField(
        _("Title"),
        max_length=200)
    title_itemprop = models.CharField(
        _("Title microdata item property"),
        name="title_itemprop",
        max_length=200,
        unique=False,
        blank=True,
        null=False,
        default="",
        editable=True,
        choices=(("ACCESS_MODE", "accessMode"),
                 ("ALTERNATE_NAME", "alternateName"),
                 ("BOOK_EDITION", "bookEdition"),
                 ("DESCRIPTION", "description"),
                 ("HEADLINE", "headline")))

    content = models.TextField(
        _("Content"),
        blank=True)
    content_itemprop = models.TextField(
        _("Content microdata item property"),
        name="content_itemprop",
        max_length=200,
        unique=False,
        blank=True,
        null=False,
        default="",
```

```
            editable=True,
            choices=(("ACCESS_MODE", "accessMode"),
                    ("ALTERNATE_NAME", "alternateName"),
                    ("BOOK_EDITION", "bookEdition"),
                    ("DESCRIPTION", "description"),
                    ("HEADLINE", "headline")))
```

Two templates are used to define how to represent the new microdata in the markup, and helper methods make use of these, so that we can easily provide the available microdata:

```
<section {{ idea.itemtype_attribute }}>
    <header {{ idea.title_itemprop_attribute }}>
        {{ idea.title }}
    </header>
    <div {{ idea.content_itemprop_attribute }}>
        {{ idea.content }}
    </div>
</section>
```

When evaluated, assuming that we have an `itemtype` (and only the `itemprop` for the title), we might see something like the following:

```
<section itemscope itemtype="//schema.org/CreativeWork">
    <header itemprop="headline">
        This is the Title
    </header>
    <div>
        Content goes here...
    </div>
</section>
```

See also

- The *Using model mixins* recipe
- The *Creating a model mixin to handle creation and modification dates* recipe
- The *Creating a model mixin to take care of meta tags* recipe
- The *Creating a model mixin to handle generic relations* recipe
- The *Creating app configuration* recipe from `Chapter 1`, *Getting Started with Django 2.1*

Using migrations

It is not true that once you have created your database structure, it won't change in the future. As development happens iteratively, you can get updates on the business requirements in the development process, and you will have to perform database schema changes along the way. With Django migrations, you don't have to change the database tables and fields manually, as most of it is done automatically, using the command-line interface.

Getting ready

Activate your virtual environment or Docker project in the command-line tool.

How to do it...

To create the database migrations, take a look at the following steps:

1. When you create models in your new `demo_app` app, you have to create an initial migration that will create the database tables for your app. This can be done by using the following command:

   ```
   (myproject_env)$ python3 manage.py makemigrations demo_app
   ```

2. The first time that you want to create all of the tables for your project, run the following command:

   ```
   (myproject_env)$ python3 manage.py migrate
   ```

   Run this command when you want to execute the new migrations for all of your apps.

3. If you want to execute the migrations for a specific app, run the following command:

   ```
   (myproject_env)$ python3 manage.py migrate demo_app
   ```

4. If you make some changes in the database schema, you will have to create a migration for that schema. For example, if we add a new `subtitle` field to the `Idea` model, we can create the migration by using the following command:

```
(myproject_env)$ python3 manage.py makemigrations \
> --name subtitle_added demo_app
```

5. Sometimes, you may have to add to or change data in the existing schema in bulk, which can be done with a data migration, instead of a schema migration. To create a data migration that modifies the data in the database table, we can use the following command:

```
(myproject_env)$ python3 manage.py makemigrations \
> --empty --name populate_subtitle demo_app
```

This creates a skeleton data migration, which you have to modify to perform the necessary data manipulation before applying it.

 Learn more about *Writing database migrations* in the official *How To* guide, found at https://docs.djangoproject.com/en/2.1/howto/writing-migrations/.

6. To list all of the available applied and unapplied migrations, run the following command:

```
(myproject_env)$ python3 manage.py showmigrations
```

The applied migrations will be listed with a `[X]` prefix. The unapplied ones will be listed with a `[ ]` prefix.

7. To list all of the available migrations for a specific app, run the same command, but pass the app name, as follows:

```
(myproject_env)$ python3 manage.py showmigrations demo_app
```

How it works...

Django migrations are instruction files for the database migration mechanism. The instruction files inform us on which database tables to create or remove, which fields to add or remove, and which data to insert, update, or delete.

There are two types of migrations in Django. One is schema migration, and the other is data migration. Schema migration should be created when you add new models, or add or remove fields. Data migration should be used when you want to fill the database with some values or massively delete values from the database. Data migrations should be created by using a command in the command-line tool, and then programmed in the migration file.

The migrations for each app are saved in their `migrations` directories. The first migration will usually be called `0001_initial.py`, and the other migrations in our example app will be called `0002_subtitle_added.py` and `0003_populate_subtitle.py`. Each migration gets a number prefix that is automatically incremented. For each migration that is executed, there is an entry that is saved in the `django_migrations` database table.

It is possible to migrate back and forth by specifying the number of the migration to which we want to migrate, as shown in the following command:

```
(myproject_env)$ python3 manage.py migrate demo_app 0002
```

This does require that each migration has both a forward and a backward action. Ideally, the backward action would exactly undo the changes made by the forward action. However, in some cases such a change would be unrecoverable, such as when the forward action removed a column from the schema, because it would destroy data. In such a case, the backward action might restore the schema, but the data would remain lost forever, or else there might not be a backward action at all.

If you want to undo all of the migrations for a specific app, you can do so by using the following command:

```
(myproject_env)$ python3 manage.py migrate demo_app zero
```

 Do not commit your migrations to version control until you have tested the forward and backward migration process, and you are sure that they will work well in other development and public website environments.

See also

- The *Working with a virtual environment* recipe in `Chapter 1`, *Getting Started with Django 2.1*
- The *Working with Docker* recipe in `Chapter 1`, *Getting Started with Django 2.1*

- The *Handling project dependencies with pip* in `Chapter 1`, *Getting Started with Django 2.1*
- The *Including external dependencies in your project* recipe in `Chapter 1`, *Getting Started with Django 2.1*
- The *Changing a foreign key to the many-to-many field* recipe

Switching from South migrations to Django migrations

If you were using Django before version 1.7 introduced database migrations into the core functionality, you have more than likely used third-party South migrations before. In this recipe, you will learn how to switch your project from South migrations to Django migrations.

Getting ready

Make sure that all apps, along with their South migrations, are up to date.

How to do it...

Execute the following steps:

1. Migrate all of your apps to the latest South migrations, as follows:

   ```
   (myproject_env)$ python3 manage.py migrate
   ```

   Remove `south` from `INSTALLED_APPS`, in the settings.

2. For each app with South migrations, delete the migration files and leave only the `migrations` directories.
3. Create new migration files with the following command:

   ```
   (my_project)$ python3 manage.py makemigrations
   ```

4. Fake the initial Django migrations, as the database schema has already been set correctly:

   ```
   (my_project)$ python3 manage.py migrate --fake-initial
   ```

5. If there are any circular relationships in the installed apps (that is, two models in different apps pointing to each other with a foreign key or many-to-many relation), apply the fake initial migrations to each of these apps separately, as follows:

```
(my_project)$ python3 manage.py migrate --fake-initial demo_app
```

How it works...

There is no conflict in the database when you are switching to the new way of dealing with the database schema changes, as the South migration history is saved in the `south_migrationhistory` database table; the Django migration history is saved in the `django_migrations` database table. The only problem is that the migration files for South have a different syntax than the Django core migrations; therefore, the South migrations have to be completely removed and replaced with Django migrations.

Thus, at first, we delete the South migration files (or they can be moved to a separate directory as backups, if preferred). Then, the `makemigrations` command recognizes the empty `migrations` directories and creates new, initial Django migrations for each app. Once these migrations are faked, the further Django migrations can be created and applied, as needed.

See also

- The *Using migrations* recipe
- The *Changing a foreign key to the many-to-many field* recipe

Changing a foreign key to the many-to-many field

This recipe is a practical example of how to change a many-to-one relation to a many-to-many relation, while preserving the already existing data. We will use both schema and data migrations in this situation.

Getting ready

Let's suppose that you have the Idea model, with a foreign key pointing to the Category model, as follows:

```python
# demo_app/models.py
from django.db import models
from django.utils.translation import ugettext_lazy as _

class Category(models.Model):
    title = models.CharField(_("Title"), max_length=200)

    def __str__(self):
        return self.title

class Idea(models.Model):
    title = model.CharField(
        _("Title"),
        max_length=200)
    category = models.ForeignKey(Category,
        verbose_name=_("Category"),
        null=True,
        blank=True,
        on_delete=models.SET_NULL)

    def __str__(self):
        return self.title
```

The initial migration should be created and executed by using the following commands:

```
(myproject_env) $ python3 manage.py makemigrations demo_app
(myproject_env) $ python3 manage.py migrate demo_app
```

How to do it...

The following steps will show you how to switch from a foreign key relation to a many-to-many relation, while preserving the already existing data:

1. Add a new many-to-many field, called categories, as follows:

```python
# demo_app/models.py
class Idea(models.Model):
    title = model.CharField(
        _("Title"),
        max_length=200)
    category = models.ForeignKey(Category,
```

```
            verbose_name=_("Category"),
            null=True,
            blank=True)
    categories = models.ManyToManyField(Category,
            verbose_name=_("Category"),
            blank=True,
            related_name="ideas")
```

2. Create and run a schema migration, in order to add the new field to the database, as shown in the following code snippet:

```
(myproject_env)$ python3 manage.py makemigrations \
> demo_app --name categories_added
(myproject_env)$ python3 manage.py migrate demo_app
```

3. Create a data migration to copy the categories from the foreign key to the many-to-many field, as follows:

```
(myproject_env)$ python3 manage.py makemigrations \
> --empty --name copy_categories demo_app
```

4. Open the newly created migration file (demo_app/migrations/0003_copy_categories.py) and define the forward migration instructions, as shown in the following code snippet:

```
# demo_app/migrations/0003_copy_categories.py
from django.db import migrations

def copy_categories(apps, schema_editor):
    cls_idea = apps.get_model("demo_app", "Idea")
    for idea in cls_idea.objects.all():
        if idea.category:
            cls_idea.categories.add(idea.category)

class Migration(migrations.Migration):
    dependencies = [
        ('demo_app', '0002_categories_added'),
    ]

    operations = [
        migrations.RunPython(copy_categories),
    ]
```

5. Run the new data migration, as follows:

```
(myproject_env)$ python3 manage.py migrate demo_app
```

6. Delete the foreign key field `category` in the `models.py` file, leaving only the new `categories` many-to-many field, as follows:

```
# demo_app/models.py
class Idea(models.Model):
    title = model.CharField(
        _("Title"),
        max_length=200)
    categories = models.ManyToManyField(Category,
        verbose_name=_("Category"),
        blank=True,
        related_name="ideas")
```

7. Create and run a schema migration, in order to delete the `categories` field from the database table, as follows:

```
(myproject_env)$ python3 manage.py makemigrations \
> demo_app --name delete_category
(myproject_env)$ python3 manage.py migrate demo_app
```

How it works...

At first, we add a new many-to-many field to the `Idea` model, and a migration is generated to update the database accordingly. Then, we create a data migration that will copy the existing relations from the foreign key `category` to the new many-to-many `categories`. Lastly, we remove the foreign key field from the model, and update the database once more.

There's more...

Our data migration currently includes only the forward action, copying the foreign key `category` as the first related item in the new `categories` relationship. Although we did not elaborate here, in a real-world scenario it would be best to include the reverse operation as well. While any `Idea` object with multiple `categories` would lose data, this could be accomplished by copying the first related item back to the `category` foreign key.

See also

- The *Using migrations* recipe
- The *Switching from South migrations to Django migrations* recipe

3
Forms and Views

In this chapter, we will cover the following topics:

- Passing HttpRequest to a form
- Utilizing the save method of a form
- Uploading images
- Creating a form layout with custom templates
- Creating a form layout with django-crispy-forms
- Filtering object lists
- Managing paginated lists
- Composing class-based views
- Generating PDF documents
- Implementing a multilingual search with Haystack and Whoosh

Introduction

While a database structure is defined in models, views provide the endpoints necessary to show content to users or to let them enter new and updated data. In this chapter, we will focus on views for managing forms, the list view, and views generating alternative outputs to HTML. In the simplest examples, we will leave the creation of URL rules and templates up to you.

Passing HttpRequest to a form

The first argument of every Django view is the `HttpRequest` object, which by convention is named `request`. It contains metadata about the request sent from a browser or other client, including such items as the current language code, user data, cookies, and session. By default, forms that are used by views accept the `GET` or `POST` data, files, initial data, and other parameters; however, they do not inherently have access to the `HttpRequest` object. In some cases, it is useful additionally to pass `HttpRequest` to the form, especially when you want to filter out the choices of form fields based on other request data, or handle saving something such as the current user or IP in the form.

In this recipe, we will see an example of a form where a person can choose a user and write a message to them. We will pass the `HttpRequest` object to the form in order to exclude the current user from the recipient choices, as we don't want anybody to write a message to themselves.

Getting ready

Let's create a new app called `email_messages` and put it in `INSTALLED_APPS` in the settings. This app will have no models, just forms and views.

How to do it...

To complete this recipe, execute the following steps:

1. Add a new `forms.py` file with the message form containing two fields: the recipient selection and message text. Also, this form will have an initialization method, which will accept the request object, and then modify `QuerySet` for the recipient's selection field:

   ```
   # email_messages/forms.py
   from django import forms
   from django.contrib.auth.models import User
   from django.utils.translation import ugettext_lazy as _


   class MessageForm(forms.Form):
       recipient = forms.ModelChoiceField(
           label=_("Recipient"),
           queryset=User.objects.all(),
           required=True)
   ```

```
message = forms.CharField(
    label=_("Message"),
    widget=forms.Textarea,
    required=True)

def __init__(self, request, *args, **kwargs):
    super().__init__(*args, **kwargs)
    self.request = request
    self.fields["recipient"].queryset = (
        self.fields["recipient"].queryset.exclude(
            pk=request.user.pk))
```

2. Create `views.py` with the `message_to_user()` and `message_sent()` view functions in order to handle the form. As you can see, the request object is passed as the first parameter to the form, as follows:

```
# email_messages/views.py
from django.contrib.auth.decorators import login_required
from django.shortcuts import render, redirect

from .forms import MessageForm


@login_required
def message_to_user(request):
    if request.method == "POST":
        form = MessageForm(request, data=request.POST)
        if form.is_valid():
            # do something with the form
            return redirect("message_sent")
    else:
        form = MessageForm(request)

    return render(request,
                  "email_messages/message_to_user.html",
                  {"form": form})


@login_required
def message_sent(request):
    return render(request,
                  "email_messages/message_sent.html")
```

3. Add a very basic template for the message form under
   `templates/email_messages/message_to_user.html`, as in the following:

```
{# email_messages/message_to_user.html #}
<form action="">
    {{ form.as_p }}
</form>
```

4. We need the template for when the message has been sent. Again, we define it
   here at `templates/email_messages/message_sent.html` with minimal
   content for demonstration:

```
{# email_messages/message_sent.html #}
<p>Thanks for sending your note!</p>
```

5. Additionally, we need to wire up the URLs so that Django will know how to
   route the requests properly. First, we will create `email_messages/urls.py`, as
   follows:

```
# email_messages/urls.py
from django.urls import path

from .views import message_to_user, message_sent

urlpatterns = [
    path('/', message_to_user, 'message_to_user'),
    path('sent/', message_sent, 'message_sent'),
]
```

6. We need to include these patterns in our `urls.py` project:

```
# project/urls.py
from django.urls import include, path

urlpatterns = [
    # ...
    path('email/', include('email_messages.urls')),
]
```

How it works...

In the initialization method of `MessageForm`, we have the `self` variable that represents the instance of the form itself, we also have the newly added `request` variable, and then we have the rest of the positional arguments (`*args`) and named arguments (`**kwargs`). We call the `super()` initialization method, passing all of the positional and named arguments to it so that the form is properly initiated. We will then assign the `request` variable to a new `request` attribute of the form for later access in other methods of the form. Finally, we modify the `queryset` attribute of the recipient's selection field, excluding the current user from the request.

In the `message_to_user` view, we will pass the `HttpRequest` object as the first argument in both situations:

- When loaded for the first time
- When the form is posted

The form is rendered via the given `message_to_user.html` template, which prints out only the markup for the form itself in our example here. In the real world, this would probably extend from a `base.html` template as described in the *Arranging the base.html template* recipe in `Chapter 4`, *Templates and JavaScript*. With our basic markup, this would look something like the following once filled in:

After submission completes successfully, we redirect to the `message_sent` named URL, which maps back to the `message_sent` view. In this, we simply render a message via the `message_sent.html` template, something like this:

See also

- The *Utilizing the save method of the form* recipe
- The *Arranging the base.html template* recipe in `Chapter 4`, *Templates and JavaScript*

Utilizing the save method of the form

To make your views clean and simple, it is good practice to move the handling of the form data to the form itself whenever this is possible and makes sense. The common practice is to have a `save()` method that will save the data, perform search, or do some other smart actions. We will extend the form that is defined in the previous recipe with the `save()` method, which will send an email to the selected recipient.

Getting ready

We will build upon the example that is defined in the *Passing HttpRequest to the form* recipe.

How to do it...

To complete this recipe, execute the following two steps:

1. From Django, import the function in order to send an email. Then, add the `save()` method to `MessageForm`. It will try to send an email to the selected recipient and will fail silently if any errors occur:

```python
# email_messages/forms.py
from django import forms
from django.contrib.auth.models import User
from django.core.mail import send_mail
from django.utils.translation import ugettext_lazy as _


class MessageForm(forms.Form):
    # ...

    def save(self):
        cleaned_data = self.cleaned_data
        user = self.request.user
        send_mail(subject=_(f"A message from {user}"),
                  message=cleaned_data["message"],
                  from_email=self.request.user.email,
                  recipient_list=[cleaned_data["recipient"].email],
                  fail_silently=True)
```

2. Call the `save()` method from the form in the view if the posted data is valid:

```python
# email_messages/views.py
from django.contrib.auth.decorators import login_required
from django.shortcuts import render, redirect

from .forms import MessageForm


@login_required
def message_to_user(request):
    if request.method == "POST":
        form = MessageForm(request, data=request.POST)
        if form.is_valid():
            form.save()
```

```
            return redirect("message_to_user_done")
    else:
        form = MessageForm(request)

    return render(request,
                "email_messages/message_to_user.html",
                {"form": form})
```

How it works...

Let's take a look at the form. The `save()` method uses the cleaned data from the form to read the recipient's email address and the message. The sender of the email is the current user from the request.

 If the email cannot be sent due to an incorrect mail server configuration or another reason, it will fail silently in this example; that is, no error will be raised. In a production site, this would probably want to be tracked somehow on the server, but we would likely still not reveal the error directly to users.

Now, let's look at the view. When the posted form is valid, the `save()` method of the form will be called before the user is redirected to the success page.

See also

- The *Passing HttpRequest to the form* recipe
- The *Uploading images* recipe

Uploading images

In this recipe, we will take a look at the easiest way to handle image uploads. You will see an example of an app where the visitors can upload images with inspirational quotes.

Getting ready

Make sure you have **Pillow** installed. Either run the following command in your virtual environment, or update your requirements file accordingly and rebuild your Docker container:

```
(myproject_env)$ pip3 install Pillow~=5.2.0
```

Then, let's create a `quotes` app and put it in `INSTALLED_APPS` in the settings. For Docker projects, you will also need to add a volume mapping to your app container in `docker-compose.yml`.

Then, we will add an `InspirationalQuote` model with three fields: the `author`, `quote`, and `picture`, as follows:

```python
# quotes/models.py
import os

from django.db import models
from django.utils.timezone import now as timezone_now
from django.utils.translation import ugettext_lazy as _


def upload_to(instance, filename):
    now = timezone_now()
    base, ext = os.path.splitext(filename)
    ext = ext.lower()
    return f"quotes/{now:%Y/%m/%Y%m%d%H%M%S}{ext}"


class InspirationalQuote(models.Model):
    class Meta:
        verbose_name = _("Inspirational Quote")
        verbose_name_plural = _("Inspirational Quotes")

    author = models.CharField(_("Author"), max_length=200)
    quote = models.TextField(_("Quote"))
    picture = models.ImageField(_("Picture"),
                                upload_to=upload_to,
                                blank=True,
                                null=True)

    def __str__(self):
        return self.quote
```

In addition, we created an `upload_to()` function, which sets the path of the uploaded picture as something similar to `quotes/2018/09/04150424140000.png`. As you can see, we use the date timestamp as the filename to ensure its uniqueness. We pass this function to the `picture` image field.

Now we can set things up to upload new images to be used for the `picture` associated with `InspirationalQuote`.

How to do it...

Execute these steps to complete the recipe:

1. Create the `forms.py` file and put a simple model form there:

```
# quotes/forms.py
from django import forms

from .models import InspirationalQuote


class InspirationalQuoteForm(forms.ModelForm):
    class Meta:
        model = InspirationalQuote
        fields = ["author", "quote", "picture", "language"]
```

2. In the `views.py` file, put a view that handles the form. Don't forget to pass the `FILES` dictionary-like object to the form. When the form is valid, trigger the `save` method as follows:

```
# quotes/views.py
from django.shortcuts import render, redirect

from .forms import InspirationalQuoteForm


def add_quote(request):
    form = InspirationalQuoteForm()
    if request.method == "POST":
        form = InspirationalQuoteForm(
            data=request.POST,
            files=request.FILES)
        if form.is_valid():
            form.save()
            return redirect("quotes-list")
        else:
```

```
        return render(request, "quotes/add_quote.html", {
            "form": form
        })
```

3. Add a rule in `urls.py` for the add form:

```
# quotes/urls.py
from django.urls import path

from .views import add_quote

urlpatterns = [
    path('add/', add_quote, name='quote_add'),
]
```

4. We also need to include the `quotes` app URLs in our project:

```
# project/urls.py
from django.urls import include, path

urlpatterns = [
    # ...
    path('quotes/', include('quotes.urls')),
]
```

5. Create a template for the view in `templates/quotes/add_quote.html`. It is very important to set the `enctype` attribute to `multipart/form-data` for the HTML form, otherwise the file upload won't work:

```
{# templates/quotes/add_quote.html #}
{% load i18n %}

{% block content %}
    <form method="post" action="" enctype="multipart/form-data">
        {% csrf_token %}
        {{ form.as_p }}
        <button type="submit">{% trans "Save" %}</button>
    </form>
{% endblock %}
```

How it works...

Django model forms are forms that are created from models. They provide all of the fields from the model so you don't need to define them manually. In the preceding example, we created a model form for the `InspirationalQuote` model. When we save the form, the form knows how to save each field in the database, as well as to upload the files and save them in the media directory. After `save`, the view returns the user to a listing of all quotes, the view for which is not discussed here.

There's more

As a bonus, we will see an example of how to generate a thumbnail out of the uploaded image. In many cases, it is sufficient to use a third-party solution such as `sorl-thumbnail` to generate thumbnails from the template layer, based on the original image. Using this technique, however, you could generate and store specific versions of the image for later use, such as the list version, mobile version, and desktop computer version.

We will add three main methods to the `InspirationalQuote` model (`quotes/models.py`). They are `save()`, `create_thumbnail()`, and `get_thumbnail_picture_url()`. Some helper functions are used by these to `get_picture_paths()`, `get_square_crop_points()` and `get_centering_points()` when creating the thumbnail.

When the model is being saved, we will trigger the thumbnail creation. When we need to show the thumbnail in a template, we can get its URL using `{{ quote.get_thumbnail_picture_url }}`. The method definitions are as follows:

```
# quotes/models.py
import os
from PIL import Image

from django.conf import settings
from django.core.files.storage import default_storage as storage
from django.db import models
from django.utils.timezone import now as timezone_now
from django.utils.translation import ugettext_lazy as _


THUMBNAIL_SIZE = getattr(settings, "QUOTES_THUMBNAIL_SIZE", 50)
THUMBNAIL_EXT = getattr(settings, "QUOTES_THUMBNAIL_EXT", None)


def get_square_crop_points(image):
```

```
    width, height = image.size
    target = width if width > height else height
    upper, lower = get_centering_points(height, target)
    left, right = get_centering_points(width, target)
    return left, upper, right, lower


def get_centering_points(size, target):
    delta = size - target
    start = int(delta) / 2
    end = start + target
    return start, end

# ...

class InspirationalQuote(models.Model):
    # ...

    def save(self, *args, **kwargs):
        super().save(*args, **kwargs)
        self.create_thumbnail()

    def create_thumbnail(self):
        if not self.picture:
            return False
        picture_path, thumbnail_path = self.get_picture_paths()
        if thumbnail_path and not storage.exists(thumbnail_path):
            try:
                picture_file = storage.open(picture_path, "r")
                image = Image.open(picture_file)
                image = image.crop(get_square_crop_points(image))
                image = image.resize((THUMBNAIL_SIZE,
                                      THUMBNAIL_SIZE),
                                     Image.ANTIALIAS)
                image.save(thumbnail_path)
            except (IOError, KeyError, UnicodeDecodeError):
                return False
        return True

    def get_thumbnail_picture_url(self):
        url = ""
        picture_path, thumbnail_path = self.get_picture_paths()

        if thumbnail_path:
            url = (storage.url(thumbnail_path)
                   if storage.exists(thumbnail_path)
                   else self.picture.url)
```

```
            return url

    def get_picture_paths(self):
        picture_path = None
        thumb_path = None

        if self.picture:
            picture_path = self.picture.name
            filename_base, filename_ext = os.path.splitext(
                picture_path)
            if THUMBNAIL_EXT:
                filename_ext = THUMBNAIL_EXT
            thumb_path = f"{filename_base}_thumbnail{filename_ext}"

        return picture_path, thumb_path

    def __str__(self):
        return self.quote
```

In the preceding methods, we are using the file storage API instead of directly juggling the filesystem, as we could then exchange the default storage with Amazon S3 buckets or other storage services and the methods will still work.

How does the creation of the thumbnail work? If we had the original file saved as quotes/2014/04/20140424140000.png, we are making sure that the quotes/2014/04/20140424140000_thumbnail.png file doesn't exist and, in that case, we are opening the original image, cropping it to a square from the center, resizing it to 50 x 50 pixels, and saving it to the storage. We can supply a QUOTES_THUMBNAIL_SIZE setting to change the resizing behavior, and we can set QUOTES_THUMBNAIL_EXT to a specific image file extension (such as ".jpg") to change the format used when saving the thumbnail.

The get_thumbnail_picture_url() method checks whether the thumbnail version exists in the storage and returns its URL. If the thumbnail version does not exist, the URL of the original image is returned as a fallback.

In this example, we only dealt with changing image size, but a more sophisticated solution might take in additional input to make changes to the center point, alter colors, or apply other effects, and much more.

See also

- The *Creating a form layout with custom templates* recipe
- The *Creating a form layout with django-crispy-forms* recipe
- The *Arranging the base.html template* recipe in Chapter 4, *Templates and JavaScript*
- The *Providing responsive images* recipe in Chapter 4, *Templates and JavaScript*

Creating a form layout with custom templates

Prior to Django 1.11, all form rendering was handled exclusively in Python code, but in that version template-based form widget rendering was introduced. In this recipe, we will examine how to use custom templates for form widgets, implement custom renderer classes for both forms and widgets, and override a widget template at the project level.

Getting ready

To demonstrate the capabilities of the Django core form rendering API, let's create a bulletin_board app and put it in INSTALLED_APPS in the settings. If you're using Docker, as described in the *Creating a Docker project structure* recipe in Chapter 1, *Getting Started with Django 2.1*, you will also need to add the new app to docker-compose.yml.

We will have a Bulletin model there with fields for bulletin_type, title, description, contact_person, phone, email, and image, as follows:

```
# bulletin_board/models.py
from django.db import models
from django.utils.translation import ugettext_lazy as

from utils import CreationModificationDateMixin


TYPE_CHOICES = (
    ('searching', _("Searching")),
    ('offering', _("Offering")),
)


class Bulletin(CreationModificationDateMixin, models.Model):
    class Meta:
```

```python
        verbose_name = _("Bulletin")
        verbose_name_plural = _("Bulletins")
        ordering = ("-created", "title",)

    bulletin_type = models.CharField(_("Type"),
                                    max_length=20,
                                    choices=TYPE_CHOICES)
    title = models.CharField(_("Title"),
                            max_length=255)
    description = models.TextField(_("Description"),
                                max_length=300)
    contact_person = models.CharField(_("Contact person"),
                                    max_length=255)
    phone = models.CharField(_("Phone"),
                            max_length=50,
                            blank=True)
    email = models.EmailField(_("Email"),
                            max_length=254,
                            blank=True)
    image = models.ImageField(_("Image"),
                            max_length=255,
                            upload_to="bulletin_board/",
                            blank=True)

    def __str__(self):
        return self.title
```

Remember to make an initial migration for the new model and run that against your database.

If you haven't done so yet, create a `base.html` template according to the example in the *Arranging the base.html template* recipe in Chapter 4, *Templates and JavaScript*. Make sure to include the Bootstrap 4 frontend framework CSS and JavaScript in the templates. To this, we'll also want to add the CSS for the Ion Icons icon set, within the `base_stylesheet` block, as follows:

```
{# templates/base.html #}
{% load static %}

{% block base_stylesheet %}
<link rel="stylesheet" type="text/css"
href="http://code.ionicframework.com/ionicons/2.0.1/css/ionicons.min.css">
{# ... #}
{% endblock %}
```

How to do it...

To complete the recipe, follow these steps:

1. Ensure that the template system will be able to find customized templates in our app by adding `django.forms` to our `INSTALLED_APPS`, using the `DjangoTemplates` backend for the `TEMPLATES` setting, and including the `APP_DIRS` flag as `True` for that engine. Aside from adding `django.forms`, these are the defaults when starting a new project:

```python
# settings.py or config/base.py
# ...
INSTALLED_APPS = [
    # ...
    'django.forms',
]
# ...
TEMPLATES = [
    {
        'BACKEND': 'django.template.backends.django.DjangoTemplates',
        'APP_DIRS': True,
        # ...
    }
]
```

2. Create `BulletinForm` in `forms.py`, as follows:

```python
# bulletin_board/forms.py
from django import forms
from django.forms.renderers import TemplatesSetting

from bulletin_board.models import Bulletin


class BulletinForm(forms.ModelForm):
    class Meta:
        model = Bulletin
        fields = ["bulletin_type", "title", "description",
                  "contact_person", "phone", "email", "image"]
        widgets = {
            "bulletin_type": forms.RadioSelect,
        }

    default_renderer = TemplatesSetting()

    def __init__(self, *args, **kwargs):
```

```
super().__init__(*args, **kwargs)

# delete empty choice for this field
self.fields["bulletin_type"].choices = \
    self.fields["bulletin_type"].choices[1:]
self.fields["bulletin_type"].widget.attrs.update({
    "class": "list-unstyled form-group",
})

self.fields["title"].widget.attrs.update({
    "class": "form-control",
})

self.fields["description"].widget.attrs.update({
    "class": "form-control",
    "rows": "3",
})

self.fields["image"].widget.template_name = \
    "bulletin_board/widgets/image.html"
self.fields["image"].widget.attrs.update({
    "class": "input-block-level clearablefileinput",
})

self.fields["contact_person"].widget.attrs.update({
    "class": "form-control",
})

self.fields["phone"].widget.template_name = \
    "bulletin_board/widgets/phone.html"
self.fields["phone"].widget.attrs.update({
    "class": "form-control",
})

self.fields["email"].widget.template_name = \
    "bulletin_board/widgets/email.html"
self.fields["email"].widget.attrs.update({
    "class": "form-control",
    "placeholder": "contact@example.com",
})
```

3. Define the customized widget templates, as referenced, for the image field:

```
{# bulletin_board/templates/bulletin_board/widgets/image.html #}
{% load i18n %}
{% include "django/forms/widgets/file.html" %}
<small class="form-text text-muted">
    {% trans "Available formats are JPG, GIF, and PNG." %}
    {% trans "Minimal size is 800 x 800 px." %}
</small>
```

Define it for the phone field:

```
{# bulletin_board/templates/bulletin_board/widgets/phone.html #}
<div class="input-group">
    <span class="input-group-prepend">
        <i class="input-group-text ioh-ios-telephone"></i>
    </span>
    {% include "django/forms/widgets/input.html" %}
</div>
```

And do the same for the email field:

```
{# bulletin_board/templates/bulletin_board/widgets/email.html #}
<div class="input-group">
    <span class="input-group-prepend">
        <i class="input-group-text ion-email"></i>
    </span>
    {% include "django/forms/widgets/input.html" %}
</div>
```

4. We'll add a basic listing view, and one for editing that uses our form, like so:

```python
# bulletin_board/views.py
from django.utils.translation import ugettext_lazy as _
from django.views.generic import ListView, FormView

from .models import Bulletin
from .forms import BulletinForm


class BulletinList(ListView):
    model = Bulletin


class BulletinEdit(FormView):
    template_name = "bulletin_board/bulletin_form.html"
    form_class = BulletinFormTemplated
```

```python
def get_form(self, *args, **kwargs):
    form = super().get_form(*args, **kwargs)
    form.fieldsets = [
        {
            "id": "main-data",
            "legend": _("Main data"),
            "fields": [
                form["bulletin_type"],
                form["title"],
                form["description"],
            ]
        },
        {
            "id": "image-fieldset",
            "legend": _("Image upload"),
            "fields": [
                form["image"]
            ],
        },
        {
            "id": "contact-info",
            "legend": _("Contact"),
            "fields": [
                form["contact_person"],
                form["phone"],
                form["email"],
            ]
        }
    ]
    return form
```

5. Create the bulletin form to pull everything together:

```html
{# bulletin_board/templates/bulletin_board/bulletin_form.html #}
{% extends "base.html" %}
{% load i18n %}

{% block content %}
<form method="POST" enctype="multipart/form-data"
    action="{{ form.action }}">
    {% csrf_token %}
    {{ form.non_field_errors }}

    {% for fieldset in form.fieldsets %}
    <fieldset{% if fieldset.id %} id="{{ fieldset.id }}"{% endif %}
            class="mb-3">
        {% if fieldset.legend %}
        <legend>{{ fieldset.legend }}</legend>
```

```
            {% endif %}
            {% for field in fieldset.fields %}
            <div class="form-group{% if field.field.required %}
                        required{% endif %}">
                <label for="{{ field.id_for_label }}">
                    {% trans field.label %}
                </label>
                {{ field }}
                {{ field.errors }}
            </div>
            {% endfor %}
        </fieldset>
        {% endfor %}

        <div class="form-actions mb-5">
            <button type="submit" class="btn btn-primary">
                {% trans "Save" %}
            </button>
        </div>
    </form>
{% endblock %}
```

6. Expose the listing and editing bulletin board views by adding URL rules:

```
# bulletin_board/urls.py
from django.urls import path

from .views import (BulletinList, BulletinEdit)


edit_view = BulletinEdit.as_view(
    success_url=reverse_lazy('bulletin-list'))
urlpatterns = [
    path('', BulletinList.as_view(), name='bulletin-list'),
    path('new/', edit_view, name='bulletin-create'),
    path('<int:pk>/edit/', edit_view, name='bulletin-edit'),
]
```

7. The bulletin board URLs need to be added to our project:

```
# myproject/urls.py
# ...
urlpatterns = [
    # ...
    path('bulletins/', include("bulletin_board.urls")),
]
```

How it works...

Historically, form rendering has been done entirely via Python code but, starting with Django 1.11, rendering has shifted to using templates. Not only does this result in a better separation of concerns, but we can also provide override templates in our apps to alter the default rendering for form widgets. As always, the form element itself is generated in a template and rendered via a view.

In `BulletinForm`, we customize `ModelForm` for the `Bulletin` model so that it contains only the fields we want. We also switch the widget for the `bulletin_type` field over from the default `Select` widget to `RadioSelect`, so that all available options will be visible at once.

On creation of the form, several augmentations are made to the fields. All of them are given added attributes for Bootstrap 4 form CSS classes. For the `bulletin_type` field, we also remove the initial empty option, since there's no point in displaying that when using the radio button widget. Finally, we provide customized template names for the `image`, `phone` and `email` fields, corresponding to the subsequent template files, which allow us to alter the markup used with more flexibility. For the phone and email fields, icons from the Ion Icon set are used as prefixes to add visual indicators of the expected input.

 In this case, the customized templates are specific to the `bulletin_board` app, but we could also customize a widget's markup more generally by providing a project-wide override of the appropriate file (such as `email.html`) under our project's `templates/django/forms/widgets/` directory.

In the `BulletinEdit` view, we build up a custom `fieldsets` property for the form object. This allows us to use looping in the subsequent `bulletin_form.html` template to create a more structured final product with `<fieldset>` blocks corresponding to the arrangement given in the view. The template provides not only `fieldsets`, but the wrapping `<form>`, a submit `<button>`, and some additional Bootstrap 4 hooks. Finally, `urls.py` uses the same view (and form) for both creation and update of bulletins, returning to the listing when a bulletin is successfully saved.

Here's what the end result might look like:

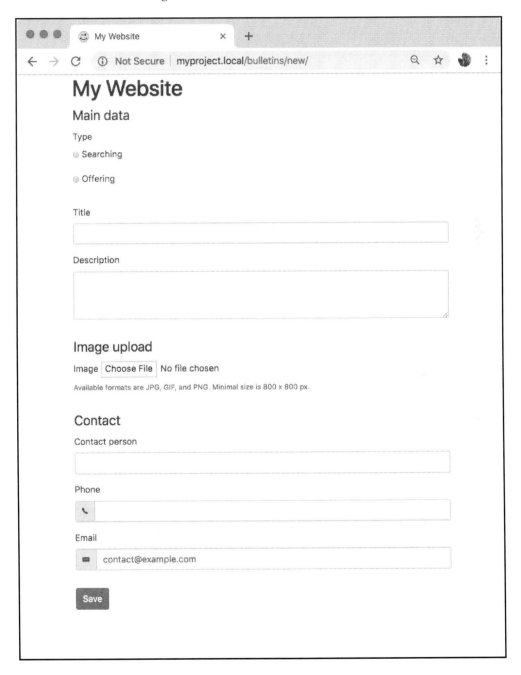

See also

- The *Uploading images* recipe
- The *Creating a form layout with django-crispy-forms* recipe
- The *Generating PDF documents* recipe
- The *Arranging the base.html template* recipe in `Chapter 4`, *Templates and JavaScript*

Creating a form layout with django-crispy-forms

The `django-crispy-forms` Django app allows you to build, customize, and reuse forms using one of the following CSS frameworks: Uni-Form, Bootstrap, or Foundation. The use of `django-crispy-forms` is somewhat analogous to fieldsets in the Django contributed administration; however, it is more advanced and customizable. You define form layout in the Python code and need not worry about how each field is presented in HTML. However, if you need to add specific HTML attributes or wrapping, you can easily do that too. Moreover, all of the markup used by `django-crispy-forms` is located in templates that can be overwritten for specific needs.

In this recipe, we will revisit the `bulletin_board` app, and see how to reproduce the layout using `django-crispy-forms` with the Bootstrap 4 version of the popular frontend framework for developing responsive, mobile-first web projects.

Getting ready

We will start with the `bulletin_board` app from the *Creating a form layout with custom templates* recipe, specifically reusing the setup from `models.py`. Next, we'll execute the following tasks one by one:

1. Make sure you have created a `base.html` template for your site. Learn more about this in the *Arranging the base.html template* recipe in `Chapter 4`, *Templates and JavaScript*.

2. Integrate the Bootstrap 4 frontend framework CSS and JS files from `http://getbootstrap.com/docs/4.1/` into the `base.html` template, adding the appropriate CDN URLs in the `base_stylesheet` and `base_js` blocks, respectively.

3. Install `django-crispy-forms` either in your virtual environment with pip or by adding it to the requirements for your Docker project and rebuilding your container. Learn more about these two approaches to development environments in the *Working with a virtual environment* and *Working with Docker* recipes from `Chapter 1`, *Getting Started with Django 2.1*, respectively.

4. Make sure that `crispy_forms` is added to `INSTALLED_APPS` and then set `bootstrap4` as the template pack to be used in this project:

```python
# settings.py or config/base.py
INSTALLED_APPS = (
    # ...
    'crispy_forms',
    'bulletin_board',
)
# ...
CRISPY_TEMPLATE_PACK = 'bootstrap4'
```

How to do it...

Follow these steps:

1. Let's add a model form for the bulletin in the app. We will attach a form helper to the form in the initialization method itself. The form helper will have the layout property that will define the layout for the form, as follows:

```python
# bulletin_board/forms.py
from django import forms
from django.utils.translation import ugettext_lazy as _

from crispy_forms import helper, layout, bootstrap

from .models import Bulletin


class BulletinForm(forms.ModelForm):
    class Meta:
        model = Bulletin
        fields = ["bulletin_type", "title", "description",
                  "contact_person", "phone", "email", "image"]
```

```python
    def __init__(self, *args, **kwargs):
        super().__init__(*args, **kwargs)

        self.fields["bulletin_type"].widget = forms.RadioSelect()
        # delete empty choice for the type
        del self.fields["bulletin_type"].choices[0]

        title = layout.Field(
            "title",
            css_class="input-block-level")
        desciption = layout.Field(
            "description",
            css_class="input-block-level",
            rows="3")
        main_fieldset = layout.Fieldset(
            _("Main data"),
            "bulletin_type",
            title,
            desciption)

        image = layout.Field(
            "image",
            css_class="input-block-level")
        format_html_template = """
            {% load i18n %}
            <p class="help-block">
            {% trans "Available formats are JPG, GIF, and PNG." %}
            {% trans "Minimal size is 800 × 800 px." %}
            </p>
            """
        format_html = layout.HTML(format_html_template)
        image_fieldset = layout.Fieldset(
            _("Image"),
            image,
            format_html,
            title=_("Image upload"),
            css_id="image_fieldset")

        contact_person = layout.Field(
            "contact_person",
            css_class="input-block-level")
        phone_field = bootstrap.PrependedText(
            "phone",
            '<i class="ion-ios-telephone"></i>',
            css_class="input-block-level")
        email_field = bootstrap.PrependedText(
            "email",
            "@",
```

```
            css_class="input-block-level",
            placeholder="contact@example.com")
        contact_info = layout.Div(
            phone_field,
            email_field,
            css_id="contact_info")
        contact_fieldset = layout.Fieldset(
            _("Contact"),
            contact_person,
            contact_info)

        submit_button = layout.Submit(
            "submit",
            _("Save"))
        actions = bootstrap.FormActions(submit_button)

        self.helper = helper.FormHelper()
        self.helper.form_action = "bulletin-change"
        self.helper.form_method = "POST"
        self.helper.layout = layout.Layout(
            main_fieldset,
            image_fieldset,
            contact_fieldset,
            actions)
```

2. To render the form in the template, we just need to load the `crispy_forms_tags` template tag library and use the `{% crispy %}` template tag, as shown in the following:

```
{# templates/bulletin_board/change_form.html #}
{% extends "base.html" %}
{% load crispy_forms_tags %}

{% block content %}
    {% crispy form %}
{% endblock %}
```

3. We'll add a basic listing view and one for editing that uses our form, like so:

```
# bulletin_board/views.py
from django.utils.translation import ugettext_lazy as _
from django.views.generic import ListView, FormView

from .models import Bulletin
from .forms import BulletinForm


class BulletinList(ListView):
```

```
        model = Bulletin


class BulletinEdit(FormView):
    template_name = "bulletin_board/change_form.html"
    form_class = BulletinForm
```

4. Expose the listing and editing bulletin board views by adding URL rules:

```
# bulletin_board/urls.py
from django.urls import path

from .views import (BulletinList, BulletinEdit)


edit_view = BulletinEdit.as_view(
    success_url=reverse_lazy('bulletin-list'))

urlpatterns = [
    path('', BulletinList.as_view(), name='bulletin-list'),
    path('<int:pk>/edit/', edit_view, name='bulletin-edit'),
]
```

5. The bulletin board URLs need to be added to our project:

```
# myproject/urls.py
# ...
urlpatterns = [
    # ...
    path('bulletins/', include("bulletin_board.urls")),
]
```

How it works...

The page with the bulletin form will look similar to the following:

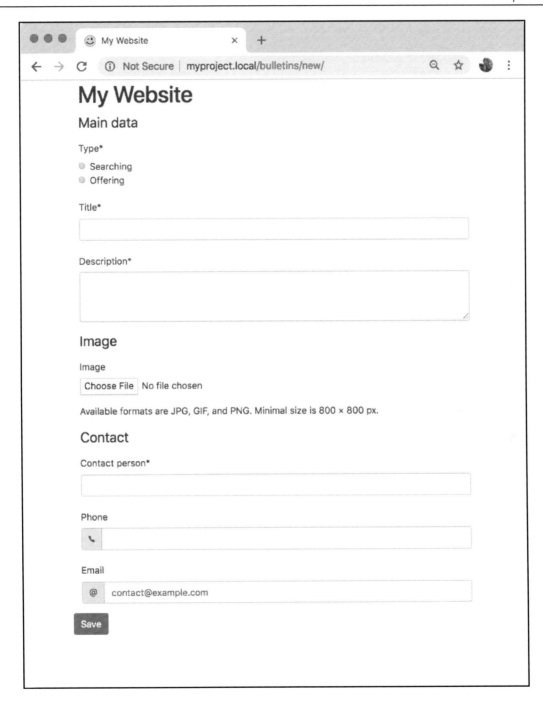

As you can see, the fields are grouped by fieldsets. The first argument of the `Fieldset` object defines the legend; the other positional arguments define the fields. You can also pass named arguments to define the HTML attributes for the fieldset; for example, for the second fieldset, we are passing `title` and `css_id` to set the `title` and `id` HTML attributes.

Fields can also have additional attributes passed by named arguments; for example, for the `description` field, we are passing `css_class` and `rows` to set the `class` and `rows` HTML attributes.

Besides the normal fields, you can pass HTML snippets as this is done with the help block for the image field. You can also have prepended text fields in the layout. For example, we added a phone icon to the **Phone** field and an @ sign for the **Email** field. As you can see from the example with the contact fields, we can easily wrap fields in the HTML `<div>` elements using the `Div` objects. This is useful when specific JavaScript needs to be applied to some form fields.

The `action` attribute for the HTML form is defined by the `form_action` property of the form helper, which can either be a named URL from your URL configuration or an actual URL string. If you use the empty string as an action, the form will be submitted to the same view, where the form is included. The `method` attribute of the HTML form is defined by the `form_method` property of the form helper. As you know, the HTML forms allow the `GET` and `POST` methods. Finally, there is a `Submit` object in order to render the submit button, which takes the name of the button as the first positional argument and the value of the button as the second argument.

There's more...

For basic usage, the given example is more than necessary. However, if you need a specific markup for the forms in your project, you can still overwrite and modify templates of the `django-crispy-forms` app, as there is no markup hard coded in the Python files, rather all of the generated markup is rendered through templates. Just copy the templates from the `django-crispy-forms` app to your project's template directory and change them as required.

See also

- The *Creating a form layout with custom templates* recipe
- The *Filtering object lists* recipe

- The *Managing paginated lists* recipe
- The *Composing class-based views* recipe
- The *Arranging the base.html template* recipe in `Chapter 4`, *Templates and JavaScript*

Filtering object lists

In web development, besides views with forms, it is typical to have object-list views and detail views. List views can simply list objects that are ordered, for example, alphabetically or by creation date; however, that is not very user-friendly with huge amounts of data. For the best accessibility and convenience, you should be able to filter the content by all possible categories. In this recipe, we will see the pattern that is used to filter list views by any number of categories.

What we'll be creating is a list view of movies that can be filtered by genre, director, actor, or rating. It will look similar to the following with Bootstrap 3 applied to it:

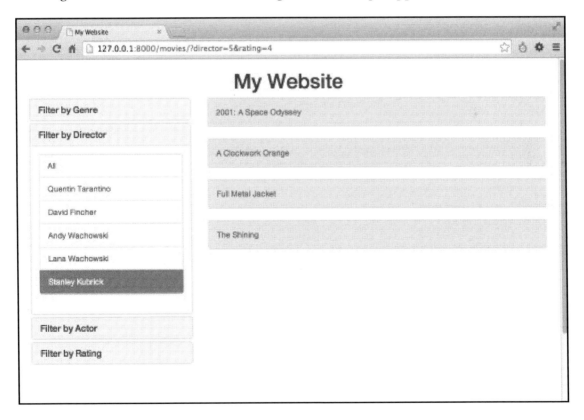

Getting ready

For the filtering example, we will use the `Movie` model with relations to genres, directors, and actors to filter by. It will also be possible to filter by ratings, which is `PositiveIntegerField` with choices. Let's create the `movies` app, put it in `INSTALLED_APPS` in the settings, and define the mentioned models in the new app, as follows:

```python
# movies/models.py
from django.db import models
from django.utils.translation import ugettext_lazy as _


RATING_CHOICES = (
    (1, "★☆☆☆☆☆☆☆☆☆"),
    (2, "★★☆☆☆☆☆☆☆☆"),
    (3, "★★★☆☆☆☆☆☆☆"),
    (4, "★★★★☆☆☆☆☆☆"),
    (5, "★★★★★☆☆☆☆☆"),
    (6, "★★★★★★☆☆☆☆"),
    (7, "★★★★★★★☆☆☆"),
    (8, "★★★★★★★★☆☆"),
    (9, "★★★★★★★★★☆"),
    (10, "★★★★★★★★★★"),
)


class Genre(models.Model):
    title = models.CharField(_("Title"),
                             max_length=100)

    def __str__(self):
        return self.title


class Director(models.Model):
    first_name = models.CharField(_("First name"),
                                  max_length=40)
    last_name = models.CharField(_("Last name"),
                                 max_length=40)

    def __str__(self):
        return f"{self.first_name} {self.last_name}"


class Actor(models.Model):
    first_name = models.CharField(_("First name"),
```

```
                                    max_length=40)
    last_name = models.CharField(_("Last name"),
                                    max_length=40)

    def __str__(self):
        return f"{self.first_name} {self.last_name}"


class Movie(models.Model):
    class Meta:
        ordering = ["title", "-release_year"]
        verbose_name = _("Movie")
        verbose_name_plural = _("Movies")

    title = models.CharField(_("Title"),
                                    max_length=255)
    genres = models.ManyToManyField(Genre,
                                        blank=True)
    directors = models.ManyToManyField(Director,
                                            blank=True)
    actors = models.ManyToManyField(Actor,
                                        blank=True)
    rating = models.PositiveIntegerField(_("Rating"),
                                            choices=RATING_CHOICES)

    def __str__(self):
        return self.title
```

If you're working with Docker, make sure to update the volumes in `docker-compose.yml` to map the movies app directory into the container, as well.

How to do it...

To complete the recipe, follow these steps:

1. We create `MovieFilterForm` with all of the possible categories to filter by:

    ```
    # movies/forms.py
    from django import forms
    from django.utils.translation import ugettext_lazy as _

    from .models import Genre, Director, Actor, RATING_CHOICES

    class MovieFilterForm(forms.Form):
        genre = forms.ModelChoiceField(
            label=_("Genre"),
    ```

```
        required=False,
        queryset=Genre.objects.all())
    director = forms.ModelChoiceField(
        label=_("Director"),
        required=False,
        queryset=Director.objects.all())
    actor = forms.ModelChoiceField(
        label=_("Actor"),
        required=False,
        queryset=Actor.objects.all())
    rating = forms.ChoiceField(
        label=_("Rating"),
        required=False,
        choices=RATING_CHOICES)
```

2. We create a `movie_list` view that will use `MovieFilterForm` to validate the request query parameters and perform the filtering for chosen categories. Note the `facets` dictionary that is used here to list the categories and also the currently selected choices:

```python
# movies/views.py
from django.conf import settings
from django.shortcuts import render

from .models import Genre, Director, Actor, Movie, RATING_CHOICES
from .forms import MovieFilterForm


def movie_list(request):
    qs = Movie.objects.order_by("title")
    form = MovieFilterForm(data=request.GET)

    facets = {
        "selected": {},
        "categories": {
            "genres": Genre.objects.all(),
            "directors": Director.objects.all(),
            "actors": Actor.objects.all(),
            "ratings": RATING_CHOICES,
        },
    }

    if form.is_valid():
        filters = (
            ("genre", "genres",),
            ("director", "directors",),
            ("actor", "actors",),
            ("rating", "rating",),
```

```
            )
            qs = filter_facets(facets, qs, form, filters)

        if settings.DEBUG:
            # Let's log the facets for review when debugging
            import logging
            logger = logging.getLogger(__name__)
            logger.info(facets)

        context = {
            "form": form,
            "facets": facets,
            "object_list": qs,
        }
        return render(request, "movies/movie_list.html", context)

    def filter_facets(facets, qs, form, filters):
        for facet, key in filters:
            value = form.cleaned_data[facet]
            if value:
                selected_value = value
                if facet == "rating":
                    rating = int(value)
                    selected_value = (rating,
                                      dict(RATING_CHOICES)[rating])
                    filter_args = {
                        f"{key}__gte": rating,
                        f"{key}__lt": rating + 1,
                    }
                else:
                    filter_args = {key: value}
                facets["selected"][facet] = selected_value
                qs = qs.filter(**filter_args).distinct()
        return qs
```

3. If you haven't done so already, create a base.html template. You can do that according to the example provided in the *Arranging the base.html template* recipe in Chapter 4, *Templates and JavaScript*.

4. For our movie list, we'll need a slight variation with a two-column layout, as follows:

```
{# base_two_columns.html #}
{% extends "base.html" %}

{% block container %}
    <div class="container">
        <div class="row">
```

```
                <div id="sidebar" class="col-md-4">
                    {% block sidebar %}{% endblock %}
                </div>
                <div id="content" class="col-md-8">
                    {% block content %}{% endblock %}
                </div>
            </div>
        </div>
    {% endblock %}
```

5. Each of the categories will follow a common pattern in the filters sidebar, so we can extract some common parts as include templates. First, we have the filter heading, corresponding to `movies/includes/filter_heading.html`, as in the following:

```
{# movies/includes/filter_heading.html #}
{% load i18n %}
<div class="panel-heading">
    <h6 class="panel-title">
        <a data-toggle="collapse" data-parent="#accordion"
            href="#collapse-{{ title|slugify }}s">{% blocktrans %}
                Filter by {{ title }}{% endblocktrans %}</a>
    </h6>
</div>
```

6. And then each filter will contain a link to reset filtering for that category, represented by `movies/includes/filter_all.html` here. This uses the `{% modify_query %}` template tag, described in the *Creating a template tag to modify request query parameters* in `Chapter 5`, *Custom Template Filters and Tags*, to generate URLs for the filters:

```
{# movies/includes/filter_all.html #}
{% load i18n utility_tags %}
<a class="list-group-item {% if not selected %}active{% endif %}"
    href="{% modify_query "page" param %}">
        {% trans "All" %}</a>
```

7. We create the `movies/movie_list.html` template for the list view itself, which will use the `facets` dictionary to list the categories and know which category is currently selected:

```
{# movies/movie_list.html #}
{% extends "base_two_columns.html" %}
{% load utility_tags %}

{% block sidebar %}
    <div class="filters panel-group" id="accordion">
```

```
{% with title="Genre" selected=facets.selected.genre %}
<div class="panel panel-default">
    {% include "movies/includes/filter_heading.html"
            with title=title %}
    <div id="collapse-{{ title|slugify }}"
        class="panel-collapse collapse in">
        <div class="panel-body"><div class="list-group">
            {% include "movies/includes/filter_all.html"
                    with param="genre" %}
            {% for cat in facets.categories.genres %}
            <a class="list-group-item
                    {% if selected == cat %}
                    active{% endif %}"
                href="{% modify_query "page"
                                    genre=cat.pk %}">
                {{ cat }}</a>
            {% endfor %}
        </div></div>
    </div>
</div>
{% endwith %}
{% with title="Director"
        selected=facets.selected.director %}
<div class="panel panel-default">
    {% include "movies/includes/filter_heading.html"
            with title=title %}
    <div id="collapse-{{ title|slugify }}"
        class="panel-collapse collapse in">
        <div class="panel-body"><div class="list-group">
            {% include "movies/includes/filter_all.html"
                    with param="director" %}
            {% for cat in facets.categories.directors %}
            <a class="list-group-item
                    {% if selected == cat %}
                    active{% endif %}"
                href="{% modify_query "page"
                                    director=cat.pk %}">
                {{ cat }}</a>
            {% endfor %}
        </div></div>
    </div>
</div>
{% endwith %}
{% with title="Actor" selected=facets.selected.actor %}
<div class="panel panel-default">
    {% include "movies/includes/filter_heading.html"
            with title=title %}
    <div id="collapse-{{ title|slugify }}"
```

```
                                class="panel-collapse collapse in">
                            <div class="panel-body"><div class="list-group">
                                {% include "movies/includes/filter_all.html"
                                        with param="actor" %}
                                {% for cat in facets.categories.actors %}
                                <a class="list-group-item
                                        {% if selected == cat %}
                                        active{% endif %}"
                                    href="{% modify_query "page"
                                                    actor=cat.pk %}">
                                    {{ cat }}</a>
                                {% endfor %}
                            </div></div>
                        </div>
                    </div>
                    {% endwith %}
                    {% with title="Rating" selected=facets.selected.rating %}
                    <div class="panel panel-default">
                        {% include "movies/includes/filter_heading.html"
                                with title=title %}
                        <div id="collapse-{{ title|slugify }}"
                            class="panel-collapse collapse">
                            <div class="panel-body"><div class="list-group">
                                {% include "movies/includes/filter_all.html"
                                        with param="rating" %}
                                {% for r_val, r_display
                                        in facets.categories.ratings %}
                                <a class="list-group-item
                                        {% if selected.0 == r_val %}
                                        active{% endif %}"
                                    href="{% modify_query "page"
                                                    rating=r_val %}">
                                    {{ r_display }}</a>
                                {% endfor %}
                            </div></div>
                        </div>
                    </div>
                    {% endwith %}
                </div>
        {% endblock %}

        {% block content %}
            <div class="movie_list">
                {% for movie in object_list %}
                    <div class="movie alert alert-info">
                        <p>{{ movie.title }}</p>
                    </div>
                {% endfor %}
```

```
    </div>
{% endblock %}
```

 NOTE: Template tags in the previous snippet have been split across lines for legibility but, in practice, template tags must be on a single line, and so cannot be split in this manner.

8. The movie list needs to be added to the URLs for the movies app:

```
# movies/urls.py
from django.urls import path

from .views import movie_list

urlpatterns = [
    path('', movie_list, name='movie-list'),
]
```

9. The movies app URLs need to be added to the project:

```
# project/urls.py
from django.urls import include, path

urlpatterns = [
    # ...
    path('movies/', include('movies.urls')),
]
```

How it works...

We are using the facets dictionary that is passed to the template context to know which filters we have and which filters are selected. To look deeper, the facets dictionary consists of two sections: the categories dictionary and the selected dictionary. The categories dictionary contains QuerySets or choices of all filterable categories. The selected dictionary contains the currently selected values for each category.

In the view, we check whether the query parameters are valid in the form and then filter the QuerySet of objects based on the selected categories. For ratings, there is custom logic to filter movies that are between the selected rating and the one above, so anything greater than or equal to 8, but less than 9. Additionally, we set the selected values to the facets dictionary, which will be passed to the template.

In the template, for each categorization from the `facets` dictionary, we list all of the categories and mark the currently selected category as active. If nothing is selected for a given category, we mark the default `"All"` link as the active one.

See also

- The *Managing paginated lists* recipe
- The *Composing class-based views* recipe
- The *Arranging the base.html template* recipe in `Chapter 4`, *Templates and JavaScript*
- The *Creating a template tag to modify request query parameters* recipe in `Chapter 5`, *Custom Template Filters and Tags*
- The *Importing data from a local CSV file* recipe in `Chapter 10`, *Data Import and Export*

Managing paginated lists

If you have dynamically changing lists of objects or their count is greater than 30 or so, you will likely need pagination in order to provide a good user experience. Instead of the full `QuerySet`, pagination provides a specific number of items in the dataset that corresponds to the appropriate size for one page. We also display links to allow users to access the other pages making up the complete set of data. Django has classes to manage paginated data, and we will see how to use them in this recipe.

Getting ready

Let's start with the forms and views of the `movies` app from the *Filtering object lists* recipe.

How to do it...

To add pagination to the list view of the movies, follow these steps:

1. Import the necessary pagination classes from Django into the `views.py` file. We will add pagination management to the `movie_list` view just after filtering. Also, we will slightly modify the context dictionary by assigning `page` to the `object_list` key:

```python
# movies/views.py
from django.conf import settings
from django.core.paginator import (EmptyPage, PageNotAnInteger,
                                    Paginator)
from django.shortcuts import render

from .models import Genre, Director, Actor, Movie, RATING_CHOICES
from .forms import MovieFilterForm


PAGE_SIZE = getattr(settings, "PAGE_SIZE", 15)


def movie_list(request):
    qs = Movie.objects.order_by("title")
    form = MovieFilterForm(data=request.GET)

    # ... filtering goes here...

    paginator = Paginator(qs, PAGE_SIZE)
    page_number = request.GET.get("page")
    try:
        page = paginator.page(page_number)
    except PageNotAnInteger:
        # If page is not an integer, show first page.
        page = paginator.page(1)
    except EmptyPage:
        # If page is out of range, show last existing page.
        page = paginator.page(paginator.num_pages)

    context = {
        "form": form,
        "facets": facets,
        "object_list": page,
    }
    return render(request, "movies/movie_list.html", context)
```

2. In the template, we will add pagination controls after the list of movies, as follows:

```html
{# templates/movies/movie_list.html #}
{# ... #}

{% block content %}
{# ... #}

{% if object_list.has_other_pages %}
<nav aria-label="Movie list pagination">
```

```
<ul class="pagination">
    {% if object_list.has_previous %}
    <li class="page-item">
        <a class="page-link"
           href="{% modify_query
                   page=object_list.previous_page_number %}">
        &laquo;</a></li>
    {% else %}
    <li class="page-item disabled">
        <span class="page-link">
            <span aria-hidden="true">&laquo;</span>
            <span class="sr-only">Previous</span></span></li>
    {% endif %}

    {% for page_number in object_list.paginator.page_range %}
        {% if page_number == object_list.number %}
        <li class="page-item active">
            <span class="page-link">{{ page_number }}
                <span class="sr-only">(current)</span></span>
        </li>
        {% else %}
        <li class="page-item">
            <a class="page-link"
               href="{% modify_query page=page_number %}">
                {{ page_number }}</a>
        </li>
        {% endif %}
    {% endfor %}

    {% if object_list.has_next %}
    <li class="page-item">
        <a class="page-link"
           href="{% modify_query
                   page=object_list.next_page_number %}">
            <span aria-hidden="true">&raquo;</span>
            <span class="sr-only">Next</span></a></li>
    {% else %}
    <li class="disabled"><span>&raquo;</span></li>
    {% endif %}
</ul>
</nav>
{% endif %}
{% endblock %}
```

 NOTE: Template tags in the previous snippet have been split across lines for legibility but, in practice, template tags must be on a single line, and so cannot be split in this manner.

How it works...

When you look at the results in the browser, you will see the pagination controls, similar to the following, is the list of movies:

How do we achieve this? When `QuerySet` is filtered out, we will create a `paginator` object passing `QuerySet` and the maximal amount of items that we want to show per page, which is 15 here. Then, we will read the current page number from the query parameter, `page`. The next step is to retrieve the current page object from `paginator`. If the page number is not an integer, we get the first page. If the number exceeds the amount of possible pages, the last page is retrieved. The page object has methods and attributes necessary for the pagination widget shown in the preceding screenshot. Also, the page object acts like `QuerySet` so that we can iterate through it and get the items from the fraction of the page.

The snippet marked in the template creates a pagination widget with the markup for the Bootstrap 3 frontend framework. We show the pagination controls only if there are more pages than the current one. We have the links to the previous and next pages, and the list of all page numbers in the widget. The current page number is marked as active. To generate URLs for the links, we use the `{% modify_query %}` template tag, which will be described later in the *Creating a template tag to modify request query parameters* recipe in `Chapter 5`, *Custom Template Filters and Tags*.

See also

- The *Filtering object lists* recipe
- The *Composing class-based views* recipe
- The *Creating a template tag to modify request query parameters* recipe in `Chapter 5`, *Custom Template Filters and Tags*

Composing class-based views

Django views are callables that take requests and return responses. In addition to function-based views, Django provides an alternative way to define views as classes. This approach is useful when you want to create reusable modular views or combine views of the generic mixins. In this recipe, we will convert the previously shown function-based `movie_list` view into a class-based `MovieListView` view.

Getting ready

Create the models, form, and template similar to the previous recipes, *Filtering object lists* and *Managing paginated lists*.

How to do it...

Follow these steps to execute the recipe:

1. Our class-based view, `MovieListView`, will inherit the Django `View` class and override the `get()` method. If we needed to support it, we could also provide a `post()` method, which is used to distinguish requests via HTTP `POST` from those by `GET`:

```python
# movies/views.py
from django.shortcuts import render
from django.core.paginator import (Paginator, EmptyPage,
                                    PageNotAnInteger)
from django.views.generic import View

from .models import Genre, Director, Actor, Movie, RATING_CHOICES
from .forms import MovieFilterForm


class MovieListView(View):
    form_class = MovieFilterForm
    template_name = "movies/movie_list.html"
    paginate_by = 15

    def get(self, request, *args, **kwargs):
        form = self.form_class(data=request.GET)
        qs, facets = self.get_queryset_and_facets(form)
        page = self.get_page(request, qs)
        context = {
```

```
            "form": form,
            "facets": facets,
            "object_list": page,
        }
        return render(request, self.template_name, context)
```

2. We will also split up the remaining majority of the logic into separate methods `get_queryset_and_facets()`, `filter_facets()`, and `get_page()`, to make the class more modular:

```python
# movies/views.py
# ...
class MovieListView(View):
    # ...
    def get_queryset_and_facets(self, form):
        qs = Movie.objects.order_by("title")

        facets = {
            "selected": {},
            "categories": {
                "genres": Genre.objects.all(),
                "directors": Director.objects.all(),
                "actors": Actor.objects.all(),
                "ratings": RATING_CHOICES,
            },
        }

        if form.is_valid():
            filters = (
                ("genre", "genres",),
                ("director", "directors",),
                ("actor", "actors",),
                ("rating", "rating",),
            )
            qs = self.filter_facets(facets, qs, form, filters)

        return qs, facets

    @staticmethod
    def filter_facets(facets, qs, form, filters):
        for facet, key in filters:
            value = form.cleaned_data[facet]
            if value:
                selected_value = value
                if facet == "rating":
                    rating = int(value)
                    selected_value = (rating,
                                      dict(RATING_CHOICES)[rating])
```

```
                            facets["selected"][facet] = selected_value
                            filter_args = {key: value}
                            qs = qs.filter(**filter_args).distinct()
                    return qs

            def get_page(self, request, qs):
                paginator = Paginator(qs, PAGE_SIZE)
                page_number = request.GET.get("page")
                try:
                    page = paginator.page(page_number)
                except PageNotAnInteger:
                    # If page is not an integer, show first page.
                    page = paginator.page(1)
                except EmptyPage:
                    # If page is out of range,
                    # show last existing page.
                    page = paginator.page(paginator.num_pages)
                return page
```

3. We will need to create a URL rule in the URL configuration using the class-based view. You may have added a rule previously for the function-based `movie_list` view, which would have been similar. To include a class-based view in the URL rules, the `as_view()` method is used, as follows:

```
# movies/urls.py
from django.urls import path

from .views import MovieListView

urlpatterns = [
    path('', MovieListView.as_view(), name="movie_list")
]
```

How it works...

The following are the things happening in the `get()` method:

- First, we create the `form` object passing the `GET` dictionary-like object to it. The `GET` object contains all of the query variables that are passed using the `GET` method.
- Then, the `form` object is passed to the `get_queryset_and_facets()` method, which returns the associated values via a tuple containing two elements: `QuerySet` and the `facets` dictionary respectively.

- The current `request` object and retrieved `QuerySet` are passed to the `get_page()` method, which returns the current page object.
- Lastly, we create a context dictionary and render the response.

There's more...

As you see, the `get()` and `get_page()` methods are largely generic so that we could create a generic `FilterableListView` class with these methods in the `utils` app. Then, in any app that requires a filterable list, we could create a class-based view that extends `FilterableListView` to handle such scenarios. This extending class would define only the `form_class` and `template_name` attributes, and the `get_queryset_and_facets()` method. Such modularity and extensibility represent two of the key benefits of how class-based views work.

See also

- The *Filtering object lists* recipe
- The *Managing paginated lists* recipe

Generating PDF documents

Django views allow you to create much more than just HTML pages. You can generate files of any type. For example, in the *Exposing settings in JavaScript* recipe in Chapter 4, *Templates and JavaScript*, our view provides its output as a JavaScript file rather than HTML. You can also create PDF documents for invoices, tickets, booking confirmations, and so on. In this recipe, we will show you how to generate résumés (curricula vitae or CVs) in PDF format using data from the database. We will be using the Pisa `xhtml2pdf` library, which is very practical as it allows you to use HTML templates to make PDF documents.

Getting ready

First of all, we need to install the `xhtml2pdf` Python library in your virtual environment:

```
(myproject_env)$ pip3 install xhtml2pdf~=0.2.3
```

Or add it to the requirements for your Docker project and rebuild the container:

```
# requirements.txt or base.txt
# ...
xhtml2pdf~=0.2.3
```

Learn more in the *Working with a virtual environment* recipe and *Working with Docker* recipe from Chapter 1, *Getting Started with Django 2.1.*

Then, let's create and add to INSTALLED_APPS a cv app containing a simple CurriculumVitae model, which combines with an Experience model that is attached to the CV through a foreign key. Remember to add the app volume in docker-compose.yml if you're using a Docker environment. The CurriculumVitae model will have fields for first name, last name, and email. The Experience model will have fields for the start and end dates of a job, the corresponding company, the position at that company, and the skills gained:

```python
# cv/models.py
from django.db import models
from django.utils.translation import ugettext_lazy as _


class CurriculumVitae(models.Model):
    class Meta:
        verbose_name = _("Curriculum Vitae")
        verbose_name_plural = _("Curricula Vitarum")

    first_name = models.CharField(_("First name"), max_length=40)
    last_name = models.CharField(_("Last name"), max_length=40)
    email = models.EmailField(_("Email"))

    def __str__(self):
        return f"{self.first_name} {self.last_name}"


class Experience(models.Model):
    class Meta:
        ordering = ("-from_date",)
        verbose_name = _("Experience")
        verbose_name_plural = _("Experiences")

    cv = models.ForeignKey(CurriculumVitae,
                           on_delete=models.CASCADE)
    from_date = models.DateField(_("From"))
    till_date = models.DateField(_("Till"), null=True, blank=True)
    company = models.CharField(_("Company"), max_length=100)
    position = models.CharField(_("Position"), max_length=100)
```

```python
skills = models.TextField(_("Skills gained"), blank=True)

def __str__(self):
    date_format = "%m/%Y"
    till = (f"{self.till_date:{date_format}}"
            if self.till_date
            else _("present"))
    start = f"{self.from_date:{date_format}}"
    return f"{start}-{till} {self.position} at {self.company}"
```

How to do it...

Execute the following steps to complete the recipe:

1. We will create the template with which the document will be rendered, as follows:

```html
{# templates/cv/cv_pdf.html #}
{% load static %}
{% get_media_prefix as MEDIA_URL %}
<!doctype html>
<html>
<head>
    <meta charset="utf-8" />
    <title>{{ cv }}</title>
    <style>
        @page {
            size: a4 portrait;
            margin: 2.5cm 1.5cm;

            @frame footer_frame {
                -pdf-frame-content: footer_content;
                bottom: 0;
                margin-left: 0;
                margin-right: 0;
                height: 1cm;
            }
        }

        #footer_content {
            color: #666;
            font-size: 10pt;
            text-align: center;
        }

        h1 { text-align: center; }
```

```
            th, td { vertical-align: top; }
            /* ... additional styles here ... */
        </style>
    </head>
    <body>
    <div>
        <h1>Curriculum Vitae for {{ cv }}</h1>

        <table><tr>
            <td>
                <h2>Contact Information</h2>
                <p><b>Email:</b> {{ cv.email }}</p>
            </td>
            <td align="right">
                <img src="{% static 'site/img/smiley.jpg' %}"
                    width="100" height="100" />
            </td>
        </tr></table>

        <h2>Experience</h2>

        {% for experience in cv.experience_set.all %}
        <h3>{{ experience.position }} at {{ experience.company }}</h3>
        <p><b>
            {{ experience.from_date|date:"F Y" }} -
            {{ experience.till_date|date:"F Y"|default:"present" }}
        </b></p>
        <p>
            <b>Skills gained</b><br>
            {{ experience.skills|linebreaksbr }}
        </p>
        {% endfor %}
    </div>
    <pdf:nextpage>
    <div>
        This is an empty page to make a paper plane.
    </div>
    <div id="footer_content">
        Document generated at {% now "Y-m-d" %} |
        Page <pdf:pagenumber> of <pdf:pagecount>
        | Smiley obtained from clipartextras.com
    </div>
    </body>
    </html>
```

2. Let's create the `download_cv_pdf()` view. This view renders the HTML template and then passes the rendered string to the `pisa` PDF creator:

```python
# cv/views.py
import os

from django.conf import settings
from django.http import HttpResponse, HttpResponseServerError
from django.shortcuts import get_object_or_404, render_to_response
from django.template.loader import render_to_string
from django.utils.text import slugify
from xhtml2pdf import pisa

from .models import CurriculumVitae


def link_callback(uri, rel):
    # convert URIs to absolute system paths
    if uri.startswith(settings.MEDIA_URL):
        path = os.path.join(settings.MEDIA_ROOT,
                            uri.replace(settings.MEDIA_URL, ""))
    elif uri.startswith(settings.STATIC_URL):
        path = os.path.join(settings.STATIC_ROOT,
                            uri.replace(settings.STATIC_URL, ""))
    else:
        # handle absolute uri (ie: http://my.tld/a.png)
        return uri

    # make sure that file exists
    if not os.path.isfile(path):
        raise Exception(
            "Media URI must start with "
            f"'{settings.STATIC_URL}' or '{settings.MEDIA_URL}'")
    return path


def download_cv_pdf(request, cv_id):
    cv = get_object_or_404(CurriculumVitae, pk=cv_id)

    response = HttpResponse(content_type="application/pdf")
    response["Content-Disposition"] = \
        f"attachment; filename='{slugify(cv, True)}.pdf'"

    html = render_to_string("cv/cv_pdf.html", {"cv": cv})
    status = pisa.CreatePDF(html,
                            dest=response,
                            link_callback=link_callback)
```

```
        if status.err:
            response = HttpResponseServerError(
                "The PDF could not be generated.")

        return response
```

3. Create a rule in `urls.py` for the view that will download a PDF document of a résumé by the ID of the `CurriculumVitae` model instance, as follows:

   # cv/urls.py
   ```
   from django.urls import path

   from .views import download_cv_pdf


   urlpatterns = [
       path('<int:pk>/pdf/', download_cv_pdf, name="cv-pdf"),
   ]
   ```

4. Add our cv URLs to the project:

   # project/urls.py
   ```
   from django.urls import include, path

   urlpatterns = [
       # ...
       path('cv/', include('cv.urls')),
   ]
   ```

How it works...

Either set up a model administration and enter details for a CV with some **Experience** entries there, or do so via the Django shell. Then, if you access the document's URL, such as at http://127.0.0.1:8000/cv/1/pdf/, you will be asked to download a PDF document that looks something similar to the following:

Curriculum Vitae for John Doe

Contact Information

Email: john.doe@example.com

Experience

Worker at Jack in the Box Not So Fine Dining

December 2012 - present

Skills gained
Contrary to popular belief, this place is not where they make Jack in the Box toys. Now I know why they asked me if I knew how to cook a hamburger in the interview!

Sumo Wrestler at Wherever

August 2012 - August 2012

Skills gained
I pursued my dream of Sumo Wrestling, only to find out that the minimum weight limit was 300 pounds. Sadly, my Sumo career did not last but I have high hopes for returning to my passion in the near future.

Local Taste Tester at Whole Foods

March 2009 - March 2011

Skills gained
Every day I went to my local Whole Foods and did quality control on all the samples. Eventually it was found that I was in fact not on the payroll, so I was escorted from the building. I even worked on weekends! Fortunately, the restraining order will be lifted soon and I will be able to return from my hiatus.

Babysitter at Home

January 2004 - March 2009

Skills gained
I was forced to babysit my little brother for years while my parents worked. He used to cry constantly, but I guess I would too if my older brother sat on me.

Document generated at 2018-04-15 | Page 1 of 2 | Smiley obtained from clipartextras.com

How does the view work? First, we load a curriculum vitae by its ID (as given in the URL) if it exists, or we raise a page-not-found error if it doesn't. Then, we create the response object with the content type for a PDF document. We set the `Content-Disposition` header to `attachment` with a filename based on the string representation for the CV. This will force the browsers to open a download prompt asking the user to save the PDF document and suggesting the specified name for the file.

 For the filename here, we are using the built-in Django utility function to slugify the `CurriculumVitae` instance (represented by the first and last name). Learn more about slugs in the *Using HTML5 data attributes* recipe from `Chapter 4`, *Templates and JavaScript*.

Next, we render the HTML template as a string, passing the curriculum vitae object into the context. For the static smiley image, we load the `static` template tag library, and use the corresponding `{% static %}` tag to output its URL. Similarly, we expose `MEDIA_URL` via the `{% get_media_prefix %}` tag from the same library, though it isn't used in the current template.

The resulting `html` string is passed to the `xhtml2pdf` PDF creation method. This method also takes a `link_callback` function, which is responsible for ensuring the sources used for images, backgrounds, or style sheets can be found by `xhtml2pdf` for inclusion in the PDF. The result is a status object indicating whether or not an error occurred. If one has, we respond with a simple error message and server error response, rather than the successful PDF response.

Let's take a look at the HTML template that is used to create this document. The template has some unusual markup tags and CSS rules. If we want to have some elements on each page of the document, we can create what are called frames for that. In the preceding example, the `<div>` tag with the `footerContent` ID is marked as a frame, which will be repeated at the bottom of each page. In a similar way, we can have a header or background image for each page. More complex layouts are also possible.

The following are the specific markup tags used in this document:

- The `<pdf:nextpage>` tag sets a manual page break
- The `<pdf:pagenumber>` tag returns the number of the current page
- The `<pdf:pagecount>` tag returns the total number of pages

The current version 0.2.3 of the Pisa `xhtml2pdf` library doesn't fully support all HTML tags and CSS rules. `http://xhtml2pdf.readthedocs.io/en/latest/reference.html` provides a listing of some things that are known to be supported, but there are no publicly accessible benchmarks to see what exactly is supported and at what level. Therefore, you would need to experiment in order to match a PDF document to design requirements. However, this library is still mighty enough for customized layouts, which can be created primarily with only knowledge of HTML and CSS.

See also

- The *Managing paginated lists* recipe
- The *Downloading authorized files* recipe

Implementing a multilingual search with Haystack and Whoosh

One of the main functionalities of content-driven websites is a full-text search. Haystack is a modular search API that supports the Solr, Elasticsearch, Whoosh, and Xapian search engines. For each model in your project that has to be findable in the search, you need to define an index that will read out the textual information from the models and place it into the backend. In this recipe, you will learn how to set up a search with Haystack and the Python-based Whoosh search engine for a multilingual website.

Getting ready

In the beginning, let's create a couple of apps with models that will be indexed in the search. Let's create an `ideas` app containing the `Category` and `Idea` models, as follows:

```python
# ideas/models.py
from django.urls import reverse, NoReverseMatch
from django.db import models
from django.utils.translation import ugettext_lazy as _

from utils.models import UrlMixin
from utils.fields import MultilingualCharField, MultilingualTextField
```

```python
class Category(models.Model):
    class Meta:
        verbose_name = _("Idea Category")
        verbose_name_plural = _("Idea Categories")

    title = MultilingualCharField(_("Title"), max_length=200)

    def __str__(self):
        return self.title


class Idea(UrlMixin):
    class Meta:
        verbose_name = _("Idea")
        verbose_name_plural = _("Ideas")

    title = MultilingualCharField(_("Title"), max_length=200)
    subtitle = MultilingualCharField(_("Subtitle"),
                                     max_length=200,
                                     blank=True)
    description = MultilingualTextField(_("Description"),
                                        blank=True)
    is_original = models.BooleanField(_("Original"))
    categories = models.ManyToManyField(Category,
                                        verbose_name=_("Categories"),
                                        blank=True,
                                        related_name="ideas")

    def __str__(self):
        return self.title

    def get_url_path(self):
        try:
            return reverse("idea_detail", kwargs={"id": self.pk})
        except NoReverseMatch:
            return ""
```

The `Idea` and `Category` models have multilingual fields, as described in the *Handling multilingual fields* recipe in Chapter 2, *Database Structure and Modeling*, which means that there is supposed to be a translation of the content for each language configured in `settings.LANGUAGES`.

Another app we can enable full-text search on is the `quotes` app from the *Uploading images* recipe. This has an `InspirationalQuote` model, but here each `quote` is stored in a simple `TextField`, so it can only be in one language and doesn't necessarily have a translation:

```python
# quotes/models.py
import os
from PIL import Image

from django.conf import settings
from django.core.files.storage import default_storage as storage
from django.db import models
from django.urls import reverse, NoReverseMatch
from django.utils.timezone import now as timezone_now
from django.utils.translation import ugettext_lazy as _

# ...

def upload_to(instance, filename):
    now = timezone_now()
    base, ext = os.path.splitext(filename)
    return f"quotes/{now:%Y/%m/%Y%m%d%H%M%S}{ext.lower()}"


class InspirationalQuote(models.Model):
    class Meta:
        verbose_name = _("Inspirational Quote")
        verbose_name_plural = _("Inspirational Quotes")

    author = models.CharField(_("Author"), max_length=200)
    quote = models.TextField(_("Quote"))
    picture = models.ImageField(_("Picture"),
                                upload_to=upload_to,
                                blank=True,
                                null=True)
    language = models.CharField(_("Language"),
                                max_length=5,
                                blank=True,
                                choices=settings.LANGUAGES)

    # ...

    def get_url_path(self):
        try:
            return reverse("quote_detail", kwargs={"id": self.pk})
        except NoReverseMatch:
            return ""

    def title(self):
```

```
        return self.quote

    def __str__(self):
        return self.quote
```

Put these two apps in `INSTALLED_APPS` in the settings, update your volumes in `docker-compose.yml` if using Docker and restart the container, create and apply database migrations, and create the model administration for these models to add some data. Also, create list and detail views for these models and plug them in the URL rules.

 If you are having any difficulty with any of these tasks, familiarize yourself with the concepts in the official Django tutorial once again: `https://docs.djangoproject.com/en/2.1/intro/tutorial01/`. For updating Docker, refer back to the *Creating a Docker project structure* recipe from `Chapter 1`, *Getting Started with Django 2.1*.

Make sure you have installed `django-haystack`, `whoosh`, and `django-crispy-forms` in your virtual environment:

```
(myproject_env)$ pip3 install django-crispy-forms~=1.7.0
(myproject_env)$ pip3 install django-haystack~=2.8.0
(myproject_env)$ pip3 install whoosh~=2.7.0
```

Or, if using Docker, just update your requirements and rebuild:

```
# requirements.txt or requirements/base.txt
# ...
django-crispy-forms~=1.7.0
django-haystack~=2.8.0
whoosh~=2.7.0
```

How to do it...

Let's set up a multilingual search with Haystack and Whoosh by executing the following steps:

1. Create a `search` app that will contain `MultilingualWhooshEngine` and search indexes for our ideas and quotes. The search engine will live in the `multilingual_whoosh_backend.py` file:

   ```
   # search/multilingual_whoosh_backend.py
   from django.conf import settings
   from django.utils import translation
   from haystack.backends.whoosh_backend import (WhooshSearchBackend,
                                                 WhooshSearchQuery,
   ```

```
                                                      WhooshEngine)
from haystack import connections
from haystack.constants import DEFAULT_ALIAS


class MultilingualWhooshSearchBackend(WhooshSearchBackend):
    def update(self, index, iterable,
               commit=True,
               language_specific=False):
        if not language_specific \
                and self.connection_alias == "default":
            current_language = (translation.get_language()
                                or settings.LANGUAGE_CODE)[:2]
            for lang_code, lang_name in settings.LANGUAGES:
                using = "default_%s" % lang_code
                translation.activate(lang_code)
                backend = connections[using].get_backend()
                backend.update(index, iterable, commit,
                               language_specific=True)
            translation.activate(current_language)
        elif language_specific:
            super().update(index, iterable, commit)


class MultilingualWhooshSearchQuery(WhooshSearchQuery):
    def __init__(self, using=DEFAULT_ALIAS):
        lang_code = translation.get_language()[:2]
        using = "default_%s" % lang_code
        super().__init__(using)


class MultilingualWhooshEngine(WhooshEngine):
    backend = MultilingualWhooshSearchBackend
    query = MultilingualWhooshSearchQuery
```

2. Let's create the search indexes, as follows:

```python
# search/search_indexes.py
from django.conf import settings
from haystack import indexes

from ideas.models import Idea
from quotes.models import InspirationalQuote


class IdeaIndex(indexes.SearchIndex,
                indexes.Indexable):
    text = indexes.CharField(document=True)

    def get_model(self):
        return Idea

    def index_queryset(self, using=None):
        """
        Used when the entire index for model is updated.
        """
        return self.get_model().objects.all()

    def prepare_text(self, idea):
        """
        Called for each language / backend
        """
        basics = [
            idea.title,
            idea.subtitle,
            idea.description,
            ]
        categories = [category.title
                      for category in idea.categories.all()]
        return "\n".join(basics + categories)


class InspirationalQuoteIndex(indexes.SearchIndex,
                              indexes.Indexable):
    text = indexes.CharField(document=True)

    def get_model(self):
        return InspirationalQuote

    def index_queryset(self, using=None):
        """
        Used when the entire index for model is updated.
        """
```

```
        if using and using != "default":
            lang_code = using.replace("default_", "")
        else:
            lang_code = settings.LANGUAGE_CODE[:2]
        return self.get_model().objects.filter(language=lang_code)

    def prepare_text(self, quote):
        """
        Called for each language / backend
        """
        return "\n".join([
            quote.author,
            quote.quote,
            ])
```

3. Configure the settings to use `MultilingualWhooshEngine`:

```python
# settings.py or config/base.py
INSTALLED_APPS = (
    # ...
    'haystack',
    # local apps
    'ideas',
    'quotes',
    'search',
    'utils',
)
# ...
LANGUAGE_CODE = 'en'
LANGUAGES = (
    ("en", "English"),
    ("de", "Deutsch"),
    ("fr", "Français"),
    ("lt", "Lietuvių kalba"),
)
# ...
HAYSTACK_CONNECTIONS = {
    'default_en': {
        'ENGINE': 'search.multilingual_whoosh_backend.'
                  'MultilingualWhooshEngine',
        'PATH': os.path.join(BASE_DIR, 'tmp/whoosh_index_en'),
    },
    'default_de': {
        'ENGINE': 'search.multilingual_whoosh_backend.'
                  'MultilingualWhooshEngine',
        'PATH': os.path.join(BASE_DIR, 'tmp/whoosh_index_de'),
    },
    'default_fr': {
```

```
        'ENGINE': 'search.multilingual_whoosh_backend.'
                  'MultilingualWhooshEngine',
        'PATH': os.path.join(BASE_DIR, 'tmp/whoosh_index_fr'),
    },
    'default_lt': {
        'ENGINE': 'search.multilingual_whoosh_backend.'
                  'MultilingualWhooshEngine',
        'PATH': os.path.join(BASE_DIR, 'tmp/whoosh_index_lt'),
    },
}
HAYSTACK_CONNECTIONS['default'] = \
    HAYSTACK_CONNECTIONS[f'default_{LANGUAGE_CODE}']
```

4. We will add a URL rule:

```
# project/urls.py
from django.conf.urls.i18n import i18n_patterns
from django.urls import include, path

urlpatterns = [
    # ...
]

urlpatterns += i18n_patterns(
    path('search/', include('haystack.urls')),
)
```

5. We will need a template for the search form and search results, as given here:

```
{# templates/search/search.html #}
{% extends "base.html" %}
{% load i18n utility_tags %}

{% block content %}
    <h2>{% trans "Search" %}</h2>
    <form method="get" action="{{ request.path }}">
        <div class="well clearfix">
            {{ form.as_p }}
            <p class="pull-right">
                <input type="submit" value="Search"
                       class="btn btn-primary">
            </p>
        </div>
    </form>

    {% if query %}
        <h3>{% trans "Results" %}</h3>
```

```
{% for result in page.object_list %}
<p>
    <a href="{{ result.object.get_url_path }}">
        {{ result.object.title }}
    </a>
</p>
{% empty %}
<p>{% trans "No results found." %}</p>
{% endfor %}

{% if page.has_previous or page.has_next %}
<nav>
    <ul class="pager">
        <li class="previous">
            {% if page.has_previous %}
            <a href="{% modify_query
                     page=page.previous_page_number %}">
            {% endif %}
            <span aria-hidden="true">&laquo;</span>
            {% if page.has_previous %}</a>{% endif %}
        </li>
        {% for num in page.paginator.page_range %}
        <li{% if num = page.number %}
            class="selected"{% endif %}>
            <a href="{% modify_query page=num %}">
                {{ num }}</a>
        </li>
        {% endfor %}
        <li class="next">
            {% if page.has_next %}
            <a href="{% modify_query
                     page=page.next_page_number %}">
            {% endif %}
                <span aria-hidden="true">&raquo;</span>
            {% if page.has_next %}</a>{% endif %}
        </li>
    </ul>
</nav>
    {% endif %}
{% endif %}
{% endblock %}
```

NOTE: Template tags in the preceding snippet have been split across lines for legibility but, in practice, template tags must be on a single line, and so cannot be split in this manner.

6. Call the `rebuild_index` management command in order to index the database data and prepare the full-text search to be used:

```
(myproject_env)$ python manage.py rebuild_index --noinput
```

How it works...

`MultilingualWhooshEngine` specifies two custom properties:

- `backend` points to `MultilingualWhooshSearchBackend`, which ensures that, for each language, the items will be indexed for each language given in the `LANGUAGES` setting, and put under the associated Haystack index location defined in `HAYSTACK_CONNECTIONS`.
- `query` references the `MultilingualWhooshSearchQuery`, whose responsibility is to ensure that, when searching for keywords, the Haystack connection specific to the current language will be used.

Each index has a field `text` field, where full-text from a specific language of a model will be stored. The model for the index is determined by the `get_model()` method, the `index_queryset()` method defines what `QuerySet` to index, and the content to search within is collected as a newline-separated string in the `prepare_text()` method.

For the template, we have incorporated a few elements of Bootstrap 3 using the out-of-the-box rendering capabilities for forms. This might be enhanced using an approach such as explained in either the *Creating a form layout with custom templates* recipe or the subsequent *Creating a form layout with django-crispy-forms* recipe from earlier in this chapter. The final search form in this case will look similar to the following:

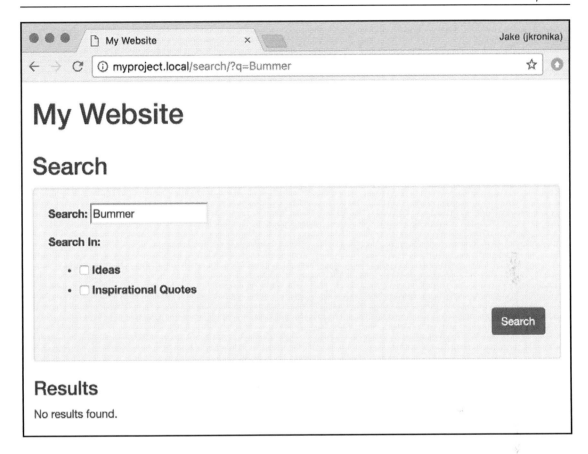

The easiest way to update the search index regularly is to call the `rebuild_index` management command, perhaps by a cron job every night. To learn about it, check the *Setting up cron jobs for regular tasks* recipe in `Chapter 11`, *Testing and Deployment*.

See also

- The *Creating a form layout with custom templates* recipe
- The *Creating a form layout with django-crispy-forms* recipe
- The *Managing paginated lists* recipe
- The *Composing class-based views* recipe
- The *Setting up cron jobs for regular tasks* recipe in `Chapter 11`, *Testing and Deployment*

4

Templates and JavaScript

In this chapter, we will cover the following topics:

- Exposing settings in JavaScript
- Arranging the base.html template
- Using HTML5 data attributes
- Opening object details in a modal dialog
- Implementing a continuous scroll
- Implementing the Like widget
- Uploading images via Ajax

Introduction

We are living in the Web 2.0 world, where social web applications and smart websites communicate between servers and clients dynamically using Ajax, refreshing whole pages only when the context changes. In this chapter, you will learn the best practices to deal with JavaScript in your templates to create a rich user experience. For responsive layouts, we will use the Bootstrap 3 frontend framework. For productive scripting, we will use the jQuery JavaScript framework.

Exposing settings in JavaScript

Each Django project has its configuration set in the `settings.py` settings file, or in `config/base.py` as described in the recipe *Configuring settings for development, testing, staging, and production environments* in Chapter 1, *Getting Started with Django 2.0*. Some of these configuration values may well be useful for functionality in the browser, and so they will also need to be set in JavaScript. As we want a single location to define our project settings and we don't want to repeat the process when setting the configuration for the JavaScript values, it is good practice to include a dynamically generated configuration file in the base template. In this recipe, we will see how to do that.

Getting ready

Make sure that you have the `request` and `i18n` context processors included in the `TEMPLATES['OPTIONS']['context_processors']` setting, as follows:

```python
# settings.py or config/base.py
TEMPLATES = [
    {
        'BACKEND': 'django.template.backends.django.DjangoTemplates',
        # ...
        'OPTIONS': {
            'context_processors': [
                # ...
                'django.template.context_processors.request',
                'django.template.context_processors.i18n',
            ],
        },
    },
]
```

Also, create the `utils` app, if you haven't done so already, and place it under `INSTALLED_APPS` in the settings:

```python
# settings.py or config/base.py
INSTALLED_APPS = [
    # ...
    'utils',
)
```

How to do it...

Follow these steps to create and include the JavaScript settings:

1. In the `views.py` of your `utils` app, create the `render_js()` view that returns a response of the JavaScript content type, as shown in the following code:

```python
# utils/views.py
from datetime import datetime, timedelta, timezone
from email.utils import format_datetime

from django.shortcuts import render
from django.views.decorators.cache import cache_control


@cache_control(public=True)
def render_js(request, template_name, cache=True, *args, **kwargs):
    response = render(request, template_name, *args, **kwargs)
    response["Content-Type"] = \
        "application/javascript; charset=UTF-8"
    if cache:
        now = datetime.now(timezone.utc)
        response["Last-Modified"] = format_datetime(now,
                                                    usegmt=True)

        # cache in the browser for 1 month
        expires = now + timedelta(days=31)
        response["Expires"] = format_datetime(expires,
                                              usegmt=True)
    else:
        response["Pragma"] = "No-Cache"
    return response
```

2. Create a `settings.js` template that returns JavaScript under the global `project_settings` variable, as follows:

```
# templates/settings.js
{% load static %}
{% get_media_prefix as MEDIA_URL %}
{% get_static_prefix as STATIC_URL %}
window.project_settings = {
    MEDIA_URL: '{{ MEDIA_URL|escapejs }}',
    STATIC_URL: '{{ STATIC_URL|escapejs }}',
    lang: '{{ LANGUAGE_CODE|escapejs }}',
    languages: { {% for lang_code, lang_name in LANGUAGES %}
        '{{ lang_code|escapejs }}': '{{ lang_name|escapejs }}'{% if
not forloop.last %},{% endif %}
```

```
        {% endfor %} }
    };
```

3. Create a URL rule to call a view that renders JavaScript settings, as follows:

```
# myproject/urls.py
from django.conf.urls.i18n import i18n_patterns
from django.urls import path

urlpatterns = [
    # ...
]

urlpatterns += i18n_patterns(
    path("js-settings/", "utils.views.render_js",
        {"template_name": "settings.js"},
        name="js_settings"),
)
```

4. Finally, if you haven't done so yet, create a base template as described in the *Arranging the base.html template* recipe. Include the rendered JavaScript settings file in the `base_js` block in that template, as shown in the following code:

```
{# templates/base.html #}
{% block base_js %}
    {# ... #}
    <script src="{% url "js_settings" %}"></script>
{% endblock %}
```

How it works...

The Django template system is very flexible; you are not limited to using templates only for HTML. In this example, we dynamically create a JavaScript file containing certain values from the settings. You can access the resulting file in your development web server via the browser at `http://localhost:8000/en/js-settings/` and its content will be something similar to the following:

```
window.project_settings = {
    MEDIA_URL: '/media/',
    STATIC_URL: '/static/20140424140000/',
    lang: 'en',
    languages: {
        'en': 'English',
        'de': 'Deutsch',
        'fr': 'Français',
        'lt': 'Lietuvi kalba'
```

```
    }
};
```

By incorporating the @cache_control decorator and the combination of Last-Modified and Expires headers, the view will be cacheable in both the server and the browser.

If you want to pass more variables to the JavaScript settings, you can either create a custom view and pass all the values to the context, or create a custom context processor and pass the values there. In the latter case, the variables will become accessible in all templates in your project, rather than only those rendered with the one specific view.

For example, let's assume you find a need to vary JavaScript behavior based on whether you are in the mobile, tablet, or desktop views, but those are determined by media queries in the CSS. Of course, it is possible to use window.matchMedia() to determine what media query our current viewport fits, but you would want to avoid duplicating the viewport sizes across both JavaScript and CSS. If you use LESS or SASS, and compile the CSS via Python, there's an easy solution using the previous method. Given variables for the MOBILE_VIEWPORT_MAX and TABLET_VIEWPORT_MAX integer values, these could be passed into the compilation system to use as variables in the LESS or SASS files, and they could also be exposed to the JavaScript to be used in the code, as shown in the following:

```
window.matchMedia("max-width:"+project_settings.MOBILE_VIEWPORT_MAX+"px")
```

 For more information on window.matchMedia(), see the MDN documentation of the method at https://developer.mozilla.org/en-US/docs/Web/API/Window/matchMedia.

See also

- The *Arranging the base.html template* recipe
- The *Using HTML5 data attributes* recipe

Arranging the base.html template

When you start working on templates, one of the first actions is to create the base.html boilerplate, which will be extended by most of the page templates in your project. In this recipe, we will demonstrate how to create such a template for multilingual HTML5 websites, with responsiveness in mind.

Responsive websites are those that provide the same base content to all devices, styled appropriately to the viewport, whether the visitor uses desktop browsers, tablets, or phones. This differs from adaptive websites, where the server attempts to determine the device type based on the user agent, then provides entirely different content, markup, and even functionality depending on how that user agent is categorized.

Getting ready

Create the `templates` directory in your project and set `TEMPLATE_DIRS` in the settings to include it, as shown here:

```python
# project/settings.py
TEMPLATES = [{
    # ...
    'DIRS': [
        # ...
        os.path.join(BASE_DIR, "templates"),
    ],
}]
```

How to do it...

Perform the following steps:

1. In the root directory of your `templates`, create a `base.html` file with the following content:

```html
{# templates/base.html #}
<!doctype html>
{% load i18n static %}
<html lang="{{ LANGUAGE_CODE }}">
<head>
    <meta charset="utf-8">
    <meta name="viewport"
        content="width=device-width, initial-scale=1">
    <title>
        {% block title %}{% endblock %}
        {% trans "My Website" %}
    </title>
    <link rel="icon" type="image/x-icon"
        href="{% static 'site/img/favicon.ico' %}">
```

```
    {% block meta_tags %}{% endblock %}

    {% block base_stylesheet %}
        <link rel="stylesheet"
href="https://stackpath.bootstrapcdn.com/bootstrap/4.1.3/css/bootst
rap.min.css"
            integrity="sha384-
MCw98/SFnGE8fJT3GXwEOngsV7Zt27NXFoaoApmYm81iuXoPkFOJwJ8ERdknLPMO"
            crossorigin="anonymous">
        <link rel="stylesheet" type="text/css" media="screen"
            href="{% static 'site/css/style.css' %}">
    {% endblock %}
    {% block stylesheet %}{% endblock %}

    {% block extrahead %}{% endblock %}
</head>
<body class="{% block bodyclass %}{% endblock %}">
{% block page %}
    <section class="wrapper">
        <header class="clearfix container">
            <h1>{% trans "My Website" %}</h1>
            {% block header_navigation %}
                {% include "utils/header_navigation.html" %}
            {% endblock %}
            {% block language_chooser %}
                {% include "utils/language_chooser.html" %}
            {% endblock %}
        </header>
        {% block container %}
        <div id="content" class="clearfix container">
            {% block content %}{% endblock %}
        </div>
        {% endblock %}
        <footer class="clearfix container">
            {% block footer_navigation %}
                {% include "utils/footer_navigation.html" %}
            {% endblock %}
        </footer>
    </section>
{% endblock %}
{% block extrabody %}{% endblock %}

{% block base_js %}
    <script src="https://code.jquery.com/jquery-3.3.1.slim.min.js"
            integrity="sha384-
q8i/X+965DzO0rT7abK41JStQIAqVgRVzpbzo5smXKp4YfRvH+8abtTE1Pi6jizo"
            crossorigin="anonymous"></script>
    <script
```

```
        src="https://cdnjs.cloudflare.com/ajax/libs/popper.js/1.14.3/umd/po
pper.min.js"
                integrity="sha384-
ZMP7rVo3mIykV+2+9J3UJ46jBk0WLaUAdn689aCwoqbBJiSnjAK/l8WvCWPIPm49"
        crossorigin="anonymous"></script>
    <script
src="https://stackpath.bootstrapcdn.com/bootstrap/4.1.3/js/bootstra
p.min.js"
                integrity="sha384-
ChfqqxuZUCnJSK3+MXmPNIyE6ZbWh2IMqE241rYiqJxyMiZ6OW/JmZQ5stwEULTy"
        crossorigin="anonymous"></script>
    <script src="{% url "js_settings" %}"></script>
{% endblock %}
{% block js %}{% endblock %}
</body>
</html>
```

2. In the same directory, create another file named `base_simple.html` for specific cases, as follows:

```
{# templates/base_simple.html #}
{% extends "base.html" %}

{% block page %}
<section class="wrapper">
    <div id="content" class="clearfix">
        {% block content %}{% endblock %}
    </div>
</section>
{% endblock %}
```

3. For the purposes of this recipe, create empty files under `templates/utils` for the `header_navigation.html`, `language_chooser.html`, and `footer_navigation.html` files.

How it works...

The base template contains the `<head>` and `<body>` sections of the HTML document, with all the details that are reused on each page of the website. Depending on the web design requirements, you can have additional base templates for different layouts. For example, we added the `base_simple.html` file, which has the same HTML `<head>` section and a very minimalistic `<body>` section, and it can be used for the login screen, password reset, or other simple pages. You can have separate base templates for other layouts as well, such as single-column, two-column, and three-column layouts, where each of them extends `base.html` and overwrites the blocks as needed.

Let's look into the details of the `base.html` template that we defined earlier.

Here are the details for the `<head>` section:

- We define UTF-8 as the default encoding to support multilingual content.
- Then, we have the viewport definition that will scale the website in the browser to use the full width. This is necessary for small-screen devices that will get specific screen layouts created with the Bootstrap frontend framework.
- Of course, there's a customizable website title, and whatever favicon you use will be shown in the browser's tab.
- We have extensible blocks for meta tags, style sheets, and whatever else might be necessary for the `<head>` section.
- We load the Bootstrap CSS, as we want to have responsive layouts, and this will also normalize basic styling for all elements for consistency across browsers.

Here are the details for the `<body>` section:

- We have the header with an overwritable navigation and a language chooser.
- We also have the main container, and within it a content block placeholder, which are to be filled by extending the templates.
- Then there is the footer, which contains the footer navigation.
- Below the footer is an empty block placeholder for additional markup, should that be needed.
- Extensible JavaScript blocks are included at the end of the `<body>` following best practices for page-load performance, much like those for the style sheets included in the `<head>`.

- Then, we load the JavaScript jQuery library that efficiently and flexibly allows us to create rich user experiences.
- We load the Bootstrap JavaScript and its dependency Popper script in the template here, as the companion to the Bootstrap CSS loaded in the `<head>`.
- We also load JavaScript settings that are rendered from a Django view, as was seen in the preceding recipe.

The base template that we created is, by no means, a static unchangeable template. You can modify the markup structure, or add to it the elements you need—for example, Google Analytics code, common JavaScript files, the Apple touch icon for iPhone bookmarks, Open Graph meta tags, Twitter Card tags, schema.org attributes, and so on. You may also want to define other blocks, depending on the requirements of your project.

There's more...

We leave it as an exercise for you to implement `header_navigation.html`, `language_chooser.html`, and `footer_navigation.html` templates in the `utils/` directory, if desired. These blocks can also be populated as described in `Chapter 8`, *Django CMS*.

See also

- The *Exposing settings in JavaScript* recipe
- The *Creating templates for Django CMS* recipe in `Chapter 8`, *Django CMS*

Using HTML5 data attributes

When you have dynamic data related to HTML **Document Object Model (DOM)** elements, often you will need to pass the values from Django to JavaScript. In this recipe, we will see a way to attach data efficiently from Django to custom HTML5 data attributes and then describe how to read the data from JavaScript with two practical examples:

- The first example will be a Google Map with a marker at a specified geographical position
- Then, we will enhance the marker to display the address in an info window when clicked

Getting ready

To get started, follow these steps:

1. Create a `location` app with a `Location` model and an associated administration, as described in the *Inserting a map into a change form* recipe in `Chapter 6`, *Model Administration*. It will include character fields for the `title`, `street`, `street2`, `city`, `country`, and `postal_code`. There also should be floating-point number fields for the `latitude` and `longitude`, and the `description` text field.

2. Augment the `Location` model to add a `slug` field for URLs, as shown here:

```
# location/models.py
class Location(models.Model):
    # ...
    _slug_definition = _(
        "The term slug comes from newspaper editing and it means "
        "a short string without any special characters; just "
        "letters, numbers, underscores, and hyphens. Slugs are "
        "generally used to create unique URLs.")
    slug = models.SlugField(_("slug"),
                            help_text=_slug_definition)
```

3. Also, we will want a method with which simply to retrieve a formatted address, for use in our templates. Add this method to the model as well:

```
# location/models.py
class Location(models.Model):
    # ...

    @property
    def address(self):
        address = [self.street]
        if self.street2:
            address.append(self.street2)
        address += [self.city, self.country, self.postal_code]
        return ", ".join(address)
```

4. For this recipe, we will replace `map_html` in the administration with an empty string. We also need to add the `slug` field to the admin. The changes will look similar to the following:

```
# location/admin.py
class LocationAdmin(admin.ModelAdmin):
    # ...
    def get_fieldsets(self, request, obj=None):
```

```
map_html = ""
# ...
fieldsets = [
    # ...
    (_("Slug"), {"fields": ("slug",)}),
]
```

5. Remember to make and run migrations for the app after updating the model. Then use the administration to enter a sample location.

How to do it...

Perform the following steps:

1. As we already have the app created, we will now need the template for the location detail:

```
{# templates/locations/location_detail.html #}
{% extends "base.html" %}
{% load static %}

{% block content %}
    <h2 class="map-title">{{ location.title }}</h2>
    <p>{{ location.description }}</p>
    <div id="map"
        data-lat="{{ location.latitude|stringformat:"f" }}"
        data-lng="{{ location.longitude|stringformat:"f" }}"
        data-address="{{ location.address }}"></div>
{% endblock %}

{% block js %}
    <script src="{% static 'site/js/location_detail.js'
%}"></script>
    <script async defer
            src="https://maps-api-ssl.google.com/maps/api/js?key={{
MAPS_API_KEY }}&callback=Location.init"></script>
{% endblock %}
```

2. Besides the template, we need the JavaScript file that will read out the HTML5 data attributes and use them accordingly, as follows:

```
// static/site/js/location_detail.js
(function(window) {
    "use strict";

    function Location() {
```

```javascript
        this.case = document.getElementById("map");
        if (this.case) {
            this.getCoordinates();
            this.getAddress();
            this.getMap();
            this.getMarker();
            this.getInfoWindow();
        }
    }

Location.prototype.getCoordinates = function() {
    this.coords = {
        lat: parseFloat(this.case.getAttribute("data-lat")),
        lng: parseFloat(this.case.getAttribute("data-lng"))
    };
};

Location.prototype.getAddress = function() {
    this.address = this.case.getAttribute("data-address");
};

Location.prototype.getMap = function() {
    this.map = new google.maps.Map(this.case, {
        zoom: 15,
        center: this.coords
    });
};

Location.prototype.getMarker = function() {
    this.marker = new google.maps.Marker({
        position: this.coords,
        map: this.map
    });
};

Location.prototype.getInfoWindow = function() {
    var self = this;
    var wrap = this.case.parentNode;
    var title = wrap.querySelector(".map-title").textContent;

    this.infoWindow = new google.maps.InfoWindow({
        content: "<h3>"+title+"</h3><p>"+this.address+"</p>"
    });

    this.marker.addListener("click", function() {
        self.infoWindow.open(self.map, self.marker);
    });
};
```

```
        var instance;
        Location.init = function() {
            // called by Google Maps service automatically once loaded
            // but is designed so that Location is a singleton
            if (!instance) {
                instance = new Location();
            }
        };

        // expose in the global namespace
        window.Location = Location;
}(window));
```

3. For the map to be displayed nicely, we need to set some CSS, as shown in the following code:

```
/* static/site/css/style.css */
#map {
    border: 1px solid #000;
    box-sizing: padding-box;
    height: 0;
    padding-bottom: calc(9 / 16 * 100%); /* 16:9 aspect ratio */
    width: 100%;
}

@media screen and (max-width: 480px) {
    #map {
        display: none; /* hide on mobile devices (esp. portrait) */
    }
}
```

4. If one is not already set up, add a detail view in `views.py`, as shown here:

```
# location/views.py
from django.conf import settings
from django.views.generic import DetailView

from .models import Location


class LocationDetail(DetailView):
    model = Location

    def get_context_data(self, **kwargs):
        context = super().get_context_data()
        context["MAPS_API_KEY"] = settings.MAPS_API_KEY
        return context
```

5. The `MAPS_API_KEY` should be passed into your application from an environment variable, rather than having it stored directly in the code under version control. This also gives you the flexibility to have separate keys for different environments. The resulting code in the settings might be as follows:

```
# settings.py
MAPS_API_KEY = os.environ.get("MAPS_API_KEY")
```

Information about the Google Maps API and instructions for creating and maintaining API keys, can be found at `https://developers.google.com/maps/`.

6. Add an associated URL rule using the `slug` field we added earlier:

```
# locations/urls.py
from django.urls import path

from .views import LocationDetail


urlpatterns = [
    path('<slug:slug>/', LocationDetail.as_view(),
        name='location-detail'),
]
```

7. Finally, make sure your `locations` app URLs are referenced in the project `urls.py`, like so:

```
# myproject/urls.py
urlpatterns = [
    # ...
    path('locations/', include('locations.urls')),
]
```

How it works...

If you open your location detail view in a browser at a URL such as
`http://localhost:8000/locations/eiffel-tower`, you will see something similar to
the following:

Clicking on the map pin will open an info window showing the title and the address of the
location:

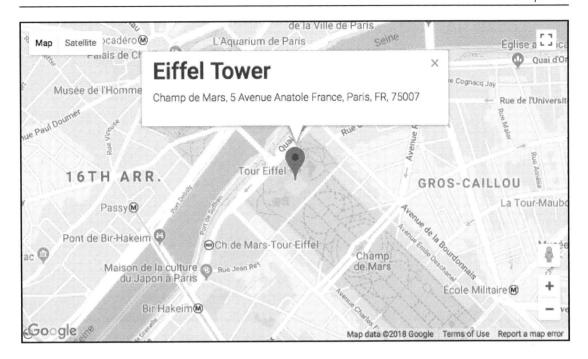

Since scrolling within maps on mobile devices can be problematic due to scroll-within-scroll issues, we have opted to hide the map on small screens (less than or equal to 480 px width), so when we resize the screen down, the map eventually becomes invisible, as in the following:

My Website
Eiffel Tower

The Eiffel Tower is a wrought iron lattice tower on the Champ de Mars in Paris, France. It is named after the engineer Gustave Eiffel, whose company designed and built the tower. – Source: wikipedia. Photo source: https://www.pexels.com/photo/picture-of-eiffel-tower-338515/

Let's take a look at the code. In the template, we have the location title and description, followed by a `<div>` element with the `map` ID, as well as the `data-lat` (latitude), `data-lng` (longitude), and `data-address` custom attributes. These make up the `content` block elements. Two `<script>` tags are added to the `js` block that comes at the end of the `<body>`—one being the `location_detail.js` described next, and the other is the Google Maps API script, to which we have passed our Maps API `key`, and the name of the `callback` to invoke when the API loads. In the `LocationDetail` view, we added our `MAPS_API_KEY` from settings as extra context, so that it could be used here.

> The `template_name` default for a `DetailView` comes from the lowercase version of the model's name, plus detail; hence, our template was named `location_detail.html`. If we wanted to use a different template, we could specify a `template_name` property for the view.

In the JavaScript, we create a `Location` class using a prototype function. This function has a static `init()` method, which is given as the callback to the Maps API. When `init()` is called, the constructor is invoked to create a new singleton `Location` instance. In the constructor function, a series of steps are taken to set up the map and its features, as in:

- First, the map `case` (container) is found by its ID. Only if that element is found do we continue.
- Next, we find the geographic coordinates using the `data-lat` and `data-lng` attributes, storing those in a dictionary as the location's `coords`. This object is in the form understood by the Maps API, and will be used later.
- The `data-address` is read next and stored directly as the address property of the location.
- From here, we start building things out, beginning with the map. To ensure that the location will be visible, we set the `center` using the `coords` pulled from data attributes earlier.
- A marker makes the location obvious on the `map`, positioned using the same `coords`.
- Finally, we build up an info window, which is a type of pop-up bubble that can be displayed directly on the map using the API. In addition to the `address` retrieved earlier, we look for the location `title` based on the `.map-title` class it was given in the template. This is added as an `<h3>` heading to the window, followed by the address as a second `<p>` paragraph. To allow the window to be displayed, we add a click event listener to the marker that will open the window.

See also

- The *Exposing settings in JavaScript* recipe
- The *Arranging the base.html template* recipe
- The *Providing responsive images* recipe
- The *Opening object details in a modal dialog* recipe
- The *Inserting a map into a change form* recipe in Chapter 6, *Model Administration*

Providing responsive images

As responsive websites have become the norm, many performance issues have arisen when it comes to providing identical content to both mobile devices and desktop computers. One very easy way to reduce the load time of a responsive site on small devices is to provide smaller images. This is where the srcset and sizes attributes, key components of responsive images, come into play.

Getting ready

Let's start with the locations app that was used in the previous recipe. We'll also want to update the administration settings accordingly, and to make sure to run migrations for the locations app as well. Then we can add a large image for the location previously created.

How to do it...

Walk through these actions to add the responsive images:

1. To create thumbnail images dynamically, we will use the sorl-thumbnail app. Install this either by directly invoking pip in a virtual environment, or through the requirements in a Docker project:

```
# requirements.txt or base.txt
# ...
sorl-thumbnail~=12.4.0
```

It will also need to be added to the INSTALLED_APPS:

```
# settings.py or config/base.py
INSTALLED_APPS = [
    # ...
    'sorl.thumbnail',
]
```

2. Once sorl_thumbnail is installed, make sure to migrate your database to add necessary schema for full thumbnail support.

3. Then, add an image field to the Location model, as follows:

```
# locations/models.py
import os
# ...
def upload_to(instance, filename):
    base, ext = os.path.splitext(filename)
    return f"locations/{instance.slug}{ext.lower()}"


class Location(models.Model):
    # ...
    image = models.ImageField(null=True,
                              upload_to=upload_to)
    # ...
```

4. Update the admin.py as shown in the following code to expose the image field, and then make/run migrations for the locations app:

```
# locations/admin.py
class LocationAdmin(admin.ModelAdmin):
    # ...
    def get_fieldsets(self, request, obj=None):
        map_html = render_to_string("admin/includes/map.html")
        fieldsets = [
            # ...
            (_("Image"), {"fields": ("image",)}),
        ]
        return fieldsets
```

5. Next we need to update the detail template to include the new image, when one exists:

```
{# templates/locations/location_detail.html #}
{% extends "base.html" %}
{% load static thumbnail %}
{% get_media_prefix as MEDIA_URL %}
```

```
{% block extrahead %}
<script src="{% static 'site/js/lib/picturefill.min.js'
%}"></script>
{% endblock %}

{% block content %}
    <h2 class="map-title">{{ location.title }}</h2>
    {% if location.image %}
    <picture>
        {% thumbnail location.image "480" as mobile_image %}
        <source media="(max-width: 480px)"
                srcset="{{ mobile_image.url }}">
        {% endthumbnail %}
        {% thumbnail location.image "768" as tablet_image_sm %}
            <source media="(max-width: 768px)"
                    srcset="{{ tablet_image_sm.url }}">
        {% endthumbnail %}
        {% thumbnail location.image "1024" as tablet_image_lg %}
            <source media="(max-width: 1024px)"
                    srcset="{{ tablet_image_lg.url }}">
        {% endthumbnail %}
        <img src="{{ MEDIA_URL }}{{ location.image.url }}"
             alt="{{ location.title }} image">
    </picture>
    {% endif %}
    {# ... #}
{% endblock %}

{# ... #}
```

6. As we can see from the previous code, we need to add a `picturefill.min.js` file to our static content, which can be downloaded following the instructions at `https://scottjehl.github.io/picturefill/`. Since this is a third-party script, it has been placed under a `lib/` subdirectory in the `static/site/js/` area.

7. Update the styles to make sure the image size is fluid:

```
# static/site/css/style.css
picture img {
    width: 100%;
}
```

8. Finally, after migrating the `location` app to add the `img` field to the database, add a location with an image via the admin, or update an existing location if you prefer.

How it works...

Responsive images are powerful, and at their base are concerned with providing different images based on media rules, which indicate the features of the displays upon which each image should be shown. The first thing we did here was to add the `sorl-thumbnail` app, which makes it easy to generate the different images needed on the fly.

Obviously, we also will need the original image source, so in our `Location` model we added an `image` field. In the `upload_to()` function, we use the `slug` when generating the storage filename, which is already required to be unique across locations, and is safe for URLs. The image is then exposed in the administration so that we can add files accordingly.

The most interesting work happens in the template, in this case. From the `sorl-thumbnail` app, we load the `thumbnail` tag library, which provides one primary `{% thumbnail %}` tag that is used later. Then, to provide support across more browsers for the `<picture>` tag that enables responsive images, we pull in the `picturefill.min.js` script. Because this is a **polyfill**—a script providing alternative support for a core feature in browsers that do not have the support natively—it needs to load and execute as early as possible for things to render properly. As such, it is added to the `extrahead` block, instead of being with the other scripts in the `base_js` or `js` blocks at the end of the `<body>`.

When a location image exists, we construct our `<picture>` element. On the surface, this is basically a container. In fact, it could have nothing inside of it besides the fallback/default `<img>` tag that appears at the end in our template, though that would not be very useful. In addition to the original image, we generate thumbnails for three different widths—`480w`, `768w`, and `1024w`—and these are then used to build additional `<source>` elements. Each source provides the `media` rule for which it should be used and a `srcset` of images from which to select. In our case, we only provide one image for each `<source>`. The location detail page now will include the image above the map and should look something like this:

When the browser loads this markup, it follows a series of steps to determine which image to load:

- The `media` rules for each `<source>` are inspected in turn, checking to see whether any one of them matches the current viewport
- When a rule matches, the `srcset` is read and the appropriate image URL is loaded and displayed
- If no rules match, the `src` of the final, default image is loaded

As a result, smaller images will be loaded on smaller viewports. For example, here we can see that the smallest size image was loaded for a viewport only 375 px wide:

For browsers that cannot understand the `<picture>` and `<source>` tags at all, the default image can still be loaded, as it is nothing more than a normal `<img>` tag.

There's more...

Responsive images can be used not only to provide targeted image sizes, but also for the differentiation of pixel density, and for compositions using imagery that is specifically curated for the design at any given viewport size (known as **art direction**). If you are interested in learning more, the **Mozilla Developer Network** (**MDN**) has a thorough article on the topic, available at `https://developer.mozilla.org/en-US/docs/Learn/HTML/Multimedia_and_embedding/Responsive_images`.

See also

- The *Arranging the base.html template* recipe
- The *Using HTML5 data attributes* recipe
- The *Opening object details in a modal dialog* recipe
- The *Inserting a map into a change form* recipe in `Chapter 6`, *Model Administration*

Opening object details in a modal dialog

In this recipe, we will create a list of links to the locations, which, when clicked, opens a Bootstrap modal dialog (we will call it a popup in this recipe) with some information about the location and the *more...* link leading to the location detail page. The content for the dialog will be loaded by Ajax. For visitors without JavaScript, the detail page will open immediately, without this intermediate step.

Getting ready

Let's start with the `locations` app that we created in the previous recipes.

In the `urls.py` file, we will have three URL rules: one for the location list, another for the location detail, and a third for the dialog, as follows:

```
# locations/urls.py
from django.urls import path

from .views import LocationList, LocationDetail


urlpatterns = [
    path('', LocationList.as_view(),
```

```
            name='location-list'),
        path('<slug:slug>/', LocationDetail.as_view(),
            name='location-detail'),
        path('<slug:slug>/popup', LocationDetail.as_view(),
            {"template_name": "location_popup.html"},
            name='location-popup'),
    ]
```

Consequently, there will be two class-based views, with the detail one being shared for both the dialog and the full detail page, as shown in the following code:

```python
# locations/views.py
from django.conf import settings
from django.views.generic import ListView, DetailView

from .models import Location


class LocationList(ListView):
 model = Location


class LocationDetail(DetailView):
    model = Location

    def get_context_data(self, **kwargs):
        context = super().get_context_data()
        context["MAPS_API_KEY"] = settings.MAPS_API_KEY
        return context
```

How to do it...

Execute these steps one by one:

1. Create a template for the location's list view with a hidden, empty modal dialog at the end. Each listed location will have custom HTML5 data attributes dealing with the pop-up information, as follows:

```
{# templates/locations/location_list.html #}
{% extends "base.html" %}
{% load i18n static %}

{% block content %}
    <h2>{% trans "Locations" %}</h2>
    <ul class="location-list">
        {% for location in location_list %}
```

```
            <li class="item">
                <a href="{% url "location-detail"
                                slug=location.slug %}"
                    data-popup-url="{% url "location-popup"
                                        slug=location.slug %}">
                    {{ location.title }}</a>
            </li>
            {% endfor %}
        </ul>
{% endblock %}

{% block extrabody %}
<div id="popup" class="modal fade" tabindex="-1" role="dialog"
        aria-hidden="true" aria-labelledby="popup-modal-title">
    <div class="modal-dialog modal-dialog-centered"
            role="document">
        <div class="modal-content">
            <div class="modal-header">
                <h4 id="popup-modal-title"
                    class="modal-title"></h4>
                <button type="button" class="close"
                        data-dismiss="modal"
                        aria-label="{% trans 'Close' %}">
                    <span aria-hidden="true">&times;</span>
                </button>
            </div>
            <div class="modal-body"></div>
        </div>
    </div>
</div>
{% endblock %}

{% block js %}
<script src="{% static 'site/js/location_list.js' %}"></script>
{% endblock %}
```

 The `template` tags in the preceding snippet have been split across lines for legibility, but in practice, `template` tags must be on a single line, and so cannot be split in this manner.

2. We need JavaScript to handle the opening of the dialog and loading the content dynamically:

    // site_static/site/js/location_list.js
    ```
    jQuery(function($) {
        var $list = $(".location-list");
    ```

```
            var $popup = $("#popup");

            $popup.on("click", ".close", function(event) {
                $popup.modal("hide");
                // do something when dialog is closed
            });

            $list.on("click", ".item a", function(event) {
                var link = this;
                var url = link.getAttribute("data-popup-url");

                if (url) {
                    event.preventDefault();

                    $(".modal-title", $popup).text(link.textContent);
                    $(".modal-body", $popup).load(url, function() {
                        $popup.on("shown.bs.modal", function () {
                            // do something when dialog is shown
                        }).modal("show");
                    });
                }
            });
        });
```

3. Finally, we will create a template for the content that will be loaded in the modal dialog, as shown in the following code:

```
{# templates/locations/location_popup.html #}
{% load i18n thumbnail %}
{% thumbnail location.image "200" as small_image %}
<p class="text-center">
    <img src="{{ small_image.url }}" class="img-thumbnail"
        alt="{{ location.title|escape }}" />
</p>
{% endthumbnail %}

<div class="modal-footer text-right">
    <a href="{% url "location-detail" slug=location.slug %}"
       class="btn btn-primary pull-right">
        {% trans "More" %}
        <span class="glyphicon glyphicon-chevron-right"></span>
    </a>
</div>
```

How it works...

If we go to the location's list view in a browser and click on one of the locations, we will see a modal dialog similar to the following:

Let's examine how this all came together. Looking first at the listing template, the `content` block is populated with an unordered list. Within this `.location-list`, we repeat an `<li>` element with the `item` CSS class for each location, which in turn contains a link. The links have a custom attribute for the `data-popup-url`, and contain the location title as the link text. Following that, we have added the placeholder pop-up markup in the `extrabody` block, and this uses a standard modal dialog markup from Bootstrap 4. The dialog contains a header with the close button and title, plus a content area for the main pop-up details. Finally, we add the JavaScript to the `js` block at the very end.

In the JavaScript, we have used the jQuery framework to take advantage of several niceties it provides. When the page is loaded, we assign an event handler `on("click")` for the `ul.location-list` element. When any `.item a` link is clicked, that event is delegated to this handler, which reads and stores the custom attribute as the `url`. When this is extracted successfully, we prevent the original click action (navigation to the full detail page) and then set up the modal for display. The new title is set for the hidden dialog box using the link's `textContent`, and the main HTML content is loaded into the modal dialog's `.content` area over Ajax. Finally, the modal is shown to the visitor using the Bootstrap4 `modal()` jQuery plugin. A separate event handler for clicks on the dialog's `button.close` reverses the process to hide the modal again.

The pop-up template simply provides a small version of the location image and a link to the full detail page. Bootstrap 4 classes are used to style the image and link.

If the JavaScript were unable to process the pop-up URL from the custom attribute, or, even worse, if the JavaScript in `location_list.js` failed to load or execute entirely, clicking on the location link would take the user to the detail page as usual. In this way, we have implemented our modal as a progressive enhancement so that the user experience is good, even in the face of failure.

See also

- The *Using HTML5 data attributes* recipe
- The *Providing responsive images* recipe
- The *Implementing a continuous scroll* recipe
- The *Implementing the Like widget* recipe

Implementing a continuous scroll

Social websites often have a feature called **continuous scrolling**, which is also known as **infinite scrolling**, as an alternative to pagination. Rather than having links to see additional sets of items separately, there are long lists of items, and, as you scroll down the page, new items are loaded and attached to the bottom automatically. In this recipe, we will see how to achieve such an effect with Django and the jScroll jQuery plugin. We'll illustrate this using a sample view showing the top 250 movies of all time from the Internet Movie Database (http://www.imdb.com/chart/top).

You can download the jScroll script, and also find extensive documentation about the plugin, from `http://jscroll.com/`.

Getting ready

Create a `movies` app such as the one described in the *Filtering object lists* recipe from `Chapter 3`, *Forms and Views*. This will have a paginated list view for the movies. For the purposes of this recipe, you can either create a `Movie` model or a list of dictionaries with the movie data. Every movie will have `title`, `release_year`, `rank`, and `rating` fields. Release years can range from 1888 through to the current year, and ratings can be any number from `0` to `10`, inclusive. The changes will be something such as the following:

```python
# movies/models.py
from datetime import datetime

from django.core.validators import (MaxValueValidator,
                                     MinValueValidator)
from django.db import models
from django.utils.translation import ugettext_lazy as _

# ...

class Movie(models.Model):
    # ...
    release_year = models.PositiveIntegerField(
        _("Release year"),
        validators=[
            MinValueValidator(1888),
            MaxValueValidator(datetime.now().year),
        ],
        default=datetime.now().year)
    rating = models.PositiveIntegerField(
        _("Rating"),
        validators=[
            MinValueValidator(0),
            MaxValueValidator(10),
        ])
    rank = models.PositiveIntegerField(
        unique=True,
        blank=False,
        null=False,
        default=0)
```

```python
@property
def rating_percentage(self):
    """Convert 0-10 rating into a 0-100 percentage"""
    return int(self.rating * 10)

def __str__(self):
    return self.title
```

How to do it...

Perform the following steps to create a continuously scrolling page:

1. First, add the top movie data to your database.

> A data migration is provided in the code files associated with the book that can be executed to add movie data to your project.

2. The next step is to create a template for the list view that will also show a link to the next page, as follows:

```html
{# templates/movies/top_movies.html #}
{% extends "base.html" %}
{% load i18n static utility_tags %}

{% block stylesheet %}
    <link rel="stylesheet" type="text/css"
        href="{% static 'movies/css/rating.css' %}">
    <link rel="stylesheet" type="text/css"
        href="{% static 'site/css/movie_list.css' %}">
{% endblock %}

{% block content %}
<h2>{% trans "Top Movies" %}</h2>
<div class="movie-list object-list">
    {% trans "IMDB rating" as rating_label %}
    {% for movie in object_list %}
        <p class="movie item alert alert-info">
            <span class="rank">{{ movie.rank }}</span>
            <span class="rating"
                title="{{ rating_label }}: {{ movie.rating }}">
            <s style="width:{{ movie.rating_percentage }}%"></s>
        </span>
            <strong class="title">{{ movie.title }}</strong>
            <span class="year">{{ movie.release_year }}</span>
```

```
        </p>
    {% endfor %}

    {% if object_list.has_next %}
        <p class="pagination">
            <a class="next_page"
                href="{% modify_query
page=object_list.next_page_number %}">
                    {% trans "More..." %}</a>
        </p>
    {% endif %}
</div>
{% endblock %}

{% block extrabody %}
    <script type="text/template" class="loader">
        <img src="{% static 'site/img/loading.gif' %}"
            alt="Loading..."></script>
{% endblock %}

{% block js %}
    <script
src="https://cdnjs.cloudflare.com/ajax/libs/jscroll/2.3.9/jquery.js
croll.min.js"></script>
    <script src="{% static 'site/js/list.js ' %}"></script>
{% endblock %}
```

 We use the Cloudflare CDN URL to load the jScroll plugin here, but if you opt to download a copy locally as a static file, use a `{% static %}` lookup to add the script to the template.

3. The second step is to add JavaScript, as shown here:

```
// site_static/site/js/list.js
jQuery(function($) {
    var $list = $(".object-list");
    var $loader = $("script[type='text/template'].loader");

    $list.jscroll({
        loadingHtml: $loader.html(),
        padding: 100,
        pagingSelector: '.pagination',
        nextSelector: 'a.next_page:last',
        contentSelector: '.item,.pagination'
    });
});
```

4. Next, we'll add some CSS to the `movies` app so that ratings can be displayed using user-friendly stars instead of just numbers:

```css
/* movies/static/movies/css/rating.css */
.rating {
    color: #c90;
    display: block;
    margin: 0;
    padding: 0;
    position: relative;
    white-space: nowrap;
    width: 10em;
}

.rating s {
    bottom: 0;
    color: #fc0;
    display: block;
    left: 0;
    overflow: hidden;
    position: absolute;
    top: 0;
    white-space: nowrap;
}
.rating s:before,
.rating s:after {
    bottom: 0;
    display: block;
    left: 0;
    overflow: hidden;
    position: absolute;
    top: 0;
}

.rating s i { visibility: hidden; }

.rating:before {
    content: "☆☆☆☆☆☆☆☆☆☆";
}
.rating s:after {
    content: "★★★★★★★★★★";
    font-size: 1.16em; /* filled stars are slightly smaller */
}
```

5. We also have some site-specific styles to add to the movie list itself:

```css
/* static/site/css/movie_list.css */
.movie { min-width: 300px; }
```

```css
.movie .rank {
    float: left;
    margin-right: .5em;
}
.movie .rank:after { content: "." }

.movie .year:before { content: "("; }
.movie .year:after { content: ")"; }

.movie .rating {
    float: right;
    margin-left: 2em;
}
```

6. To support all the same capabilities of the default list, but have the correct ordering and limit to only the top 250 movies, we need to add a customized view. It will also override the template to render with:

```python
# movies/views.py
# ...
class TopMoviesView(MovieListView):
    template_name = "movies/top_movies.html"

    def get_queryset_and_facets(self, form):
        qs, facets = super().get_queryset_and_facets(form)
        qs = qs.order_by("rank")
        qs.filter(rank__gte=1, rank__lte=250)
        return qs, facets
```

7. And, finally, let's add a new URL rule to the top 250 listing:

```python
# movies/urls.py
from django.urls import path

from .views import MovieListView, TopMoviesView

urlpatterns = [
    # ...
    path('top/', TopMoviesView.as_view(), name='top-movies'),
]
```

Remember to pull the new static file into the static directory. This can be done by copying the files over manually, but this is made easier with the collectstatic management command. Just be careful you have made edits directly under your project's static folder, as those will be overwritten.

How it works...

When you open the movie list view in a browser, the predefined number of items set to `paginate_by` in the view (that is, 15) is shown on the page. As you scroll down, an additional page's worth of items and the next pagination link are loaded automatically and appended to the item container. The pagination link uses the `{% modify_query %}` custom template tag from the *Creating a template tag to modify request query parameters* recipe in `Chapter 5`, *Customizing Template Filters and Tags* to generate an adjusted URL based on the current one, but pointing to the correct next page number:

Scrolling down further, the third page of the items is loaded and attached at the bottom. This continues until there are no more pages left to load, which is signified by not having loaded any next pagination link in the final group.

Upon the initial page load, the element with the `object-list` CSS class, which contains the items and pagination links, will become a jScroll object through the code in the `list.js`. In fact, this implementation is generic enough that it could be used to enable continuous scrolling for any list display following a similar markup structure.

The following options are given to define its features:

- `loadingHtml`: This sets the markup that jScroll will inject at the end of the list while loading a new page of items. In our case, it is an animated loading indicator, and it is drawn from the HTML contained in a `<script type="text/template">` tag directly in the markup. By giving this type attribute, the browser will not try to execute it as it would a normal JavaScript, and the content inside remains invisible to the user.
- `padding`: When the scroll position of the page is within this distance of the end of the scrolling area, a new page should be loaded. Here, we've set it at 100 pixels.
- `pagingSelector`: A CSS selector that indicates what HTML elements in the `object_list` are pagination links. These will be hidden in browsers where the jScroll plugin activates so that the continuous scroll can take over loading additional pages, but users in other browsers will still be able to navigate by clicking on the pagination normally.
- `nextSelector`: This CSS selector finds the HTML element(s) from which to read the URL of the next page.
- `contentSelector`: Another CSS selector. This specifies which HTML elements should be extracted from the Ajax-loaded content and added to the container.

The `rating.css` inserts unicode star characters and overlaps the outlines with filled-in versions to create the rating effect. Using a width equivalent to the rating value's percentage of the maximum (*10* in this case), the filled-in stars cover the right amount of space on top of the hollow ones, allowing for decimal ratings. In the markup, a `title` attribute and a nested `<i>` tag are given with text equivalents so that the ratings remain accessible, such as to those using screen readers.

Finally, the `movie_list.css` uses something called **floats** to position the rank to the far left and the rating to the far right, even though in the markup they come before the movie's title. The rating is enhanced by adding a period following the plain numeric value, and the year is wrapped in parentheses.

There's more

You might note that it would have been easy to include the rating and the year punctuation enhancements directly in the template, but this has been done via CSS to make the treatment as flexible as possible. For instance, try replacing the site-specific `.rank` styles with the following:

```css
/* static/site/css/movie_list.css */
.movie { position: relative; }
.movie .rank {
    background-color: rgba(0, 0, 0, 0.2);
    color: #fff;
    font-size: .5em;
    text-align: center;
    line-height: 1em;
    padding: .25em .5em;
    position: absolute;
    left: .5em;
    top: .5em;
    border-radius: 1em;
}
```

This will move the movie rank out of the flow of the rest of the text and gives it a badge-like appearance, with rounded corners and smaller text. In doing so, the movie titles are all aligned neatly on the left, even when they break across multiple lines. If we had included the period in the markup, there would be no way to omit it when providing this style:

Although in this case the flexibility is purely for design choices, there may be more critical needs for it. As an example, it may be that different treatment is required depending on the locale the site is being viewed in, such as right-to-left text. It also can have a beneficial impact on content accessibility— this is a growing concern, as **Web Content Accessibility Guidelines (WCAG)** become increasingly enforced. Because of all of these reasons, shifting responsibility for things such as punctuation and other such augmentations to the design layer is useful in cases such as this one.

There are other styling enhancements possible here too, such as changing the display for small screens to account for the narrow available space, and taking advantage of more advanced CSS layout approaches. Examples of these are included in the source code accompanying this book.

See also

- The *Filtering object lists* recipe in Chapter 3, *Forms and Views*
- The *Managing paginated lists* recipe in Chapter 3, *Forms and Views*
- The *Composing class-based views* recipe in Chapter 3, *Forms and Views*
- The *Exposing settings in JavaScript* recipe
- The *Creating a template tag to modify request query parameters* recipe in Chapter 5, *Customizing Template Filters and Tags*

Implementing the Like widget

Websites, in general, and most commonly those with a social component, often have integrated Facebook, Twitter, and Google+ widgets to *Like* and *Share* content. In this recipe, we will guide you through the building of a similar Django app that will save information in your database whenever a user likes something. You will be able to create specific views based on the things that are liked on your website. We will similarly create a **Like** widget with a two-state button and badge showing the number of total likes. The following are the states:

- This is an inactive state, where you can click on a button to activate it:

- This is an active state, where you can click on a button to deactivate it:

Changes in the state of the widget will be handled by Ajax calls.

Getting ready

First, create a `likes` app and add it to your INSTALLED_APPS (and to your app's volumes in `docker-compose.yml` if you are using Docker). Then, set up a `Like` model, which has a foreign-key relation to the user who is liking something and a generic relationship to any object in the database. We will use `ObjectRelationMixin`, which we defined in the *Creating a model mixin to handle generic relations* recipe in `Chapter 2`, *Database Structure and Modeling*. If you don't want to use the mixin, you can also define a generic relation in the following model yourself:

```
# likes/models.py
from django.db import models
from django.utils.translation import ugettext_lazy as _
from django.conf import settings

from utils.models import (CreationModificationDateMixin,
                          object_relation_mixin_factory)


class Like(CreationModificationDateMixin,
          object_relation_mixin_factory(is_required=True)):
    class Meta:
        verbose_name = _("like")
        verbose_name_plural = _("likes")
        ordering = ("-created",)

    user = models.ForeignKey(settings.AUTH_USER_MODEL)

    def __str__(self):
        return _(u"%(user)s likes %(obj)s") % {
            "user": self.user,
            "obj": self.content_object,
        }
```

Also, make sure that the request context processor is set in the settings. We also need an authentication middleware in the settings for the currently logged-in user to be attached to the request:

```
# settings.py or config/base.py
MIDDLEWARE = [
    # ...
    'django.contrib.auth.middleware.AuthenticationMiddleware',
]
TEMPLATES = [
    {
        # ...
        'OPTIONS': {
            'context_processors': [
                # ...
                'django.template.context_processors.request',
            ],
        },
    },
]
```

Remember to create and run a migration to set up the database accordingly for the new *Like* model.

How to do it...

Execute these steps one by one:

1. In the `likes` app, create a `templatetags` directory with an empty `__init__.py` file to make it a Python module. Then, add the `likes_tags.py` file, where we'll define the `{% like_widget %}` template tag as follows:

```
# likes/templatetags/likes_tags.py
from django import template
from django.contrib.contenttypes.models import ContentType
from django.template.loader import render_to_string

from likes.models import Like

register = template.Library()


class ObjectLikeWidget(template.Node):
    def __init__(self, var):
```

```
                    self.var = var

          def render(self, context):
              liked_object = self.var.resolve(context)
              ct = ContentType.objects.get_for_model(liked_object)
              user = context["request"].user

              if not user.is_authenticated:
                  return ""

              context.push(object=liked_object,
                           content_type_id=ct.pk)
              # is_liked_by_user=liked_by(liked_object,
              # user),
              # count=liked_count(liked_object))
              output = render_to_string("likes/includes/widget.html",
                                        context.flatten())
              context.pop()
              return output


    # TAGS

    @register.tag
    def like_widget(parser, token):
        try:
            tag_name, for_str, var_name = token.split_contents()
        except ValueError:
            tag_name = "%r" % token.contents.split()[0]
            raise template.TemplateSyntaxError(
                f"{tag_name} tag requires a following syntax: "
                f"{{% {tag_name} for <object> %}}")
        var = template.Variable(var_name)
        return ObjectLikeWidget(var)
```

2. Also, we'll add filters in the same file to get the like status for a user and the total number of likes for a specified object:

```
# likes/templatetags/likes/likes_tags.py
# ...

# FILTERS

@register.filter
def liked_by(obj, user):
    ct = ContentType.objects.get_for_model(obj)
    liked = Like.objects.filter(user=user,
                                content_type=ct,
```

```
                                          object_id=obj.pk)
        return liked.count() > 0


    @register.filter
    def liked_count(obj):
        ct = ContentType.objects.get_for_model(obj)
        likes = Like.objects.filter(content_type=ct,
                                    object_id=obj.pk)
        return likes.count()
```

3. In the URL rules, we need a rule for a view, which will handle the liking and unliking using Ajax:

```
# likes/urls.py
from django.urls import path

from .views import json_set_like


urlpatterns = [
    path("<int:content_type_id>/<int:object_id>/",
        json_set_like,
        name="json-set-like")
]
```

4. Make sure to map the URLs to the project as well:

```
# project/urls.py
from django.urls import include, path
# ...

urlpatterns = [
    # ...
    path('like/', include('likes.urls')),
]
```

5. Then, we need to define the view, as shown in the following code:

```
# likes/views.py
import json

from django.contrib.contenttypes.models import ContentType
from django.http import HttpResponse
from django.views.decorators.cache import never_cache
from django.views.decorators.csrf import csrf_exempt

from .models import Like
```

```
from .templatetags.likes_tags import liked_count


@never_cache
@csrf_exempt
def json_set_like(request, content_type_id, object_id):
    """
    Sets the object as a favorite for the current user
    """
    result = {
        "success": False,
    }
    if request.user.is_authenticated and request.method == "POST":
        content_type = ContentType.objects.get(id=content_type_id)
        obj = content_type.get_object_for_this_type(pk=object_id)

        like, is_created = Like.objects.get_or_create(
            content_type=ContentType.objects.get_for_model(obj),
            object_id=obj.pk,
            user=request.user)
        if not is_created:
            like.delete()

        result = {
            "success": True,
            "action": "add" if is_created else "remove",
            "count": liked_count(obj),
        }

    json_str = json.dumps(result, ensure_ascii=False)
    return HttpResponse(json_str, content_type="application/json")
```

6. In the template for the list or detail view of any object, we can add the `template` tag for the widget. Let's add the widget to the location detail that we created in the previous recipes, as follows:

```
{# templates/locations/location_detail.html #}
{% extends "base.html" %}
{% load likes_tags static thumbnail %}

{% block content %}
    <h2 class="map-title">{{ location.title }}</h2>
    {% if request.user.is_authenticated %}
        {% like_widget for location %}
    {% endif %}
    {# ... #}
{% endblock %}
```

```
{% block js %}
    <script src="{% static 'likes/js/widget.js' %}"></script>
    {# ... #}
{% endblock %}
```

7. Then, we need a template for the widget, as shown in the following code:

```
{# templates/likes/includes/widget.html #}
{% load i18n %}
<p class="like-widget">
    <button type="button"
            class="like-button btn btn-primary
                   {% if is_liked_by_user %} active{% endif %}"
            data-href="{% url "json_set_like"
                             content_type_id=content_type_id
                             object_id=object.pk %}"
            data-remove-label="{% trans "Like" %}"
            data-add-label="{% trans "Unlike" %}">
        {% if is_liked_by_user %}
            <span class="glyphicon glyphicon-star"></span>
            {% trans "Unlike" %}
        {% else %}
            <span class="glyphicon glyphicon-star-empty"></span>
            {% trans "Like" %}
        {% endif %}
    </button>
    <span class="like-badge badge badge-secondary">
        {{ count }}</span>
</p>
```

 The `template` tags in the preceding snippet have been split across lines for legibility, but in practice, `template` tags must be on a single line, and so they cannot be split in this manner.

8. Finally, we create JavaScript to handle the liking and unliking action in the browser, as follows:

```
// static/likes/js/widget.js
(function($) {
    var star = {
        add: '<span class="glyphicon glyphicon-star"></span>',
        remove: '<span class="glyphicon glyphicon-star-empty"></span>'
    };

    $(document).on("click", ".like-button", function() {
        var $button = $(this);
```

```
        var $widget = $button.closest(".like-widget");
        var $badge = $widget.find(".like-badge");

        $.post($button.data("href"), function(data) {
            if (data.success) {
                var action = data.action; // "add" or "remove"
                var label = $button.data(action + "-label");

                $button[action + "Class"]("active");
                $button.html(star[action] + " " + label);

                $badge.html(data.count);
            }
        }, "json");
    });
}(jQuery));
```

How it works...

For any `object` in your website, you can now use the `{% like_widget for object %}` template tag. It generates a widget that will show the liked state based on whether and how the current logged-in user has responded to the object.

The *Like* button has three custom HTML5 data attributes:

- `data-href` supplies a unique, object-specific URL to change the current state of the widget.
- `data-add-text` is the translated text to be displayed when the *Like* association has been added (Unlike)
- `data-remove-text` is similarly the translated text for when the *Like* association has been removed (Like)

In the JavaScript, *Like* buttons are recognized by the `like-button` CSS class. An event listener, attached to the document, watches for `click` events from any such button found in the page, and then posts an Ajax call to the URL specified by the `data-href` attribute.

The specified view (`json_set_like`) accepts two parameters, the content type ID and the primary key of the liked object. The view checks whether a `Like` exists for the specified object, and if it does, the view removes it; otherwise, the `Like` object is added. As a result, the view returns a JSON response with the `success` status, the `action` that was taken for the *Like* object (*add* or *remove*), and the total `count` of Likes for the object across all users. Depending on the action that is returned, JavaScript will show an appropriate state for the button.

You can debug the Ajax responses in the browser's developer tools, generally in the Network tab. If any server errors occur while developing, and you have DEBUG turned on in your settings, you will see the error traceback in the preview of the response. Otherwise, you will see the returned JSON, as shown in the following screenshot:

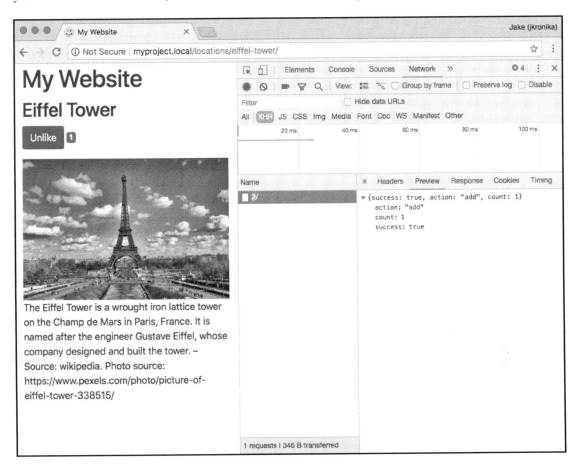

See also

- The *Opening object details in a modal dialog* recipe
- The *Implementing a continuous scroll* recipe
- The *Uploading images by Ajax* recipe

- The *Creating a model mixin to handle generic relations* recipe in Chapter 2, *Database Structure and Modelling*
- Chapter 5, *Customizing Template Filters and Tags*

Uploading images via Ajax

With default file input fields, it quickly becomes obvious that there is a lot we could do to improve the user experience. First, only the path to the selected file is displayed within the field, whereas people want to see what they have chosen right after selecting the file. Second, the file input itself is generally too narrow to show much of the path selected, and reads from the left end. As a result, the filename is rarely visible within the field. Finally, if the form has validation errors, nobody wants to select the files again; the file should still be selected in the form with validation errors. In this recipe, we will see how to do this.

Getting ready

Let's start with the quotes app that we created for the *Uploading images* recipe in Chapter 3, *Forms and Views*. We will reuse the model, and the view for adding a quote; however, we'll add views for handling the uploads, augmenting the form, and adding templates and JavaScript too.

Our own JavaScript will rely upon some external libraries, so those need to be downloaded:

- From the jQuery File Upload widget available at https://blueimp.github.io/jQuery-File-Upload/, download and extract the 9.21.0 version. From the js/ folder in the extracted contents, we'll need jquery.fileupload.css, jquery.fileupload.js, and jquery.fileupload-ui.js. This utility also requires the jquery.ui.widget.js in turn, which is made available in a vendor/ subdirectory alongside the other files.
- jQuery file upload makes use of the JavaScript templates system to provide something akin to Django templates, but in the browser. In support of this, we will need to get the tmpl.min.js file from that project, accessible at https://blueimp.github.io/JavaScript-Templates/.

Place the JavaScript files under static/site/js/lib, and static/site/css/lib is where the CSS should live. With that, we're ready to begin.

How to do it...

Let's refine the form for inspirational quotes so that it can support Ajax uploads, using the following steps:

1. First of all, add the following to your settings:

```
# settings.py or config/base.py
# ...
UPLOAD_URL = f'{MEDIA_URL}upload/'
UPLOAD_ROOT = os.path.join(MEDIA_ROOT, 'upload')
```

> If you want, you can also update the .gitignore file under the MEDIA_ROOT to avoid committing anything to the UPLOAD_ROOT, just by adding /upload/ as a new line.

2. Then, in the quotes app, we will define a custom file storage system for uploads using the new setting:

```
# quotes/storages.py
from django.conf import settings
from django.core.files.storage import import FileSystemStorage


upload_storage = FileSystemStorage(location=settings.UPLOAD_ROOT)
```

3. Getting to the form, we'll update it to add a hidden picture_path field dynamically:

```
# quotes/forms.py
# ...
class InspirationalQuoteForm(forms.ModelForm):
    # ...
    picture_path = forms.CharField(max_length=255,
                                   widget=forms.HiddenInput(),
                                   required=False)
```

4. Then, we will override the save() method in the form, as follows:

```
# quotes/forms.py
class InspirationalQuoteForm(forms.ModelForm):
    # ...
    def save(self, commit=True):
        instance = super().save(commit=commit)
        picture = self.cleaned_data["picture"]
        path = self.cleaned_data["picture_path"]
```

```
        if not picture and path:
            try:
                picture = upload_storage.open(path)
                instance.picture.save(path, picture, False)
                os.remove(path)
            except FileNotFoundError:
                pass
        instance.save()
        return instance
```

5. In addition to the previously defined views in the quotes app, we'll add
   an upload_quote_picture view, as shown in the following code:

```
# quotes/views.py
from datetime import datetime
import os

from django.core.files.base import ContentFile
from django.http import HttpResponse
from django.shortcuts import render, redirect
from django.template.loader import render_to_string
from django.utils.translation import ugettext_lazy as _
from django.views.decorators.csrf import csrf_protect
from django.views.generic import DetailView, ListView

from .models import InspirationalQuote
from .forms import InspirationalQuoteForm
from .storages import upload_storage

# ...

def _upload_to(request, filename):
    user = (f"user-{request.user.pk}"
            if request.user.is_authenticated
            else "anonymous")

    return os.path.join("quotes",
                        user,
                        f"{datetime.now():%Y/%m/%d}",
                        filename)


@csrf_protect
def upload_quote_picture(request):
    status_code = 400
    data = {
        "files": [],
        "error": _("Bad request"),
```

```
    }
if request.method == "POST" \
        and request.is_ajax() \
        and "picture" in request.FILES:
    image_types = [f"image/{x}" for x in [
        "gif", "jpg", "jpeg", "pjpeg", "png"
    ]]
    picture = request.FILES["picture"]
    if picture.content_type not in image_types:
        status_code = 405
        data["error"] = _("Invalid image format")
    else:
        upload_to = _upload_to(request, picture.name)
        name = upload_storage.save(upload_to,
                                ContentFile(picture.read()))
        picture = upload_storage.open(name)
        status_code = 200
        del data["error"]
        picture.filename = os.path.basename(picture.name)
        data["files"].append(picture)

json_data = render_to_string("quotes/upload.json", data)
return HttpResponse(json_data,
                    content_type="application/json",
                    status=status_code)
```

6. Similarly, there needs to be the delete_quote_picture view to handle the removal of the uploads:

```
# quotes/views.py
# ...

@csrf_protect
def delete_quote_picture(request, filename):
    if request.method == "DELETE" \
            and request.is_ajax() \
            and filename:
        try:
            upload_to = _upload_to(request, filename)
            upload_storage.delete(upload_to)
        except FileNotFoundError:
            pass
    json = render_to_string("quotes/upload.json", {"files": []})
    return HttpResponse(json,
                        content_type="application/json",
                        status=200)
```

7. We set the URL rules for the new upload and deletion views, as follows:

```
# quotes/urls.py
from django.urls import path

from .views import (add_quote,
                     QuotesList,
                     upload_quote_picture,
                     delete_quote_picture)


urlpatterns = [
    # ...
    path('upload/', upload_quote_picture,
        name='quote-picture-upload'),
    path('upload/<str:filename>', delete_quote_picture,
        name='quote-picture-delete'),
]
```

8. The new views render their JSON output via a new template, so we can define that file next:

```
{# templates/quotes/upload.json #}
{% load thumbnail %}
{
  {% if error %}"error": "{{ error }}",{% endif %}
  "files": [{% for file in files %}
    {
      "name": "{{ file.filename }}",
      "size": {{ file.size }},
      "deleteType": "DELETE",
      "deleteUrl": "{% url 'quote-picture-delete'
filename=file.filename %}",
      "thumbnailUrl": "{% thumbnail file '200x200' %}",
      "type": "{{ file.content_type }}",
      "path": "{{ file.name }}"
    }{% if not forloop.last %},{% endif %}
  {% endfor %}]
}
```

9. Now we move on to create the JavaScript template that will be used to display a file we have selected for upload:

```
{# templates/quotes/includes/tmpl-upload.html #}
{% verbatim %}
<script type="text/x-tmpl" id="template-upload">
{% for (var i=0, file; file=o.files[i]; i++) { %}
<tr class="template-upload">
    <td><span class="preview"></span></td>
    <td>
        <p class="name">{%=file.name%}</p>
        <strong class="error text-danger"></strong>
    </td>
    <td>
        <p class="size">{%=o.options.i18n('Processing...') %}</p>
    </td>
    <td width="20%">
        <div role="progressbar" aria-valuenow="0"
            aria-valuemin="0" aria-valuemax="100"
            class="progress progress-striped active"><div
                class="progress-bar progress-bar-success"
                style="width:0%;"></div></div>
    </td>
    <td>
    {% if (!i && !o.options.autoUpload) { %}
        <button class="btn btn-primary start">
            <i class="ion-upload"></i>
            <span>{%=o.options.i18n('Start') %}</span>
        </button>
    {% } %}
    {% if (!i) { %}
        <button class="btn btn-warning cancel">
            <i class="ion-close-circled"></i>
            <span>{%=o.options.i18n('Cancel') %}</span>
        </button>
    {% } %}
    </td>
</tr>
{% } %}
</script>
{% endverbatim %}
```

10. There is also a corresponding JavaScript template for displaying the file once it has been uploaded successfully:

```
{# templates/quotes/includes/tmpl-download.html #}
{% verbatim %}
<script type="text/x-tmpl" id="template-download">
```

```
{% for (var i=0, file; file=o.files[i]; i++) { %}
    <tr class="template-download">
        <td>
            <span class="preview">
    {% if (file.thumbnailUrl) { %}
                <a href="{%=file.url%}" data-gallery
                    title="{%=file.name%}"
                    download="{%=file.name%}">
                     <img src="{%=file.thumbnailUrl%}"></a>
    {% } %}
            </span>
        </td>
        <td>
            <p class="name">
    {% if (file.url) { %}
                <a href="{%=file.url%}"
                    {%=file.thumbnailUrl?'data-gallery':''%}
                    title="{%=file.name%}"
                    download="{%=file.name%}">
                     <img src="{%=file.thumbnailUrl%}"></a>
    {% } else { %}
                <span>{%=file.name%}</span>
    {% } %}
            </p>
    {% if (file.error) { %}
            <div>
                <span class="label label-danger">
                    {%=o.options.i18n('Error') %}</span>
                {%=file.error%}
            </div>
    {% } %}
        </td>
        <td><span class="size">
            {%=o.formatFileSize(file.size)%}
        </span></td>
        <td>
    {% if (file.deleteUrl) { %}
            <button data-type="{%=file.deleteType%}"
                    data-url="{%=file.deleteUrl%}"
                    {% if (file.deleteWithCredentials) { %}
                    data-xhr-fields='{"withCredentials":true}'
                    {% } %}
                    class="btn btn-danger delete">
                <i class="ion-trash-a"></i>
                <span>{%=o.options.i18n('Remove') %}</span>
            </button>
    {% } else { %}
            <button class="btn btn-warning cancel">
```

```
                    <i class="ion-close-circled"></i>
                    <span>{%=o.options.i18n('Cancel') %}</span>
                </button>
        {% } %}
            </td>
        </tr>
    {% } %}
    </script>
    {% endverbatim %}
```

11. These new includes, and the supporting CSS and JS need to be added to the form markup. Let's update that template now, as follows:

```
{# templates/quotes/add_quote.html #}
{% extends "base.html" %}
{% load i18n static %}

{% block stylesheet %}
<link rel="stylesheet" type="text/css"
 href="{% static 'site/css/lib/jquery.fileupload.css' %}">
{% endblock %}

{% block content %}
    <form method="post" action="" enctype="multipart/form-data"
        class="change-quote">
        {% csrf_token %}
        {{ form.as_p }}
        <button type="submit">{% trans "Save" %}</button>
    </form>
{% endblock %}

{% block extrabody %}
{% include "quotes/includes/tmpl-upload.html" %}
{% include "quotes/includes/tmpl-download.html" %}
{% endblock %}

{% block js %}
<script src="{% static 'site/js/lib/tmpl.min.js' %}"></script>
<script src="{% static 'site/js/lib/jquery.ui.widget.js'
%}"></script>
<script src="{% static 'site/js/lib/jquery.fileupload.js'
%}"></script>
<script src="{% static 'site/js/lib/jquery.fileupload-ui.js'
%}"></script>
<script src="{% static 'quotes/js/uploader.js' %}"></script>
{% endblock %}
```

12. Then, let's set up the JavaScript file that integrates the Ajax upload functionality as a progressive enhancement:

```javascript
// static/quotes/js/uploader.js
(function($) {
    var SELECTORS = {
        CSRF_TOKEN: "input[name='csrfmiddlewaretoken']",
        PICTURE: "input[type='file'][name='picture']",
        PATH: "input[name='picture_path']"
    };

    var DEFAULTS = {
        labels: {
            "Select": "Select File"
        }
    };

    function Uploader(form, uploadUrl, options) {
        if (form && uploadUrl) {
            this.form = form;
            this.url = uploadUrl;

            this.processOptions(options);
            this.gatherFormElements();
            this.wrapFileField();
            this.setupFileUpload();
        }
    }

    Uploader.prototype.mergeObjects = function(source, target) {
        var self = this;
        Object.keys(source).forEach(function(key) {
            var sourceVal = source[key];
            var targetVal = target[key];
            if (!target.hasOwnProperty(key)) {
                target[key] = sourceVal;
            } else if (typeof sourceVal === "object"
                    && typeof targetVal === "object") {
                self.mergeObjects(sourceVal, targetVal);
            }
        });
    };

    Uploader.prototype.processOptions = function(options) {
        options = options || {};
        this.mergeObjects(DEFAULTS, options);
        this.options = options;
    };
```

```
Uploader.prototype.gatherFormElements = function() {
    this.csrf = this.form.querySelector(SELECTORS.CSRF_TOKEN);
    this.picture = this.form.querySelector(SELECTORS.PICTURE);
    this.path = this.form.querySelector(SELECTORS.PATH);

    this.createButton();
    this.createContainer();
};

Uploader.prototype.createButton = function() {
    var label = this.options.labels["Select Picture"];
    this.button = document.createElement("button");
    this.button.appendChild(document.createTextNode(label));
    this.button.setAttribute("type", "button");
    this.button.classList.add(
        "btn", "btn-primary", "fileinput-button");
};

Uploader.prototype.createContainer = function() {
    this.container = document.createElement("table");
    this.container.setAttribute("role", "presentation");
    this.container.classList.add("table", "table-striped");

    this.list = document.createElement("tbody");
    this.list.classList.add("files");
    this.container.appendChild(this.list);
};

Uploader.prototype.wrapFileField = function() {
    this.picture.parentNode.insertBefore(
        this.button, this.picture);
    this.button.appendChild(this.picture);
    this.button.parentNode.insertBefore(
        this.container, this.button);
};

Uploader.prototype.setupFileUpload = function() {
    var self = this;
    var safeMethodsRE = /^(GET|HEAD|OPTIONS|TRACE)$/;
    $.ajaxSettings.beforeSend = (function(existing) {
        var csrftoken = document.cookie.replace(
                /^(?:.*;)?csrftoken=(.*?)(?:;.*)?$/, "$1");
        return function(xhr, settings) {
            if (!safeMethodsRE.test(settings.type)
                    && !this.crossDomain) {
                xhr.setRequestHeader("X-CSRFToken", csrftoken);
            }
        }
```

```
$(this.form).fileupload({
    url: this.url,
    dataType: 'json',
    acceptFileTypes: /^image\/(gif|p?jpeg|jpg|png)$/,
    autoUpload: false,
    replaceFileInput: true,
    messages: self.options.labels,
    maxNumberOfFiles: 1
}).on("fileuploaddone", function(e, data) {
    self.path.value = data.result.files[0].path;
}).on("fileuploaddestroy", function(e, data) {
    self.path.value = "";
});
};

    window.Uploader = Uploader;
}(jQuery));
```

13. Finally, we add one last integration piece to the change form template:

```
{# templates/quotes/add_quote.html #}
{% block js %}
{# ... #}
<script>
jQuery(function($){
    if (typeof Uploader !== "undefined") {
        var form = document.querySelector("form.change-quote");
        var uploadUrl = "{% url 'quote-picture-upload' %}";
        new Uploader(form, uploadUrl, {
            "labels": {
                "Select Picture": "{% trans 'Select Picture' %}",
                "Cancel": "{% trans 'Cancel' %}",
                "Remove": "{% trans 'Remove' %}",
                "Error": "{% trans 'Error' %}",
                "Processing...": "{% trans 'Processing...' %}",
                "Start": "{% trans 'Start' %}"
            }
        });
    }
});
</script>
{% endblock %}
```

How it works...

If the JavaScript fails to execute, the form remains completely usable just as it was before, but when JavaScript runs properly, we get an enhanced form with the file field replaced by a simple button, as shown here:

When an image is selected by clicking on the **Select Picture** button, the result in the browser will look similar to the following screenshot:

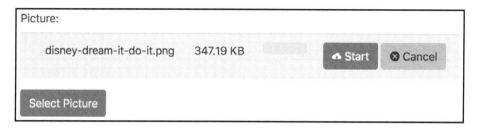

Clicking on the **Start** button in this new row triggers the Ajax upload process, and we then see a preview of the image that has been attached, as shown in the following screenshot. We can see here that the upload-related action buttons are also replaced with a **Remove** button, which would trigger deletion of the uploaded file:

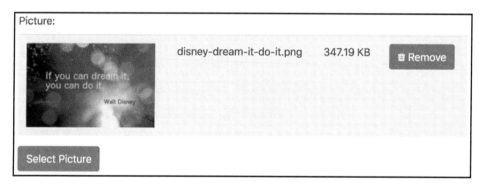

The same form will work using the normal file input if JavaScript somehow is unable to run as expected. Let's run backwards through the steps to dig deeper into the process and to see how it works.

In the changed form, we load the scripts and CSS that support the jQuery File Upload widget, as well as our own Uploader code. When the page is ready, we instantiate the Uploader that will enable the Ajax submission enhancements, providing it with a reference to the form element, the URL corresponding to our upload view, and translated labels for each of the action buttons.

As part of functionality given by the JavaScript templates utilities, the translation dictionary keys will serve as fallback values, if the translation is invalid.

The Uploader is where the majority of the work happens. When initialized, it goes through a series of steps, as follows:

- Processing and merging any provided options with the DEFAULTS
- Gathering the elements within the form that are needed for handling uploads—specifically, the csrfmiddlewaretoken hidden field, the picture file input field, and the picture_path hidden field
- Dynamically creating the Select <button> element and a container <table> that will hold the uploaded files list
- Wrapping the file input in the Select button and adding the container above it
- Setting up the jQuery File Upload widget

The really interesting work happens in this final step. We'll dive a bit deeper into that here:

- First, the X-CSRFToken header is set by default in the Ajax settings, so that the upload and delete requests will be accepted.
- Next, the widget is initialized for the form. Settings such as the upload URL, acceptable MIME types, and translated labels are passed along.
- And last, but not least, event listeners are set up to update the picture_path field value properly when an image has either been uploaded or removed. These listen for the fileuploaddone and fileuploaddestroy custom widget events, which correspond respectively to those two actions, but there are many other events available, too.

On page load, the Uploader is initialized and Ajax enhancements are applied. When a user clicks on the **Select** button, the file input is triggered and the usual file selection window opens. After selection, a row is added to the files list using the content provided by the tmpl_upload.html include, which shows the filename, human-friendly file size, and the action buttons. If the user clicks the **Cancel** button, that row is removed without ever uploading the file.

After clicking the **Start** button, the Ajax upload request kicks off, and the upload view stores the image under the UPLOAD_ROOT, returning the appropriate JSON data as generated from the upload.json template. This data is used to replace the existing file row with a new one generated from the tmpl_download.html include. The new row contains a preview thumbnail, the filename, the file size, and a **Remove** button.

Examining the two JavaScript template includes more closely, we can see that their content is wrapped by `{% verbatim %}` Django template tags. This is done because the JavaScript template syntax is very similar to the core Django template syntax, and it would confuse Django and cause errors. Similarly to Django, there are `{% ... %}` tags that can contain JavaScript expressions, and we can use `{%=... %}` to output variables. By default, context data is nested under a global `o` variable.

The outermost tag in the includes initiates a loop over a files list in that context data. This list corresponds to the list created in the JSON returned by the upload and delete views. As we can see, the `upload.json` also uses a loop to generate its content, so it would be trivial to use a similar implementation to handle a multiple-image case.

In the `delete_quote_picture` view, a valid Ajax request should use the `DELETE` method, and the filename to be deleted is parameterized as part of the URL. We use the same upload storage system that initially saves the images in order to delete them. The view always returns a valid JSON object containing an empty file list, so the form will update to remove the uploaded image, even if there is an issue with the server.

As for the `upload_quote_picture` view, there is more strict processing, and by default, we assume a bad request. When the request itself is valid, we reinforce the image type restrictions on the server, which is always a good practice. For valid types, we save the picture using the upload storage system, and add the result to the files list. We also dynamically add a filename property containing only the base name of the file, to pass along and ultimately display in the file list.

After a picture has been selected and uploaded, and the form is submitted, the quote instance will be saved initially with no picture. In the custom save-handling for the form, though, we check for a `picture_path`, which would indicate that an upload took place. Using the same upload storage, we open the given path and save that as the picture for the quote. Afterward, since the uploaded image is no longer needed, it is deleted. Any changes are saved back to the instance, which is then returned.

See also

- The *Uploading images* recipe in `Chapter 3`, *Forms and Views*
- The *Opening object details in a modal dialog* recipe
- The *Implementing a continuous scroll* recipe
- The *Implementing the Like widget* recipe
- The *Making forms secure from cross-site request forgery (CSRF)* recipe in `Chapter 7`, *Security and Performance*

5
Customizing Template Filters and Tags

In this chapter, we will cover the following topics:

- Following conventions for your own template filters and tags
- Creating a template filter to show how many days have passed since a post
- Creating a template filter to extract the first media object
- Creating a template filter to humanize URLs
- Creating a template tag to include a template, if it exists
- Creating a template tag to load a QuerySet in a template
- Creating a template tag to parse content as a template
- Creating a template tag to modify request query parameters

Introduction

As you know, Django has an extensive template system with features such as template inheritance, filters to change the representation of values, and tags for presentational logic. Moreover, Django allows you to add your own template filters and tags to your apps. Custom filters or tags should be located in a template tag library file under the `templatetags` Python package in your app. Then, your template tag library can be loaded in any template with the `{% load %}` template tag. In this chapter, we will create several useful filters and tags that will give more control to template editors.

To see the template tags of this chapter in action, create either a virtual environment or a Docker project, extract the code provided for this chapter there, run the development server, and visit the appropriate URL for the development site in a browser. With a virtual environment, this would be `http://127.0.0.1:8000/en/`, whereas with Docker, you can set any hostname in your `docker-compose.yml` and map it via the `/etc/hosts` file. For the purposes of this chapter, we will assume the Docker URL is set to `http://myproject.local/en/`.

Following conventions for your own template filters and tags

Custom template filters and tags can become a total mess if you don't have persistent guidelines to follow. Template filters and tags should serve template editors as much as possible. They should be both handy and flexible. In this recipe, we will take a look at some conventions that should be used when enhancing the functionality of the Django template system.

How to do it...

Follow these conventions for Django template system extensions:

1. Don't create or use custom template filters or tags when the logic for the page fits better in the view, context processors, or model methods. When your content is context-specific, such as a list of objects or object-detail view, load the object in the view. If you need to show some content on every page, create a context processor. Use custom methods of the model instead of template filters when you need to get some properties of an object that are not related to the context of the template.

2. Name the `template`-tag library with the `_tags` suffix. When your app is named differently than your `template`-tag library, you can avoid ambiguous package-importing problems.

3. In the newly created library, separate the filters from the tags, for example, using comments as shown in the following code:

```
# utils/templatetags/utility_tags.py
from django import template
register = template.Library()
```

```
"""TAGS"""

# .. your tags go here...


"""FILTERS"""

# .. your filters go here...
```

4. When creating advanced custom template tags, make sure that their syntax is easy to remember by including the following constructs that can follow the tag name:

   - `for [app_name.model_name]`: Include this construct to use a specific model
   - `using [template_name]`: Include this construct to use a template for the output of the template tag
   - `limit [count]`: Include this construct to limit the results to a specific amount
   - `as [context_variable]`: Include this construct to save the results to a context variable that can be reused multiple times

5. Try to avoid multiple values that are defined positionally in the template tags, unless they are self-explanatory. Otherwise, this will likely confuse template developers.

6. Make as many resolvable arguments as possible. Strings without quotes should be treated as context variables that need to be resolved or as short words that remind you of the structure of the template tag components.

See also

- The *Creating a template filter to show how many days have passed since a post* recipe
- The *Creating a template tag to load a QuerySet in a template* recipe

Creating a template filter to show how much time has passed since a post was published

Not all people keep track of the date, and it can be easy to miscalculate it when trying to determine the difference between dates in your head. When talking about creation or modification dates, it is convenient to read a more human-readable time difference. For example, the blog entry was posted *3 days ago*, the news article was published *today*, and the user last logged in *yesterday*. In this recipe, we will create a template filter named date_since, which converts dates to humanized time differences based on days, weeks, months, or years.

Getting ready

Create the utils app, and put it under INSTALLED_APPS in the settings, if you haven't done that yet. Then, create a templatetags Python package in this app (Python packages are directories with an empty __init__.py file).

How to do it...

Create a utility_tags.py file with the following content:

```python
# utils/templatetags/utility_tags.py
from datetime import datetime

from django import template
from django.utils import timezone
from django.utils.translation import ugettext_lazy as _

register = template.Library()


"""FILTERS"""


@register.filter(is_safe=True)
def date_since(value):
    """
    Returns a human-friendly difference between today and value
    (adapted from https://www.djangosnippets.org/snippets/116/)
    """
    today = timezone.now().date()
```

```
        if isinstance(value, datetime):
            value = value.date()
        diff = today - value
        diff_years = int(diff.days / YEAR)
        diff_months = int(diff.days / MONTH)
        diff_weeks = int(diff.days / WEEK)
        diff_map = [
            ("year", "years", diff_years,),
            ("month", "months", diff_months,),
            ("week", "weeks", diff_weeks,),
            ("day", "days", diff.days,),
        ]
        for parts in diff_map:
            (interval, intervals, count,) = parts
            if count > 1:
                return _(f"{count} {intervals} ago")
            elif count == 1:
                return _("yesterday") \
                    if interval == "day" \
                    else _(f"last {interval}")
        if diff.days == 0:
            return _("today")
        else:
            # Date is in the future; return formatted date.
            return f"{value:%B %d, %Y}"
```

How it works...

If you use this filter in a template, as shown in the following code, it will render something similar to *yesterday*, *last week*, or *5 months ago*:

```
{% load utility_tags %}
{{ object.published|date_since }}
```

You can apply this filter to values of the date and datetime types.

Each template tag library has a register where filters and tags are collected. Django filters are functions registered by the @register.filter decorator. In this case, we pass the parameter is_safe=True to indicate that our filter will not introduce any unsafe HTML markup.

By default, the filter in the template system will be named the same as the function or other callable object. If you want, you can set a different name for the filter by passing the name to the decorator, as follows:

```
@register.filter(name="humanized_date_since", is_safe=True)
def date_since(value):
    # ...
```

The filter itself is fairly self-explanatory. At first, the current date is read. If the given value of the filter is of the `datetime` type, its `date` is extracted. Then, the difference between `today` and the extracted value is calculated based on the `YEAR`, `MONTH`, `WEEK`, or `days` intervals. Depending on the `count`, different string results are returned, falling back to displaying a formatted date if the `value` is in the future.

There's more...

If required, we could cover other stretches of time, too, as in *20 minutes ago, 5 hours ago*, or even *1 decade ago*. To do so, we would add more intervals to the existing `diff_map` set, and to show the difference in time, we would need to operate on `datetime` values instead of the date values.

See also

- The *Creating a template filter to extract the first media object* recipe
- The *Creating a template filter to humanize URLs* recipe

Creating a template filter to extract the first media object

Imagine that you are developing a blog overview page, and for each post you want to show images, music, or videos in that page taken from the content. In such a case, you need to extract the `<figure>`, `<img>`, `<object>`, `<embed>`, `<video>`, `<audio>`, and `<iframe>` tags from the HTML content of the post, as stored on a field of the post model. In this recipe, we will see how to perform this using regular expressions in the `first_media` filter.

Getting ready

We will start with the `utils` app that should be set in `INSTALLED_APPS` in the settings and the `templatetags` package in this app.

How to do it...

In the `utility_tags.py` file, add the following content:

```python
# utils/templatetags/utility_tags.py
import re

from django import template
from django.utils.safestring import mark_safe

register = template.Library()


"""FILTERS"""

MEDIA_CLOSED_TAGS = "|".join([
    "figure", "object", "video", "audio", "iframe"])
MEDIA_SINGLE_TAGS = "|".join(["img", "embed"])
MEDIA_TAGS_REGEX = re.compile(
    r"<(?P<tag>" + MEDIA_CLOSED_TAGS + ")[\S\s]+?</(?P=tag)>|" +
    r"<(" + MEDIA_SINGLE_TAGS + ")[^>]+>",
    re.MULTILINE)


@register.filter
def first_media(content):
    """
    Returns the chunk of media-related markup from the html content
    """
    tag_match = MEDIA_TAGS_REGEX.search(content)
    media_tag = ""
    if tag_match:
        media_tag = tag_match.group()
    return mark_safe(media_tag)
```

How it works...

If the HTML content in the database is valid, when you put the following code in the template, it will retrieve the media tags from the content field of the object; otherwise, an empty string will be returned if no media is found:

```
{% load utility_tags %}
{{ object.content|first_media }}
```

Regular expressions are a powerful feature to search/replace patterns of text. At first, we define lists of all the supported media tag names, split into groups for those that have both opening and closing tags (MEDIA_CLOSED_TAGS), and those that are self-closed (MEDIA_SINGLE_TAGS). From these lists, we generate the compiled regular expression as MEDIA_TAGS_REGEX. In this case, we search for all the possible media tags, allowing for them to occur across multiple lines.

Let's see how this regular expression works, as follows:

- Alternating patterns are separated by the pipe (|) symbol.
- There are two groups within the patterns—first of all, those with both opening and closing *normal* tags (<figure>, <object>, <video>, <audio>, <iframe>, and <picture>), and then one final pattern for what are called self-closing or void tags (<img> and <embed>).
- For the possibly multiline normal tags, we will use the [\S\s]+? pattern that matches any symbol at least once; however, we do this as few times as possible until we find the string that goes after it.
  Therefore, <figure[Ss]+?</figure> searches for the start of the <figure> tag and everything after it, until it finds the closing the </figure> tag.
- Similarly, with the [^>]+ pattern for self-closing tags, we search for any symbol except the right-angle bracket (possibly better known as a greater than symbol, that is to say, >) at least once and as many times as possible, until we encounter such a bracket indicating the closure of the tag.

The re.MULTILINE flag ensures that matches can be found even if they span multiple lines in the content. Then, in the filter, we perform a search using this regular expression pattern. By default, in Django, the result of any filter will show the <, >, and & symbols escaped as the <, >, and & entities, respectively. In this case, however, we use the mark_safe() function to indicate that the result is safe and HTML-ready, so that any content will be rendered without escaping. Because the originating content is user input, we do this instead of passing is_safe=True when registering the filter, as we need to explicitly certify that the markup is safe.

There's more...

If you are interested in regular expressions, you can learn more about them in the official Python documentation at `https://docs.python.org/3/library/re.html`.

See also

- The *Creating a template filter to show how many days have passed since a post was published* recipe
- The *Creating a template filter to humanize URLs* recipe

Creating a template filter to humanize URLs

Web users commonly recognize URLs without the protocol (`http://`) or trailing slash (`/`), and, similarly, they will enter URLs in this fashion in address fields. In this recipe, we will create a `humanize_url` filter that is used to present URLs to the user in a shorter format, truncating very long addresses, similar to what Twitter does with the links in tweets.

Getting ready

Similar to the previous recipes, we will start with the `utils` app that should be set in `INSTALLED_APPS` in the settings and contain the `templatetags` package.

How to do it...

In the `FILTERS` section of the `utility_tags.py` template library in the `utils` app, let's add the `humanize_url` filter and register it, as shown in the following code:

```python
# utils/templatetags/utility_tags.py
import re

from django import template

register = template.Library()


"""FILTERS"""
```

```
@register.filter
def humanize_url(url, letter_count):
    """
    Returns a shortened human-readable URL
    """
    letter_count = int(letter_count)
    re_start = re.compile(r"^https?://")
    re_end = re.compile(r"/$")
    url = re_end.sub("", re_start.sub("", url))
    if len(url) > letter_count:
        url = f"{url[:letter_count - 1]}..."
    return url
```

How it works...

We can use the `humanize_url` filter in any template, as follows:

```
{% load utility_tags %}
<a href="{{ object.website }}" target="_blank">
    {{ object.website|humanize_url:40 }}
</a>
```

The filter uses regular expressions to remove the leading protocol and trailing slash, shortens the URL to the given amount of letters, and adds an ellipsis to the end after truncating it if the full URL doesn't fit the specified letter count. For example, for the URL `https://docs.djangoproject.com/en/2.1/ref/request-response/`, the 40-character humanized version would be `docs.djangoproject.com/en/2.1/ref/reque...`

See also

- The *Creating a template filter to show how many days have passed since a post was published* recipe
- The *Creating a template filter to extract the first media object* recipe
- The *Creating a template tag to include a template if it exists* recipe

Creating a template tag to include a template if it exists

Django provides the {% include %} template tag that allows one template to render and include another template. However, in situations when an error is raised because the template to include does not exist, rendering will outright fail. In this recipe, we will create a {% try_to_include %} template tag that includes another template if it exists, and fails silently by rendering as an empty string otherwise.

Getting ready

We will start again with the utils app that is installed and ready for custom template tags.

How to do it...

Advanced custom template tags consist of two things:

- A function that parses the arguments of the template tag
- The Node class that is responsible for the logic of the template tag as well as the output

Perform the following steps to create the {% try_to_include %} template tag:

1. First, let's create the function parsing the template tag arguments, as follows:

```
# utils/templatetags/utility_tags.py
from django import template
from django.template.loader import import get_template

register = template.Library()


"""TAGS"""


@register.tag
def try_to_include(parser, token):
    """
    Usage: {% try_to_include "sometemplate.html" %}
    This will fail silently if the template doesn't exist.
    If it does exist, it will be rendered with the current context.
```

```
"""
try:
    tag_name, template_name = token.split_contents()
except ValueError:
    tag_name = token.contents.split()[0]
    raise template.TemplateSyntaxError(
        f"{tag_name} tag requires a single argument")
return IncludeNode(template_name)
```

2. Then, we need a custom `IncludeNode` class in the same file, extending from the base `template.Node`, as follows:

```
# utils/templatetags/utility_tags.py
# ...
class IncludeNode(template.Node):
    def __init__(self, template_name):
        self.template_name = template.Variable(template_name)

    def render(self, context):
        try:
            # Loading the template and rendering it
            included_template = self.template_name.resolve(context)
            if isinstance(included_template, str):
                included_template = get_template(included_template)
            rendered_template = included_template.render(context)
        except (template.TemplateDoesNotExist,
                template.VariableDoesNotExist,
                AttributeError):
            rendered_template = ""
        return rendered_template
```

How it works...

The `{% try_to_include %}` template tag expects one argument, that is, `template_name`. Therefore, in the `try_to_include()` function, we try to assign the split contents of the token only to the `tag_name` variable (which is `try_to_include`) and the `template_name` variable. If this doesn't work, a `TemplateSyntaxError` is raised. The function returns the `IncludeNode` object, which gets the `template_name` field, and stores it as a template `Variable` object for later use.

In the `render()` method of `IncludeNode`, we resolve the `template_name` variable. If a context variable was passed to the template tag, its value will be used here for `template_name`. If a quoted string was passed to the template tag, then the content within the quotes will be used for `included_template`, whereas a string corresponding to a context variable will be resolved into its string equivalent for the same.

Lastly, we will try to load the template, using the resolved `included_template` string and render it with the current template context. If that doesn't work, an empty string is returned.

There are at least two situations where we could use this template tag:

- When including a template whose path is defined in a model, as follows:

```
{% load utility_tags %}
{% try_to_include object.template_path %}
```

- When including a template whose path is defined with the `{% with %}` template tag somewhere high in the template context variable's scope. This is especially useful when you need to create custom layouts for plugins in the placeholder of a template in Django CMS:

```
{# templates/cms/start_page.html #}
{% with editorial_content_template_path=
            "cms/plugins/editorial_content/start_page.html" %}
    {% placeholder "main_content" %}
{% endwith %}
```

When the placeholder is filled, the context variable is then read and the template can be safely included, if available:

```
{# templates/cms/plugins/editorial_content.html #}
{% load utility_tags %}

{% if editorial_content_template_path %}
    {% try_to_include editorial_content_template_path %}
{% else %}
  <div>
      <!-- Some default presentation of
            editorial content plugin -->
  </div>
{% endif %}
```

The template tags in the previous snippet have been split across lines for legibility, but in practice, template tags must be on a single line, and so they cannot be split in this manner.

There's more...

You can use the `{% try_to_include %}` tag in any combination with the default `{% include %}` tag to include the templates that extend other templates. This is beneficial for large-scale portals, where you have different kinds of lists in which complex items share the same structure as widgets but have a different source of data.

For example, in the artist list template, you can include the artist item template, as follows:

```
{% load utility_tags %}
{% for object in object_list %}
    {% try_to_include "artists/includes/artist_item.html" %}
{% endfor %}
```

This template will extend from the item base, as follows:

```
{# templates/artists/includes/artist_item.html #}
{% extends "utils/includes/item_base.html" %}

{% block item_title %}
    {{ object.first_name }} {{ object.last_name }}
{% endblock %}
```

The item base defines the markup for any item and also includes a `Like` widget, as follows:

```
{# templates/utils/includes/item_base.html #}
{% load likes_tags %}

<h3>{% block item_title %}{% endblock %}</h3>
{% if request.user.is_authenticated %}
    {% like_widget for object %}
{% endif %}
```

See also

- The *Implementing the Like widget* recipe in chapter 4, *Templates and JavaScript*
- The *Creating a template tag to load a QuerySet in a template* recipe
- The *Creating a template tag to parse content as a template* recipe

- The *Creating a template tag to modify request query parameters* recipe
- The *Creating templates for Django CMS* recipe in `Chapter 8`, *Django CMS*
- The *Writing your own CMS plugin* recipe in `Chapter 8`, *Django CMS*

Creating a template tag to load a QuerySet in a template

Generally, the content that should be shown on a web page will be defined in the context by views. If the content is to be shown on every page, it is logical to create a context processor to make it available globally. Another situation is when you need to show additional content such as the latest news or a random quote on some pages, for example, the starting page or the details page of an object. In this case, you can load the necessary content with a custom `{% load_objects %}` template tag, which we will implement in this recipe.

Getting ready

Once again, we will start with the `utils` app, which should be installed and ready for custom template tags.

How to do it...

An advanced custom template tag consists of a function that parses the arguments that are passed to the tag, and the `Node` class that renders the output of the tag or modifies the template context. Perform the following steps to create the `{% load_objects %}` template tag:

1. First, let's create the function that handles parsing the template tag arguments, as follows:

```
# utils/templatetags/utility_tags.py
from django import template
from django.apps import apps

register = template.Library()


"""TAGS"""
```

```
@register.tag
def load_objects(parser, token):
    """
    Gets a queryset of objects of the model specified by app and
    model names

    Usage:
        {% load_objects [<manager>.]<method>
                        from <app_name>.<model_name>
                        [limit <amount>]
                        as <var_name> %}

    Examples:
        {% load_objects latest_published from people.Person
                        limit 3 as people %}
        {% load_objects site_objects.all from news.Article
                        as articles %}
        {% load_objects site_objects.all from news.Article
                        limit 3 as articles %}
    """
    limit_count = None
    try:
        (tag_name, manager_method,
         str_from, app_model,
         str_limit, limit_count,
         str_as, var_name) = token.split_contents()
    except ValueError:
        try:
            (tag_name, manager_method,
             str_from, app_model,
             str_as, var_name) = token.split_contents()
        except ValueError:
            tag_name = token.contents.split()[0]
            raise template.TemplateSyntaxError(
                f"{tag_mame} tag requires the following syntax: "
                f"{{% {tag_mame} [<manager>.]<method> from "
                "<app_name>.<model_name> [limit <amount>] "
                "as <var_name> %}")
    try:
        app_name, model_name = app_model.split(".")
    except ValueError:
        raise template.TemplateSyntaxError(
            "load_objects tag requires application name "
            "and model name, separated by a dot")
    model = apps.get_model(app_name, model_name)
    return ObjectsNode(model, manager_method, limit_count,
                       var_name)
```

2. Then, we will create the custom `ObjectsNode` class in the same file, extending from the base `template.Node`, as shown in the following code:

```python
class ObjectsNode(template.Node):
    def __init__(self, model, manager_method, limit, var_name):
        self.model = model
        self.manager_method = manager_method
        self.limit = template.Variable(limit) if limit else None
        self.var_name = var_name

    def render(self, context):
        if "." in self.manager_method:
            manager, method = self.manager_method.split(".")
        else:
            manager = "_default_manager"
            method = self.manager_method

        model_manager = getattr(self.model, manager)
        fallback_method = self.model._default_manager.none
        qs = getattr(model_manager, method, fallback_method)()
        limit = None
        if self.limit:
            try:
                limit = self.limit.resolve(context)
            except template.VariableDoesNotExist:
                limit = None
        context[self.var_name] = qs[:limit] if limit else qs
        return ""
```

How it works...

The `{% load_objects %}` template tag loads a QuerySet defined by the method of the manager from a specified app and model, limits the result to the specified count, and saves the result to the given context variable.

The following code is the simplest example of how to use the template tag that we have just created. It will load all news articles in any template, using the following snippet:

```
{% load utility_tags %}
{% load_objects all from news.Article as all_articles %}
{% for article in all_articles %}
    <a href="{{ article.get_url_path }}">{{ article.title }}</a>
{% endfor %}
```

This is using the `all()` method of the default `objects` manager of the `Article` model, and it will sort the articles by the `ordering` attribute defined in the `Meta` class of the model.

A more advanced example would be required to create a custom manager with a custom method to query the objects from the database. A **manager** is an interface that provides the database query operations to models. Each model has at least one manager called `objects` by default. As an example, let's create an `Artist` model that has a draft or a published status and a new `custom_manager` that allows you to select random published artists:

```python
# artists/models.py
from django.db import models
from django.utils.translation import ugettext_lazy as _


STATUS_CHOICES = (
    ("draft", _("Draft")),
    ("published", _("Published")),
)


class ArtistManager(models.Manager):
    def random_published(self):
        return self.filter(status="published").order_by("?")


class Artist(models.Model):
    # ...
    status = models.CharField(_("Status"),
                              max_length=20,
                              choices=STATUS_CHOICES)
    custom_manager = ArtistManager()
```

To load a random published artist, you add the following snippet to any template:

```
{% load utility_tags %}
{% load_objects custom_manager.random_published
            from artists.Artist limit 1 as random_artists %}
{% for artist in random_artists %}
   {{ artist.first_name }} {{ artist.last_name }}
{% endfor %}
```

Template tags in the previous snippet have been split across lines for legibility, but in practice, template tags must be on a single line, and so cannot be split in this manner.

Let's look at the code of the `{% load_objects %}` template tag. In the parsing function, there are two allowed forms for the tag—with or without a limit. The string is parsed, and if the format is recognized, the components of the template tag are passed to the `ObjectNode` class.

In the `render()` method of the `Node` class, we check the manager's name and its method's name. If no manager is specified, `_default_manager` will be used, which is an automatic property of any model injected by Django and points to the first available `models.Manager()` instance. In most cases, `_default_manager` will be the `objects` manager. After that, we will call the method of the manager and fall back to empty `QuerySet` if the method doesn't exist. If a limit is defined, we resolve the value of it and limit `QuerySet` accordingly. Lastly, we will save the resulting `QuerySet` to the context variable as given by `var_name`.

See also

- The *Creating a template tag to include a template if it exists* recipe
- The *Creating a template tag to parse content as a template* recipe
- The *Creating a template tag to modify request query parameters* recipe

Creating a template tag to parse content as a template

In this recipe, we will create the `{% parse %}` template tag, which will allow you to put template snippets in the database. This is valuable when you want to provide different content for authenticated and unauthenticated users, when you want to include a personalized salutation or you don't want to hardcode the media paths in the database.

Getting ready

As usual, we will start with the `utils` app that should be installed and ready for custom template tags.

How to do it...

An advanced custom template tag consists of a function that parses the arguments that are passed to the tag, and a `Node` class that renders the output of the tag or modifies the template context. Perform the following steps to create them `{% parse %}` template tag:

1. First, let's create the function parsing the arguments of the template tag, as follows:

```python
# utils/templatetags/utility_tags.py
from django import template

register = template.Library()


"""TAGS"""


@register.tag
def parse(parser, token):
    """
    Parses a value as a template and prints or saves to a variable

    Usage:
        {% parse <template_value> [as <variable>] %}

    Examples:
        {% parse object.description %}
        {% parse header as header %}
        {% parse "{{ MEDIA_URL }}js/" as js_url %}
    """
    bits = token.split_contents()
    tag_name = bits.pop(0)
    try:
        template_value = bits.pop(0)
        var_name = None
        if len(bits) >= 2:
            str_as, var_name = bits[:2]
    except ValueError:
        raise template.TemplateSyntaxError(
```

```
            f"{tag_name} tag requires the following syntax: "
            f"{{% {tag_name} <template_value> [as <variable>] %}}")
    return ParseNode(template_value, var_name)
```

2. Then, we will create the custom `ParseNode` class in the same file, extending from the base `template.Node`, as shown in the following code:

```
class ParseNode(template.Node):
    def __init__(self, template_value, var_name):
        self.template_value = template.Variable(template_value)
        self.var_name = var_name

    def render(self, context):
        template_value = self.template_value.resolve(context)
        t = template.Template(template_value)
        context_vars = {}
        for d in list(context):
            for var, val in d.items():
                context_vars[var] = val
        req_context = template.RequestContext(context["request"],
                                              context_vars)
        result = t.render(req_context)
        if self.var_name:
            context[self.var_name] = result
            result = ""
        return result
```

How it works...

The `{% parse %}` template tag allows you to parse a value as a template and render it immediately or save it as a context variable.

If we have an object with a description field, which can contain template variables or logic, we can parse and render it using the following code:

```
{% load utility_tags %}
{% parse object.description %}
```

It is also possible to define a value to parse using a quoted string, as shown in the following code:

```
{% load static utility_tags %}
{% get_static_prefix as STATIC_URL %}
{% parse "{{ STATIC_URL }}site/img/" as img_path %}
<img src="{{ img_path }}someimage.png" alt="" />
```

Let's take a look at the code of the `{% parse %}` template tag. The parsing function checks the arguments of the template tag bit by bit. At first, we expect the `parse` name and the template value. If there are still more bits in the token, we expect the combination of an optional `as` word followed by the context variable name. The template value and the optional variable name are passed to the `ParseNode` class.

The `render()` method of that class first resolves the value of the template variable and creates a template object out of it. The context vars are copied and a request context is generated, which the template is rendered. If the variable name is defined, the result is saved to it and an empty string is rendered; otherwise, the rendered template is shown immediately.

See also

- The *Creating a template tag to include a template if it exists* recipe
- The *Creating a template tag to load a QuerySet in a template* recipe
- The *Creating a template tag to modify request query parameters* recipe

Creating a template tag to modify request query parameters

Django has a convenient and flexible system to create canonical and clean URLs just by adding regular expression rules to the URL configuration files. However, there is a lack of built-in mechanisms with which to manage query parameters. Views such as search or filterable object lists need to accept query parameters to drill down through the filtered results using another parameter or to go to another page. In this recipe, we will create `{% modify_query %}`, `{% add_to_query %}`, and `{% remove_from_query %}` template tags, which let you add, change, or remove the parameters of the current query.

Getting ready

Once again, we start with the `utils` app that should be set in `INSTALLED_APPS` and contain the `templatetags` package.

Also, make sure that you have the request context processor added to the `context_processors` list in the `TEMPLATES` settings under `OPTIONS`, as follows:

```python
# settings.py or config/base.py
TEMPLATES = [
    {
        # ...
        'OPTIONS': {
            'context_processors': [
                'django.template.context_processors.request',
                # ...
            ]
        }
    }
]
```

How to do it...

For these template tags, we will be using the `simple_tag` decorator that parses the components and requires you to just define the rendering function, as follows:

1. First, let's add a helper method for putting together the query strings that each of our tags will output:

```python
# utils/templatetags/utility_tags.py
from urllib.parse import urlencode

from django import template
from django.utils.encoding import force_str

register = template.Library()


def construct_query_string(context, query_params):
    # empty values will be removed
    query_string = context["request"].path
    if len(query_params):
        encoded_params = urlencode([
            (key, force_str(value))
            for (key, value) in query_params if value
```

```
        ]).replace("&", "&amp;")
        query_string += f"?{encoded_params}"
    return query_string


"""TAGS"""
# ...
```

2. Then, we will create the `{% modify_query %}` template tag:

```
@register.simple_tag(takes_context=True)
def modify_query(context, *params_to_remove, **params_to_change):
    """Renders a link with modified current query parameters"""
    query_params = []
    get_data = context["request"].GET
    for key, last_value in get_data.items():
        value_list = get_data.getlist(key)
        if key not in params_to_remove:
            # don't add key-value pairs for params_to_remove
            if key in params_to_change:
                # update values for keys in params_to_change
                query_params.append((key, params_to_change[key]))
                params_to_change.pop(key)
            else:
                # leave existing parameters as they were
                # if not mentioned in the params_to_change
                for value in value_list:
                    query_params.append((key, value))
    # attach new params
    for key, value in params_to_change.items():
        query_params.append((key, value))
    return construct_query_string(context, query_params)
```

3. Next, let's create the `{% add_to_query %}` template tag:

```
@register.simple_tag(takes_context=True)
def add_to_query(context, *params_to_remove, **params_to_add):
    """Renders a link with modified current query parameters"""
    query_params = []
    # go through current query params..
    get_data = context["request"].GET
    for key, last_value in get_data.items():
        value_list = get_data.getlist(key)
        if key not in params_to_remove:
            # don't add key-value pairs which already
            # exist in the query
            if (key in params_to_add
                    and params_to_add[key] in value_list):
```

```
                        params_to_add.pop(key)
                    for value in value_list:
                        query_params.append((key, value))
            # add the rest key-value pairs
            for key, value in params_to_add.items():
                query_params.append((key, value))
            return construct_query_string(context, query_params)
```

4. Lastly, let's create the {% remove_from_query %} template tag:

```
@register.simple_tag(takes_context=True)
def remove_from_query(context, *args, **kwargs):
    """Renders a link with modified current query parameters"""
    query_params = []
    # go through current query params..
    get_data = context["request"].GET
    for key, last_value in get_data.items():
        value_list = get_data.getlist(key)
        # skip keys mentioned in the args
        if key not in args:
            for value in value_list:
                # skip key-value pairs mentioned in kwargs
                if not (key in kwargs and
                        str(value) == str(kwargs[key])):
                    query_params.append((key, value))
    return construct_query_string(context, query_params)
```

How it works...

All the three created template tags behave similarly. At first, they read the current query parameters from the request.GET dictionary-like QueryDict object to a new list of (key, value) query_params tuples. Then, the values are updated depending on the positional arguments and keyword arguments. Lastly, the new query string is formed via the helper method defined first. In this process, all spaces and special characters are URL-encoded, and the ampersands connecting the query parameters are escaped. This new query string is returned to the template.

To read more about the QueryDict objects, refer to the official Django documentation
at https://docs.djangoproject.com/en/2.1/ref/request-response/#querydict-objects.

Let's take a look at an example of how the `{% modify_query %}` template tag can be used. Positional arguments in the template tag define which query parameters are to be removed, and the keyword arguments define which query parameters are to be updated in the current query. If the current URL is `http://127.0.0.1:8000/artists/?category=fine-art&page=5`, we can use the following template tag to render a link that goes to the next page:

```
{% load utility_tags %}
<a href="{% modify_query page=6 %}">6</a>
```

The following snippet is the output rendered using the preceding template tag:

```
<a href="/artists/?category=fine-art&amp;page=6">6</a>
```

We can also use the following example to render a link that resets pagination and goes to another category, `sculpture`, as follows:

```
{% load utility_tags %}
<a href="{% modify_query "page" category="sculpture" %}">
    Sculpture</a>
```

So, the rendered output rendered using the preceding template tag would be as shown in this snippet:

```
<a href="/artists/?category=sculpture">
    Sculpture</a>
```

With the `{% add_to_query %}` template tag, you can add parameters step-by-step with the same name. For example, if the current URL is `http://127.0.0.1:8000/artists/?category=fine-art`, you can add another category, *Sculpture*, with the help of the following snippet:

```
{% load utility_tags %}
<a href="{% add_to_query category="sculpture" %}">
    + Sculpture</a>
```

This will be rendered in the template, as shown in the following snippet:

```
<a href="/artists/?category=fine-art&amp;category=sculpture">
    + Sculpture</a>
```

Lastly, with the help of the `{% remove_from_query %}` template tag, you can remove the parameters step-by-step with the same name. For example, if the current URL is `http://127.0.0.1:8000/artists/?category=fine-art&category=sculpture`, you can remove the `Sculpture` category with the help of the following snippet:

```
{% load utility_tags %}
<a href="{% remove_from_query category="sculpture" %}">
    - Sculpture</a>
```

This will be rendered in the template as follows:

```
<a href="/artists/?category=fine-art">
    - Sculpture</a>
```

See also

- The *Filtering object lists* recipe in `Chapter 3`, *Forms and Views*
- The *Creating a template tag to include a template if it exists* recipe
- The *Creating a template tag to load a QuerySet in a template* recipe
- The *Creating a template tag to parse content as a template* recipe

6
Model Administration

In this chapter, we will cover the following topics:

- Customizing columns on the change list page
- Creating admin actions
- Developing change list filters
- Customizing default admin settings
- Inserting a map on a change form

Introduction

The Django framework comes with a built-in administration system for your data models. With very little effort, you can set up filterable, searchable, and sortable lists for browsing your models, and you can configure forms to add and manage data. In this chapter, we will go through the advanced techniques to customize administration, by developing some practical cases.

Customizing columns on the change list page

The change list views in the default Django administration system let you have an overview of all of the instances of the specific models. By default, the `list_display` model admin property controls the fields that are shown in different columns. Additionally, you can implement custom admin methods that will return the data from relations or display custom HTML. In this recipe, we will create a special function, for use with the `list_display` property, that shows an image in one of the columns of the list view. As a bonus, we will make one field directly editable in the list view, by adding the `list_editable` setting.

Getting ready

To start, make sure that `django.contrib.admin` is in `INSTALLED_APPS` in the settings, and hook up the `admin` site in the URL configuration, as follows:

```python
# project/urls.py
from django.contrib import admin
from django.urls import include, path

urlpatterns = [
    path('admin/', admin.site.urls),
    # ...
]
```

Next, create a new `products` app, and put it under `INSTALLED_APPS`, adding the volume to the Docker Compose configuration if needed. This app will have the `Product` and `ProductPhoto` models, where one product might have multiple photos. For this example, we will also be using `UrlMixin`, which was defined in the *Creating a model mixin with URL-related methods* recipe, in `Chapter 2`, *Database Structure and Modeling*.

Let's create the `Product` and `ProductPhoto` models in the `models.py` file, as follows:

```python
# products/models.py
import os

from django.urls import reverse, NoReverseMatch
from django.db import models
from django.utils.timezone import now as timezone_now
from django.utils.translation import ugettext_lazy as _

from utils.models import UrlMixin


def product_photo_upload_to(instance, filename):
    now = timezone_now()
    slug = instance.product.slug
    base, ext = os.path.splitext(filename)
    return f"products/{slug}/{now:%Y%m%d%H%M%S}{ext.lower()}"


class Product(UrlMixin):
    class Meta:
        verbose_name = _("Product")
        verbose_name_plural = _("Products")

    title = models.CharField(_("title"),
                             max_length=200)
    slug = models.SlugField(_("slug"),
                            max_length=200)
    description = models.TextField(_("description"),
                                   blank=True)
    price = models.DecimalField(_("price (€)"),
                                max_digits=8,
                                decimal_places=2,
                                blank=True,
                                null=True)

    def get_url_path(self):
        try:
            return reverse("product_detail",
                           kwargs={"slug": self.slug})
        except NoReverseMatch:
            return ""

    def __str__(self):
        return self.title
```

```
class ProductPhoto(models.Model):
    class Meta:
        verbose_name = _("Photo")
        verbose_name_plural = _("Photos")

    product = models.ForeignKey(Product,
                                on_delete=models.CASCADE)
    photo = models.ImageField(_("photo"),
                              upload_to=product_photo_upload_to)

    def __str__(self):
        return self.photo.name
```

Don't forget to make and run an initial migration for the new `products` app, once your models are in place.

How to do it...

We will create a simple administration for the `Product` model that will have instances of the `ProductPhoto` model attached to the product as inlines.

In the `list_display` property, we will include the `first_photo()` method of the model admin, which will be used to show the first photo from the many-to-one relationship.

1. Let's create an `admin.py` file, with the following content:

```
# products/admin.py
from django.contrib import admin
from django.template.loader import render_to_string
from django.utils.text import mark_safe
from django.utils.translation import ugettext_lazy as _

from .models import Product, ProductPhoto


class ProductPhotoInline(admin.StackedInline):
    model = ProductPhoto
    extra = 0


class ProductAdmin(admin.ModelAdmin):
    list_display = ["get_photo", "title", "price"]
    list_display_links = ["title",]
```

```
        list_editable = ["price"]

        fieldsets = (
            (_("Product"), {
                "fields": ("title", "slug", "description", "price"),
            }),
        )
        prepopulated_fields = {"slug": ("title",)}
        inlines = [ProductPhotoInline]

        def get_photo(self, obj):
            project_photos = obj.productphoto_set.all()[:1]
            if project_photos.count() > 0:
                photo_preview = render_to_string(
                    "products/includes/photo-preview.html",
                    {
                        "photo": project_photos[0],
                        "size": "100",
                        "product": obj,
                        "target": "preview",
                    });
                return mark_safe(photo_preview)
            return ""
        get_photo.short_description = _("Preview")


    admin.site.register(Product, ProductAdmin)
```

2. Now, we have to create the template that is used to generate the `photo_preview`, as follows:

```
{# products/includes/photo-preview.html #}
{% load thumbnail %}
<a href="{% url 'product-detail' slug=product.slug %}"
   target="{{ target }}">
  <img src="{% thumbnail photo size %}"
        alt="{{ product.title }} preview"></a>
```

3. In order for the URL lookup to work properly, we will have to create a detail view and wire it up. Let's start with the view, as follows:

```
# products/views.py
from django.views.generic import DetailView

from .models import Product


class ProductDetail(DetailView):
    model = Product
```

4. Now, wire the view up in a URLconf for the products app, as follows:

```
# products/urls.py
from django.urls import path

from .views import ProductDetail

urlpatterns = [
    path('<slug:slug>/', ProductDetail.as_view(),
        name='product-detail'),
]
```

5. Finally, include the app URLs in the project configuration, as follows:

```
# project/urls.py
from django.urls import include, path

urlpatterns = [
    # ...
    path('products/', include('products.urls')),
]
```

How it works...

If you add a few products with photos, and then look at the product administration list in the browser, it will look similar to the following screenshot:

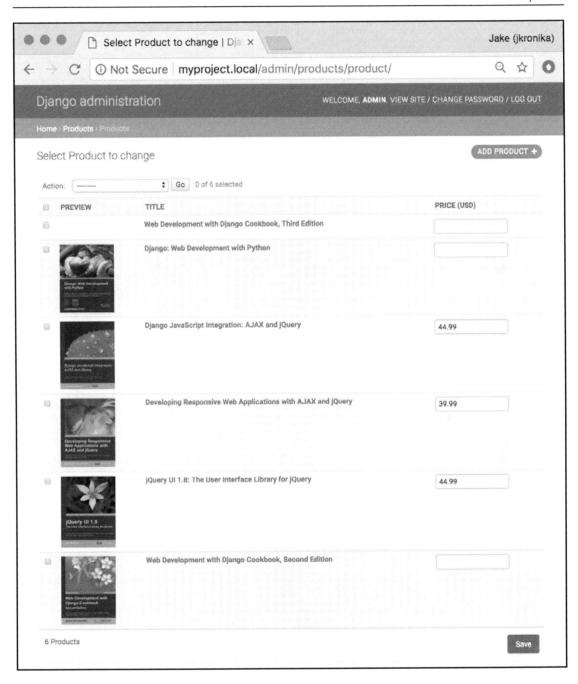

The `list_display` property is usually used to define the fields to display in the administration list view; for example, `title` and `price` are fields of the `Product` model. Besides the normal field names, though, the `list_display` property also accepts the following:

- A function, or another `callable`
- The name of an attribute of the admin model
- The name of an attribute of the model

In Python, `callable` is a function, method, or class that implements the `__call__()` method. You can check whether a variable is `callable` by using the `callable()` function.

When using callables in `list_display`, each one will get the model instance passed as the first argument. Therefore, in our example, we have defined the `get_photo()` method in the model admin class, and that receives the `Product` instance as `obj`. The method tries to get the first `ProductPhoto` object from the many-to-one relationship, and, if it exists, it returns HTML generated from the `include` template, with the `<img>` tag linked to the detail page for `Product`.

You can set several attributes for the callables that you use in `list_display`. The `short_description` attribute of the callable defines the title shown at the top of the column, for instance. When content will not sort naturally, the `admin_order_field` attribute can be set to another field name, optionally using a hyphen prefix to indicate a reversed sort order.

Finally, the **Price** field is made editable by including it in the `list_editable` setting, and, as there are editable fields, a **Save** button is introduced at the bottom, to save the whole list of products.

There's more...

With some minor adjustments, the photo preview template used here could also be used in product listing and detail views, to display one or more of the photos associated with each product. We leave that as an exercise for you.

See also

- The *Creating a model mixin with URL-related methods* recipe, in `Chapter 2`, *Database Structure and Modeling*
- The *Creating admin actions* recipe
- The *Developing change list filters* recipe

Creating admin actions

The Django administration system provides actions that we can execute for selected items in the list. There is one action given, by default, and it is used to delete selected instances. In this recipe, we will create an additional action for the list of the `Product` model, which will allow the administrators to export selected products to Excel spreadsheets.

Getting ready

We will start with the `products` app that we created in the previous recipe.

Make sure that you have the `openpyxl` module installed in your virtual environment, to create an Excel spreadsheet, as follows:

```
(myproject_env)$ pip3 install openpyxl~=2.5.0
```

If you are using a Docker project, add the dependency to your requirements and rebuild the container, as follows:

```
# requirements.txt or requirements/base.txt
# ...
openpyxl~=2.5.0
```

How to do it...

Admin actions are functions that take three arguments, as follows:

- The current `ModelAdmin` value
- The current `HttpRequest` value
- The `QuerySet` value containing the selected items

Perform the following steps to create a custom admin action to export a spreadsheet:

1. Create an `export_xlsx()` function in the `admin.py` file of the `products` app, as follows:

```
# products/admin.py
from copy import copy
from openpyxl import Workbook
from openpyxl.styles import Alignment, NamedStyle, builtins
from openpyxl.styles.numbers import FORMAT_NUMBER
from openpyxl.writer.excel import save_virtual_workbook

from django.http.response import HttpResponse
from django.utils.translation import ugettext_lazy as _
# ... other imports ...

def export_xlsx(modeladmin, request, queryset):
    wb = Workbook()
    ws = wb.active
    ws.title = "Products"

    number_alignment = Alignment(horizontal="right")
    wb.add_named_style(NamedStyle("Identifier",
                                  alignment=number_alignment,
                                  number_format=FORMAT_NUMBER))
    wb.add_named_style(NamedStyle("Normal Wrapped",
                                  alignment=Alignment(
                                      wrap_text=True)))

    number_headline_1 = copy(builtins.styles["Headline 1"])
```

```python
number_headline_1.name = "Number Headline 1"
number_headline_1.alignment = number_alignment
wb.add_named_style(number_headline_1)

class Config():
    def __init__(self,
                 heading,
                 width=None,
                 heading_style="Headline 1",
                 style="Normal Wrapped"):
        self.heading = heading
        self.width = width
        self.heading_style = heading_style
        self.style = style

column_config = {
    "A": Config("ID",
                width=10,
                heading_style="Number Headline 1",
                style="Identifier"),
    "B": Config("Title", width=30),
    "C": Config("Description", width=60),
    "D": Config("Price ($)",
                width=15,
                heading_style="Number Headline 1",
                style="Currency"),
    "E": Config("Preview", width=100, style="Hyperlink"),
}

# Set up column widths, header values and styles
for col, conf in column_config.items():
    ws.column_dimensions[col].width = conf.width

    column = ws[f"{col}1"]
    column.value = conf.heading
    column.style = conf.heading_style

# Add products
for obj in queryset.order_by("pk"):
    project_photos = obj.productphoto_set.all()[:1]
    url = ""
    if project_photos:
        url = project_photos[0].photo.url

    data = [obj.pk, obj.title, obj.description, obj.price, url]
    ws.append(data)

    row = ws.max_row
```

```
            for row_cells in ws.iter_cols(min_row=row, max_row=row):
                for cell in row_cells:
                    cell.style = column_config[cell.column].style

        mimetype = "application/vnd.openxmlformats-
    officedocument.spreadsheetml.sheet"
        charset = "utf-8"
        response = HttpResponse(
            content=save_virtual_workbook(wb),
            content_type=f"{mimetype}; charset={charset}",
            charset=charset)
        response["Content-Disposition"] = "attachment;
    filename=products.xlsx"
        return response


    export_xlsx.short_description = _("Export XLSX")
```

2. Then, add the `actions` setting to `ProductAdmin`, as follows:

```
class ProductAdmin(admin.ModelAdmin):
    # ...
    actions = [export_xlsx]
```

How it works...

If you take a look at the product administration list page in the browser, you will see a new action called **Export XLSX**, along with the default **Delete selected Products** action, as shown in the following screenshot:

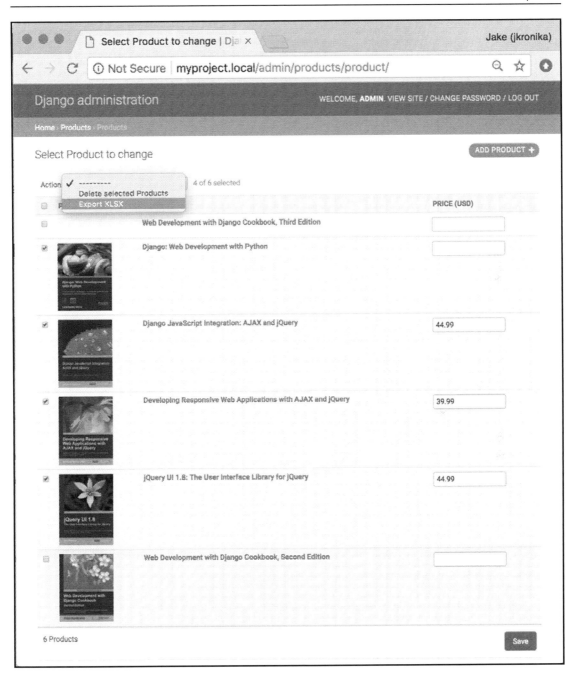

To create the spreadsheet export response, we use the `openpyxl` Python module to create an OpenOffice XML file compatible with Excel and other spreadsheet software.

First, a workbook is created, and the active worksheet is selected, for which we set the title to `Products`. Because there are common styles that we will want to use throughout the worksheet, these are set up as named styles, so that they can be applied by name to each cell, as appropriate. For the `id` and `price` headers, the base `Headline 1` style is copied, aligned right, and stored under a new name, `Number Headline 1`. These styles, the column headings, and the column widths are stored as `Config` objects, and a `column_config` dictionary maps column letter keys to the objects. This is then iterated over, to set up the headers and column widths.

 The value given for the column width can be an integer or decimal, and it indicates the quantity of the widest number in the normal style's font that should fit on a single line, adjusted to account for the spacing and gridlines of each cell.

We use the `append()` method of the sheet to add the content for each of the selected products in `QuerySet`, ordered by ID, including the URL of the first photo for the product, when photos are available. The product data is then individually styled by iterating over each of the cells in the just-added row, once again referring to `column_config` to apply styles consistently.

By default, admin actions do something with `QuerySet`, and redirect the administrator back to the change list page. However, for more complex actions like these, `HttpResponse` can be returned. The `export_xlsx()` function saves a virtual copy of the workbook to `HttpResponse`, with the content type and character set appropriate to the **Office Open XML (OOXML)** spreadsheet. Using the `Content-Disposition` header, we set the response to be downloadable as `products.xlsx`. The resulting sheet can be opened in Excel, and will look similar to the following:

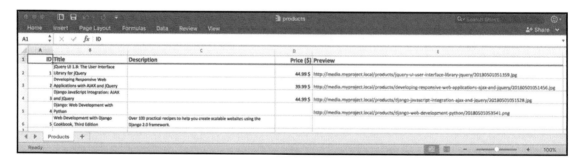

See also

- The *Customizing columns on the change list page* recipe
- The *Developing change list filters* recipe
- Chapter 9, *Data Import and Export*

Developing change list filters

If you want the administrators to be able to filter the change list by date, relation, or field choices, you have to use the `list_filter` property for the admin model. Additionally, there is the possibility of having custom-tailored filters. In this recipe, we will add a filter that allows you to select products by the number of photos attached to them.

Getting ready

Let's start with the `products` app that we created in the *Customizing columns on the change list page* recipe.

How to do it...

Execute the following steps:

1. In the `admin.py` file, create a `PhotoFilter` class extending from `SimpleListFilter`, as follows:

```
# products/admin.py
# ... all previous imports go here ...
from django.db import models

ZERO = "zero"
ONE = "one"
MANY = "many"


class PhotoFilter(admin.SimpleListFilter):
    # Human-readable title which will be displayed in the
    # right admin sidebar just above the filter options.
    title = _("photos")

    # Parameter for the filter that will be used in the
```

```
# URL query.
parameter_name = "photos"

def lookups(self, request, model_admin):
    """
    Returns a list of tuples, akin to the values given for
    model field choices. The first element in each tuple is the
    coded value for the option that will appear in the URL
    query. The second element is the human-readable name for
    the option that will appear in the right sidebar.
    """
    return (
        (ZERO, _("Has no photos")),
        (ONE, _("Has one photo")),
        (MANY, _("Has more than one photo")),
    )

def queryset(self, request, queryset):
    """
    Returns the filtered queryset based on the value
    provided in the query string and retrievable via
    `self.value()`.
    """
    qs = queryset.annotate(
        num_photos=models.Count("productphoto"))

    if self.value() == ZERO:
        qs = qs.filter(num_photos=0)
    elif self.value() == ONE:
        qs = qs.filter(num_photos=1)
    elif self.value() == MANY:
        qs = qs.filter(num_photos__gte=2)
    return qs
```

2. Then, add a list filter to `ProductAdmin`, as shown in the following code:

```
class ProductAdmin(admin.ModelAdmin):
    # ...
    list_filter = ["price", PhotoFilter]
```

How it works...

The list filter, based on the **price (USD)** field plus the custom one that we just created, will be shown in the sidebar of the product list, as follows:

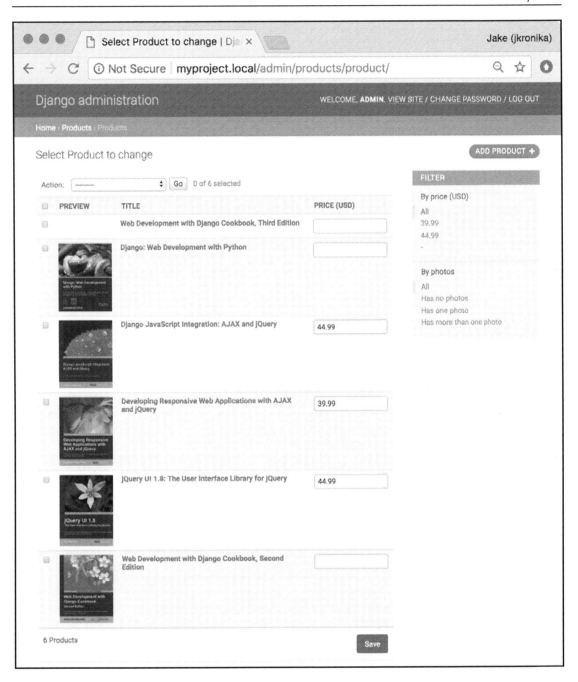

The `PhotoFilter` class has translatable title and query parameter names as properties. It also has two methods, as follows:

- The `lookups()` method that defines the choices of the filter
- The `queryset()` method that defines how to filter `QuerySet` objects when a specific value is selected

In the `lookups()` method, we define three choices, as follows:

- There are no photos
- There is one photo
- There is more than one photo attached

In the `queryset()` method, we use the `annotate()` method of `QuerySet` to select the count of photos for each product. This count of the photos is then filtered according to the selected choice.

 To learn more about the aggregation functions, such as `annotate()`, refer to the official Django documentation at `https://docs.djangoproject.com/en/2.1/topics/db/aggregation/`.

See also

- The *Customizing columns on the change list page* recipe
- The *Creating admin actions* recipe
- The *Customizing default admin settings* recipe

Customizing default admin settings

Django apps, as well as third-party apps, come with their own administration settings; however, there is a mechanism to switch these settings off and use your own, preferred administration settings. In this recipe, you will learn how to exchange the standard administration settings from the `django.contrib.auth` app with custom administration settings of your own.

Getting ready

Create a custom_admin app, and put this app under INSTALLED_APPS, in the settings. For
Docker projects, add it to the docker-compose.yml app volumes.

How to do it...

1. First, add the following content to the new admin.py file in the custom_admin
   app, to set up extended admin settings for user administration:

```python
# custom_admin/admin.py
from django.contrib import admin
from django.contrib.auth.admin import (User, UserAdmin,
                                        Group, GroupAdmin)
from django.contrib.contenttypes.models import ContentType
from django.urls import reverse
from django.utils.text import mark_safe
from django.utils.translation import ugettext_lazy as _


class UserAdminExtended(UserAdmin):
    list_display = ("username", "email",
                    "first_name", "last_name",
                    "is_active", "is_staff",
                    "date_joined", "last_login")
    list_filter = ("is_active", "is_staff", "is_superuser",
                   "date_joined", "last_login")
    ordering = ("last_name", "first_name", "username")
    save_on_top = True


admin.site.unregister(User)
admin.site.register(User, UserAdminExtended)
```

2. Then, add an extension for group administration, as well:

```python
class GroupAdminExtended(GroupAdmin):
    list_display = ("__str__", "display_users")
    save_on_top = True

    def display_users(self, obj):
        links = []
        for user in obj.user_set.all():
            ct = ContentType.objects.get_for_model(user)
            rule_name = f"admin:{ct.app_label}_{ct.model}_change"
            url = reverse(rule_name, args=(user.id,))
            user_name = (
                    f"{user.first_name} {user.last_name}".strip()
                    or user.username)
            links.append(f"""
            <a href="{url}" target="_blank">{user_name}</a>
            """)
        return mark_safe("<br />".join(links))
    display_users.allow_tags = True
    display_users.short_description = _("Users")


admin.site.unregister(Group)
admin.site.register(Group, GroupAdminExtended)
```

How it works...

The default user administration list looks similar to the following screenshot:

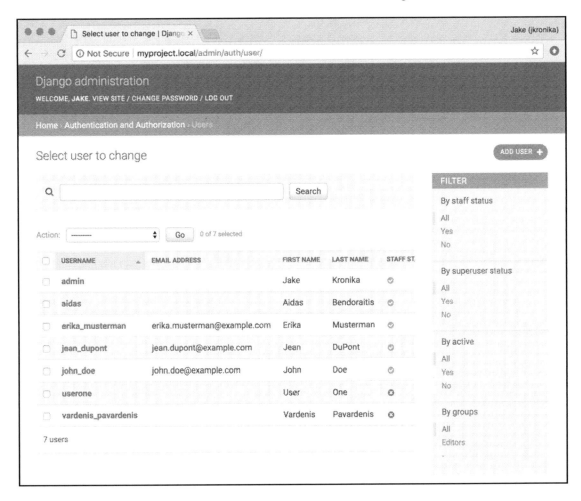

The default group administration list looks similar to the following screenshot:

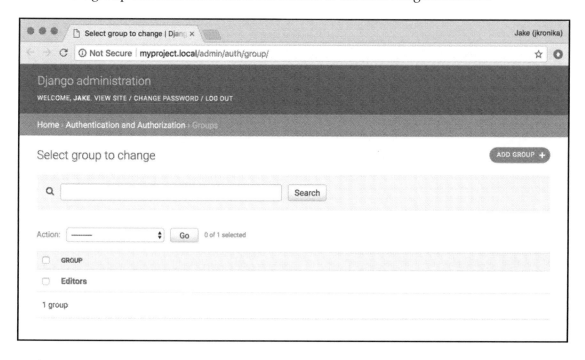

In this recipe, we created two model admin classes, `UserAdminExtended` and `GroupAdminExtended`, which extend the contributed `UserAdmin` and `GroupAdmin` classes respectively, and overwrite some of the properties. Then, we unregistered the existing administration classes for the `User` and `Group` models, and registered the new, modified ones.

The following screenshot shows how the user administration will now look:

The modified user administration settings show more fields than the default settings in the list view, add additional filters and ordering options, and show **Submit** buttons at the top of the editing form.

In the change list of the new group administration settings, we will display the users that are assigned to the specific groups. In the browser, this will look similar to the following screenshot:

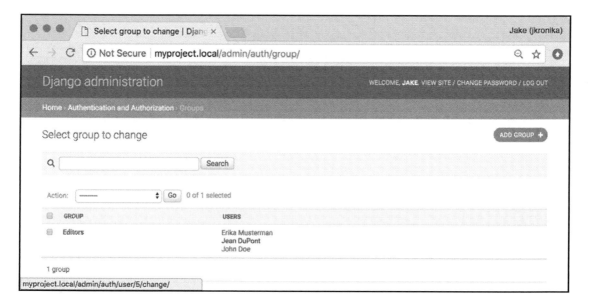

See also

- The *Customizing columns on the change list page* recipe
- The *Inserting a map into a change form* recipe

Inserting a map into a change form

Google Maps offers a JavaScript API to insert maps into your websites. In this recipe, we will create a `locations` app with the `Location` model and extend the template of the change form, in order to add a map where an administrator can find and mark the geographical coordinates of a location.

Getting ready

We will start with a `locations` app, which should be put under `INSTALLED_APPS`, in the settings. Create `Location` model there, with a `title`, `description`, `address`, and geographical coordinates, as follows:

```python
# locations/models.py
from django.db import models
from django.utils.translation import ugettext_lazy as _

COUNTRY_CHOICES = (
    ("US", _("United States")),
    ("UK", _("United Kingdom")),
    ("CA", _("Canada")),
    ("DE", _("Germany")),
    ("FR", _("France")),
    ("LT", _("Lithuania")),
)


class Location(models.Model):
    class Meta:
        verbose_name = _("Location")
        verbose_name_plural = _("Locations")

    title = models.CharField(_("title"),
                             max_length=255,
                             unique=True)
    description = models.TextField(_("description"), blank=True)
    street = models.CharField(_("street address"),
                              max_length=255,
                              blank=True)
    street2 = models.CharField(_("street address (line 2)"),
                               max_length=255,
                               blank=True)
    postal_code = models.CharField(_("postal code"),
                                   max_length=10,
                                   blank=True)
    city = models.CharField(_("city"),
                            max_length=255,
                            blank=True)
    country = models.CharField(_("country"),
                               max_length=2,
                               blank=True,
                               choices=COUNTRY_CHOICES)
    _latitude_definition = _(
        "Latitude (Lat.) is the angle between any point and the "
```

```
            "equator (north pole is at 90°; south pole is at -90°).")
    latitude = models.FloatField(_("latitude"),
                                    blank=True,
                                    null=True,
                                    help_text=_latitude_definition)
    _longitude_definition = _(
        "Longitude (Long.) is the angle east or west of a point "
        "on Earth at Greenwich (UK), which is the international "
        "zero-longitude point (longitude = 0°). The anti-meridian "
        "of Greenwich (the opposite side of the planet) is both "
        "180° (to the east) and -180° (to the west).")
    longitude = models.FloatField(_("longitude"),
                                    blank=True,
                                    null=True,
                                    help_text=_longitude_definition)

    def __str__(self):
        return self.title
```

How to do it...

The administration of the `Location` model is as simple as it can be. Perform the following steps:

1. Let's create the administration settings for the `Location` model. Note that we are using the `get_fieldsets()` method to define the field sets, with a description rendered from a template, as follows:

```
# locations/admin.py
from django.contrib import admin
from django.template.loader import render_to_string
from django.utils.translation import ugettext_lazy as _

from .models import Location


class LocationAdmin(admin.ModelAdmin):
    save_on_top = True
    list_display = ("title", "street", "description")
    search_fields = ("title", "street", "description")

    def get_fieldsets(self, request, obj=None):
        map_html = render_to_string("admin/includes/map.html")
        fieldsets = [
            (_("Main Data"), {"fields": ("title",
                                        "description")}),
```

```
                (_("Address"), {"fields": ("street",
                                           "street2",
                                           "postal_code",
                                           "city",
                                           "country",
                                           "latitude",
                                           "longitude")}),
            (_("Map"), {"description": map_html, "fields": []}),
        ]
        return fieldsets
```

```
    admin.site.register(Location, LocationAdmin)
```

2. To create a custom change form template, add a new `change_form.html` file under `admin/locations/location/`, in your `templates` directory. This template will extend from the default `admin/change_form.html` template, and will overwrite the `extrastyle` and `field_sets` blocks, as follows:

```
{# templates/admin/locations/location/change_form.html #}
{% extends "admin/change_form.html" %}
{% load i18n static admin_modify admin_static admin_urls %}

{% block extrastyle %}
    {{ block.super }}
    <link rel="stylesheet" type="text/css"
          href="{% static 'site/css/location.css' %}" />
{% endblock %}

{% block field_sets %}
    {% for fieldset in adminform %}
        {% include "admin/includes/fieldset.html" %}
    {% endfor %}
    <script type="text/javascript"
src="http://maps.google.com/maps/api/js?language=en"></script>
    <script type="text/javascript"
            src="{% static 'site/js/location.js' %}"></script>
{% endblock %}
```

3. Then, we have to create the template for the map that will be inserted in the `Map` field set, as follows:

```
{# templates/admin/locations/includes/map.html #}
{% load i18n %}
<div class="form-row map">
    <div class="canvas">
        <!-- THE GMAPS WILL BE INSERTED HERE DYNAMICALLY -->
```

```
        </div>
        <ul class="locations"></ul>
        <div class="btn-group">
            <button type="button"
                    class="btn btn-default locate-address">
                {% trans "Locate address" %}
            </button>
            <button type="button"
                    class="btn btn-default remove-geo">
                {% trans "Remove from map" %}
            </button>
        </div>
    </div>
</div>
```

4. Of course, the map won't be styled by default. Therefore, we will have to add some CSS, as shown in the following code:

```
/* static/locations/css/map.css */
.map {
    box-sizing: border-box;
    width: 98%;
}
.map .canvas,
.map ul.locations,
.map .btn-group {
    margin: 1rem 0;
}
.map .canvas {
    border: 1px solid #000;
    box-sizing: padding-box;
    height: 0;
    padding-bottom: calc(9 / 16 * 100%); /* 16:9 aspect ratio */
    width: 100%;
}
.map .canvas:before {
    color: #eee;
    color: rgba(0, 0, 0, 0.1);
    content: "map";
    display: block;
    font-size: 5rem;
    line-height: 5rem;
    margin-top: -25%;
    padding-top: calc(50% - 2.5rem);
    text-align: center;
}
.map ul.locations {
    padding: 0;
}
```

```
.map ul.locations li {
    border-bottom: 1px solid #ccc;
    list-style: none;
}
.map ul.locations li:first-child {
    border-top: 1px solid #ccc;
}
.map .btn-group .btn.remove-geo {
    float: right;
}
```

5. Next, let's create a `change_form.js` JavaScript file, which will need to be added to the project's static files, either by directly copying or by using the `collectstatic` management command. We don't want to pollute the environment with global variables; therefore, we will start with a closure, to make a private scope for variables and functions.

 A closure is a function scope within which variables that are not accessible to the outer scope can be defined, but where the enclosing scope variables can be accessed.

We will be using jQuery in this file (as jQuery comes with the contributed administration system and makes the work easy and cross-browser), as follows:

```
// static/locations/js/change_form.js
(function ($, undefined) {
    var gettext = window.gettext || function (val) {
        return val;
    };
    var $map, $foundLocations, $lat, $lng, $street, $street2,
        $city, $country, $postalCode, gMap, gMarker;

    // ...this is where all the further JavaScript functions go...

}(django.jQuery));
```

6. We will create JavaScript functions and add them to `change_form.js`, one by one. The `getAddress4search()` function will collect the `address` string from the address fields that can be used later for geocoding, as follows:

```
function getAddress4search() {
    var sStreetAddress2 = $street2.val();
    if (sStreetAddress2) {
        sStreetAddress2 = " " + sStreetAddress2;
    }
```

```
            return [
                $street.val() + sStreetAddress2,
                $city.val(),
                $country.val(),
                $postalCode.val()
            ].join(", ");
    }
```

7. The `updateMarker()` function will take the latitude and longitude arguments and draw or move a marker on the map. It will also make the marker draggable, as follows:

```
function updateMarker(lat, lng) {
    var point = new google.maps.LatLng(lat, lng);

    if (!gMarker) {
        gMarker = new google.maps.Marker({
            position: point,
            map: gMap
        });
    }

    gMarker.setPosition(point);
    gMap.panTo(point, 15);
    gMarker.setDraggable(true);

    google.maps.event.addListener(gMarker, "dragend", function() {
        var point = gMarker.getPosition();
        updateLatitudeAndLongitude(point.lat(), point.lng());
    });
}
```

8. The `updateLatitudeAndLongitude()` function, referenced in the preceding `dragend` event listener, takes the latitude and longitude arguments and updates the values for the fields with the `id_latitude` and `id_longitude` IDs, as follows:

```
function updateLatitudeAndLongitude(lat, lng) {
    var precision = 1000000;
    $lat.val(Math.round(lng * precision) / precision);
    $lng.val(Math.round(lat * precision) / precision);
}
```

9. The `autocompleteAddress()` function gets the results from Google Maps geocoding, and lists them under the map, in order to select the correct one; or, if there is just one result, it updates the geographical position and address fields, as follows:

```
function autocompleteAddress(results) {
    var $item = $('<li/>');
    var $link = $('<a href="#"/>');

    $foundLocations.html("");
    results = results || [];

    if (results.length) {
        results.forEach(function (result, i) {
            $link.clone()
                .html(result.formatted_address)
                .click(function (event) {
                    event.preventDefault();
                    updateAddressFields(result.address_components);

                    var point = result.geometry.location;
                    updateLatitudeAndLongitude(
                        point.lat(), point.lng());
                    updateMarker(point.lat(), point.lng());
                    $foundLocations.hide();
                })
                .appendTo($item.clone().appendTo($foundLocations));
        });
        $link.clone()
            .html(gettext("None of the above"))
            .click(function(event) {
                event.preventDefault();
                $foundLocations.hide();
            })
            .appendTo($item.clone().appendTo($foundLocations));
    } else {
        $foundLocations.hide();
    }
}
```

10. The `updateAddressFields()` function takes a nested dictionary, with the address components as an argument, and fills in all of the address fields, as follows:

```
function updateAddressFields(addressComponents) {
    var streetName, streetNumber;
    var typeActions = {
        "locality": function(obj) {
            $city.val(obj.long_name);
        },
        "street_number": function(obj) {
            streetNumber = obj.long_name;
        },
        "route": function(obj) {
            streetName = obj.long_name;
        },
        "postal_code": function(obj) {
            $postalCode.val(obj.long_name);
        },
        "country": function(obj) {
            $country.val(obj.short_name);
        }
    };

    addressComponents.forEach(function(component) {
        var action = typeActions[component.types[0]];
        if (typeof action === "function") {
            action(component);
        }
    });

    if (streetName) {
        var streetAddress = streetName;
        if (streetNumber) {
            streetAddress += " " + streetNumber;
        }
        $street.val(streetAddress);
    }
}
```

11. Finally, we have the initialization function, which is called on the page load. It attaches the `onclick` event handlers to the buttons, creates a Google Map, and, initially, marks the geoposition that is defined in the `latitude` and `longitude` fields, as follows:

```
$(function(){
    $map = $(".map");

    $foundLocations = $map.find("ul.locations").hide();
    $lat = $("#id_latitude");
    $lng = $("#id_longitude");
    $street = $("#id_street");
    $street2 = $("#id_street2");
    $city = $("#id_city");
    $country = $("#id_country");
    $postalCode = $("#id_postal_code");

    $map.find("button.locate-address")
        .click(function(event) {
            var oGeocoder = new google.maps.Geocoder();
            oGeocoder.geocode(
                {address: getAddress4search()},
                function (results, status) {
                    if (status === google.maps.GeocoderStatus.OK) {
                        autocompleteAddress(results);
                    } else {
                        autocompleteAddress(false);
                    }
                }
            );
        });

    $map.find("button.remove-geo")
        .click(function() {
            $lat.val("");
            $lng.val("");
            gMarker.setMap(null);
            gMarker = null;
        });
```

```
gMap = new google.maps.Map($map.find(".canvas").get(0), {
    scrollwheel: false,
    zoom: 16,
    center: new google.maps.LatLng(51.511214, -0.119824),
    disableDoubleClickZoom: true
});

google.maps.event.addListener(gMap, "dblclick", function(event)
{
    var lat = event.latLng.lat();
    var lng = event.latLng.lng();
    updateLatitudeAndLongitude(lat, lng);
    updateMarker(lat, lng);
});

if ($lat.val() && $lng.val()) {
    updateMarker($lat.val(), $lng.val());
}
});
```

How it works...

If you look at the location change form in the browser, you will see a map shown in a field set, followed by the field set containing the address fields, as shown in the following screenshot:

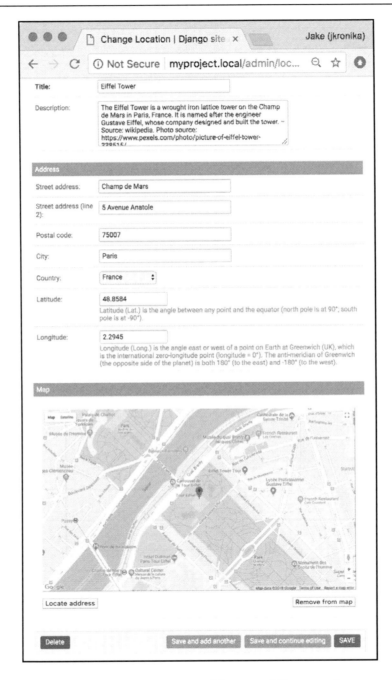

Under the map, there are two buttons: **Locate address** and **Remove from map**.

When you click on the **Locate address** button, the geocoding is called in order to search for the geographical coordinates of the entered address. The result of the geocoding is one or more addresses, with `latitudes` and `longitudes` listed in a nested dictionary format. To see the structure of the nested dictionary in the console of the developer tools, put the following line at the beginning of the `autocompleteAddress()` function:

```
console.log(JSON.stringify(results, null, 4));
```

If there is just one result, the missing postal code or other missing address fields are populated, `latitude` and `longitude` are filled in, and a marker is put at a specific place on the map. If there are more results, the entire list is shown under the map, with the option to select the correct one, as shown in the following screenshot:

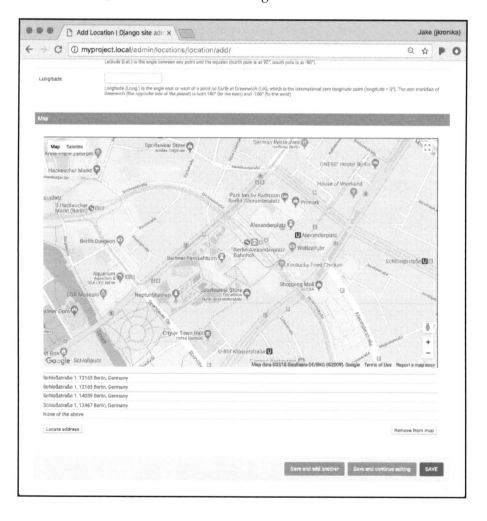

Then, the administrator can move the marker on the map by dragging and dropping. Also, a double-click anywhere on the map will update the geographical coordinates and the marker position.

Finally, if the **Remove from map** button is clicked, the geographical coordinates are cleaned, and the marker is removed.

See also

- The *Using HTML5 data attributes* recipe, in Chapter 4, *Templates and JavaScript*

7

Security and Performance

In this chapter, we will cover the following topics:

- Making forms secure from Cross Site Request Forgery (CSRF)
- Implementing password validation
- Downloading authorized files
- Authenticating with Auth0
- Caching the method return value
- Using Memcached to cache Django views
- Using Redis to cache Django views

Introduction

Software that inappropriately exposes sensitive information, makes the user suffer through interminable wait times, or requires extensive amounts of hardware will never last. As a result, it is our responsibility as developers to make sure that applications are secure and performant. In this chapter, we will examine just some of the many ways to keep your users (and yourself) safe while operating within Django applications. Then, we'll cover a few options for caching that can reduce processing and get data to users at a lower expense in both money and time.

Making forms secure from Cross Site Request Forgery (CSRF)

Without proper precautions, malicious sites could potentially invoke requests against your site that would result in undesired changes on your server, such as affecting a user's authentication, altering content, or accessing sensitive information. Django comes bundled with a system for preventing CSRF attacks such as these, and we'll review that in this recipe.

Getting ready

Start with the `email_messages` app that was created in the *Passing the HttpRequest to a form* recipe from `Chapter 3`, *Forms and Views*.

How to do it...

In order to enable CSRF prevention in Django, follow these steps:

1. Make sure that `CsrfViewMiddleware` is included in your project settings, as shown here:

```
# settings.py or base.py
MIDDLEWARE = [
    # ...
    'django.middleware.csrf.CsrfViewMiddleware',
]
```

2. Make sure the form view is rendered using the request context. For example, in the existing `email_messages` app, we have this:

```
# email_messages/views.py
# ...

@login_required
def message_to_user(request):
    # ...

    return render(request,
                  "email_messages/message_to_user.html",
                  {"form": form}
```

3. Update the form template for the form to extend from base.html, making sure it uses the POST method and includes the csrf_token tag:

```
{# templates/email_messages/message_to_user.html #}
{% extends "base.html" %}
{% load i18n %}

{% block content %}
<form action="" method="POST">
    {% csrf_token %}
    {{ form.as_p }}
    <p>
        <button type="submit">{% trans "Send" %}</button>
    </p>
</form>
{% endblock %}
```

How it works...

Django uses a hidden field approach to prevent CSRF attacks. A token is generated on the server, based on a combination of request-specific and randomized information. Through CsrfViewMiddleware, this token is automatically made available via the request context.

While it is not recommended that this middleware be disabled, it is possible to mark individual views to get the same behavior by applying the csrf_protect decorator:

```
from django.views.decorators.csrf import csrf_protect

@csrf_protect
def my_protected_form():
    # ...
```

Similarly, we can mark individual views as exempt from CSRF checks, even when the middleware is enabled, using the csrf_exclude decorator:

```
from django.views.decorators.csrf import csrf_exclude

@csrf_exclude
def my_unsecured_form():
    # ...
```

The built-in `{% csrf_token %}` tag generates the hidden input field that provides the token. It is considered invalid to include the token for forms that submit requests using the `GET`, `HEAD`, `OPTIONS`, or `TRACE` methods, as any requests using those methods should not cause side effects in the first place. In most cases, web forms that will require CSRF protection will be `POST` forms.

When a protected form using an unsafe method is submitted without the required token, Django's built-in form validation will recognize this and reject the request outright. Only those submissions containing a token with a valid value will be allowed to proceed. As a result, external sites will be unable to effect changes on your server, since they won't be able to know and include the currently valid token value.

There's more...

In many cases, it is desirable to enhance a form so that it can submit over Ajax. These also need to be protected using CSRF tokens, and while it is possible to inject the token as extra data in each request, using such an approach requires developers to remember to do so for each and every `POST`. An alternative using a CSRF token header exists and it makes things more efficient.

First, the token value needs to be retrieved, and how we do this depends upon the value of the `CSRF_USE_SESSIONS` setting. When it is `True`, the token is stored in the session rather than a cookie, and so we must use the `{% csrf_token %}` tag to include it in the DOM. We can then read that element to retrieve the data in JavaScript:

```
var csrfInput = document.querySelector("[name='csrfmiddlewaretoken']");
var csrfToken = csrfTokenInput && csrfTokenInput.value;
```

When the `CSRF_USE_SESSIONS` setting is in the default `False` state, the preferred source of the token value is the `csrftoken` cookie. While it is possible to roll your own cookie manipulation methods, there are many utilities available that simplify the process. For example, we can extract the token easily by name using the js-cookie API, available at `https://github.com/js-cookie/js-cookie`, as shown here:

```
var token = Cookies.get("crsftoken");
```

Once the token is extracted, it needs to be set as the `CSRF-Token` header value for `XmlHttpRequest`. Although this might be done separately for each request, doing so has the same drawbacks as adding the data to the request parameters for each request. Instead, we might use jQuery and its facility for attaching data to all requests automatically before they are sent, like so:

```
CSRF_SAFE_METHODS = ["GET", "HEAD", "OPTIONS", "TRACE"];
$.ajaxSetup({
    beforeSend: function(xhr, settings) {
        if (CSRF_SAFE_METHODS.indexOf(settings.type) < 0
                && !this.crossDomain) {
            xhr.setRequestHeader("X-CSRFToken", csrftoken);
        }
    }
});
```

See also

- The *Implementing password validation* recipe
- The *Downloading authorized files* recipe
- The *Authenticating with Auth0* recipe

Implementing password validation

Among the items at the top of the list of software security failures is the choice of insecure passwords by users. In this recipe, we will see how to enforce minimum password requirements through both built-in and custom password validators, so that users are guided toward setting up more secure authentication.

Getting ready

Open the project's `settings.py` file and locate the `AUTH_PASSWORD_VALIDATORS` setting. Also, create a new `auth_extra` app containing a `password_validation.py` file.

How to do it...

Follow these steps to set up stronger password validation for your project:

1. Let's customize the settings for the validators included with Django by adding options:

```
# settings.py or base.py
# ...
AUTH_PASSWORD_VALIDATORS = [
    {
        'NAME': 'django.contrib.auth.password_validation.'
                'UserAttributeSimilarityValidator',
        'OPTIONS': {
            'max_similarity': 0.5,
        },
    },
    {
        'NAME': 'django.contrib.auth.password_validation.'
                'MinimumLengthValidator',
        'OPTIONS': {
            'min_length': 12,
        }
    },
    {
        'NAME': 'django.contrib.auth.password_validation.'
                'CommonPasswordValidator',
    },
    {
        'NAME': 'django.contrib.auth.password_validation.'
                'NumericPasswordValidator',
    },
]
```

2. Let's add a new `auth_extra` app and include it in `INSTALLED_APPS`. Fill in the `password_validation.py` file in the new app also, as follows:

```
# auth_extra/password_validation.py
from django.core.exceptions import ValidationError
from django.utils.translation import gettext as _


class MaximumLengthValidator:
    def __init__(self, max_length=24):
        self.max_length = max_length

    def validate(self, password, user=None):
```

```python
        if len(password) > self.max_length:
            raise ValidationError(
                self.get_help_text(pronoun="this"),
                code="password_too_long",
                params={'max_length': self.max_length},
            )

    def get_help_text(self, pronoun="your"):
        return _(f"{pronoun.capitalize()} password must contain "
                 f"no more than {max_length} characters")


class SpecialCharacterInclusionValidator:
    DEFAULT_SPECIAL_CHARACTERS = ('$', '%', ':', '#', '!')

    def __init__(self, special_chars=DEFAULT_SPECIAL_CHARACTERS):
        self.special_chars = special_chars

    def validate(self, password, user=None):
        has_specials_chars = False
        for char in self.special_chars:
            if char in password:
                has_specials_chars = True
                break
        if not has_specials_chars:
            raise ValidationError(
                self.get_help_text(pronoun="this"),
                code="password_missing_special_chars"
            )

    def get_help_text(self, pronoun="your"):
        return _(f"{pronoun.capitalize()} password must contain at"
                 " least one of the following special characters: "
                 f"{', '.join(self.special_chars)}"),
```

3. Then, add the new validators to the settings:

```python
# settings.py or base.py
# ... existing imports ...
from auth_extra.password_validation import \
    SpecialCharacterInclusionValidator

# ...
AUTH_PASSWORD_VALIDATORS = [
    # ...
    {
        'NAME': 'auth_extra.password_validation.'
                'MaximumLengthValidator',
```

```
        'OPTIONS': {
            'max_length': 32,
        },
    },
    {
        'NAME': 'auth_extra.password_validation.'
                'SpecialCharacterInclusionValidator',
        'OPTIONS': {
            'special_chars': ('{', '}', '^', '&') +
                SpecialCharacterInclusionValidator.
                DEFAULT_SPECIAL_CHARACTERS
        }
    },
]
```

How it works...

Django ships with its own set of default validators:

- `UserAttributeSimilarityValidator` ensures that any password chosen is not too similar to certain attributes of the user. By default, the similarity ratio is set to 0.7 and the attributes checked are the username, first and last name, and email address. If any of these attributes contains multiple parts, each part is checked independently as well.
- `MinimumLengthValidator` checks that the password entered is at least the minimum number of characters in length. By default, passwords must be eight or more characters long.
- `CommonPasswordValidator` refers to a file containing a list of passwords that are often used, and hence are insecure. The list Django uses by default contains 1,000 such passwords.
- `NumericPasswordValidator` verifies that the password entered is not made up entirely of numbers.

When you use `startproject` to create a new project, these are added with their default options as the initial set of validators. We see here how these options can be adjusted for our project needs, increasing the minimum length of passwords to 12 characters.

For `UserAttributeSimilarityValidator`, we have also reduced `max_similarity` to 0.6, which means that passwords must differ more greatly from user attributes than the default.

Looking at `password_validation.py`, we have defined two new validators:

- `MaximumLengthValidator` is very similar to the built-in one for minimum length, ensuring that the password is no longer than a default of 24 characters.
- `SpecialCharacterInclusionValidator` checks that one or more special characters—defined as the $, %, :, #, and ! symbols by default—are found within the given password.

Each `validator` class has two required methods:

- The `validate()` method performs the actual checks against the `password` argument. Optionally, a second `user` argument will be passed when a user has been authenticated.
- We also must provide a `get_help_text()` method, which returns a string describing the validation requirements for the user.

Finally, we add the new validators to the settings, overriding the defaults to allow up to a 32-character maximum length, and to add the symbols {, }, ^, and & to the default special character list.

There's more...

The validators provided in `AUTH_PASSWORD_VALIDATORS` are executed automatically for `createsuperuser` and `changepassword` management commands, and in built-in forms used to reset or change passwords. There can be times that you will want to use the same validation for custom password management code, though. Django provides functions for that level of integration, also, under the contributed Django `auth` app's `password_validation` module.

First, let's examine the functions that allow you to retrieve instances of validation classes:

- We can retrieve a set of `validator` instances, one for each class represented in a given configuration list, with `get_password_validators()`, as follows:

```
from django.contrib.auth.password_validation import (
    get_password_validators)
# ...
config = [{
    'NAME': 'auth_extra.password_validation.'
            'MaximumLengthValidator'
}]
max_length_validator = get_password_validators(config)[0]
```

- If we want to get instances for each of the default set of validators defined in our settings, we could use the same method and pass in the AUTH_PASSWORD_VALIDATORS setting:

```
from django.conf import settings
from django.contrib.auth.password_validation import (
    get_password_validators)
# ...
default_validators = get_password_validators(
    settings.AUTH_PASSWORD_VALIDATORS)
```

- However, Django makes this common case easy by providing a shorthand method to retrieve the default set, as in the following:

```
from django.contrib.auth.password_validation import (
    get_default_password_validators)
# ...
default_validators = get_default_password_validators()
```

Starting with a set of validators instances, then, Django provides the following functions for extracting help text from each:

- We can simply get the basic help text, like so:

```
from django.contrib.auth.password_validation import (
    get_default_password_validators,
    password_validators_help_texts)
# ...
default_validators = get_default_password_validators()
help_texts = password_validators_help_texts(validators)
```

- Since Django deals mainly with web applications, it is likely that the help text will need to be output as HTML. Though we could iterate over help_texts and wrap them in any markup we wanted, a handy method is provided to get help text automatically as an unordered list:

```
from django.contrib.auth.password_validation import (
    get_default_password_validators,
    password_validators_help_text_html)
# ...
validators = get_default_password_validators()
help_html = password_validators_help_text_html(validators)
```

Most commonly, though, we would want to apply the validation and prevent insecure passwords from being created. There are functions available for that as well:

- To apply validation, we can invoke the validate_password() function, handling any ValidationError raised when validation fails as needed. Optionally, a third argument can specify a different list of validators instances, but the default validators are used if it is omitted, as in the following example:

```
from django.contrib.auth.password_validation import (
    validate_password)
from django.core.exceptions import ValidationError
# ...
try:
    validate_password(password, request.user)
except ValidationError:
    # ... handle validation failures ...
```

- In some cases, validator behavior when a password is initially set may differ from that when the password is later altered. While validate_password() is appropriate upon creation, a separate function is provided for handling updates, so that validators execute the appropriate logic in each case:

```
from django.contrib.auth.password_validation import (
    password_changed)
from django.core.exceptions import ValidationError
# ...
try:
    password_changed(password, request.user)
except ValidationError:
    # ... handle validation failures ...
```

See also

- The *Downloading authorized files* recipe
- The *Authenticating with Auth0* recipe

Downloading authorized files

Sometimes, you might need to allow only specific people to download intellectual property from your website. For example, music, videos, literature, or other artistic works should be accessible only to paid members. In this recipe, you will learn how to restrict image downloads only to authenticated users using the contributed Django `auth` app.

Getting ready

To start, create the `quotes` app as in the *Uploading images* recipe from `Chapter 3`, *Forms and Views*.

How to do it...

Execute these steps one by one:

1. Create the view that will require authentication to download a file, as follows:

```
# quotes/views.py
import os

from django.contrib.auth.decorators import login_required
from django.http import FileResponse
from django.shortcuts import get_object_or_404
from django.utils.text import slugify

from .models import InspirationalQuote


@login_required(login_url="user-login")
def download_quote_picture(request, pk):
    quote = get_object_or_404(InspirationalQuote, pk=pk)
    try:
        filename, extension = os.path.splitext(
            quote.picture.file.name)
        extension = extension[1:] # remove the dot
        response = FileResponse(
            quote.picture.file,
            content_type=f"image/{extension}")
        author = slugify(quote.author)[:100]
        excerpt = slugify(quote.quote)[:100]
        response["Content-Disposition"] = \
            "attachment; filename=" \
```

```
            f"{author}---{excerpt}.{extension}"
        except ValueError:
            response = HttpResponseNotFound(
                content='Picture unavailable')
        return response
```

2. Add the download view to the URL configuration:

```
# quotes/urls.py
from django.urls import path


urlpatterns = [
    # ...
    path('<int:pk>/download', download_quote_picture,
        name='quote-picture-download'),
]
```

3. We need to set up the login view in our project URLs:

```
# myproject/urls.py
from django.conf.urls.i18n import i18n_patterns
from django.contrib.auth.views import LoginView
from django.urls import include, path

urlpatterns = [
    # ...
    path('login/', LoginView.as_view(), name='user-login'),
]

urlpatterns += i18n_patterns(
    # ...
    path('quotes/', include('quotes.urls')),
)
```

4. Let's create a template for the login form, as shown in the following:

```
{# templates/registration/login.html #}
{% extends "base.html" %}
{% load i18n static %}

{% block stylesheet %}
<link rel="stylesheet" href="{% static 'site/css/login.css' %}">
{% endblock %}

{% block content %}
<div class="container">
    <form method="POST" action="{% url 'user-login' %}"
```

```
              class="form-signin">
        {% csrf_token %}
        <h2 class="my-3">{% trans "Please sign in" %}</h2>

        {{ form.non_field_errors }}

        <fieldset class="mb-3" required>
            <div class="control-group username required mb-3">
                <label for="{{ form.username.id_for_label }}"
                        class="control-label requiredField">
                    {% trans form.username.label %}
                </label>
                <div class="controls">
                    {{ form.username }}
                    {{ form.username.errors }}
                </div>
            </div>
            <div class="control-group password required mb-3">
                <label for="{{ form.password.id_for_label }}"
                        class="control-label requiredField">
                    {% trans form.password.label %}
                </label>
                <div class="controls">
                    {{ form.password }}
                    {{ form.password.errors }}
                </div>
            </div>
        </fieldset>
        {{ form.next }}
        <div class="form-actions mb-5 text-right">
            <button type="submit" class="btn btn-lg btn-primary">
                {% trans "Login" %}
            </button>
        </div>
    </form>
</div>
{% endblock %}
```

5. Create the `login.css` file to add some additional style to the login form, if desired. Basic styles will be provided by Bootstrap already, if the library has been loaded, as in the example:

```
form.form-signin {
    background-color: rgba(0, 0, 0, 0.1);
    box-shadow: 0 0 10px 5px rgba(0, 0, 0, 0.25);
    margin: 0 auto;
    max-width: 400px;
    padding: 50px;
}

.controls input {
    border: 0;
    box-shadow: 0 0 4px 2px rgba(0, 0, 0, 0.15);
    font-size: 1.5rem;
    padding: .25em .5em;
    width: 100%;
}
```

6. You should restrict users from bypassing Django and downloading restricted files directly. To do so on an Apache web server, you can put a `.htaccess` file in the `media/quotes` directory, using the following content if you are running Apache 2.2:

```
# media/quotes/.htaccess
Order deny,allow
Deny from all
```

You would use the following content instead when running Apache 2.4:

```
# media/quotes/.htaccess
Require all denied
```

How it works...

The `download_quote_picture()` view streams the picture from a specific inspirational quote. The `Content-Disposition` header that is set to `attachment` makes the file downloadable instead of being immediately shown in the browser. The filename for the file is also set in this header, and will be something similar to `walt-disney---if-you-can-dream-it-you-can-do-it.png`. As a bonus, if the quote has no picture, a 404 page is shown with a very simple message, as follows:

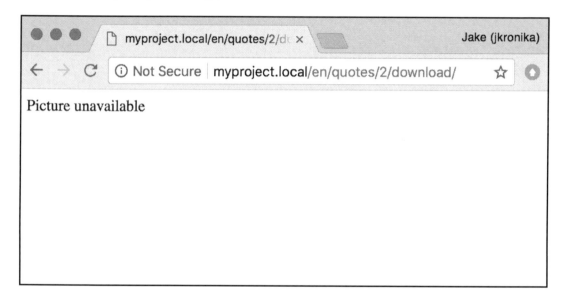

The `@login_required` decorator will redirect the visitor to the login page if he or she tries to access the downloadable file without being logged in. As we want to have a nice Bootstrap-style login form, we are using customized Bootstrap markup in our `login.html` override template, which is automatically rendered through `LoginView` for the login form.

Depending on the custom CSS applied, the login form might look similar to the following:

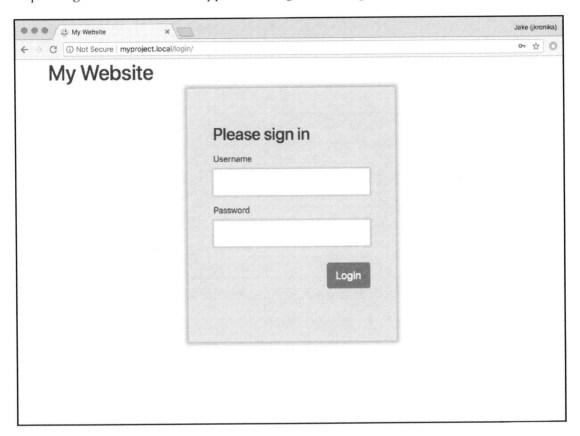

See also

- The *Uploading images* recipe from Chapter 3, *Forms and Views*
- The *Creating a form layout with custom templates* recipe from Chapter 3, *Forms and Views*
- The *Creating a form layout with django-crispy-forms* recipe from Chapter 3, *Forms and Views*
- The *Arranging the base.html template* recipe from Chapter 4, *Templates and JavaScript*
- The *Implementing password validation* recipe
- The *Adding a dynamic watermark to images* recipe

Adding a dynamic watermark to images

Sometimes, it is desirable to allow users to see images, but keep them from being able to redistribute them due to intellectual property and artistic rights. In this recipe, we will see how to apply a watermark to images that are displayed on your site.

Getting ready

To start, create the `quotes` app as in the *Uploading images* recipe from `Chapter 3`, *Forms and Views*.

How to do it...

Follow these steps to apply a watermark to displayed quote images:

1. Add the `django-watermark` app to your Docker project requirements file (or install it directly if using a virtual environment):

   ```
   # requirements.txt or requirements/base.txt
   # ...
   django-watermark~=0.1.8
   ```

2. Make sure that the new app is included in the `INSTALLED_APPS` setting:

   ```
   # project/settings.py
   # ...
   INSTALLED_APPS = [
       # ...
       'watermarker',
   ]
   ```

3. Once you make and run any necessary migrations, open the **administration** interface to add a watermark. Using a transparent PNG file works best. Here's what the form might look like:

4. Next, add a detail template to the `quotes` app:

```
{# templates/quotes/inspirationalquote_detail.html #}
{% extends "base.html" %}
{% load i18n watermark %}

{% block content %}
<h2>{% trans "Inspirational Quote" %}</h2>

{% if inspirationalquote.picture %}
<img src="{{ inspirationalquote.picture.url|watermark:"Basic Two-
Tone,opacity=35,tile=1,position=BL,rotation=30" }}" alt="">
{% endif %}
<blockquote>
    <h3>{{ inspirationalquote.quote }}</h3>
    <cite>{{ inspirationalquote.author }}</cite>
</blockquote>
{% endblock %}
```

5. And we will also need a listing template:

```
{# templates/quotes/inspirationalquote_list.html #}
{% extends "base.html" %}
{% load i18n thumbnail %}
```

```
{% block content %}
<h2>{% trans "Inspirational Quotes" %}</h2>
{% if inspirationalquote_list.count == 0 %}
    <p>{% trans "No quotes to show!" %}</p>
{% else %}
    <ul class="quote-list">
        {% for quote in inspirationalquote_list %}
        <li>
            {% if quote.picture %}
            <a href="{% url 'quote-detail' pk=quote.pk %}">
                <img src="{% thumbnail quote.picture '100x100' %}"
                    alt="" class="align-right"></a>
            {% endif %}
            <p>{{ quote.quote|truncatechars:20 }}</p>
        </li>
        {% endfor %}
    </ul>
{% endif %}
{% endblock %}
```

6. The views associated with these templates are trivial and can be created as follows:

```
# quotes/views.py
from django.views.generic import DetailView, ListView

from .models import InspirationalQuote


class QuoteList(ListView):
    model = InspirationalQuote


class QuoteDetail(DetailView):
    model = InspirationalQuote
```

7. Add URL rules for the listing and detail views:

```
# quotes/urls.py
from django.urls import path

from .views import QuoteList, QuoteDetail


urlpatterns = [
    path('', QuoteList.as_view(),
        name='quotes-list'),
    path('<int:pk>/', QuoteDetail.as_view(),
```

```
                    name='quote-detail'),
        # ...
    ]
```

How it works...

If we go to the root URL for the quotes app, we should see the list of current quotes, with thumbnail images and the first four words of the quote, both linked to the detail page. Clicking through to the detail, we should see the full-size image masked by our watermark, similar to this:

Let's examine how this was done. In the detail template, the `src` attribute for the `<img>` tag uses the inspirational quote's photo URL, as usual, but with the watermark filter applied. Within this filter is where all of the magic happens, as dictated by the options passed to it through its string argument, as copied here:

```
"Basic Two-Tone,opacity=35,tile=1,position=BL,rotation=30"
```

Let's examine each of these options to see how it was done:

- First is the required name of the watermark, as was entered into the administration area; `Basic Two-Tone` in this case. This tells the filter what watermark image to apply.
- Additional options are separated by commas, all of which have defaults, and can come in any order or be omitted entirely. The first of these optional configurations used here sets the opacity of the applied watermark to 35%.
- We want the watermark to be repeated across the entire image, so we tell the filter to tile it by setting the associated option to 1 (`True`) next.
- To have the best result, the starting position for each watermark may differ, and may be set to any of the corners (`BL` for lower-left, `TR` for upper-right, and so on), centered (`C`), or at a specific point using percentages or pixels (for example, `50%x100` to center horizontally 100 px below the top edge).
- Finally, the original watermark here is rotated by 30 degrees to give it a slightly more active effect.

There's more...

In addition to the options used here, there are a few more available for the filter:

- Using `grayscale=1` will remove all color from the watermark.
- By default, the filename used for a watermarked image will not include the original one, making it impossible for users to guess the URL of the image without watermarks. This can be turned off by setting `obscure=0`.
- If the position is not specified, the starting point of the watermark will be randomized. By default, the first position is cached for use in all subsequent requests. Turning off this setting with `random_position_once=0` will cause the watermark to be positioned randomly on every request.
- The quality of the watermarked image can also be controlled by setting the corresponding option to a number representing the percentage quality. The default would be `quality=85`.
- The watermark can also be scaled via the scale option, with values of `F` (full watermark visible), `R` (watermark at a specified ratio in size to the original image), or a positive decimal factor.

The defaults for some options can be set project-wide in the settings, too:

- When using `scale=R`, the `WATERMARK_PERCENTAGE` setting controls the scaling, with a default value of 30, indicating a 30% ratio.
- Default quality can be set via `WATERMARK_QUALITY`.
- If all image URLs should be based on the original filename, it might be appropriate to use `WATERMARK_OBSCURE_ORIGINAL=False` in the settings.
- Finally, when every request for an image should get a freshly positioned watermark, the `WATERMARK_RANDOM_POSITION_ONCE` setting can be given as `False`.

See also

- The *Downloading authorized files* recipe

Authenticating with Auth0

As the number of services people interact with daily increases, so does the number of usernames and passwords that they need to remember. Beyond just that, each additional place where user information is stored is another place that it could be stolen from, in the event of a security breach. To help mitigate this, services such as Auth0 allow you to consolidate authentication services on a single, secure platform.

In addition to support of username and password credentials, Auth0 has the ability to connect users via social platforms such as Google and Facebook. There is even enterprise-level support including that for **Lightweight Directory Access Protocol (LDAP)** and **Active Directory (AD)**. In this recipe, you'll learn how to connect an Auth0 application to Django, integrating it to handle user authentication.

Getting ready

If you haven't done so yet, create an Auth0 application at `https://auth0.com/` and configure it following the instructions there. We switch need to install some dependencies in the project.

Update your virtual environment or Docker project's requirements to include the Auth0 dependencies, as follows:

```
# requirements.txt or base.txt
# ...
python-dotenv~=0.8.0
requests~=2.18.0
social-auth-app-django~=2.1.0
```

For a virtual environment, install each of these individually using `pip3 install ...`, as usual. For Docker projects, make sure to build and restart your containers after updating the requirements.

How to do it...

To connect Auth0 to your Django project, follow these steps:

1. Create a new `external_auth` app module (empty for now), and add both it and the social auth app it to `INSTALLED_APPS`, like so:

```
# settings.py or base.py
INSTALLED_APPS = [
    # ...
    'social_django',
    'external_auth',
]
```

2. Now, add the Auth0 settings required by the `social_django` app, which will be similar to the following:

```
# settings.py or base.py
import os

# ...

SOCIAL_AUTH_AUTH0_DOMAIN = os.environ.get('AUTH0_DOMAIN')
SOCIAL_AUTH_AUTH0_KEY = os.environ.get('AUTH0_KEY')
SOCIAL_AUTH_AUTH0_SECRET = os.environ.get('AUTH0_SECRET')
SOCIAL_AUTH_AUTH0_SCOPE = ['openid', 'profile']
SOCIAL_AUTH_TRAILING_SLASH = False
```

More information about scopes can be found in the associated documentation at https://auth0.com/docs/scopes/current.

The values for the domain, key, and secret are application-specific, and are available in your Auth0 application's settings.

Sensitive settings can be added via environment variables to keep them secure. At minimum, this should be done for the SOCIAL_AUTH_AUTH0_SECRET.

3. We need to create a backend for the Auth0 connection, as in the following example:

```python
# external_auth/backends.py
import requests

from social_core.backends.oauth import BaseOAuth2


class Auth0(BaseOAuth2):
    name = "auth0"
    SCOPE_SEPARATOR = " "
    ACCESS_TOKEN_METHOD = "POST"
    EXTRA_DATA = [
        ("picture", "picture")
    ]

    def authorization_url(self):
        return f"https://{self.setting('DOMAIN')}/authorize"

    def access_token_url(self):
        return f"https://{self.setting('DOMAIN')}/oauth/token"

    def get_user_id(self, details, response):
        return details['user_id']

    def get_user_details(self, response):
        url = f"https://{self.setting('DOMAIN')}/userinfo"
        headers = {
            "authorization": f"Bearer {response['access_token']}"
        }
        resp = requests.get(url, headers=headers)
        userinfo = resp.json()
```

```
                    return {
                        "username": userinfo["nickname"],
                        "first_name": userinfo["name"],
                        "picture": userinfo["picture"],
                        "user_id": userinfo["sub"]
                    }
```

4. Add the backend to your AUTHENTICATION_BACKENDS setting, as in the following:

```
# settings.py or config/base.py
AUTHENTICATION_BACKENDS = [
    'external_auth.backends.Auth0',
    'django.contrib.auth.backends.ModelBackend',
]
```

5. Create a dashboard view for users to land on when they log in, as follows:

```
# external_auth/views.py
from django.views.generic import TemplateView


class DashboardView(TemplateView):
    template_name = "external_auth/dashbaord.html"

    def dispatch(self, request, *args, **kwargs):
        self.request = request
        return super().dispatch(request, *args, **kwargs)

    def get_context_data(self, **kwargs):
        user = self.request.user
        auth0_user = user.social_auth.get(provider="auth0")
        context = super().get_context_data(**kwargs)
        context["user_id"] = auth0_user.uid
        context["name"] = user.first_name
        context["picture"] = auth0_user.extra_data["picture"]
        return context
```

6. Create a dashboard template accordingly:

```
{# templates/external_auth/dashboard.html #}
{% extends "base.html" %}

{% block content %}
<h2>Welcome {{ name }}</h2>
{% if picture %}
<p>
    <img src="{{ picture }}" alt="">
```

```
</p>
{% endif %}
<p>
    You are now logged in as {{ user_id }}.
    <a href="{% url 'auth:logout' %}"
       class="btn btn-primary btn-sm btn-logout">
        Logout</a>
</p>
{% endblock %}
```

7. Set up a URL rule for the dashboard, like so:

```python
# external_auth/urls.py
from django.contrib.auth.decorators import login_required
from django.urls import include, path

from .views import DashboardView


urlpatterns = [
    # ...
    path('', login_required(DashboardView.as_view()),
        name='auth-dashboard'),
]
```

8. And then add entries for authentication to the project:

```python
# project/urls.py
from django.contrib.auth.urls import urlpatterns as auth_patterns
from django.urls import include, path

urlpatterns = [
    # ...
    path('dashboard/', include('external_auth.urls')),
    path('', include((auth_patterns, 'auth'))),
    path('', include('social_django.urls',
        namespace='social')),
]
```

9. We can configure the login and logout URL settings, as follows:

```python
# settings or config/base.py
LOGIN_URL = '/login/auth0'
LOGIN_REDIRECT_URL = '/dashboard/'
LOGOUT_REDIRECT_URL = '/'
```

How it works...

If we point a browser to the `/dashboard/` path for our project domain (for example, `http://myproject.local/dashboard/`), we will be required to log in first, as a result of applying the `login_required` decorator to the class-based `Dashboard` view in the `urls.py` project. A series of redirects by the authentication system will bring us to an Auth0 login screen similar to the following:

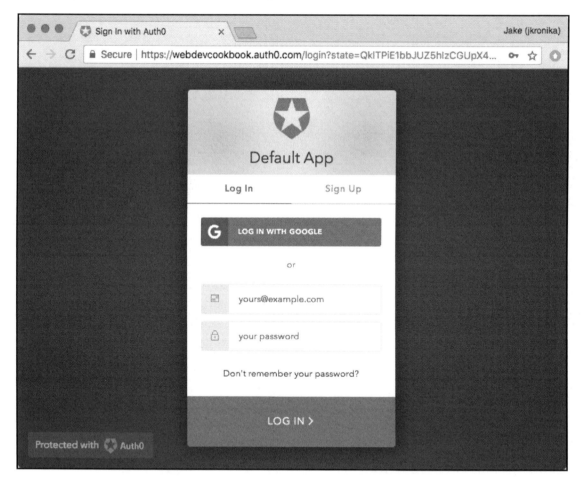

This much is enabled out of the box by Django—the integration of the `social_django` app, and configuration of its associated `SOCIAL_AUTH_*` settings.

As we can see, there is support for OpenID login through Google already in place. Other social logins such as Facebook or LinkedIn can be easily configured through the Auth0 system.

Once a successful login is completed, the Auth0 backend receives the data from the response and processes it. The associated data is attached to the user object associated with the request. In the dashboard view, reached as a result of authentication proceeding to `LOGIN_REDIRECT_URL`, user details are extracted and added to the template context. `dashboard.html` is then rendered, and the result might appear as something like this:

The logout button presented on the dashboard will proceed to log the user back out, ultimately taking them to the configured `LOGOUT_REDIRECT_URL`.

There's more...

In addition to simple login handling, as shown here, Auth0 provides a multitude of more advanced features, including the following:

- Single sign-on across applications
- Connectivity to LDAP and AD systems

- Multi-factor authentication for an increased level of security
- Support for a variety of passwordless logins, even fingerprint scanning

See also

- The *Implementing password validation* recipe
- The *Downloading authorized files* recipe

Caching the method return value

If you call a model method with heavy calculations or database queries multiple times in the request-response cycle, the performance of the view might be very slow. In this recipe, you will learn about a pattern that you can use to cache the return value of a method for later repetitive use. Note that we are not using the Django cache framework here, only what Python provides us by default.

Getting ready

Choose an app with a model that has a time-consuming method that will be used repetitively in the same request-response cycle.

How to do it...

Perform the following steps:

1. This is a pattern that you can use to cache a method return value of a model for repetitive use in views, forms, or templates, as follows:

```
class SomeModel(models.Model):
    # ...
    def some_expensive_function(self):
        if not hasattr(self, "_expensive_value_cached"):
            # do some heavy calculations...
            # ... and save the result to result variable
            self._expensive_value_cached = result
        return self._expensive_value_cached
```

2. For example, let's create a `get_thumbnail_url()` method for the `ViralVideo` model created in the *Using database query expressions* recipe in `Chapter 11`, *Bells and Whistles*:

```python
# viral_videos/models.py
import re
# ... other imports ...


class ViralVideo(CreationModificationDateMixin, UrlMixin):
    # ...
    def get_thumbnail_url(self):
        if not hasattr(self, "_thumbnail_url_cached"):
            url_pattern = re.compile(
                r'src="https://www.youtube.com/embed/([^"]+)"'
            )
            match = url_pattern.search(self.embed_code)
            self._thumbnail_url_cached = ""
            if match:
                video_id = match.groups()[0]
                self._thumbnail_url_cached = \
                    f"http://img.youtube.com/vi/{video_id}/0.jpg"

        return self._thumbnail_url_cached
```

How it works...

In the generic example, the method checks whether the `_expensive_value_cached` attribute exists for the model instance. If it doesn't exist, the time-consuming calculations are done and the result is assigned to this new attribute. At the end of the method, the cached value is returned. Of course, if you have several weighty methods, you will need to use different attribute names to save each calculated value.

You can now use something such as `{{ object.some_expensive_function }}` in the header and footer of a template, and the time-consuming calculations will be done just once.

In a template, you can also use the function in both the `{% if %}` condition and the output of the value, as follows:

```
{% if object.some_expensive_function %}
    <span class="special">
        {{ object.some_expensive_function }}
    </span>
{% endif %}
```

In this example, we are checking the thumbnail of a YouTube video by parsing the URL of the video's embed code, getting its ID, and then composing the URL of the thumbnail image. Then, you can use it in a template as follows:

```
{% if video.get_thumbnail_url %}
    <figure>
        <img src="{{ video.get_thumbnail_url }}"
            alt="{{ video.title }}">
        <figcaption>{{ video.title }}</figcaption>
    </figure>
{% endif %}
```

There's more...

This approach only works if the method is called without arguments, such that the result will always be the same, but what if the input varies? Since Python 3.2, there is a decorator we can use to provide basic **Least Recently Used** (**LRU**) caching of method calls based on a hash of the arguments (at least those that are hashable).

For example, let's look at a contrived and trivial example with a function that takes in two values and returns the result of some expensive logic:

```
def busy_bee(a, b):
    # expensive logic
    return result
```

If we had such a function, and wanted to provide a cache to store the result of commonly used input variations, we could do so easily with the `lru_cache` decorator from the `functools` package, as follows:

```
from functools import lru_cache

@lru_cache(maxsize=100, typed=True)
def busy_bee(a, b):
    # ...
```

Now, we have provided a caching mechanism that will store up to `100` results under keys hashed from the input. The `typed` option was added in Python 3.3 and, by specifying `True`, we have made it so that a call having *a=1* and *b=2.0* will be stored separately from one with *a=1.0* and *b=2*. Depending on how the logic operates and what the return value is, such variation may or may not be appropriate.

 Learn more about the `lru_cache` decorator in the `functools` documentation at `https://docs.python.org/3/library/functools.html#functools.lru_cache`.

We could use this decorator for the examples earlier in this recipe to simplify the code, though we would probably use `maxsize` of 1 since there are no input variations to deal with, as in the following:

```python
# viral_videos/models.py
from functools import lru_cache
# ... other imports ...


class ViralVideo(CreationModificationDateMixin, UrlMixin):
    # ...
    @lru_cache(maxsize=1)
    def get_thumbnail_url(self):
        # ...
```

See also

- Refer to `Chapter 4`, *Templates and JavaScript*, for more details
- The *Using Memcached to cache Django views* recipe
- The *Using Redis to cache Django views* recipe

Using Memcached to cache Django views

Django provides a possibility to speed up the request-response cycle by caching the most expensive parts such as database queries or template rendering. The fastest and most reliable caching natively supported by Django is the memory-based cache server Memcached. In this recipe, you will learn how to use Memcached to cache a view for the `viral_videos` app, created in the *Using database query expressions* recipe in `Chapter 11`, *Bells and Whistles*.

Getting ready

There are several things to do in order to prepare caching for your Django project. First, let's examine how this would be done for a virtual environment project:

1. Install the `memcached` server, as follows:

    ```
    $ wget http://memcached.org/files/memcached-1.5.7.tar.gz
    $ tar -zxvf memcached-1.4.23.tar.gz
    $ cd memcached-1.4.23
    $ ./configure && make && make test && sudo make install
    ```

2. Start the `memcached` server, as shown in the following:

    ```
    $ memcached -d
    ```

3. Install Memcached Python bindings in your virtual environment, as follows:

    ```
    (myproject_env)$ pip3 install python-memcached~=1.59.0
    ```

If using a Docker environment, follow these steps instead:

1. Update your `docker-compose.yml` file to associate a Memcached container with your app, as in the following:

    ```
    # docker-compose.yml
    version: '3'
    services:
      # ...
      memcached:
        image: 'memcached:1.5'
      app:
        # ...
        environment:
          # ...
          - "CACHE_LOCATION=memcached:11211"
    ```

2. Include the Memcached Python bindings in the requirements for your app container, like so:

    ```
    # requirements.txt or requirements/base.txt
    # ...
    python-memcached~=1.59.0
    ```

3. Stop, build, and restart your containers.

How to do it...

To integrate caching for your specific views, perform the following steps:

1. Set `CACHES` in the project settings, as follows:

```
CACHES = {
    'memcached': {
        'BACKEND': 'django.core.cache.backends.'
                   'memcached.MemcachedCache',
        'LOCATION': os.environ.get('CACHE_LOCATION',
                                   '127.0.0.1:11211'),
        "TIMEOUT": 60, # 1 minute
        "KEY_PREFIX": os.environ.get('CACHE_KEY',
                                     'myproject_production'),
    },
}
CACHES['default'] = CACHES['memcached']
```

2. Modify the views of the `viral_videos` app, as follows:

```
# viral_videos/views.py
from django.views.decorators.cache import cache_page
from django.views.decorators.vary import vary_on_cookie


@vary_on_cookie
@cache_page(60)
def viral_video_detail(request, id):
    # ...
```

> If you follow the Redis setup in the next recipe, there is no change whatsoever in the `views.py` file. That shows how we can change the underlying caching mechanism at will without ever needing to modify the code that uses it.

How it works...

Now, if you access the first viral video (such as at `/en/viral-videos/1/`) and refresh the page a few times, you will see that the number of impressions changes only once a minute. This is because each request is cached for 60 seconds for every user. We set caching for the view using the `@cache_page` decorator.

Memcached is a key-value store and it uses the full URL by default to generate the key for each cached page. When two visitors access the same page simultaneously, the first visitor's request would receive the page generated by the Python code, and the second one would get the same HTML code but from the Memcached server.

In our example, to ensure that each visitor gets treated separately even if they access the same URL, we are using the @vary_on_cookie decorator. This decorator checks the uniqueness of the Cookie header of the HTTP request.

 Learn more about Django's cache framework from the official documentation at https://docs.djangoproject.com/en/2.1/topics/cache/. Similarly, more details on Memcached can be found at https://memcached.org/.

See also

- The *Caching the method return value* recipe
- The *Using Redis to cache Django views* recipe
- The *Using database query expressions* recipe in Chapter 11, *Bells and Whistles*

Using Redis to cache Django views

Although Memcached is well established in the market as a caching mechanism, and well supported by Django, an alternate system that provides all the functionality of Memcached and more is Redis. Here, we'll revisit the process from the *Using Memcached to cache Django views* recipe, and learn how to do the same using Redis instead.

Getting ready

There are several things to do in order to prepare caching for your Django project. First, let's examine how this would be done for a virtual environment project:

1. Install Redis server, as follows:

```
$ wget http://download.redis.io/releases/redis-4.0.9.tar.gz
$ tar -zxvf redis-4.0.9.tar.gz
$ cd redis-4.0.9
$ make
```

2. Create a configuration file to run Redis as a LRU key/value cache, like Memcached is:

```
# config/redis.conf
maxmemory 100mb
maxmemory-policy allkeys-lru
```

3. Start Redis server using the custom configuration, as shown in the following:

```
$ cd src
$ ./redis-server /path/to/config/redis.conf
```

4. Install the Redis cache backend for Django in your virtual environment, as follows:

```
(myproject_env)$ pip3 install django-redis~=4.9.0
```

If using a Docker environment, follow these steps instead:

1. Update your docker-compose.yml file to associate a Redis container with your app, as in the following:

```
# docker-compose.yml
version: '3'
services:
  # ...
  redis:
    image: 'redis:4.9'
    volumes:
      - './config/redis.conf:/usr/local/etc/redis/redis.conf'
  app:
    # ...
    environment:
      # ...
      - 'CACHE_LOCATION=redis://redis:6379'
```

2. Include the Redis cache backend for Django in the requirements for your app container, like so:

```
# requirements.txt or requirements/base.txt
# ...
django-redis~=4.9.0
```

3. Stop, build, and restart your containers.

How to do it...

To integrate caching for your specific views, perform the following steps:

1. Set CACHES in the project settings, as follows:

```
CACHES = {
    # ...
    'redis': {
        'BACKEND': 'django_redis.cache.RedisCache',
        'LOCATION': os.environ.get('CACHE_LOCATION',
                                   'redis://127.0.0.1:6379/1'),
        "TIMEOUT": 60, # 1 minute
        "KEY_PREFIX": os.environ.get('CACHE_KEY',
                                     'myproject_production'),
        'OPTIONS': {
            'CLIENT_CLASS': 'django_redis.client.DefaultClient',
            'IGNORE_EXCEPTIONS': True,
        },
    },
}
CACHES['default'] = CACHES['redis']
```

2. Modify the views of the viral_videos app, as follows:

```
# viral_videos/views.py
from django.views.decorators.cache import cache_page
from django.views.decorators.vary import vary_on_cookie


@vary_on_cookie
@cache_page(60)
def viral_video_detail(request, id):
    # ...
```

If you followed the Memcached setup from the previous recipe, there is no change whatsoever in the views.py here. That shows how we can change the underlying caching mechanism at will without ever needing to modify the code that uses it.

How it works...

Now, if you access the first viral video (such as at /en/viral-videos/1/) and refresh the page a few times, you will see that the number of impressions changes only once a minute. This is because each request is cached for 60 seconds for every user. We set caching for the view using the @cache_page decorator.

Just like Memcached, Redis is a key-value store, and when used for caching it generates the key for each cached page based on the full URL. When two visitors access the same page simultaneously, the first visitor's request would receive the page generated by the Python code, and the second one would get the same HTML code but from the Redis server.

In our example, to ensure that each visitor gets treated separately even if they access the same URL, we are using the @vary_on_cookie decorator. This decorator checks the uniqueness of the Cookie header of the HTTP request.

 Learn more about Django's cache framework from the official documentation at https://docs.djangoproject.com/en/2.1/topics/cache/. Similarly, more details on Redis can be found at https://redis.io/.

There's more...

While Redis is able to handle caching in the same manner as Memcached, there are a multitude of additional options for the caching algorithm built right in to the system. In addition to caching, Redis can also be used as a database or message store. It supports a variety of data structures, transactions, pub/sub, and automatic failover, among other things.

Through the django-redis backend, Redis can also be configured as the session backend with almost no effort, like so:

```
# settings.py or config/base.py
SESSION_ENGINE = 'django.contrib.sessions.backends.cache'
SESSION_CACHE_ALIAS = 'default'
```

See the documentation of django-redis at http://niwinz.github.io/django-redis/latest/ for more possibilities.

See also

- The *Caching the method return value* recipe
- The *Using Memcached to cache Django views* recipe
- The *Using database query expressions* recipe in Chapter 11, *Bells and Whistles*

8
Django CMS

In this chapter, we will cover the following recipes:

- Creating templates for Django CMS
- Structuring the page menu
- Converting an app to a CMS app
- Attaching your own navigation
- Writing your own CMS plugin
- Adding new fields to the CMS page

Introduction

Django CMS is an open source content management system that is based on Django and was created by Divio AG, Switzerland. Django CMS takes care of a website's structure, provides navigation menus, makes it easy to edit page content in the frontend, and supports using multiple languages on a website. You can also extend it to suit your own needs by using the provided hooks. To create a website, you have to create a hierarchical structure of pages, where each page has a template. Templates have placeholders that can be assigned different plugins with the content. Using special template tags, the menus can be generated out of the hierarchical page structure. The CMS takes care of mapping URLs to specific pages.

In this chapter, we will look at Django CMS 3.6 from a developer's perspective. You will see what is necessary for the templates to function, and we will take a look at the possible page structure for header and footer navigation. You will also learn how to attach the URL rules of an app to a CMS page tree node. Then, we will attach custom navigation to the page menu and create our own CMS content plugins. Finally, you will learn how to add new fields to the CMS pages.

At the time of writing, Django CMS 3.6 has not yet been released, and several plugins are also incompatible with Django 2.*x*. The examples have been written based on the in-development version, which is slated to be released as version 3.6, soon after this book is published.

In this book, we won't guide you through all of the bits and pieces of using Django CMS, but by the end of this chapter, you will be aware of its purpose and use. The rest can be learned from the official documentation at http://docs.django-cms.org/en/latest/, and by trying out the frontend user interface of the CMS.

Creating templates for Django CMS

For every page in your page structure, you have to choose a template from the list of templates that are defined in the settings. In this recipe, we will look at the minimum requirements for the templates.

Getting ready

If you want to start a new Django CMS project, execute the following commands in a virtual environment, and answer all of the prompted questions:

```
(myproject_env)$ pip3 install djangocms-installer
(myproject_env)$ djangocms -p project/myproject myproject
```

Here, project/myproject is the path where the project will be created, and myproject is the project name.

On the other hand, if you want to integrate Django CMS into an existing project, check the official documentation at http://docs.django-cms.org/en/latest/how_to/install.html. If you are working with a Docker project, a good place to start from is the *Minimally-required applications and settings* section. We will proceed by modifying our existing example project, with this integration already completed.

How to do it...

We will update the Bootstrap-powered `base.html` template, so that it contains everything that Django CMS needs. Then, we will create and register two templates, `default.html` and `start.html`, to choose from for CMS pages:

1. First, we will update the base template that we created in the *Arranging the base.html template* recipe in `Chapter 4`, *Templates and JavaScript*, as follows:

```
{# templates/base.html #}
<!doctype html>
{% load i18n static cms_tags sekizai_tags menu_tags %}
<html lang="{{ LANGUAGE_CODE }}">
<head>
    <meta charset="utf-8">
    <meta name="viewport"
        content="width=device-width, initial-scale=1">
    <title>
        {% block title %}{% endblock %}{% trans "My Website" %}
    </title>
    <link rel="icon" type="image/x-icon"
        href="{% static 'site/img/favicon.ico' %}">

    {% block meta_tags %}{% endblock %}

    {% render_block "css" %}
    {% block base_stylesheet %}
        <link rel="stylesheet" type="text/css"
href="http://code.ionicframework.com/ionicons/2.0.1/css/ionicons.mi
n.css">
        <link rel="stylesheet"
href="https://stackpath.bootstrapcdn.com/bootstrap/4.1.3/css/bootst
rap.min.css"
            integrity="sha384-
MCw98/SFnGE8fJT3GXwEOngsV7Zt27NXFoaoApmYm81iuXoPkFOJwJ8ERdknLPMO"
            crossorigin="anonymous">
        <link rel="stylesheet" type="text/css" media="screen"
            href="{% static 'site/css/style.css' %}">
    {% endblock %}
    {% block stylesheet %}{% endblock %}

    {% block extrahead %}{% endblock %}
</head>
<body class="{% block bodyclass %}{% endblock %}">
{% cms_toolbar %}
{% block page %}
<section class="wrapper">
```

```
    <header class="clearfix container navbar navbar-expand-lg
                   navbar-light bg-light mb-4 mx-0">
        <h1 class="navbar-brand col mb-0">{% trans "My Website"
%}</h1>
        <nav role="navigation" class="navbar-nav col-10">
            {% block header_navigation %}
            <ul class="navbar-nav col">
                {% show_menu_below_id "start-page" 0 1 1 1 %}
            </ul>
            {% endblock %}
            {% block language_chooser %}
            <ul class="navbar-nav col-3">
                {% language_chooser %}
            </ul>
            {% endblock %}
        </nav>
    </header>
    {% block container %}
    <div id="content" class="clearfix container">
        {% block content %}{% endblock %}
    </div>
    {% endblock %}
    <footer class="clearfix container">
        {% block footer_navigation %}
        <nav class="navbar navbar-default" role="navigation">
            <ul class="nav navbar-nav">
                {% show_menu_below_id "footer-navigation" 0 1 1 1
%}
            </ul>
        </nav>
        {% endblock %}
    </footer>
</section>
{% endblock %}
{% block extrabody %}{% endblock %}

{% block base_js %}
    <script src="https://code.jquery.com/jquery-3.3.1.min.js"
            integrity="sha256-
FgpCb/KJQlLNfOu91ta32o/NMZxltwRo8QtmkMRdAu8="
            crossorigin="anonymous"></script>
    <script
src="https://cdnjs.cloudflare.com/ajax/libs/popper.js/1.14.3/umd/po
pper.min.js"
            integrity="sha384-
ZMP7rVo3mIykV+2+9J3UJ46jBk0WLaUAdn689aCwoqbBJiSnjAK/l8WvCWPIPm49"
            crossorigin="anonymous"></script>
    <script
```

```
        src="https://stackpath.bootstrapcdn.com/bootstrap/4.1.3/js/bootstra
        p.min.js"
                    integrity="sha384-
        ChfqqxuZUCnJSK3+MXmPNIyE6ZbWh2IMqE241rYiqJxyMiZ60W/JmZQ5stwEULTy"
                    crossorigin="anonymous"></script>
            <script src="{% url "js_settings" %}"></script>
        {% endblock %}
        {% block js %}{% endblock %}
        {% render_block "js" %}
        </body>
        </html>
```

2. Then, we will create a cms directory under templates and add two templates for CMS pages, the first of which is default.html, for normal pages:

```
{# templates/cms/default.html #}
{% extends "base.html" %}
{% load cms_tags %}

{% block title %}{% page_attribute "page_title" %} - {% endblock %}

{% block meta_tags %}
    <meta name="description"
          content="{% page_attribute meta_description %}"/>
{% endblock %}

{% block content %}
    <h1>{% page_attribute "page_title" %}</h1>
    <div class="row">
        <div class="col-md-8">{% placeholder main_content %}</div>
        <div class="col-md-4">{% placeholder sidebar %}</div>
    </div>
{% endblock %}
```

3. Then, we will add start.html for the home page, as follows:

```
{# templates/cms/start.html #}
{% extends "base.html" %}
{% load cms_tags %}

{% block meta_tags %}
    <meta name="description"
          content="{% page_attribute meta_description %}"/>
{% endblock %}

{% block content %}
```

```
{% comment %}
Here goes very customized website-specific content like
slideshows, latest tweets, latest news, latest profiles, etc.
{% endcomment %}
{% endblock %}
```

4. Finally, we will set the paths of these two templates in the settings, as shown in the following code snippet:

```
# settings.py or conf/base.py
from django.utils.translation import ugettext_lazy as _
# ...
CMS_TEMPLATES = (
    ("cms/default.html", _("Default")),
    ("cms/start.html", _("Homepage")),
)
```

How it works...

As usual, the `base.html` template is the main template that is extended by all of the other templates. In this template, Django CMS uses the `{% render_block %}` template tag from the `django-sekizai` module to inject CSS and JavaScript into the templates that create a toolbar and other administration widgets in the frontend. We will insert the `{% cms_toolbar %}` template tag at the beginning of the `<body>` section; that's where the toolbar will be placed. We will use the `{% show_menu_below_id %}` template tag to render the header and footer menus from the specific page menu trees. Also, we will use the `{% language_chooser %}` template tag to render the language chooser that switches to the same page in different languages. All of the navigation is enhanced with Bootstrap 4 classes, for the navbar and other styling.

The `default.html` and `start.html` templates that are defined in the `CMS_TEMPLATES` setting will be available as a choice when creating a CMS page. In these templates, for each area that needs to have dynamically entered content, add a `{% placeholder %}` template tag (when you need page-specific content) or `{% static_placeholder %}` (when you need the content that is shared among different pages). Logged in administrators can add content plugins to the placeholders when they switch from the **Live** mode to the **Draft** mode in the CMS toolbar and switch to the **Structure** section.

Once the settings are correctly configured, the templates are in place, and all CMS-related static files have been collected, the default page content should look something like the following:

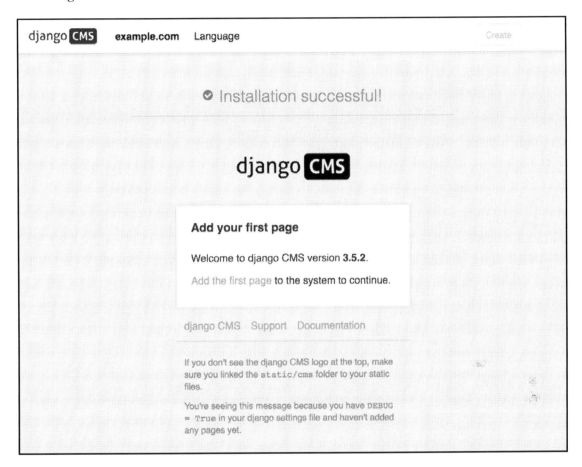

See also

- The *Arranging the base.html template* recipe in Chapter 4, *Templates and JavaScript*
- The *Structuring the page menu* recipe

Structuring the page menu

In this recipe, we will discuss some guidelines for defining the tree structures for the pages on your website.

Getting ready

It is a good practice to set the available languages for your website before creating the structure of your pages (although the Django CMS database structure also allows you to add new languages later on). Beside LANGUAGES, make sure that you have CMS_LANGUAGES set in your settings. The CMS_LANGUAGES setting defines which languages should be active for each Django site, as follows:

```
# conf/base.py or settings.py
# ...
gettext = lambda s: s

LANGUAGES = (
    ("en", "English"),
    ("de", "Deutsch"),
    ("fr", "Français"),
    ("lt", "Lietuvių kalba"),
)

CMS_LANGUAGES = {
    "default": {
        "public": True,
        "hide_untranslated": False,
        "redirect_on_fallback": True,
    },
    1: [
        {
```

```
                "public": True,
                "code": "en",
                "hide_untranslated": False,
                "name": gettext("en"),
                "redirect_on_fallback": True,
            },
            {
                "public": True,
                "code": "de",
                "hide_untranslated": False,
                "name": gettext("de"),
                "redirect_on_fallback": True,
            },
            {
                "public": True,
                "code": "fr",
                "hide_untranslated": False,
                "name": gettext("fr"),
                "redirect_on_fallback": True,
            },
            {
                "public": True,
                "code": "lt",
                "hide_untranslated": False,
                "name": gettext("lt"),
                "redirect_on_fallback": True,
            },
        ],
    }
```

How to do it...

The page navigation is set in tree structures. The first tree is the main tree, and, contrary to the other trees, the root node of the main tree is not reflected in the URL structure. The root node of this tree is the home page of the website. Usually, this page has a specific template, where you add the content aggregated from different apps, for example, a slideshow, actual news, newly registered users, the latest tweets, or other latest or featured objects.

For a convenient way to render items from different apps, check the *Creating a template tag to a QuerySet in a template* recipe in `Chapter 5`, *Custom Template Filters and Tags*.

1. If your website has multiple navigation types, such as a top, meta, and footer navigation, give an ID to the root node of each tree in the **Advanced Settings** of the page. This ID will be used in the base template with the `{% show_menu_below_id %}` template tag. The **Advanced Settings** will look something like the following:

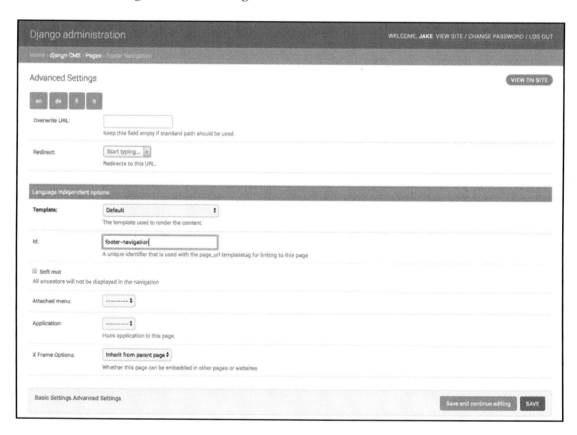

You can read more about this and other menu-related template tags in the official documentation at
`http://docs.django-cms.org/en/latest/reference/navigation.html`.

2. The first tree defines the main structure of the website. If you want a page under the root-level URL (for example, `/en/search/` but not `/en/meta/search/`), put this page under the home page. If you don't want a page to be shown in the menu, as it will be linked from an icon or widget, just hide it from the menu.

3. The footer navigation usually shows items different from the top navigation, with some of the items being repeated. For example, the page for developers will only be shown in the footer, whereas the page for news will be shown in both the header and footer. For all of the repeated items, just create a page with the **Redirect** setting in the advanced settings of the page and set it to the original page in the main tree. By default, when you create a secondary tree structure, all pages under the root of that tree will include the slug of the root page in their URL paths. If you want to skip the slug of the root in the URL path, you will need to set the **Overwrite URL** setting in the advanced settings of the page; for example, the developers page should be under `/en/developers/`, not `/en/secondary/developers/`.

How it works...

Finally, your page structure will look similar to the following screenshot (of course, the page structure can be much more complex, too):

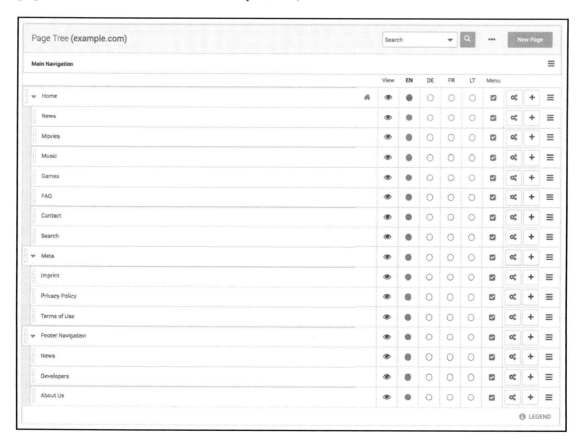

See also

- The *Creating a template tag to load a QuerySet in a template* recipe in `Chapter 5,` *Custom Template Filters and Tags*
- The *Creating templates for Django CMS* recipe
- The *Attaching your own navigation* recipe

Converting an app to a CMS app

The simplest Django CMS website will have the whole page tree created by using an administration interface. However, for real-world cases, you will probably need to show forms or lists of your modeled objects under some page nodes. If you have created an app that is responsible for some types of objects on your website, such as `movies`, you can easily convert it to a Django CMS app and attach it to one of the pages. This will ensure that the root URL of the app is translatable and the menu item is highlighted when selected. In this recipe, we will convert the `movies` app to a CMS app.

Getting ready

Let's start with the `movies` app that we created in the *Filtering object lists* recipe in `Chapter 3,` *Forms and Views*.

How to do it...

Follow these steps to convert a usual `movies` Django app to a Django CMS app:

1. First of all, remove or comment out the inclusion of the URL configuration of the app, as it will be included by `apphook` in Django CMS, as follows:

```
# myproject/urls.py
# ...
urlpatterns = [
    # ...
    # remove or comment out the inclusion of app's urls
    # path("movies/", include("movies.urls")),
    # ...
]
```

2. Create a `cms_apps.py` file in the `movies` directory and create `MoviesApphook` there, as follows:

```python
# movies/cms_apps.py
from cms.app_base import CMSApp
from cms.apphook_pool import apphook_pool
from django.utils.translation import ugettext_lazy as _


@apphook_pool.register
class MoviesApphook(CMSApp):
    app_name = "movies"
    name = _("Movies")

    def get_urls(self, page=None, language=None, **kwargs):
        return ["movies.urls"]
```

3. By default, the CMS will automatically discover your apphooks by searching each app in `INSTALLED_APPS` for the preceding magic file. If you only want to wire in specific apps instead, you can set the newly created `apphook` in the `CMS_APPHOOKS` settings, as shown in the following code:

```python
# settings.py or config/base.py
CMS_APPHOOKS = (
    # ...
    "movies.cms_apps.MoviesApphook",
)
```

4. Finally, in all of the movie templates, change the first line to extend from the template of the current CMS page, instead of extending `base.html`, as follows:

```
{# templates/movies/movies_list.html #}
{% comment %}
Change {% extends "base.html" %} to: {% endcomment %}
{% extends CMS_TEMPLATE %}
```

How it works...

The apphooks are the interfaces that join the URL configuration of apps to the CMS pages. The apphooks need to extend from CMSApp. To define the name, which will be shown in the **Application** selection list under the **Advanced Settings** of a page, put the path of the apphook in the CMS_APPHOOKS project setting (only if automatic discovery is not desired), and restart the web server. The apphook will appear as one of the applications in the advanced page settings, as shown in the following screenshot:

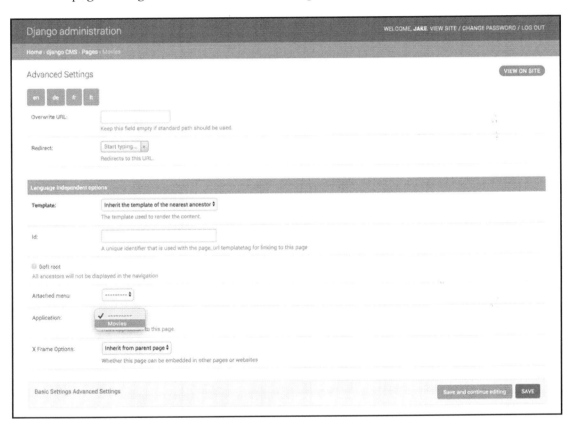

After selecting an application for a page and publishing it, you must restart the server for the URLs to take effect, unless you have included `cms.middleware.utils.ApphookReloadMiddleware` as close to the start of your `MIDDLEWARE` list as possible, in `settings.py`. This middleware handles reloading the application automatically; in many cases, a restart would otherwise be necessary.

The templates of the app should extend the page template if you want them to contain the placeholders or attributes of the page, such as the `title` or the `description` meta tags.

See also

- The *Filtering object lists* recipe in Chapter 3, *Forms and Views*
- The *Attaching your own navigation* recipe

Attaching your own navigation

Once you have an app hooked in the CMS pages, all of the URL paths under the page node will be controlled by the `urls.py` file of the app. To add some menu items under this page, you need to add a dynamic branch of navigation to the page tree. In this recipe, we will improve the `movies` app that was converted for CMS use in the previous recipe, and we will add new navigation items under the **Movies** page.

Getting ready

Suppose that we have a URL configuration for different lists of movies—editor's picks, commercial movies, and independent movies - as shown in the following code:

```
# movies/urls.py
from django.shortcuts import redirect
from django.urls import path
from django.conf.urls.i18n import i18n_patterns
```

```
from .views import (FeaturedMoviesView, CommercialMoviesView,
                    IndependentMoviesView, TopMoviesView,
 MovieDetailView)


urlpatterns = i18n_patterns(
    # path('', movie_list, name='movie-list'),
    path('', lambda request: redirect('featured-movies')),
    path('editors-picks/', FeaturedMoviesView.as_view(),
        name='featured-movies'),
    path('commercial/', CommercialMoviesView.as_view(),
        name='commercial-movies'),
    path('independent/', IndependentMoviesView.as_view(),
        name='independent-movies'),
    path('top/', TopMoviesView.as_view(),
        name='top-movies'),
    path('movie/', lambda request: redirect('featured-movies')),
    path('movie/<slug:slug>/', MovieDetailView.as_view(),
        name='movie-detail'),
)
```

The `Movie` model would need to include a few new, simple fields, as follows:

```
# movies/models.py
# ...other imports...
from django.db import models

# ...

class Movie(models.Model):
    # ...
    featured = models.BooleanField(default=False)
    commercial = models.BooleanField(default=False)
    independent = models.BooleanField(default=False)
    # ...
```

To support the added differentiation, we also extend `MovieListView` to provide the additional view filtering variations, as follows:

```
# movies/views.py
# ...other imports...
from django.views.generic import View

# ...
```

```
class MovieListView(View):
    # ...


class FeaturedMoviesView(MovieListView):
    def get_queryset_and_facets(self, form):
        qs, facets = super().get_queryset_and_facets(form)
        qs.filter(featured=True)
        return qs, facets


class CommercialMoviesView(MovieListView):
    def get_queryset_and_facets(self, form):
        qs, facets = super().get_queryset_and_facets(form)
        qs.filter(commercial=True)
        return qs, facets


class IndependentMoviesView(MovieListView):
    def get_queryset_and_facets(self, form):
        qs, facets = super().get_queryset_and_facets(form)
        qs.filter(independent=True)
        return qs, facets
```

The MovieDetailView will be defined as follows:

```
# movies/views.py
# ...other imports...
from django.views.generic import DetailView

# ...

class MovieDetailView(DetailView):
    model = Movie
    template_name = "movies/movie_detail.html"
```

How to do it...

Follow these two steps to attach the **Editor's Picks**, **Commercial Movies**, and **Independent Movies** menu choices to the navigational menu under the **Movies** page:

1. Create a `cms_menus.py` file in the `Movies` app and add the `MoviesMenu` class, as follows:

```python
# movies/cms_menus.py
from django.urls import reverse
from django.utils.translation import ugettext_lazy as _
from cms.menu_bases import CMSAttachMenu
from menus.base import NavigationNode
from menus.menu_pool import menu_pool


@menu_pool.register_menu
class MoviesMenu(CMSAttachMenu):
    name = _("Movies Menu")

    def get_nodes(self, request):
        nodes = [
            NavigationNode(title=_("Editor Picks"),
                           url=reverse("movies:featured-movies"),
                           id=1),
            NavigationNode(title=_("Commercial Movies"),
                           url=reverse("movies:commercial-movies"),
                           id=2),
            NavigationNode(title=_("Independent Movies"),
                           url=reverse("movies:independent-
movies"),
                           id=3),
            NavigationNode(title=_("Top 250 Movies"),
                           url=reverse("movies:top-movies"),
                           id=4),
        ]
        return nodes
```

2. Restart the web server, then edit the **Advanced Settings** of the **Movies** page and select the **Movies** menu for the **Attached menu** setting, which resembles the following screenshot:

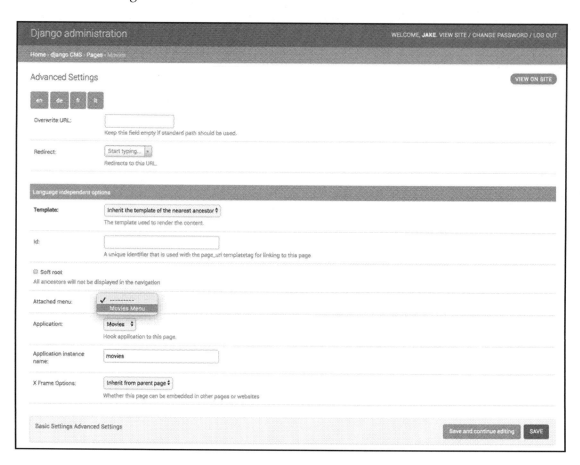

Restarts can often be avoided if you include the `cms.middleware.utils.ApphookReloadMiddleware` as close to the start of your `MIDDLEWARE` list as possible in `settings.py`. This middleware handles reloading the application automatically in many cases when a restart would otherwise be necessary.

How it works...

In the frontend, you will see the new menu items attached to the **Movies** page item in the navigation, similar to the result shown in the following screenshot:

Dynamic menus that can be attached to pages need to extend CMSAttachMenu, define the name by which they will be selected, and define the get_nodes() method that returns a list of NavigationNode objects. The NavigationNode class takes at least three parameters, as follows:

- The title of the menu item
- The URL path of the menu item
- The ID of the node

In this case, we have used reverse() lookups for the URLs (including the app name as a prefix) so that the lookup can find the right mappings from movies/urls.py. The IDs can be chosen freely, with the only requirement being that they have to be unique among this attached menu. The other optional parameters, available but not used here, are as follows:

- parent_id: This is the ID of the parent node, if you want to create a hierarchical dynamic menu.
- parent_namespace: This is the name of another menu, if this node is to be attached to a different menu tree; for example, the name of this menu is MoviesMenu.

- `attr`: This is a dictionary of the additional attributes that can be used in a template or menu modifier.
- `visible`: This sets whether or not the menu item should be visible.

For other examples of attachable menus, refer to the official documentation at `http://docs.django-cms.org/en/latest/how_to/menus.html`.

See also

- The *Structuring the page menu* recipe
- The *Converting an app to a CMS app* recipe

Writing your own CMS plugin

Django CMS comes with a lot of content plugins that can be used in template placeholders, such as text, flash, picture, and Google Maps plugins. However, for more structured and better styled content from your own models, you will need custom plugins, which are not too difficult to implement. In this recipe, we will look at how to create a new plugin and have a custom layout for its data, depending on the chosen template of the page.

Getting ready

Let's create an `editorial` app and mention it in the `INSTALLED_APPS` setting. Also, we will need to create a `cms/magazine.html` template and add it to the `CMS_TEMPLATES` setting, with the `Magazine` label. You can simply duplicate the `cms/default.html` template for this.

How to do it...

To create the `EditorialContent` plugin, follow these steps:

1. In the `models.py` file of the newly created app, add the `EditorialContent` model extending from `CMSPlugin`, after which you will need to make and run migrations against the database. The `EditorialContent` model will have fields to store the `Title`, `Subtitle`, `Description`, `Website`, `Image`, `Image Caption`, and a CSS class:

```python
# editorial/models.py
import os

from django.db import models
from django.utils.translation import ugettext_lazy as _
from django.utils.timezone import now as tz_now
from cms.models import CMSPlugin


def upload_to(instance, filename):
    now = tz_now()
    filename_base, filename_ext = os.path.splitext(filename)
    return "editorial/%s%s" % (
        now.strftime("%Y/%m/%Y%m%d%H%M%S"),
        filename_ext.lower())


class EditorialContent(CMSPlugin):
    title = models.CharField(_("Title"),
                             max_length=255)
    subtitle = models.CharField(_("Subtitle"),
                                max_length=255,
                                blank=True)
    description = models.TextField(_("Description"),
                                   blank=True)
    website = models.CharField(_("Website"),
                               max_length=255,
                               blank=True)

    image = models.ImageField(_("Image"),
                              max_length=255,
                              upload_to=upload_to,
                              blank=True)
    image_caption = models.TextField(_("Image Caption"),
                                     blank=True)

    css_class = models.CharField(_("CSS Class"),
```

```
                                          max_length=255,
                                          blank=True)

        def __str__(self):
            return self.title

        class Meta:
            ordering = ["title"]
            verbose_name = _("Editorial content")
            verbose_name_plural = _("Editorial contents")
```

2. In the same app, create a `cms_plugins.py` file and add
   an `EditorialContentPlugin` class extending `CMSPluginBase`. This class is a
   little bit like `ModelAdmin`; it defines the appearance of administration settings
   for the plugin:

   ```python
   # editorial/cms_plugins.py
   from django.utils.translation import ugettext as _
   from cms.plugin_base import CMSPluginBase
   from cms.plugin_pool import plugin_pool

   from .models import EditorialContent


   class EditorialContentPlugin(CMSPluginBase):
       model = EditorialContent
       module = _("Editorial")
       name = _("Editorial Content")
       render_template = "cms/plugins/editorial_content.html"

       fieldsets = (
           (_("Main Content"), {
               "fields": (
                   "title", "subtitle", "description",
                   "website"),
               "classes": ["collapse open"]
           }),
           (_("Image"), {
               "fields": ("image", "image_caption"),
               "classes": ["collapse open"]
           }),
           (_("Presentation"), {
               "fields": ("css_class",),
               "classes": ["collapse closed"]
           }),
       )
   ```

```
def render(self, context, instance, placeholder):
    context.update({
        "object": instance,
        "placeholder": placeholder,
    })
    return context


plugin_pool.register_plugin(EditorialContentPlugin)
```

3. To specify which plugins go to which placeholders, rather than having plugins be available to all placeholders, you have to define the CMS_PLACEHOLDER_CONF setting. You can also define some extra context for the templates of the plugins that are rendered in a specific placeholder. Let's allow EditorialContentPlugin for the main_content placeholder and set the editorial_content_template context variable for the main_content placeholder in the cms/magazine.html template, as follows:

```
# settings.py
# ...other imports...
from django.utils.text import gettext_lazy as gettext
# ...
CMS_PLACEHOLDER_CONF = {
    "main_content": {
        "name": gettext("Main Content"),
        "plugins": (
            "EditorialContentPlugin",
            "TextPlugin",
        ),
    },
    "cms/magazine.html main_content": {
        "name": gettext("Magazine Main Content"),
        "plugins": (
            "EditorialContentPlugin",
            "TextPlugin"
        ),
        "extra_context": {
            "editorial_content_template":
                "cms/plugins/editorial_content/magazine.html",
        }
    },
}
```

4. Then, we will create two templates. One of them will be the
   `editorial_content.html` template. It checks whether the
   `editorial_content_template` context variable exists. If the variable exists,
   the template specified by the variable is included. Otherwise, it renders the
   default layout for editorial content:

```
{# templates/cms/plugins/editorial_content.html #}
{% load i18n %}

{% if editorial_content_template %}
{% include editorial_content_template %}
{% else %}
<div class="card bg-light mb-3 {% if object.css_class %}
        {{ object.css_class }}{% endif %}">
    <!-- editorial content for non-specific placeholders -->
    <figure class="figure">
        {% if object.image %}
        <img src="{{ object.image.url }}"
            class="figure-img img-fluid"
            alt="{{ object.image_caption|striptags }}">
        {% endif %}
        {% if object.image_caption %}
        <figcaption class="figure-caption text-center">
            {{ object.image_caption|safe }}
        </figcaption>
        {% endif %}
    </figure>
    <div class="card-body">
        <h3 class="card-title">{% if object.website %}
            <a href="{{ object.website }}">
                {{ object.title }}</a>{% else %}
            {{ object.title }}{% endif %}</h3>
        <h4 class="card-subtitle">{{ object.subtitle }}</h4>
        <div class="card-text">{{ object.description|safe }}</div>
    </div>
</div>
{% endif %}
```

5. The second template is a specific template for the EditorialContent plugin in the cms/magazine.html template. There's nothing too fancy here - just a change to the background color and the removal of the outer border via the bg-white border-0 Bootstrap-specific CSS classes for the container card container to make the main content plugin stand out:

```
{# templates/cms/plugins/editorial_content/magazine.html #}
{% load i18n %}
<div class="card bg-white border-0{% if object.css_class %}
           {{ object.css_class }}{% endif %}">
    <!-- editorial content for non-specific placeholders -->
    <figure class="figure">
        {% if object.image %}
        <img src="{{ object.image.url }}"
            class="figure-img img-fluid"
            alt="{{ object.image_caption|striptags }}">
        {% endif %}
        {% if object.image_caption %}
        <figcaption class="figure-caption text-center">
            {{ object.image_caption|safe }}
        </figcaption>
        {% endif %}
    </figure>
    <div class="card-body">
        <h3 class="card-title">{% if object.website %}
            <a href="{{ object.website }}">
                {{ object.title }}</a>{% else %}
            {{ object.title }}{% endif %}</h3>
        <h4 class="card-subtitle">{{ object.subtitle }}</h4>
        <div class="card-text">{{ object.description|safe }}</div>
    </div>
</div>
```

How it works...

If you go to the **Preview** mode of any CMS page and click on the **Toggle structure** panel (via the button at the far right of the CMS toolbar), you can add the **Editorial Content** plugin to a placeholder, as follows:

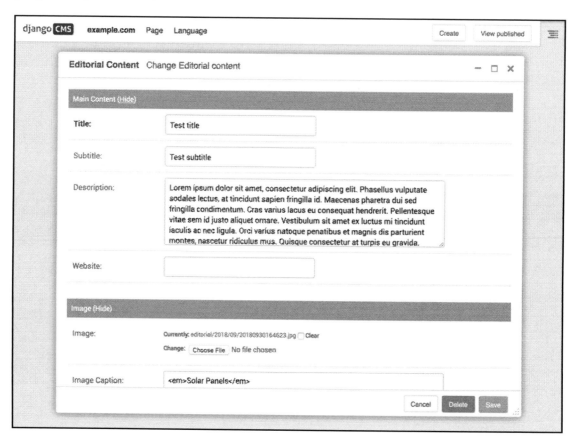

The content of this plugin will be rendered with a specified template, and it can also be customized, depending on the template of the page where the plugin is chosen. For example, choose the `cms/magazine.html` template for the **News** page, and then add the **Editorial Content** plugin. The **News** page might look similar to the following screenshot:

Here, the **Test title** with an image and description is the custom plugin inserted into the `main_content` placeholder in the `magazine.html` page template. If the page template were different, the plugin would be rendered with the same style as the plugin content in the sidebar, having a gray background and border. However, this differentiation could be much greater via making further modifications to the `editorial_content.html` template or providing other specialized templates.

See also

- The *Creating templates for Django CMS* recipe
- The *Structuring the page menu* recipe

Adding new fields to the CMS page

CMS pages have several multilingual fields, such as the title, slug, menu title, page title, description meta tag, and overwrite URL. They also have several common language-agnostic fields, such as the template, the ID used in the template tags, the attached application, and the attached menu. However, that might not be enough for more complex websites. Thankfully, Django CMS features a manageable mechanism to add new database fields for CMS pages. In this recipe, you will see how to add fields for the CSS classes, for the navigational menu items and page body.

Getting ready

Let's create the `cms_extensions` app and put it under `INSTALLED_APPS` in the settings.

How to do it...

To create a CMS page extension with the CSS class fields for the navigational menu items and page body, follow these steps:

1. In the `models.py` file, create a `CSSExtension` class extending `PageExtension`, registered in `extension_pool` and containing fields for the menu item's CSS class and `<body>` CSS class, as follows:

```python
# cms_extensions/models.py
from django.db import models
from django.utils.translation import ugettext_lazy as _
from cms.extensions import PageExtension
from cms.extensions.extension_pool import extension_pool

MENU_ITEM_CSS_CLASS_CHOICES = (
    ("featured", ".featured"),
)

BODY_CSS_CLASS_CHOICES = (
```

```
        ("serious", ".serious"),
        ("playful", ".playful"),
    )


    @extension_pool.register
    class CSSExtension(PageExtension):
        menu_item_css_class = models.CharField(
            _("Menu Item CSS Class"),
            max_length=200,
            blank=True,
            choices=MENU_ITEM_CSS_CLASS_CHOICES)
        body_css_class = models.CharField(
            _("Body CSS Class"),
            max_length=200,
            blank=True,
            choices=BODY_CSS_CLASS_CHOICES)
```

2. After migrating to incorporate the extension model into the database, add an `admin.py` file. In that file, register the minimum administration options for the CSSExtension model that we just created, as follows:

```
# cms_extensions/admin.py
from django.contrib import admin
from cms.extensions import PageExtensionAdmin
from .models import CSSExtension


class CSSExtensionAdmin(PageExtensionAdmin):
    pass


admin.site.register(CSSExtension, CSSExtensionAdmin)
```

3. Then, we need to show the CSS extension in the toolbar for each page. The code will need to check whether the user has the permission to change the current page; if so, it loads the page menu from the current toolbar and adds a new menu item, **CSS**, with the link to create or edit `CSSExtension`. This can be done by putting the following code into the `cms_toolbars.py` file of the app:

```python
# cms_extensions/cms_toolbars.py
from cms.api import get_page_draft
from cms.toolbar_pool import toolbar_pool
from cms.toolbar_base import CMSToolbar
from cms.utils.page_permissions import user_can_change_page
from django.urls import reverse, NoReverseMatch
from django.utils.translation import ugettext_lazy as _

from .models import CSSExtension


@toolbar_pool.register
class CSSExtensionToolbar(CMSToolbar):
    page = None

    def populate(self):
        # always use draft if we have a page
        self.page = get_page_draft(self.request.current_page)

        if not self.page:
            # Nothing to do
            return

        # check if user has page edit permission
        if user_can_change_page(user=self.request.user,
                                page=self.page):
            try:
                extension = CSSExtension.objects.get(
                    extended_object_id=self.page.id)
            except CSSExtension.DoesNotExist:
                extension = None

            try:
                if extension:
                    url = reverse(
                        "admin:cms_extensions_cssextension_change",
                        args=(extension.pk,))
                else:
                    url = reverse(
                        "admin:cms_extensions_cssextension_add")
                    url = f"{url}?extended_object={self.page.pk}"
```

```
        except NoReverseMatch:
            # not in urls
            pass
    else:
        not_edit_mode = not self.toolbar.edit_mode_active
        current_page_menu = self.toolbar.\
            get_or_create_menu("page")
        current_page_menu.add_modal_item(
            _("CSS"),
            url=url,
            disabled=not_edit_mode)
```

4. As we want to access the CSS extension in the navigation menu, in order to attach a CSS class, we need to create a menu modifier in the cms_menus.py file of the same app:

```
# cms_extensions/cms_menus.py
from cms.models import Page
from menus.base import Modifier
from menus.menu_pool import menu_pool


@menu_pool.register_modifier
class CSSModifier(Modifier):
    def modify(self, request, nodes, namespace, root_id, post_cut,
                breadcrumb):
        if post_cut:
            return nodes
        for node in nodes:
            try:
                page = Page.objects.get(pk=node.id)
            except:
                continue
            try:
                page.cssextension
            except:
                pass
            else:
                node.cssextension = page.cssextension
        return nodes
```

5. Then, we add the body CSS class to the `<body>` element in the `base.html` template, as follows:

```
{# templates/base.html #}
{# ... #}
<body class="{% block bodyclass %}{% endblock %}
            {% if request.current_page.css_extension %}
            {{ request.current_page.cssextension.body_css_class }}
            {% endif %}">
{# ... #}
```

6. Next, we will override the `menu.html` file, which is the default template for the navigation menu, to work with Bootstrap 4 and add the menu item's CSS class, like so:

```
{# templates/menu/menu.html #}
{% load menu_tags %}

{% for child in children %}
<li class="nav-item{% if child.selected %}
            selected{% endif %}{% if child.ancestor %}
            ancestor{% endif %}{% if child.sibling %}
            sibling{% endif %}{% if child.descendant %}
            descendant{% endif %}{% if child.children %}
            dropdown{% endif %}{% if child.cssextension %}
            {{ child.cssextension.menu_item_css_class }}{% endif
%}">
    {% if child.children %}
    <a id="dropdown-{{ child.get_menu_title|slugify }}"
       class="nav-link dropdown-toggle{% if child.selected %}
            active{% endif %}" href="#"
       role="button" data-toggle="dropdown"
       aria-haspopup="true" aria-expanded="false">
        {{ child.get_menu_title }}</a>
    <ul class="dropdown-menu"
        aria-labelledby="dropdown-{{ child.get_menu_title|slugify
}}">
        {% show_menu from_level to_level extra_inactive
extra_active template "" "" child %}
    </ul>
    {% else %}
    <a class="nav-link{% if child.selected %}
            active{% endif %}"
       href="{{
child.attr.redirect_url|default:child.get_absolute_url }}">
        {{ child.get_menu_title }}</a>
    {% endif %}
```

```
</li>
{% endfor %}
```

7. Finally, make and run migrations for the `cms_extensions` app, as follows:

```
(myproject_env)$ python3 manage.py makemigrations cms_extensions
(myproject_env)$ python3 manage.py migrate cms_extensions
```

How it works...

The `PageExtension` class is a model mixin with a one-to-one relationship with the `Page` model. To be able to administrate the custom extension model in Django CMS, there is a specific `PageExtensionAdmin` class to extend. Then, in the `cms_toolbars.py` file, we create the `CSSExtensionToolbar` class, inheriting from the `CMSToolbar` class, to create an item in the Django CMS toolbar. In the `populate()` method, we perform the general routine to check the page permissions, and then, we add a **CSS** menu item to the toolbar.

If the current user has permission to edit the page, they will see a **CSS** option in the toolbar, under the **Page** menu item, as shown in the following screenshot:

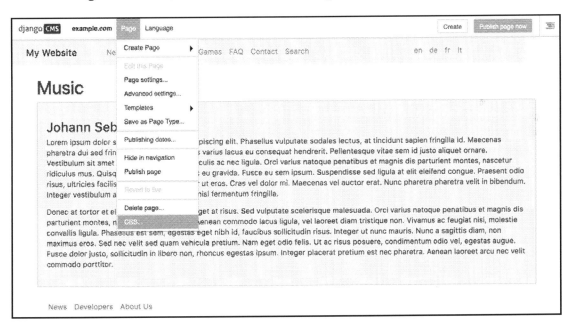

When the administrator clicks on the new menu item, a pop-up window will open, and they will be able to select the CSS classes for the navigation menu item and body, as shown in the following screenshot:

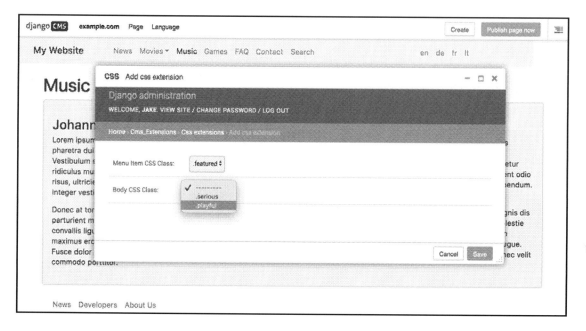

To show a specific CSS class from the page extension in the navigation menu, we need to attach the CSSExtension object to the navigation items. Then, these objects can be accessed in the menu.html template, as in {{ child.cssextension }}. In the end, you will see some navigation menu items highlighted, such as the **Music** item shown in the following screenshot (depending on your CSS):

It is much simpler to show a specific CSS class for `<body>` of the current page. We can use `{{ request.current_page.cssextension.body_css_class }}` right away, as the extension is attached to the page by Django CMS automatically.

See also

- The *Creating templates for Django CMS* recipe

Hierarchical Structures

9

In this chapter, we will cover the following recipes:

- Creating hierarchical categories with django-mptt
- Creating a category administration interface with django-mptt-admin
- Rendering categories in a template with django-mptt
- Using a single selection field to choose a category in forms with django-mptt
- Using a checkbox list to choose multiple categories in forms with django-mptt
- Creating hierarchical categories with django-treebeard
- Creating a basic category administration interface with django-treebeard

Introduction

Whether you build your own forum, threaded comments, or categorization system, there will be a moment when you need to save hierarchical structures in the database. Although the tables of relational databases (such as MySQL and PostgreSQL) are of a flat manner, there is a fast and effective way to store hierarchical structures. It is called **Modified Preorder Tree Traversal** (**MPTT**). MPTT allows you to read the tree structures without recursive calls to the database.

At first, let's get familiar with the terminology of the tree structures. A tree data structure is a nested collection of nodes, starting at the root node and having references to child nodes. There is a restriction that no node references back to create a loop and no reference is duplicated. The following are some other terms to learn:

- **Parent** is any node that has references to child nodes.
- **Descendants** are the nodes that can be reached by recursively traversing from a parent to its children. Therefore, a node's descendants will be its child, the child's children, and so on.

- **Ancestors** are the nodes that can be reached by recursively traversing from a child to its parent. Therefore, a node's ancestors will be its parent, the parent's parent, and so on up to the root.
- **Siblings** are nodes with the same parent.
- **Leaf** is a node without children.

Now, I'll explain how MPTT works. Imagine that you lay out your tree horizontally with the root node at the top. Each node in the tree has left and right values. Imagine them as small left and right handles on the left and right-hand side of the node. Then, you walk (traverse) around the tree counterclockwise, starting from the root node and mark each left or right value that you find with a number: 1, 2, 3, and so on. It will look similar to the following diagram:

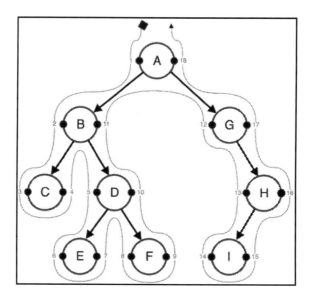

In the database table of this hierarchical structure, you have a title, left value, and right value for each node.

Now, if you want to get the subtree of the **B** node with **2** as the left value and **11** as the right value, you will have to select all of the nodes that have a left value between **2** and **11**. They are **C**, **D**, **E**, and **F**.

To get all of the ancestors of the **D** node with **5** as the left value and **10** as the right value, you have to select all of the nodes that have a left value that is less than **5** and a right value that is more than **10**. These would be **B** and **A**.

To get the number of the descendants for a node, you can use the following formula: *descendants = (right - left - 1) / 2.*

Therefore, the number of descendants for the **B** node can be calculated as shown in the following formula: *(11 - 2 - 1) / 2 = 4.*

If we want to attach the **E** node to the **C** node, we will have to update the left and right values only for the nodes of their first common ancestor, the **B** node. Then, the **C** node will still have **3** as the left value; the **E** node will get **4** as the left value and **5** as the right value; the right value of the **C** node will become **6**; the left value of the **D** node will become **7**; the left value of the **F** node will stay **8**; and the others will also remain the same.

Similarly, there are other tree-related operations with nodes in MPTT. It might be too complicated to manage all this by yourself for every hierarchical structure in your project. Luckily, there is a Django app called `django-mptt` that has a long history of handling these algorithms, and provides an easy API to handle the tree structures. Another app `django-treebeard` has also been tried and tested, and gained additional traction as a powerful alternative when it replaced MPTT in Django CMS 3.1. In this chapter, you will learn how to use these helper apps.

Creating hierarchical categories with django-mptt

To illustrate how to deal with MPTT, we will build on top of the `movies` app from the *Filtering object lists* recipe in `Chapter 3`, *Forms and Views*. In our changes, we will add a hierarchical `Category` model and update the `Movie` model to have a many-to-many relationship with the categories. Alternatively, you can create the app fresh, using only the content shown here to implement a very basic version of the `Movie` model from scratch.

Getting ready

To get started, perform the following steps:

1. Install `django-mptt` in your virtual environment using the following command (or add the same to your requirements file and rebuild if using a Docker project):

```
(myproject_env)$ pip3 install django-mptt~=0.9.1
```

2. Create the `movies` app if you have not done so already. Add the `movies` app as well as `mptt` to `INSTALLED_APPS` in the settings, as follows:

```python
# settings.py or config/base.py
INSTALLED_APPS = (
    # ...
    "mptt",
    "movies",
)
```

How to do it...

We will create a hierarchical `Category` model and tie it to the `Movie` model, which will have a many-to-many relationship with the categories, as follows:

1. Open the `models.py` file and add a `Category` model that extends `mptt.models.MPTTModel` and `CreationModificationDateMixin`, which we defined in Chapter 2, *Database Structure*. In addition to the fields coming from the mixins, the `Category` model will need to have a `parent` field of the `TreeForeignKey` type and a `title` field:

```python
# movies/models.py
from django.db import models
from django.utils.translation import ugettext_lazy as _
from mptt.models import MPTTModel
from mptt.fields import TreeForeignKey, TreeManyToManyField

from utils.models import CreationModificationDateMixin

RATING_CHOICES = (
    # ...
)


class Category(MPTTModel, CreationModificationDateMixin):
    class Meta:
        ordering = ["tree_id", "lft"]
        verbose_name = _("Category")
        verbose_name_plural = _("Categories")

    class MPTTMeta:
        order_insertion_by = ["title"]

    parent = TreeForeignKey("self",
                            on_delete=models.CASCADE,
```

```
                              blank=True,
                              null=True,
                              related_name="children")
        title = models.CharField(_("Title"),
                                  max_length=200)

    # ...
```

2. Update the `Movie` model to extend `CreationModificationDateMixin`. Also, make sure a `title` field is included and a `categories` field of the `TreeManyToManyField` type:

```
class Movie(models.Model):
    # ...
    categories = TreeManyToManyField(Category,
                                     verbose_name=_("Categories"))
    # ...
```

3. Update your database by making migrations and running them for the `movies` app:

```
(myproject_env)$ python3 manage.py makemigrations movies
(myproject_env)$ python3 manage.py migrate movies
```

How it works...

The `MPTTModel` mixin will add the `tree_id`, `lft`, `rght`, and `level` fields to the `Category` model. The `tree_id` field is used as you can have multiple trees in the database table. In fact, each root category is saved in a separate tree. The `lft` and `rght` fields store the left and right values used in the MPTT algorithms. The `level` field stores the node's depth in the tree. The root node will be level `0`. Through the `order_insertion_by` meta option specific to MPTT, we ensure that when new categories are added they stay in alphabetical order by `title`.

Besides new fields, the `MPTTModel` mixin adds methods to navigate through the tree structure similar to how you navigate through DOM elements using JavaScript. These methods are listed as follows:

- If you want to get the ancestors of a category, use the following code. Here, the `ascending` parameter defines from which direction to read the nodes (the default is `False`), and the `include_self` parameter defines whether to include the category itself in `QuerySet` (the default is `False`):

  ```
  ancestor_categories = category.get_ancestors(ascending=False,
                                               include_self=False)
  ```

- To just get the root category, use the following code:

  ```
  root = category.get_root()
  ```

- If you want to get the direct children of a category, use the following code:

  ```
  children = category.get_children()
  ```

- To get all of the descendants of a category, use the following code. Here, the `include_self` parameter again defines whether or not to include the category itself in `QuerySet`:

  ```
  descendants = category.get_descendants(include_self=False)
  ```

- If you want to get the descendant count without querying the database, use the following code:

  ```
  descendants_count = category.get_descendant_count()
  ```

- To get all `siblings`, call the following method:

  ```
  siblings = category.get_siblings(include_self=False)
  ```

- Root categories are considered siblings of other root categories.
- To just get the previous and next siblings, call the following methods:

  ```
  previous_sibling = category.get_previous_sibling()
  next_sibling = category.get_next_sibling()
  ```

- Also, there are methods to check whether the category is root, child, or leaf, as follows:

```
category.is_root_node()
category.is_child_node()
category.is_leaf_node()
```

All these methods can be used either in the views, templates, or management commands. If you want to manipulate the tree structure, you can also use the insert_at() and move_to() methods. In this case, you can read about them and the tree manager methods at http://django-mptt.readthedocs.io/en/stable/models.html.

In the preceding models, we used TreeForeignKey and TreeManyToManyField. These are similar to ForeignKey and ManyToManyField, except that they show the choices indented in hierarchies in the administration interface.

Also, note that in the Meta class of the Category model, we order the categories by tree_id and then by the lft value in order to show the categories naturally in the tree structure.

See also

- The *Working with Docker* recipe in Chapter 1, *Getting Started with Django 2.0*
- The *Creating a model mixin to handle creation and modification dates* recipe in Chapter 2, *Database Structure*
- The *Structuring the page menu* recipe in Chapter 7, *Django CMS*
- The *Creating a category administration interface with django-mptt-admin* recipe

Creating a category administration interface with django-mptt-admin

The django-mptt app comes with a simple model administration mixin that allows you to create the tree structure and list it with indentation. To reorder trees, you need to either create this functionality yourself or use a third-party solution. One app that can help you to create a draggable administration interface for hierarchical models is django-mptt-admin. Let's take a look at it in this recipe.

Getting ready

First, set up the `movies` app as described in the *Creating hierarchical categories with django-mptt* recipe earlier in this chapter. Then, we need to have the `django-mptt-admin` app installed by performing the following steps:

1. Install the app in your virtual environment using the following command, or add it to your requirements and rebuild for a Docker project:

```
(myproject_env)$ pip3 install django-mptt-admin~=0.6.0
```

2. Put it in `INSTALLED_APPS` in the settings, as follows:

```
# settings.py or config/base.py
INSTALLED_APPS = (
    # ...
    'django_mptt_admin',
)
```

3. Make sure that the static files for `django-mptt-admin` are available to your project:

```
(myproject_env)$ python3 manage.py collectstatic
```

How to do it...

Create an `admin.py` in which we define the administration interface for the `Category` model. It will extend `DjangoMpttAdmin` instead of `admin.ModelAdmin`, as follows:

```python
# movies/admin.py
from django.contrib import admin
from django_mptt_admin.admin import DjangoMpttAdmin

from .models import Category

class CategoryAdmin(DjangoMpttAdmin):
    list_display = ["title", "created", "modified"]
    list_filter = ["created"]


admin.site.register(Category, CategoryAdmin)
```

How it works...

The administration interface for the categories will have two modes: tree view and grid view. Your tree view will look similar to the following screenshot:

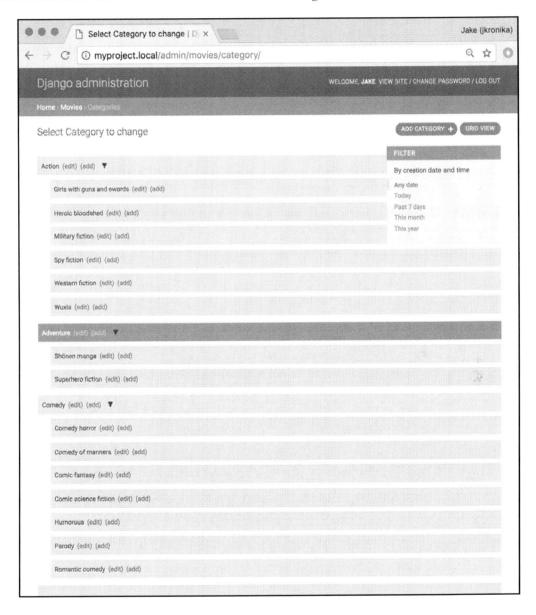

The tree view uses the `jqTree` jQuery library for node manipulation. You can expand and collapse categories for a better overview. To reorder them or change the dependencies, you can drag and drop the titles in this list view. During reordering, the user interface looks similar to the following screenshot:

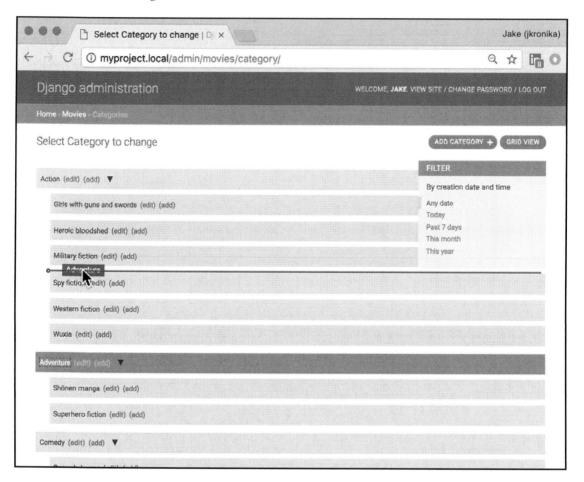

 Note that any usual list-related settings such as `list_display` or `list_filter` will be ignored. Also, any ordering driven by the `order_insertion_by` meta property will be overridden by manual sorting.

If you want to filter categories, sort them by a specific field, or apply admin actions, you can switch to the grid view, which shows the default category change list, as in the following:

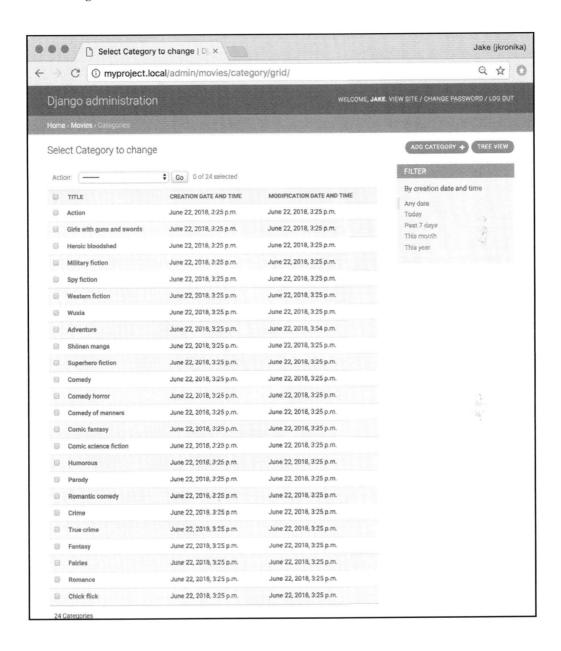

See also

- The *Creating hierarchical categories with django-mptt* recipe
- The *Creating a category administration interface with django-treebeard* recipe

Rendering categories in a template with django-mptt

Once you have created categories in your app, you need to display them hierarchically in a template. The easiest way to do this with MPTT trees, as described in the *Creating hierarchical categories with django-mptt* recipe, is to use the `{% recursetree %}` template tag from the `django-mptt` app. We will show you how to do that in this recipe.

Getting ready

Make sure that your `movies` app has the `Category` model created, as per the *Creating hierarchical categories with django-mptt* recipe, and some categories are entered in the database.

How to do it...

Pass `QuerySet` of your hierarchical categories to the template and then use the `{% recursetree %}` template tag as follows:

1. Create a view that loads all the categories and passes them to a template:

```
# movies/views.py
# ...other imports...
from django.shortcuts import render

from .models import Category

# ...

class MovieCategoryListView(View):
    template_name = "movies/movie_category_list.html"

    def get(self, request, *args, **kwargs):
        context = {
```

```
                    "categories": Category.objects.all(),
            }
            return render(request, self.template_name, context)
```

2. Create a template with the following content to output the hierarchy of categories:

```
{# templates/movies/category_list.html #}
{% extends "base.html" %}
{% load mptt_tags %}

{% block content %}
    <ul class="root">
        {% recursetree categories %}
            <li>
                {{ node.title }}
                {% if not node.is_leaf_node %}
                    <ul class="children">
                        {{ children }}
                    </ul>
                {% endif %}
            </li>
        {% endrecursetree %}
    </ul>
{% endblock %}
```

3. Create a URL rule to show the view:

```
# movies/urls.py
# ...other imports...
from django.urls import path

from .views import MovieCategoryListView


urlpatterns = [
    # ...
    path('category/', MovieCategoryListView.as_view(),
        name='category_list')
]
```

How it works...

The template will be rendered as nested lists, as shown in the following screenshot:

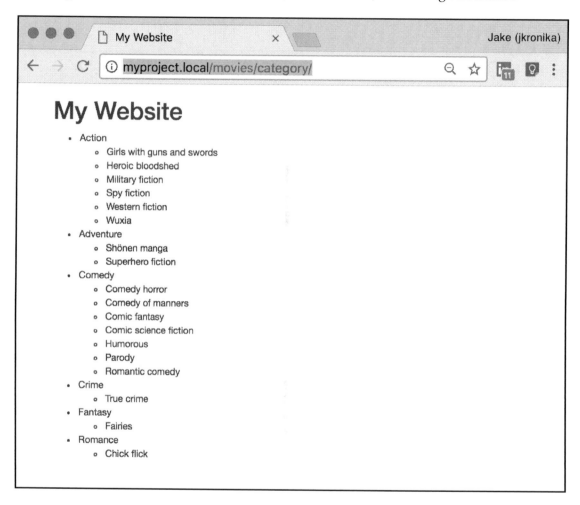

The {% recursetree %} block template tag takes QuerySet of the categories and renders the list using the template content nested within the tag. There are two special variables used here:

- The node variable is an instance of the Category model whose fields or methods can be used to add specific CSS classes or HTML5 data-* attributes for JavaScript, such as {{ node.get_descendent_count }}, {{ node.level }}, or {{ node.is_root }}
- Secondly, we have a children variable that defines where the rendered child nodes of the current category will be placed

There's more...

If your hierarchical structure is very complex, with more than 20 depth levels, it is recommended to use the full_tree_for_model and drilldown_tree_for_node iterative tags or the non-recursive, tree_info template filter. For more information on how to do this, refer to the official documentation at https://django-mptt.readthedocs.io/en/latest/templates.html#iterative-tags.

See also

- The *Using HTML5 data attributes* recipe in Chapter 4, *Templates and JavaScript*
- The *Creating hierarchical categories with django-mptt* recipe
- The *Creating hierarchical categories with django-treebeard* recipe
- The *Using a single selection field to choose a category in forms with django-mptt* recipe

Using a single selection field to choose a category in forms with django-mptt

What happens if you want to show category selection in a form? How will the hierarchy be presented? In django-mptt, there is a special TreeNodeChoiceField form field that you can use to show the hierarchical structures in a selected field. Let's take a look at how to do this.

Getting ready

We will start with the `movies` app that we defined in the previous recipes.

How to do it...

Let's enhance the filter form for movies that we created in the *Filtering object lists* recipe in `Chapter 3`, *Forms and Views*, adding a field for filtering by category:

1. In the `forms.py` file of the `movies` app, create a form with a category field as follows:

```python
# movies/forms.py
from django import forms
from django.utils.translation import ugettext_lazy as _
from django.utils.html import mark_safe
from mptt.forms import TreeNodeChoiceField

from .models import Category


class MovieFilterForm(forms.Form):
    # ...
    category = TreeNodeChoiceField(
        label=_("Category"),
        queryset=Category.objects.all(),
        required=False,
        level_indicator=mark_safe("    "))
```

2. We should already have created `MovieListView`, an associated URL rule, and the `movie_list.html` template to show this form. Add the `Category` filter to the template, as follows:

```html
{# templates/movies/movie_list.html #}
{# ... #}
{% block sidebar %}
   <div class="filters panel-group" id="accordion">
       {# ... #}
       {% with title="Category" %}
       <div class="panel panel-default">
           {% include "movies/includes/filter_heading.html" with
           title=title %}
           <div id="collapse-{{ title|slugify }}"
               class="panel-collapse collapse">
               <div class="panel-body"><div class="list-group">
```

```
                {{ form.category }}
            </div></div>
        </div>
      </div>
      {% endwith %}
    </div>
  {% endblock %}
  {# ... #}
```

How it works...

The category selection drop-down menu will look similar to the following:

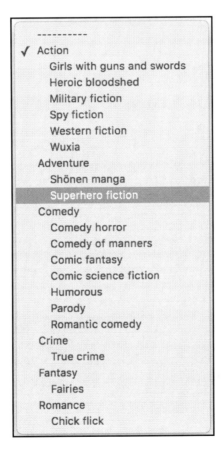

`TreeNodeChoiceField` acts like `ModelChoiceField`; however, it shows hierarchical choices as indented. By default, `TreeNodeChoiceField` represents each deeper level prefixed by three dashes, `---`. In our example, we have changed the level indicator to be four non-breaking spaces (the ` ` HTML entities) by passing the `level_indicator` parameter to the field. To ensure that the non-breaking spaces aren't escaped, we use the `mark_safe()` function.

See also

- The *Rendering categories in a template with django-mptt* recipe
- The *Using a checkbox list to choose multiple categories in forms with django-mptt* recipe

Using a checkbox list to choose multiple categories in forms with django-mptt

When one or more categories need to be selected at once in a form, you can use the `TreeNodeMultipleChoiceField` multiple selection field that is provided by django-mptt. However, multiple selection fields (for example, `<select multiple>`) are not very user friendly from an interface point of view, as the user needs to scroll and hold control keys while clicking in order to make multiple choices. Especially when there are a fairly large number of items to choose from, the user wants to select several at once, or the user has accessibility handicaps, such as poor motor control, that can lead to a really awful user experience. A much better approach is to provide a checkbox list from which to choose the categories. In this recipe, we will create a field that allows you to show the hierarchical tree structure as indented checkboxes in the form.

Getting ready

We will start with the `movies` app that we defined in the previous recipes and the `utils` app that you should have in your project.

How to do it...

To render an indented list of categories with checkboxes, we will create and use a new
MultipleChoiceTreeField form field and also create an HTML template for this field.
The specific template will be passed to the crispy_forms layout in the form. To do this,
perform the following steps:

1. In the utils app, add a fields.py file (or update it if one already exists) and
    create a MultipleChoiceTreeField form field that
    extends ModelMultipleChoiceField, as follows:

    ```python
    # utils/fields.py
    # ...other imports...
    from django import forms

    # ...

    class MultipleChoiceTreeField(forms.ModelMultipleChoiceField):
        widget = forms.CheckboxSelectMultiple

        def label_from_instance(self, obj):
            return obj
    ```

2. Use the new field with the categories to choose from in a new form for movie
    creation. Also, in the form layout, pass a custom template to the categories field,
    as shown in the following:

    ```python
    # movies/forms.py
    from django import forms
    from django.utils.translation import ugettext_lazy as _
    from crispy_forms.helper import FormHelper
    from crispy_forms import layout, bootstrap

    from utils.fields import MultipleChoiceTreeField
    from .models import Movie, Category


    class MovieForm(forms.ModelForm):
        class Meta:
            model = Movie

        categories = MultipleChoiceTreeField(
            label=_("Categories"),
            required=False,
            queryset=Category.objects.all())
    ```

```python
def __init__(self, *args, **kwargs):
    super().__init__(*args, **kwargs)

    self.helper = FormHelper()
    self.helper.form_action = ""
    self.helper.form_method = "POST"
    self.helper.layout = layout.Layout(
        layout.Field("title"),
        layout.Field(
            "categories",
            template="utils/checkbox_multi_select_tree.html"),
        bootstrap.FormActions(
            layout.Submit("submit", _("Save")),
        )
    )
```

3. Create a template for a Bootstrap-style checkbox list, as shown in the following:

```html
{# templates/utils/checkbox_multi_select_tree.html #}
{% load crispy_forms_filters %}
{% load l10n %}

<div id="div_{{ field.auto_id }}"
    class="form-group{% if wrapper_class %}
        {{ wrapper_class }}{% endif %}
        {% if form_show_errors and field.errors %}
        has-error{% endif %}
        {% if field.css_classes %}
        {{ field.css_classes }}{% endif %}">
    {% if field.label and form_show_labels %}
        <label for="{{ field.id_for_label }}"
            class="control-label {{ label_class }}
                {% if field.field.required %}
                requiredField{% endif %}">
            {{ field.label|safe }}{% if field.field.required %}
                <span class="asteriskField">*</span>{% endif %}
        </label>
    {% endif %}

    <div class="controls {{ field_class }}"{% if flat_attrs %}
        {{ flat_attrs|safe }}{% endif %}>
        {% include 'bootstrap3/layout/field_errors_block.html' %}

        {% for choice_value, choice_instance
            in field.field.choices %}
        <label class="form-check checkbox{% if inline_class
                    %}-{{ inline_class }}{% endif %}
                level-{{ choice_instance.level }}">
```

```
                <input type="checkbox" class="form-check-input"
                    {% if choice_value in field.value
                        or choice_value|stringformat:'s'
                            in field.value
                        or choice_value|stringformat:'s' ==
                            field.value|stringformat:'s'
                    %} checked{% endif %}
                    name="{{ field.html_name }}"
                    id="id_{{field.html_name}}_{{forloop.counter}}"
                    value="{{ choice_value|unlocalize }}"
                {{ field.field.widget.attrs|flatatt }}>
                <span>{{ choice_instance }}</span>
            </label>
            {% endfor %}

            {% include "bootstrap3/layout/help_text.html" %}
        </div>
    </div>
```

 Template tags in the snippet above have been split across lines for legibility, but in practice template tags must be on a single line, and so cannot be split in this manner.

4. Create a new view for adding a movie, using the form we just created:

```
# movies/views.py
# ...other imports...
from django.views.generic import FormView

from .forms import MovieForm

# ...

class MovieAdd(FormView):
    template_name = 'movies/add_form.html'
    form_class = MovieForm
    success_url = '/'
```

5. Add the associated template to show the **Add Movie** form with the {% crispy %} template tag, whose usage you can learn more about in the *Creating a form layout with django-crispy-forms* recipe in Chapter 3, *Forms and Views*:

```
{# templates/movies/add_form.html #}
{% extends "base.html" %}
{% load i18n static crispy_forms_tags %}
```

```
{% block stylesheet %}
<link rel="stylesheet" type="text/css"
    href="{% static 'site/css/movie_add.css' %}">
{% endblock %}

{% block content %}
    <h2>{% trans "Add Movie" %}</h2>
    <div id="form_add_movie">
        {% crispy form %}
    </div>
{% endblock %}
```

6. We also need a URL rule pointing to the new view, as follows:

```
# movies/urls.py
# ...other imports...
from django.urls import path

from .views import MovieAdd

# ...

urlpatterns = [
    # ...
    path('add/', views.MovieAdd.as_view(),
        name="add_movie"),
]
```

7. Add rules to your CSS file to indent the labels using the classes generated in the checkbox tree field template, such as .level-0, .level-1, and .level-2, by setting the margin-left parameter. Make sure that you have a reasonable amount of these CSS classes for the expected maximum depth of trees in your context, as follows:

```
/* static/site/movie_add.css */
.level-0 {
    margin-left: 0;
}
.level-1 {
    margin-left: 20px;
}
.level-2 {
    margin-left: 40px;
}
```

How it works...

As a result, we get the following form:

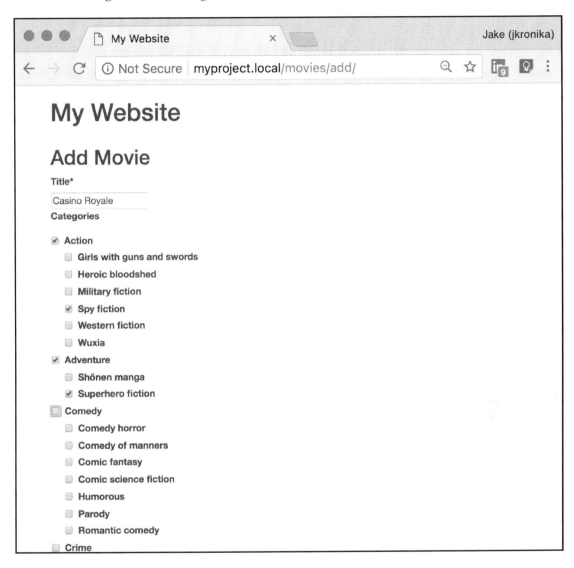

Contrary to the default behavior of Django, which hardcodes field generation in Python code, the `django-crispy-forms` app uses templates to render the fields. You can browse them under `crispy_forms/templates/bootstrap3`, and copy some of them to an analogous path in your project's template directory to overwrite them when necessary.

In our movie creation form, we pass a custom template for the categories field that will add the `.level-*` CSS classes to the `<label>` tag, wrapping the checkboxes. One problem with the normal `CheckboxSelectMultiple` widget is that when rendered it only uses choice values and choice texts, whereas we need other properties of the category such as the depth level. To solve this, we also created a custom `MultipleChoiceTreeField` form field, which extends `ModelMultipleChoiceField` and overrides the `label_from_instance` method to return the category instance itself, instead of its Unicode representation. The template for the field looks complicated; however, it is mostly a combination of a common field template (`crispy_forms/templates/bootstrap3/field.html`) and multiple checkbox field template (`crispy_forms/templates/bootstrap3/layout/checkboxselectmultiple.html`), with all the necessary Bootstrap markup. We just made a slight modification to add the `.level-*` CSS classes.

There's more...

One thing to note here is that this approach using the `.level-*` classes is not very scalable. The more trees one has, the more classes need to be created, and at some point it is quite possible that a new level could be added that is more than the classes provide for.

To provide a more robust solution, a nested markup structure similar to the tree recursion used for tree display in the *Rendering categories in a template with django-mptt* recipe might be used. We leave this as an investigation and exercise for the reader.

See also

- The *Creating a form layout with django-crispy-forms* recipe in Chapter 3, *Forms and Views*
- The *Rendering categories in a template with django-mptt* recipe
- The *Using a single selection field to choose a category in forms* recipe

Creating hierarchical categories with django-treebeard

There are several algorithms for tree structures, each with its own benefits. An app called `django-treebeard`, an alternative to *django-mptt*, which is used by Django CMS, provides support for three tree forms:

- **Adjacency List** trees are simple structures, where each node has a `parent` attribute. Although read operations are fast, this comes at the cost of slow writes.
- **Nested Sets** trees and MPTT trees are the same; they structure nodes as sets nested beneath the parent. This structure also provides very fast read access, at the cost of more expensive writing and deletion, particularly when writes require some particular ordering.
- **Materialized Path** trees are built with each node in the tree having an associated path attribute, which is a string indicating the full path from the root to the node—much like a URL path indicates where to find a particular page on a website. This is the most efficient approach supported.

As a demonstration of the support it has for all of these algorithms, we will use `django-treebeard` and its consistent API. We will extend the `ideas` app from the *Implementing a multilingual search with Haystack and Whoosh* recipe in `Chapter 3`, *Forms and Views*. In our changes, we will simply enhance the `Category` model with support for hierarchy via one of the supported tree algorithms.

Getting ready

To get started, perform the following steps:

1. Install `django-treebeard` in your virtual environment using the following command (or add the same to your requirements file and rebuild if using a Docker project):

   ```
   (myproject_env)$ pip3 install django-treebeard~=4.3.0
   ```

2. Create the ideas app if you have not done so already. Add the ideas app as well as treebeard to INSTALLED_APPS in the settings, as follows:

```
# settings.py or config/base.py
INSTALLED_APPS = (
    # ...
    "treebeard",
    "ideas",
)
```

How to do it...

We will enhance the Category model using the Materialized Path algorithm, as follows:

1. Open the models.py file and update the Category model to extend treebeard.mp_tree.MP_Node instead of the standard Django Model. It should also inherit from CreationModificationDateMixin, which we defined in Chapter 2, *Database Structure*. In addition to the fields coming from the mixins, the Category model will need to have a title field:

```
# ideas/models.py
from django.urls import reverse, NoReverseMatch
from django.db import models
from django.utils.translation import ugettext_lazy as _
from treebeard.mp_tree import MP_Node

from utils.models import CreationModificationDateMixin, UrlMixin
from utils.fields import (MultilingualCharField,
                          MultilingualTextField)


class Category(MP_Node, CreationModificationDateMixin):
    class Meta:
        verbose_name = _("Idea Category")
        verbose_name_plural = _("Idea Categories")

    node_order_by = ["title",]

    title = MultilingualCharField(_("Title"), max_length=200)

    def __str__(self):
        return self.title

    # ...
```

2. This will require an update to the database, so next we'll need to migrate the `ideas` app:

```
(myproject_env)$ python3 manage.py makemigrations ideas
(myproject_env)$ python3 manage.py migrate ideas
```

3. With the use of abstract model inheritance, `treebeard` tree nodes can be related to other models using the standard relationships. As such, the `Idea` model can continue to have a simple `ManyToManyField` relation to `Category`:

```
# ideas/models.py
class Idea(UrlMixin):
    # ...
    categories = models.ManyToManyField(Category,
                                        blank=True,
                                        related_name="ideas",
                                        verbose_name=_(
                                            "Categories"))

    # ...
```

How it works...

The `MP_Node` abstract model provides the `path`, `depth`, `numchild`, `steplen`, and `alphabet` fields to the `Category` model that are necessary for constructing the tree:

- The `depth` and `numchild` fields provide metadata about a node's location and descendants
- The `path` field is indexed, allowing database queries against it using `LIKE` to be very fast
- The `path` is built of fixed-length encoded segments, where the size of each segment is determined by the `steplen` value (which defaults to 4), and the encoding uses characters found in the given `alphabet` (defaults to Latin alphanumeric)
- The `node_order_by` field defines a list of fields used for ordering nodes in the tree, and is respected by all tree operations

The path, depth, and numchild fields should be treated as read-only. Also, steplen, alphabet, and node_order_by values should never be changed after saving the first object to a tree; otherwise, the data will be corrupted.

Besides new fields, the MP_Node abstract class adds methods for navigation through the tree structure. Some important examples of these methods are listed as follows:

- If you want to get the ancestors of a category, which are returned as queryset of ancestors from the root to the parent of the current node, use the following code:

```
ancestor_categories = category.get_ancestors()
```

- To just get the root category, which is identified by having depth of 1, use the following code:

```
root = category.get_root()
```

- If you want to get the direct children of a category, use the following code:

```
children = category.get_children()
```

- To get all the descendants of a category, returned as queryset of all children and their children, and so on, but not including the current node itself, use the following code:

```
descendants = category.get_descendants()
```

- If you want to get just the descendant count, use the following code:

```
descendants_count = category.get_descendant_count()
```

- To get all of the siblings, including the reference node, call the following method:

```
siblings = category.get_siblings()
```

- Root categories are considered to be siblings of other root categories.
- To just get the previous and next siblings, call the following methods, where get_prev_sibling() will return None for the leftmost sibling, as will get_next_sibling() for the rightmost one:

```
previous_sibling = category.get_prev_sibling()
next_sibling = category.get_next_sibling()
```

- Also, there are methods to check whether the category is `root`, `leaf`, or related to another node, as follows:

```
category.is_root()
category.is_leaf()
category.is_child_of(node)
category.is_descendant_of(node)
category.is_sibling_of(node)
```

There's more...

This recipe only scratches the surface of the power of `django-treebeard` and its Materialized Path trees. There are many other methods available for navigation as well as construction of the trees. In addition, the API for Materialized Path trees is largely identical to those for Nested Sets trees and Adjacency List trees, which are available simply by implementing your model with the `NS_Node` or `AL_Node` abstract classes, respectively, instead of using `MP_Node`.

 Read the `django-treebeard` API documentation for a complete listing of the available properties and methods for each of the tree implementations at `https://django-treebeard.readthedocs.io/en/latest/api.html`.

See also

- The *Implementing a multilingual search with Haystack and Whoosh* recipe in `Chapter 3`, *Forms and Views*
- The *Creating hierarchical categories with django-mptt* recipe
- The *Creating a category administration interface with django-treebeard* recipe

Creating a basic category administration interface with django-treebeard

The django-treebeard app provides its own TreeAdmin, extending from the standard ModelAdmin. This allows you to view tree nodes hierarchically in the administration interface, with interface features dependent upon the tree algorithm used. Let's take a look in this recipe.

Getting ready

First, set up the ideas app and django-treebeard as described in the *Creating hierarchical categories with django-treebeard* recipe earlier in this chapter. Also, make sure that the static files for django-treebeard are available to your project:

```
(myproject_env)$ ./manage.py collectstatic
```

How to do it...

Create an administration interface for the Category model from the ideas app that extends treebeard.admin.TreeAdmin instead of admin.ModelAdmin, as follows:

```python
# ideas/admin.py
from django.contrib import admin
from treebeard.admin import TreeAdmin


from .models import Category


class CategoryAdmin(TreeAdmin):
    list_display = ("title", "created", "modified",)
    list_filter = ("created",)


admin.site.register(Category, CategoryAdmin)
```

How it works...

The administration interface for the categories will have two modes, dependent upon the tree implementation used. For Materialized Path and Nested Sets trees, an advanced user interface is provided, as seen here:

This advanced view allows you to expand and collapse categories for a better overview, as has been done for **Recipes** and **Prose**. To reorder them or change the dependencies, you can drag and drop the titles. During reordering, the user interface looks similar to the following screenshot:

If you apply filtering or sorting of categories by a specific field, the advanced functionality is disabled, but the more attractive look and feel of the advanced interface remains. We can see this intermediate view here, where only categories created **Today** are shown:

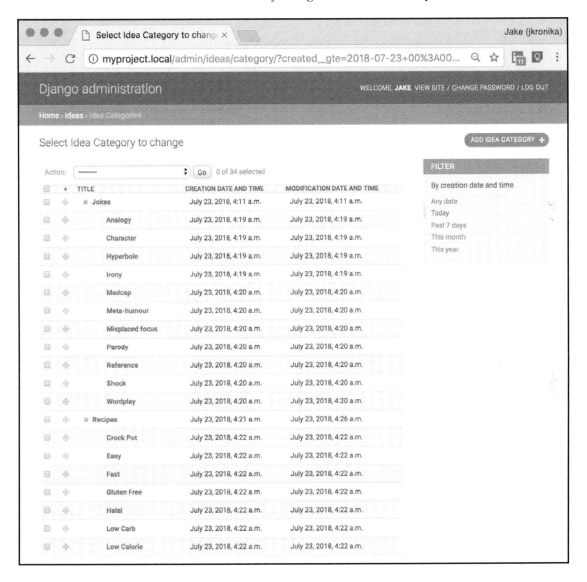

However, if your tree uses the Adjacency List algorithm, a basic UI is provided with a less aesthetic presentation and none of the toggling or reordering functionality given in the advanced UI.

More details about the `django-treebeard` administration, including a screenshot of the basic interface, can be found in their documentation here `https://django-treebeard.readthedocs.io/en/latest/admin.html`.

See also

- The *Creating hierarchical categories with django-mptt* recipe
- The *Creating hierarchical categories with django-treebeard* recipe
- The *Creating a category administration interface with django-mptt-admin* recipe

10
Importing and Exporting Data

In this chapter, we will cover the following recipes:

- Importing data from a local CSV file
- Importing data from a local Excel file
- Importing data from an external JSON file
- Importing data from an external XML file
- Creating filterable RSS feeds
- Using Tastypie to create an API
- Using Django REST framework to create an API

Introduction

There are times when your data needs to be transported from a local format to the database, imported from external resources, or provided to third parties. In this chapter, we will take a look at some practical examples of how to write management commands and APIs to do this.

Importing data from a local CSV file

The **comma-separated values (CSV)** format is probably the simplest way to store tabular data in a text file. In this recipe, we will create a management command that imports data from a CSV file to a Django database. We will need a CSV list of movies. You can easily create such files with Excel, Calc, or another spreadsheet application.

Getting ready

Create a `movies` app with the `Movie` model containing the following fields: `title`, `release_year`, `rating`, and `rank`. You may already have such an app created if you worked through the *Filtering object lists* recipe in `Chapter 3`, *Forms and Views*. If you've just created the app, make sure to add it under `INSTALLED_APPS` in the settings and migrate your database.

 Movie data can be obtained from the IMDb Top Movies list, though other sources also exist. For the IMDb data, see `https://www.imdb.com/chart/top`.

How to do it...

Follow these steps to create and use a management command that imports movies from a local CSV file:

1. In the `movies` app, create a `management` directory and then a `commands` directory in the new `management` directory. Put empty `__init__.py` files in both new directories to make them Python packages.

2. Add an `import_movies_from_csv.py` file there with the following content:

```python
# movies/management/commands/import_movies_from_csv.py
import csv
from django.core.management.base import BaseCommand

from movies.models import Movie


SILENT, NORMAL, VERBOSE, VERY_VERBOSE = 0, 1, 2, 3


class Command(BaseCommand):
    help = ("Imports movies from a local CSV file. Expects each"
            " row in the CSV to contain a single movie's"
            " title, release year, rating and rank.")

    def add_arguments(self, parser):
        # Positional arguments
        parser.add_argument("file_path",
                            nargs=1,
                            type=str)
```

```
def handle(self, *args, **options):
    verbosity = options.get("verbosity", NORMAL)
    file_path = options["file_path"][0]

    if verbosity >= NORMAL:
        self.stdout.write("=== Importing movies ===")

    with open(file_path) as f:
        reader = csv.reader(f)
        for row in enumerate(reader):
            index, (title, release_year, rating, rank) = row
            if index == 0:
                # let's skip the column headers
                continue
            movie, created = Movie.objects.get_or_create(
                title=title,
                release_year=release_year,
                rank=rank,
                rating=rating)
            if verbosity >= NORMAL:
                self.stdout.write(
                    f"{movie.rank}. {movie.title}")
```

3. To run the import, call the following in the command line:

```
(myproject_env)$ python3 manage.py import_movies_from_csv \
> data/top-movies.csv
```

How it works...

For a management command, we need to create a `Command` class deriving from `BaseCommand` and overwriting the `add_arguments()` and `handle()` methods. The `help` attribute defines the help text for the management command. It can be seen when you type the following in the command line:

```
(myproject_env)$ python3 manage.py help import_movies_from_csv
```

Django management commands use the built-in argparse module to parse the passed arguments. The `add_arguments()` method defines what positional or named arguments should be passed to the management command. In our case, we will add a positional `file_path` argument of Unicode type. By `nargs` set to the `1` attribute, we allow only one value.

To learn about the other arguments that you can define and how to do this, refer to the official `argparse` documentation at `https://docs.python.org/2/library/argparse.html#the-add-argument-method`.

At the beginning of the `handle()` method, the `verbosity` argument is checked. Verbosity defines how much terminal output the command should provide, from 0, not giving any, to 3, providing extensive logging. You can pass this argument to the command as follows:

```
(myproject_env)$ python3 manage.py import_movies_from_csv \
> ../data/top-movies.csv --verbosity=0
```

Then, we also expect the filename as the first positional argument. The `options["file_path"]` returns a list of the values defined in the `nargs`; therefore, it is one value in this case.

We open the given file and pass its pointer to `csv.reader`. The first line in the file is assumed to contain headings for each of the columns, so it is skipped. Then, for each additional line in the file, we will create a new `Movie` object, if a matching movie doesn't exist yet. Our command only supports two levels of output verbosity, and we default the level to `--verbosity=1`, so the management command will print out the imported movie ranks and titles to the console, unless you set `--verbosity=0`.

If you want to debug the errors of a management command while developing it, pass the `--traceback` parameter for it. If an error occurs, you will see the full stack trace of the problem.

Assuming we invoked the command with `--verbosity=1` or higher, the start of the sort of output we could expect might be as follows:

```
(myproject_env)$ python3 manage.py import_movies_from_csv \
> ../data/movies.csv --verbosity=1
=== Importing movies ===
1. The Shawshank Redemption
2. The Godfather
3. The Godfather: Part II
4. The Dark Knight
5. 12 Angry Men
6. Schindler's List
7. The Lord of the Rings: The Return of the King
8. Pulp Fiction
9. The Good, the Bad and the Ugly
10. Fight Club
...
```

There's more...

You can learn more about the CSV library from the official documentation at `https://docs.python.org/2/library/csv.html`.

It also is possible to generalize this command into a form usable for any app and model. To do so, we need to accept the app and model to import to as additional arguments. Also, the first row (the column headings) has to be provided and contain the model field names. From these, in combination with the row data, we construct a `kwargs` object and pass that to get or create an instance of the appropriate app model. We leave the implementation of such a generalized command as an exercise for the reader.

See also

- The *Filtering object lists* recipe in `Chapter 3`, *Forms and Views*
- The *Importing data from a local Excel file* recipe

Importing data from a local Excel file

Another popular format for storing tabular data is an Excel spreadsheet. In this recipe, we will import movies from a file of this format.

Getting ready

Let's start with the `movies` app that we created in the previous recipe. Install the `openpyxl` package to read Excel files, as follows:

```
(project_env)$ pip3 install openpyxl~=2.5.0
```

How to do it...

Follow these steps to create and use a management command that imports movies from a local XLSX file:

1. If you haven't done so, in the `movies` app, create a `management` directory, and then a `commands` subdirectory beneath it. Add empty `__init__.py` files in both of the new directories to make them Python packages.

2. Add an `import_movies_from_xlsx.py` file with the following content:

```python
# movies/management/commands/import_movies_from_xlsx.py
from django.core.management.base import BaseCommand
from openpyxl import load_workbook

from movies.models import Movie


SILENT, NORMAL, VERBOSE, VERY_VERBOSE = 0, 1, 2, 3

class Command(BaseCommand):
    help = ("Imports movies from a local XLSX file. "
            "Expects title, release year, rating and rank.")

    def add_arguments(self, parser):
        # Positional arguments
        parser.add_argument("file_path",
                            nargs=1,
                            type=str)

    def handle(self, *args, **options):
        verbosity = options.get("verbosity", NORMAL)
        file_path = options["file_path"][0]

        wb = load_workbook(filename=file_path)
        ws = wb.worksheets[0]

        if verbosity >= NORMAL:
            self.stdout.write("=== Importing movies ===")

        index = 0
        rows = ws.iter_rows(min_row=2) # skip the column captions
        for row in rows:
            index += 1
            row_values = [cell.value for cell in row]
            (title, release_year, rating, rank) = row_values
            movie, created = Movie.objects.get_or_create(
                title=title,
```

```
                    release_year=release_year,
                    rating=rating,
                    rank=rank)
            if verbosity >= NORMAL:
                self.stdout.write(f"{movie.rank}. {movie.title}")
```

3. To run the import, call the following in the command line:

```
(myproject_env)$ python3 manage.py import_movies_from_xlsx \
> ../data/bottom-movies.xlsx
```

How it works...

The principle of importing from an XLSX file is the same as with CSV. We open the file, read it row by row, and create the `Movie` objects from the provided data. Here is a detailed explanation:

- Excel files are workbooks containing sheets as different tabs.
- We are using the `openpyxl` library to open a file passed as a positional argument to the command. Then, we read the first sheet from the workbook.
- Afterward, we will read the rows one by one (except the first row with the column titles) and create the `Movie` objects from them.
- Once again, the management command will print out the imported movie titles to the console, unless you set `--verbosity=0`.

There's more...

You can learn more about how to work with Excel files at http://www.python-excel.org/.

See also

- The *Creating admin actions* recipe in Chapter 6, *Model Administration*
- The *Importing data from a local CSV file* recipe
- The *Importing data from an external JSON file* recipe

Importing data from an external JSON file

The Last.fm music website has an API under the `http://ws.audioscrobbler.com/` domain that you can use to read the albums, artists, tracks, events, and more. The API allows you to either use the JSON or XML format. In this recipe, we will import the top tracks tagged disco using the JSON format.

Getting ready

Follow these steps to import data in the JSON format from Last.fm:

1. To use Last.fm, you need to register and get an API key. The API key can be created at `http://www.last.fm/api/account/create`.

2. The API key has to be set in the settings as `LAST_FM_API_KEY`. We recommend providing it as an environment variable and drawing that into your settings as shown here:

   ```
   # settings.py or config/base.py
   import os
   # ...
   LAST_FM_API_KEY = os.environ.get('LAST_FM_API_KEY')
   ```

3. Also, install the `requests` library in your virtual environment using the following command:

   ```
   (myproject_env)$ pip install requests~=2.19.1
   ```

4. Let's check the structure of the JSON endpoint for the top disco tracks (`http://ws.audioscrobbler.com/2.0/?method=tag.gettoptracks&tag=disco&api_key=xxx&format=json`), which should look something like this:

   ```json
   {
       "tracks":{
           "track":[
               {
                   "name":"Billie Jean",
                   "duration":"293",
                   "mbid":"f980fc14-e29b-481d-ad3a-5ed9b4ab6340",
   "url":"https://www.last.fm/music/Michael+Jackson/_/Billie+Jean",
                   "streamable":{
                       "#text":"0",
                       "fulltrack":"0"
                   },
                   "artist":{
   ```

```
                    "name":"Michael Jackson",
                    "mbid":"f27ec8db-af05-4f36-916e-3d57f91ecf5e",
                    "url":"https://www.last.fm/music/Michael+Jackson"
                },
                "image":[
                    {
"#text":"https://lastfm-img2.akamaized.net/i/u/34s/7a9b0f69d51f41a8
88ef29df9cfe3594.png",
                        "size":"small"
                    },
                    {
"#text":"https://lastfm-img2.akamaized.net/i/u/64s/7a9b0f69d51f41a8
88ef29df9cfe3594.png",
                        "size":"medium"
                    },
                    {
"#text":"https://lastfm-img2.akamaized.net/i/u/174s/7a9b0f69d51f41a
888ef29df9cfe3594.png",
                        "size":"large"
                    },
                    {
"#text":"https://lastfm-img2.akamaized.net/i/u/300x300/7a9b0f69d51f
41a888ef29df9cfe3594.png",
                        "size":"extralarge"
                    }
                ],
                "@attr":{
                    "rank":"1"
                }
            },
            ...
        ],
        "@attr":{
            "tag":"disco",
            "page":"1",
            "perPage":"50",
            "totalPages":"577",
            "total":"28810"
        }
    }
}
```

We want to read the track `name`, `artist`, `URL`, and medium-sized images (shown here in bold).

How to do it...

Follow these steps to create a `Track` model and a management command, which imports the top tracks from Last.fm to the database:

1. Let's create a `music` app and add it to the `INSTALLED_APPS`. For Docker projects, make sure to map the volume and restart the app container as well.

2. Then, create a `models.py` file with a simple `Track` model as follows:

```python
# music/models.py
import os

from django.utils.translation import ugettext_lazy as _
from django.db import models
from django.utils.text import slugify


def upload_to(instance, filename):
    filename_base, filename_ext = os.path.splitext(filename)
    artist = slugify(instance.artist)
    track = slugify(instance.name)
    return f"tracks/{artist}--{track}{filename_ext.lower()}"


class Track(models.Model):
    class Meta:
        verbose_name = _("Track")
        verbose_name_plural = _("Tracks")

    name = models.CharField(_("Name"),
                            max_length=250)
    artist = models.CharField(_("Artist"),
                              max_length=250)
    url = models.URLField(_("URL"))
    image = models.ImageField(_("Image"),
                              upload_to=upload_to,
                              blank=True,
                              null=True)

    def __str__(self):
        return f"{self.artist} - {self.name}"
```

3. Next, make and run migrations for the music app to get your database ready for the import:

```
(myproject_env)$ python3 manage.py makemigrations music
(myproject_env)$ python3 manage.py migrate music
```

4. Then, create the management command as shown here:

```python
# music/management/commands/import_top_tracks_from_lastfm_json.py
import os, requests
from io import BytesIO

from django.conf import settings
from django.core.files import File
from django.core.management.base import BaseCommand
from django.utils.encoding import force_text

from music.models import Track


SILENT, NORMAL, VERBOSE, VERY_VERBOSE = 0, 1, 2, 3
API_URL = "http://ws.audioscrobbler.com/2.0/"


class Command(BaseCommand):
    help = "Imports top tracks from last.fm as JSON."
    verbosity = NORMAL

    def add_arguments(self, parser):
        # Named (optional) arguments
        parser.add_argument("--max_pages",
                            type=int,
                            default=0)

    def handle(self, *args, **options):
        self.verbosity = options.get("verbosity", self.verbosity)
        max_pages = options["max_pages"]

        params = {
            "method": "tag.gettoptracks",
            "tag": "disco",
            "api_key": settings.LAST_FM_API_KEY,
            "format": "json",
        }

        r = requests.get(API_URL, params=params)
        response_dict = r.json()
        pages = int(response_dict.get("tracks", {})
                                 .get("@attr", {})
                                 .get("totalPages", 1))
        if max_pages > 0:
            pages = min(pages, max_pages)

        if self.verbosity >= NORMAL:
```

```
                    self.stdout.write(
                        f"=== Importing {pages} page(s) of tracks ===")

                self.save_page(response_dict)
                for page_number in range(2, pages + 1):
                    params["page"] = page_number
                    r = requests.get(API_URL, params=params)
                    response_dict = r.json()
                    self.save_page(response_dict)

            def save_page(self, data):
                # ...
```

5. As the list is paginated, we will implement the `save_page()` method in the
   `Command` class to save a single page of tracks. This method takes the dictionary
   with the top tracks from a single page as a parameter, as follows:

```
    def save_page(self, data):
        for track_dict in data.get("tracks", {}).get("track"):
            if not track_dict:
                continue

            name = track_dict.get("name", "")
            artist = track_dict.get("artist", {}).get("name", "")
            url = track_dict.get("url", "")
            track, created = Track.objects.get_or_create(
                name=force_text(name),
                artist=force_text(artist),
                url=force_text(url))

            image_dict = track_dict.get("image", None)
            if created and image_dict:
                image_url = image_dict[1]["#text"]
                image_response = requests.get(image_url)
                track.image.save(
                    os.path.basename(image_url),
                    File(BytesIO(image_response.content)))

            if self.verbosity >= NORMAL:
                self.stdout.write(f" - {str(track)}")
```

6. To run the import, call the following in the command line:

```
(myproject_env)$ python3 manage.py
import_top_tracks_from_lastfm_json \
> --max_pages=3
```

How it works...

The option named `max_pages` argument limits the imported data to three pages. Just skip it, or explicitly pass 0 (zero) if you want to download all the available top tracks.

 Beware that there are around 30,000 pages as detailed in the `totalPages` value, and this will take a long time, and a lot of processing.

Using the `requests.get()` method, we read the data from Last.fm, passing the `params` query parameters. The response object has a built-in method called `json()`, which converts a JSON string to a parsed dictionary object.

We read the total pages value from this dictionary and then save the first page of results. Then, we get the second and later pages one by one and save them. If the number of pages to get is only 1, the range returned is empty, so we do not end up retrieving additional pages.

One interesting part in the import is downloading and saving the image. Here, we also use `requests.get()` to retrieve the image data and then we pass it to `File` through `StringIO`, which is accordingly used in the `image.save()` method. The first parameter of `image.save()` is a filename that will be overwritten anyway by the value from the `upload_to` function and is necessary only for the file extension.

If the command is invoked with a `--verbosity=1` or higher, then a list of the tracks created by the import will be output, using the string representation of the `Track` object.

There's more...

You can learn more about how to work with Last.fm at `https://www.last.fm/api`.

See also

- The *Importing data from a local CSV file* recipe
- The *Importing data from an external XML file* recipe

Importing data from an external XML file

Just as we showed what could be done with JSON in the preceding recipe, the `Last.fm` file also allows you to take data from its services in XML format. In this recipe, we will show you how to do this.

Getting ready

To prepare importing top tracks from `Last.fm` in the XML format, follow these steps:

1. Start with the first three steps from the *Getting ready* section in the *Importing data from an external JSON file* recipe.

2. Then, let's check the structure of the XML endpoint for the top folk tracks (for example, `http://ws.audioscrobbler.com/2.0/?method=tag.gettoptrac ks&tag=disco&api_key=xxx&format=xml`, but with a real API key) as follows:

```xml
<?xml version="1.0" encoding="UTF-8" ?>
<lfm status="ok">
    <tracks tag="folk" page="1" perPage="50" totalPages="2729"
total="136432">
        <track rank="1">
            <name>Hurt</name>
            <duration>218</duration>
            <mbid>25d8de5e-3662-4ffd-8dea-511a696ac3e7</mbid>
            <url>https://www.last.fm/music/Johnny+Cash/_/Hurt</url>
            <streamable fulltrack="0">0</streamable>
            <artist>
                <name>Johnny Cash</name>
                <mbid>d43d12a1-2dc9-4257-a2fd-0a3bb1081b86</mbid>
                <url>https://www.last.fm/music/Johnny+Cash</url>
            </artist>
            <image size="small">
https://lastfm-img2.akamaized.net/i/u/34s/08dfab76ecc847f0862a950f9
63f5596.png
            </image>
            <image size="medium">
https://lastfm-img2.akamaized.net/i/u/64s/08dfab76ecc847f0862a950f9
63f5596.png
            </image>
            <image size="large">
https://lastfm-img2.akamaized.net/i/u/174s/08dfab76ecc847f0862a950f
963f5596.png
            </image>
            <image size="extralarge">
```

```
https://lastfm-img2.akamaized.net/i/u/300x300/08dfab76ecc847f0862a9
50f963f5596.png
                </image>
        </track>
        ...
    </tracks>
</lfm>
```

How to do it...

Execute the following steps one by one to import the top tracks from Last.fm in the XML format:

1. First, perform the first three steps from the *How to do it...* section in the *Importing data from an external JSON file* recipe, if you haven't already.

2. Then, create an import_music_from_lastfm_xml.py management command. We will be using the ElementTree XML API that comes with Python to parse the XML nodes, as follows:

```python
# music/management/commands/import_music_from_lastfm_xml.py
import os, requests
from io import BytesIO
from xml.etree import ElementTree

from django.core.management.base import BaseCommand
from django.utils.encoding import force_text
from django.conf import settings
from django.core.files import File

from music.models import Track


SILENT, NORMAL, VERBOSE, VERY_VERBOSE = 0, 1, 2, 3
API_URL = "http://ws.audioscrobbler.com/2.0/"


class Command(BaseCommand):
    help = "Imports top tracks from last.fm as XML."
    verbosity = NORMAL

    def add_arguments(self, parser):
        # Named (optional) arguments
        parser.add_argument("--max_pages",
                            type=int,
                            default=0)
```

```python
    def handle(self, *args, **options):
        self.verbosity = options.get("verbosity", self.verbosity)
        max_pages = options["max_pages"]

        params = {
            "method": "tag.gettoptracks",
            "tag": "folk",
            "api_key": settings.LAST_FM_API_KEY,
            "format": "xml",
        }

        r = requests.get(API_URL, params=params)
        root = ElementTree.fromstring(r.content)

        pages = int(root.find("tracks").attrib
                        .get("totalPages", 1))
        if max_pages > 0:
            pages = min(pages, max_pages)

        if self.verbosity >= NORMAL:
            self.stdout.write(
                f"=== Importing {pages} page(s) of tracks ===")

        self.save_page(root)

        for page_number in range(2, pages + 1):
            params["page"] = page_number
            r = requests.get(API_URL, params=params)
            root = ElementTree.fromstring(r.content)
            self.save_page(root)

    def save_page(self, root):
        # ...
```

3. As the list is paginated, we will implement the `save_page()` method in the
   `Command` class to save a single page of tracks. This method takes the root node of
   the XML as a parameter, as shown here:

```python
    def save_page(self, root):
        for track_node in root.findall("tracks/track"):
            if not track_node:
                continue

            name = track_node.find("name").text
            artist = track_node.find("artist/name").text
            url = track_node.find("url").text
            track, created = Track.objects.get_or_create(
                name=force_text(name),
```

```
                       artist=force_text(artist),
                       url=force_text(url))

           image_node = track_node.find("image[@size='medium']")
           if created and image_node is not None:
               image_url = image_node.text
               image_response = requests.get(image_url)
               track.image.save(
                   os.path.basename(image_url),
                   File(BytesIO(image_response.content)))

           if self.verbosity >= NORMAL:
               self.stdout.write(f" - {track}")
```

4. To run the import, call the following in the command line:

```
(myproject_env)$ python manage.py import_music_from_lastfm_xml \
> --max_pages=3
```

How it works...

The process is analogous to the JSON approach. Using the `requests.get()` method, we read the data from `Last.fm`, passing the query parameters as `params`. The XML content of the response is passed to the `ElementTree` parser, and the root node is returned.

The `ElementTree` nodes have the `find()` and `findall()` methods, where you can pass XPath queries to filter out specific subnodes.

The following is a table of the available XPath syntax supported by `ElementTree`:

XPath Syntax Component	Meaning
tag	This selects all the child elements with the given tag.
*	This selects all the child elements.
.	This selects the current node.
//	This selects all the subelements on all the levels beneath the current element.
..	This selects the parent element.
[@attrib]	This selects all the elements that have the given attribute.
[@attrib='value']	This selects all the elements for which the given attribute has the given value.

[tag]	This selects all the elements that have a child named *tag*. Only immediate children are supported.
[position]	This selects all the elements that are located at the given position. The position can either be an integer (1 is the first position), the last () expression (for the last position), or a position relative to the last position (for example, last ()-1).

Therefore, using `root.find("tracks").attrib.get("totalPages", 1)`, we read the total amount of pages, defaulting to one if the data is missing somehow. We will save the first page and then go through the other pages one by one and save them too.

In the `save_page()` method, `root.findall("tracks/track")` returns an iterator through the <track> nodes under the <tracks> node. With `track_node.find("image[@size='medium']")`, we get the medium-sized image.

There's more...

If you worked with both the JSON and XML import recipes, you will notice that there are a large number of similarities between the two management commands. We leave it as an exercise to generalize the implementation into a single command to `import_music_from_lastfm`, which could differentiate its behavior based on receiving additional arguments for the format, tag, or even the API method.

You can learn more from the following links:

- Read about how to work with Last.fm at `https://www.last.fm/api`.
- Read about XPath at `https://en.wikipedia.org/wiki/XPath`.
- The full documentation of `ElementTree` can be found at `https://docs.python.org/2/library/xml.etree.elementtree.html`.

See also

- The *Importing data from an external JSON file* recipe

Creating filterable RSS feeds

Django comes with a syndication feed framework that allows you to create RSS and Atom feeds easily. RSS and Atom feeds are XML documents with specific semantics. They can be subscribed in an RSS reader, such as Feedly, or they can be aggregated in other websites, mobile applications, or desktop applications. In this recipe, we will create BulletinFeed, which provides a bulletin board with images. Moreover, the results will be filterable by URL query parameters.

Getting ready

Start by creating the bulletin_board app from the *Creating a form layout with custom template* recipe in Chapter 3, *Forms and Views*. Specifically, follow the steps in the *Getting ready* section to set up the models.

How to do it...

We will augment the Bulletin model and add an RSS feed to it. We will be able to filter the RSS feed by type or category so that it is possible to only subscribe to the bulletins that are, for example, offering used books:

1. In the models.py file of this app, add the Category model, like so:

```python
# bulletin_board/models.py
# ...

class Category(models.Model):
    class Meta:
        verbose_name = _("Category")
        verbose_name_plural = _("Categories")

    title = models.CharField(_("Title"), max_length=200)

    def __str__(self):
        return self.title
```

2. We'll then augment the `Bulletin` model to add a foreign key relationship with `Category`, and to apply the `UrlMixin` we created in the *Creating a model mixin with URL-related methods* recipe in Chapter 2, *Database Structure and Modeling*, as follows:

```
# bulletin_board/models.py
# import ...
from django.urls import reverse

from utils.models import CreationModificationDateMixin, UrlMixin

# ...

class Bulletin(CreationModificationDateMixin, UrlMixin):
    class Meta:
        verbose_name = _("Bulletin")
        verbose_name_plural = _("Bulletins")
        ordering = ("-created", "title",)

    category = models.ForeignKey(Category,
                                 null=True,
                                 verbose_name=_("Category"),
                                 on_delete=models.SET_NULL)
    # ...

    def get_url_path(self):
        try:
            path = reverse("bulletin_detail",
                           kwargs={"pk": self.pk})
        except:
            # the apphook is not attached yet
            return ""
        else:
            return path
```

3. Migrate the `bulletin_board` app to update the database according to the model changes.

4. Then, create `BulletinFilterForm` that allows the visitor to filter the bulletins by type and category, as follows:

```
# bulletin_board/forms.py
# ...other imports...
from django import forms
from django.utils.translation import ugettext_lazy as _

from .models import Bulletin, Category, TYPE_CHOICES
```

```
TYPE_FILTER_CHOICES = (("", "----------"),) + TYPE_CHOICES


class BulletinFilterForm(forms.Form):
    bulletin_type = forms.ChoiceField(
        label=_("Bulletin Type"),
        required=False,
        choices=TYPE_FILTER_CHOICES)
    category = forms.ModelChoiceField(
        label=_("Category"),
        required=False,
        queryset=Category.objects.all())

# ...
```

5. Add a feeds.py file with the BulletinFeed class, as shown here:

```
# bulletin_board/feeds.py
from django.contrib.syndication.views import Feed
from django.urls import reverse

from .models import Bulletin, TYPE_CHOICES
from .forms import BulletinFilterForm


class BulletinFeed(Feed):
    description_template = \
        "bulletin_board/feeds/bulletin_description.html"

    def get_object(self, request, *args, **kwargs):
        form = BulletinFilterForm(data=request.GET)
        obj = {}
        if form.is_valid():
            obj = {"query_string": request.META["QUERY_STRING"]}
            for field in ["bulletin_type", "category"]:
                value = form.cleaned_data.get(field, None)
                obj[field] = value
        return obj

    def title(self, obj):
        title_parts = ["Bulletin Board"]

        # add type "Searching" or "Offering"
        type_key = obj.get("bulletin_type", False)
        type = dict(TYPE_CHOICES).get(type_key, False) \
            if type_key else ""
        if type:
            title_parts.append(type)
```

```
        # add category
        category = obj.get("category", False)
        if category:
            title_parts.append(category.title)

        return " - ".join(title_parts)

    def link(self, obj):
        return self.get_named_url("bulletin-list", obj)

    def feed_url(self, obj):
        return self.get_named_url("bulletin-rss", obj)

    @staticmethod
    def get_named_url(name, obj):
        url = reverse(name)
        qs = obj.get("query_string", False)
        if qs:
            url = f"{url}?{qs}"
        return url

    def item_pubdate(self, item):
        return item.created

    def items(self, obj):
        type = obj.get("bulletin_type", False)
        category = obj.get("category", False)

        qs = Bulletin.objects.order_by("-created")
        if type:
            qs = qs.filter(bulletin_type=type).distinct()
        if category:
            qs = qs.filter(category=category).distinct()
        return qs[:30]
```

6. Create a template for the bulletin description that will be provided in the feed, as shown here:

```
{# templates/bulletin_board/feeds/bulletin_description.html #}
{% if obj.image %}
<p>
    <a href="{{ obj.get_url }}">
        <img src="{{ MEDIA_URL }}{{ obj.image.url }}"
            alt="" /></a>
</p>
{% endif %}
<p>{{ obj.description }}</p>
```

7. Create a URL configuration for the `bulletin_board` app, or update the existing one, and include it in the root URL configuration. The result should include the new feed URL rule, as follows:

```
# templates/bulletin_board/urls.py
from django.urls import path, reverse_lazy

from .feeds import BulletinFeed
from .views import (BulletinList, BulletinDetail)


urlpatterns = [
    path('', BulletinList.as_view(),
        name='bulletin-list'),
    path('<int:pk>/', BulletinDetail.as_view(),
        name='bulletin-detail'),
    path('rss/', BulletinFeed(),
        name='bulletin-rss'),
    # ...
]
```

8. You will also need views for the filterable list and details of the bulletins:

```
# bulletin_board/views.py
# ...other imports...
from django.views.generic import ListView, DetailView

from .models import Bulletin

# ...

class BulletinList(ListView):
    model = Bulletin


class BulletinDetail(DetailView):
    model = Bulletin

# ...
```

9. Next, add a `Bulletins` listing page template, including the RSS feed link, as follows:

```
{# templates/bulletin_board/bulletin_list.html #}
{% extends "base.html" %}
{% load i18n %}

{% block content %}
```

```
<h2>{% trans "Bulletins" %}</h2>
{% if bulletin_list.count == 0 %}
<p>
    No bulletins to show! Why don't you
    <a href="{% url "bulletin-create" %}">
        create a new bulletin</a>?
</p>
{% else %}
<dl class="bulletin-list">
    {% for bulletin in bulletin_list %}
    <dt>
        <a href="{% url "bulletin-detail" pk=bulletin.pk %}">
            {{ bulletin.title }}</a>
        {% if request.user.is_authenticated %}
        <a class="btn btn-outline-secondary btn-sm"
            href="{% url "bulletin-edit" pk=bulletin.pk %}">
            Edit</a>
        {% endif %}
    </dt>
    <dd>
        {% if bulletin.description %}
        <p>{{ bulletin.description }}</p>
        {% endif %}
    </dd>
    {% endfor %}
</dl>
<p>
    <a href="{% url "bulletin-rss" %}?{{ request.META.QUERY_STRING
}}">
        RSS Feed</a>
</p>
{% endif %}
{% endblock %}
```

10. Finally, add a `Bulletins` detail page template, which can reuse the same `bulletin_description.html` template, as shown here:

```
{# templates/bulletin_board/bulletin_detail.html #}
{% extends "base.html" %}
{% load i18n %}

{% block content %}
<h1>
    {{ object.bulletin_type|capfirst }}:
    <strong>{{ object.title }}</strong>
    {% if request.user.is_authenticated %}
    <a class="btn btn-outline-secondary btn-sm"
        href="{% url "bulletin-edit" pk=bulletin.pk %}">Edit</a>
```

```
        {% endif %}
</h1>

{% if category %}
<p><em>{{ object.category.title }}</em></p>
{% endif %}

{% include "bulletin_board/feeds/bulletin_description.html" with
obj=object %}

<h3>Contact {{ object.contact_person }}</h3>

{% if object.phone or object.email %}
    {% if object.phone %}
    <p>Phone: {{ object.phone }}</p>
    {% endif %}

    {% if object.email %}
    <p>Email: <a href="mailto:{{ object.email }}?subject={{
object.title|escape }}">
        {{ object.email }}</p>
    {% endif %}
{% endif %}

<p><a href="{% url "bulletin-list" %}">Back to Listing</a></p>
{% endblock %}
```

How it works...

If you have some data in the database and you open
http://127.0.0.1:8000/bulletin-board/rss/?bulletin_type=offering&catego
ry=4 in your browser, you will get an RSS feed of bulletins with the Offering type and the
category ID of 4. The Feed class takes care of automatically generating the XML markup for
the RSS feed.

The BulletinFeed class has the get_objects() method that takes the current
HttpRequest and defines the obj dictionary used in other methods of the same class. The
obj dictionary contains the bulletin type, the category, and the current query string.

The `title()` method returns the title of the feed. It can either be generic or related to the selected bulletin type or category. The `link()` method returns the link to the original bulletin list with the filtering done. The `feed_url()` method returns the URL of the current feed. The `items()` method does the filtering itself and returns a filtered `QuerySet` of bulletins. Finally, the `item_pubdate()` method returns the creation date of the bulletin.

To see all the available methods and properties of the `Feed` class that we are extending, refer to the following documentation at
`https://docs.djangoproject.com/en/2.1/ref/contrib/syndication/#feed-class-refer`
`ence`.

The other parts of the code are self-explanatory.

See also

- The *Creating a model mixin with URL-related methods* recipe in `Chapter 2`, *Database Structure and Modeling*
- The *Creating a model mixin to handle creation and modification dates* recipe in `Chapter 2`, *Database Structure and Modeling*
- The *Creating a form layout with custom template* recipe in `Chapter 3`, *Forms and Views*
- The *Using Tastypie to create an API* recipe

Using Tastypie to create an API

Tastypie is a framework for Django for creating a web service **Application Program Interface (API)**. It supports the full set of `HTTP` protocol methods (`GET`/`POST`/`PUT`/`DELETE`/`PATCH`) to deal with online resources. It also supports different types of authentication and authorization, serialization, caching, throttling, and so on. In this recipe, you will learn how to provide bulletins to third parties for reading; that is, we will implement only the `GET` HTTP method here.

Getting ready

First of all, install `tastypie` in your virtual environment using the following command (or add to your requirements file for a Docker project):

```
(myproject_env)$ pip install django-tastypie~=0.14.0
```

Add `tastypie` to `INSTALLED_APPS` in the settings. Then, enhance the `bulletin_board` app that we worked with in the *Creating filterable RSS feeds* recipe.

How to do it...

We will create an API for bulletins and inject it in the URL configuration as follows:

1. In the `bulletin_board` app, create an `api.py` file with two resources, `CategoryResource` and `BulletinResource`, as follows:

```python
# bulletin_board/api.py
from tastypie import fields
from tastypie.authentication import ApiKeyAuthentication
from tastypie.authorization import ReadOnlyAuthorization
from tastypie.resources import (ModelResource,
                                ALL,
                                ALL_WITH_RELATIONS)

from .models import Category, Bulletin


class CategoryResource(ModelResource):
    class Meta:
        queryset = Category.objects.all()
        resource_name = "categories"
        fields = ["title"]
        allowed_methods = ["get"]
        authentication = ApiKeyAuthentication()
        authorization = ReadOnlyAuthorization()
        filtering = {
            "title": ALL,
        }


class BulletinResource(ModelResource):
    class Meta:
        queryset = Bulletin.objects.all()
        resource_name = "bulletins"
```

```
                    fields = [
                        "bulletin_type", "category", "title",
                        "description", "contact_person", "phone",
                        "email", "image"
                    ]
                    allowed_methods = ["get"]
                    authentication = ApiKeyAuthentication()
                    authorization = ReadOnlyAuthorization()
                    filtering = {
                        "bulletin_type": ALL,
                        "title": ALL,
                        "category": ALL_WITH_RELATIONS,
                        "created": ["gt", "gte", "exact", "lte", "lt"],
                    }

                category = fields.ForeignKey(CategoryResource, "category",
                                             null=True,
                                             blank=True,
                                             full=True)
```

2. In the main URL configuration, include the API URLs, as follows:

```
# project/urls.py
# ...other imports...
from django.conf import settings
from django.urls import include, path
from tastypie.api import Api

from bulletin_board.api import BulletinResource, CategoryResource

v1_api = Api(api_name="v1")
v1_api.register(CategoryResource())
v1_api.register(BulletinResource())

urlpatterns = [
    path('admin/', admin.site.urls),
    path("api/", include(v1_api.urls)),
    path('bulletins/', include('bulletin_board.urls')),
    # ...
]
```

3. Create a Tastypie API key for the admin user in the model administration. To do this, navigate to **Tastypie** | **Api key** | **Add Api key**, select the admin user, and save the entry. This will generate a random API key, as shown in the following screenshot:

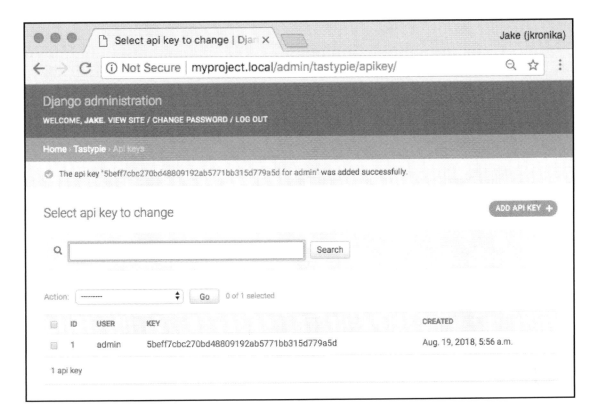

4. Then, you can open this URL to see the JSON response in action:
`http://127.0.0.1:8000/api/v1/bulletins/?format=json&username=ad min&api_key=xxx`
Simply replace `xxx` with your API key, and `admin` with the appropriate username if necessary, and the result should appear something like the following (formatted here using the JSONView extension for Chrome):

How it works...

Each endpoint of Tastypie should have a class extending `ModelResource` defined. Similar to the Django models, the configuration of the resource is set in the `Meta` class:

- The `queryset` parameter defines the `QuerySet` of objects to list.
- The `resource_name` parameter defines the name of the URL endpoint for reverse lookup.
- The `fields` parameter lists out the fields of the model that should be shown in the API. Alternatively, `excludes` can be used to blacklist fields instead.

- The `allowed_methods` parameter lists the request methods, such as GET, POST, PUT, DELETE, and PATCH (this being the default set). It is also possible to specify a different set of `list_allowed_methods` for listings, and `detail_allowed_methods` for individual records.
- The `authentication` parameter defines how third parties can authenticate themselves when connecting to the API. The available options are `Authentication` (default), `BasicAuthentication`, `ApiKeyAuthentication`, `SessionAuthentication`, `DigestAuthentication`, `OAuthAuthentication`, `MultiAuthentication`, or your own custom authentication. In our case, we are using `ApiKeyAuthentication` as we want each user to use `username` and `api_key`.
- The `authorization` parameter answers the authorization question: is permission granted to this user to take the stated action? The possible choices are `Authorization`, `ReadOnlyAuthorization`, `DjangoAuthorization`, or your own custom authorization. In our case, we are using `ReadOnlyAuthorization`, as we only want to allow read access to the users.
- The `filtering` parameter defines which fields you can use to filter lists via the URL query parameters. For example, with the current configuration, you can filter the items by titles that contain the word `movie`:
  `http://127.0.0.1:8000/api/v1/bulletins/format=json&username=admin&api_key=xxx&title__contains=movie`.

Also, there is a `category` foreign key that is defined in `BulletinResource` with the `full=True` argument, meaning that the full list of category fields will be shown in the bulletin resource instead of an endpoint link.

Besides JSON, Tastypie allows you to use other formats such as XML, YAML, and bplist.

There is a lot more that you can do with APIs using Tastypie. To find out more details, check the official documentation at
`http://django-tastypie.readthedocs.org/en/latest/`.

See also

- The *Creating filterable RSS feeds* recipe
- The *Using Django REST framework to create an API* recipe

Using Django REST framework to create an API

Besides Tastypie, the Django REST framework is a newer and fresher framework for creating an API for your data transfers to and from third parties. This framework has more extensive documentation and a Django-centric implementation, helping make it more maintainable. Therefore, if you have to choose between Tastypie or the Django REST Framework, we recommend the latter. In this recipe, you will learn how to use the Django REST Framework to allow your project partners, mobile clients, or Ajax-based website to access data on your site to create, read, update, and delete content as appropriate.

Getting ready

First of all, install Django REST Framework in your virtual environment using the following command (or, for Docker projects, add it to your requirements file and rebuild):

```
(myproject_env)$ pip install djangorestframework~=3.8.2
```

Add `rest_framework` to `INSTALLED_APPS` in the settings. Then, enhance the `bulletin_board` app that we defined in the *Creating filterable RSS feeds* recipe. You will also want to collect the static files provided by the Django REST Framework for the pages it provides to be as nicely styled as possible:

```
(myproject_env)$ python3 manage.py collectstatic
```

How to do it...

To integrate a new REST API in our `bulletin_board` app, execute the following steps:

1. Add configurations for the Django REST Framework to the settings as shown here:

```
# settings.py or conf/base.py
REST_FRAMEWORK = {
    "DEFAULT_PERMISSION_CLASSES": [
        "rest_framework.permissions."
        "DjangoModelPermissionsOrAnonReadOnly"
    ],
```

```
    "DEFAULT_PAGINATION_CLASS":
        "rest_framework.pagination.LimitOffsetPagination",
    "PAGE_SIZE": 100,
}
```

2. In the `bulletin_board` app, create the `serializers.py` file with the following content:

```python
# bulletin_board/serializers.py
from rest_framework import serializers

from .models import Category, Bulletin


class CategorySerializer(serializers.ModelSerializer):
    class Meta:
        model = Category
        fields = ["id", "title"]


class BulletinSerializer(serializers.ModelSerializer):
    class Meta:
        model = Bulletin
        fields = ["id", "bulletin_type", "title",
                  "description", "contact_person", "phone",
                  "email", "image", "category"]

    category = CategorySerializer()

    def create(self, validated_data):
        category_data = validated_data.pop('category')
        category, created = Category.objects.get_or_create(
            title=category_data['title'])
        bulletin = Bulletin.objects.create(category=category,
                                           **validated_data)
        return bulletin

    def update(self, instance, validated_data):
        category_data = validated_data.pop('category')
        category, created = Category.objects.get_or_create(
            title=category_data['title'])
        for fname, fvalue in validated_data.items():
            setattr(instance, fname, fvalue)
        instance.category = category
        instance.save()
        return instance
```

3. Add two new class-based views to the `views.py` file in the `bulletin_board` app:

```python
# bulletin_board/views.py
from rest_framework import generics

from .models import Bulletin
from .serializers import BulletinSerializer

# ...

class RESTBulletinList(generics.ListCreateAPIView):
    queryset = Bulletin.objects.all()
    serializer_class = BulletinSerializer


class RESTBulletinDetail(generics.RetrieveUpdateDestroyAPIView):
    queryset = Bulletin.objects.all()
    serializer_class = BulletinSerializer
```

4. Finally, plug in the new views to the project URL configuration:

```python
# project/urls.py
from django.urls import include, path
from bulletin_board.views import (RESTBulletinList,
                                  RESTBulletinDetail)

urlpatterns = [
    # ...
    path("api-auth/",
        include("rest_framework.urls",
               namespace="rest_framework")),
    path("rest-api/bulletin-board/",
        RESTBulletinList.as_view(),
        name="rest_bulletin_list"),
    path("rest-api/bulletin-board/<int:pk>",
        RESTBulletinDetail.as_view(),
        name="rest_bulletin_detail"),
]
```

How it works...

What we created here is an API for the bulletin board, where you can read a paginated bulletin list, create a new bulletin, and read, change, or delete a single bulletin by ID. Reading is allowed without authentication, but you have to have a user account with the appropriate permissions to add, change, or delete a bulletin. The Django REST Framework provides you with a web-based API documentation that is shown when you access the API endpoints in a browser via GET. Without logging in, the framework would display something like this:

Here's how you can approach the created API:

URL	HTTP Method	Description
`/rest-api/bulletin-board/`	GET	List bulletins paginated by 100.
`/rest-api/bulletin-board/`	POST	Create a new bulletin if the requesting user is authenticated and authorized to create bulletins.
`/rest-api/bulletin-board/1/`	GET	Get a bulletin with the 1 ID.
`/rest-api/bulletin-board/1/`	PUT	Update a bulletin with the 1 ID, if the user is authenticated and authorized to change bulletins.
`/rest-api/bulletin-board/1/`	DELETE	Delete the bulletin with the 1 ID, if the user is authenticated and authorized to delete bulletins.

You might ask how you would use the API practically. For example, we might use the `curl` command to create a new bulletin via the command line, as follows:

```
(myproject_env)$ curl "http://127.0.0.1:8000/rest-api/bulletin-board/" \
> -d bulletin_type=searching -d title=TEST -d contact_person=TEST \
> -d category.title=TEST -d description=TEST -u admin
Enter host password for user 'admin':
{"id":2,"bulletin_type":"searching","category":{"id":2,"title":"TEST"},"tit
le":"TEST","description":"TEST","contact_person":"TEST","phone":"","email":
"","image":null}
```

The same could be done via Postman, which provides a user-friendly interface for submitting requests, as seen here:

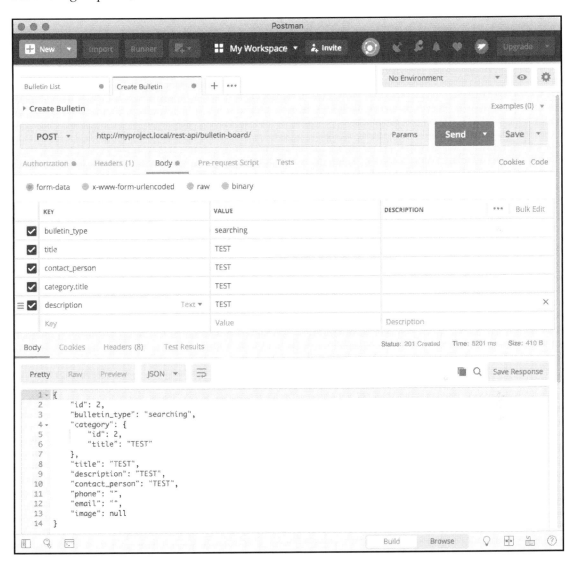

You can also try out the APIs via integrated forms under the framework-generated API documentation, when logged in, as shown in the following screenshot:

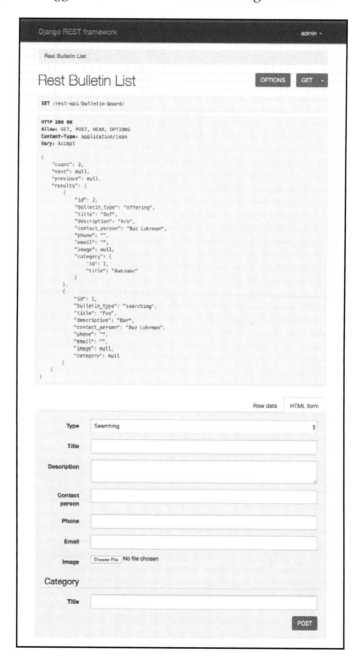

Let's take a quick look at how the code that we wrote works. In the settings, we have set the access to be dependent on the permissions of the Django system. For anonymous requests, only reading is allowed. Other access options include allowing any permission to everyone, allowing any permission only to authenticated users, allowing any permission to staff users, and so on. The full list can be found at
`http://www.django-rest-framework.org/api-guide/permissions/`.

Then, in the settings, pagination is set. The current option is to have the `limit` and `offset` parameters as in an SQL query. Other options are to have either the pagination by page numbers for rather static content or cursor pagination for real-time data. We set the default pagination to 100 items per page.

Later, we define serializers for categories and bulletins. They handle the data that will be shown in the output or validated by the input. To handle category retrieval or saving, we have to overwrite the `create()` and `update()` methods of `BulletinSerializer`. There are various ways to serialize relations in Django REST Framework, and we chose the most verbose one in our example. To read more about how to serialize relations, refer to the documentation at `http://www.django-rest-framework.org/api-guide/relations/`.

After defining the serializers, we created two class-based views to handle the API endpoints and plugged them into the URL configuration. In the URL configuration, we have a rule (`/api-auth/`) for browsable API pages, login, and logout.

See also

- The *Creating filterable RSS feeds* recipe
- The *Using Tastypie to create an API* recipe
- The *Testing an API created using Django REST framework* recipe in `Chapter 11`, *Testing and Deployment*

11
Bells and Whistles

In this chapter, we will cover the following recipes:

- Using the Django shell
- Using database query expressions
- Monkey patching the `slugify()` function for better internationalization support
- Toggling the Debug Toolbar
- Using `ThreadLocalMiddleware`
- Using signals to notify administrators about new entries
- Checking for missing settings

Introduction

In this chapter, we will go over several important bits and pieces that will help you to better understand and utilize Django. We will provide an overview of how to use the Django shell to experiment with the code, before writing it in the files. You will be introduced to monkey patching, also known as guerrilla patching, which is a powerful feature of dynamic languages, such as Python and Ruby. Full-text search capabilities will be revealed, and you will learn how to debug your code and check its performance. Then, you will learn how to access the currently logged-in user (and other request parameters) from any module. Also, you will learn how to handle signals and create system checks. Get ready for an interesting programming experience!

Using the Django shell

With the virtual environment activated and your project directory selected as the current directory, enter the following command in your command-line tool:

```
(myproject_env)$ python3 manage.py shell
```

If you are using a Docker project, this process is similar; however, first you need to connect to your app:

```
$ docker-compose exec app /bin/bash
/usr/src/app# python3 manage.py shell
```

By executing the preceding command, you will get into an interactive Python shell, configured for your Django project, where you can play around with the code, inspect the classes, try out methods, or execute scripts on the fly. In this recipe, we will go over the most important functions that you need to know in order to work with the Django shell.

Getting ready

You can install either IPython or bpython to provide additional interface options for Python shells, or you can install both, if you want a choice. These will highlight the syntax for the output of your Django shell, and will add some other helpers. Install them by using one of the following commands for a virtual environment, or add them to your requirements and rebuild for a Docker project:

```
(myproject_env)$ pip3 install ipython~=6.5.0
(myproject_env)$ pip3 install bpython~=0.17.1
```

How to do it...

Learn the basics of using the Django shell by following these instructions:

1. Run the Django shell by typing the following command:

    ```
    (myproject_env)$ python3 manage.py shell
    ```

    If you have installed IPython or bpython, it will automatically become the default interface when you are entering the shell. You can also use a particular interface by adding the -i <interface> option to the preceding command. The prompt will change, according to which interface you use. The following screenshot shows what an IPython shell might look like, starting with In [1] as the prompt:

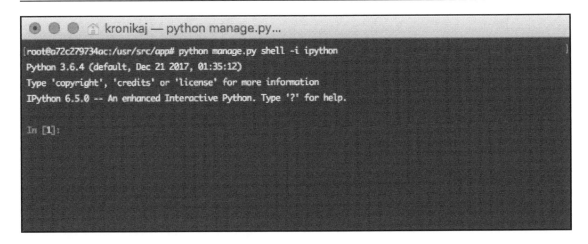

If you use `bpython`, the shell will be shown with the >>> prompt, along with code highlighting and text autocompletion when typing, as follows:

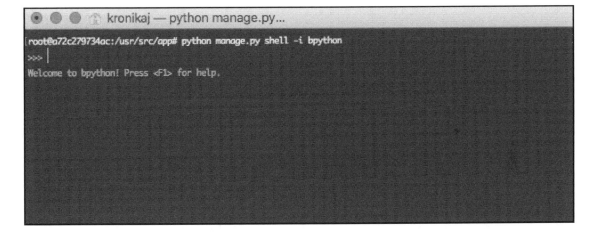

The default Python interface shell looks as follows, also using the >>> prompt, but with a preamble that provides information about the system:

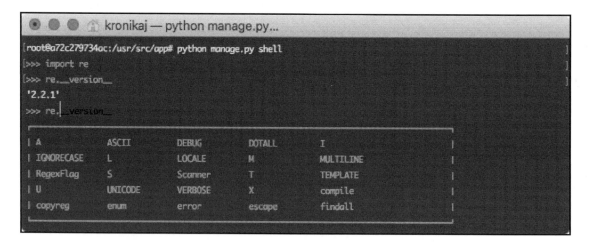

2. Now, you can import classes, functions, or variables, and play around with them. For example, to see the version of an installed module, you can import the module and then try to read its __version__, VERSION, or version properties (shown using bpython, and demonstrating both its highlighting and autocompletion features), as follows:

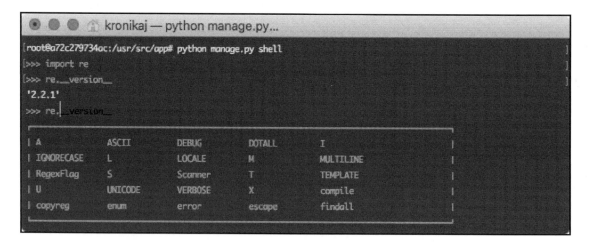

3. To get a comprehensive description of a module, class, function, method, keyword, or documentation topic, use the `help()` function. You can either pass a string with the path to a specific entity, or the entity itself, as follows:

```
>>> help("django.forms")
```

This will open the help page for the `django.forms` module. Use the arrow keys to scroll the page up and down. Press *Q* to get back to the shell.

If you run `help()` without the parameters, it opens an interactive help page. There, you can enter any path of a module, class, function, and so onto, and get information on what it does and how to use it. To quit the interactive help, press *Ctrl + D*.

4. The following is an example of passing an entity to the `help()` function, shown with `IPython`:

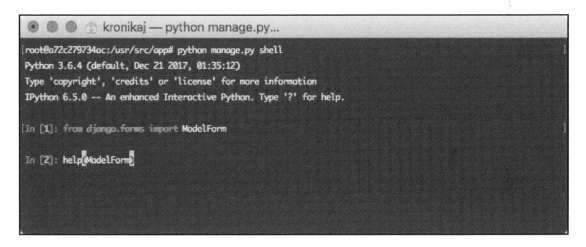

Doing so will open a help page for the `ModelForm` class, as follows:

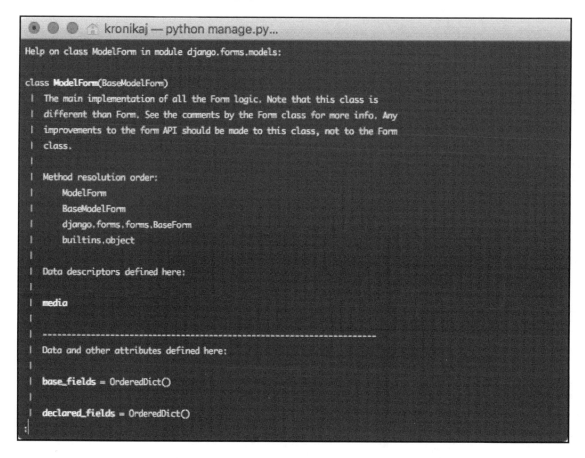

5. To quickly see what fields and values are available for a model instance, use the `__dict__` attribute. Also, use the `pprint()` function to get the dictionaries printed in a more readable format (not just one long line), as shown in the following screenshot. Note that when we are using `__dict__`, we don't get many-to-many relationships. However, this might be enough for a quick overview of the fields and values:

```
●  ●  ●  🏠 kronikaj — python manage.py...

[root@o72c279734ac:/usr/src/app# python manage.py shell -i bpython
[>>> from django.contrib.contenttypes.models import ContentType
[>>> content_type = ContentType.objects.all()[0]
[>>> content_type.__dict__
{'_state': <django.db.models.base.ModelState object at 0x7f8eb5d8f278>, 'id': 1, 'app_label': 'admin', 'model': '
logentry'}
[>>> from pprint import pprint
[>>> pprint(content_type.__dict__)
{'_state': <django.db.models.base.ModelState object at 0x7f8eb5d8f278>,
 'app_label': 'admin',
 'id': 1,
 'model': 'logentry'}
```

6. To get all of the available properties and methods of an object, you can use the `dir()` function, as follows:

```
●  ●  ●  🏠 kronikaj — python manage.py...

[>>> dir(ContentType)
['DoesNotExist', 'MultipleObjectsReturned', '__class__', '__delattr__', '__dict__', '__dir__', '__doc__', '__eq__
', '__format__', '__ge__', '__getattribute__', '__getstate__', '__gt__', '__hash__', '__init__', '__init_subclass
__', '__le__', '__lt__', '__module__', '__ne__', '__new__', '__reduce__', '__reduce_ex__', '__repr__', '__setattr
__', '__setstate__', '__sizeof__', '__str__', '__subclasshook__', '__weakref__', '_check_column_name_clashes', '_
check_field_name_clashes', '_check_fields', '_check_id_field', '_check_index_together', '_check_local_fields', '_
check_long_column_names', '_check_m2m_through_same_relationship', '_check_managers', '_check_model', '_check_mode
l_name_db_lookup_clashes', '_check_ordering', '_check_swappable', '_check_unique_together', '_do_insert', '_do_up
date', '_get_FIELD_display', '_get_next_or_previous_by_FIELD', '_get_next_or_previous_in_order', '_get_pk_val', '
_get_unique_checks', '_meta', '_perform_date_checks', '_perform_unique_checks', '_save_parents', '_save_table', '
_set_pk_val', 'app_label', 'check', 'clean', 'clean_fields', 'date_error_message', 'delete', 'from_db', 'full_cle
an', 'get_all_objects_for_this_type', 'get_deferred_fields', 'get_object_for_this_type', 'id', 'like_set', 'liked
', 'logentry_set', 'model', 'model_class', 'name', 'natural_key', 'objects', 'owner', 'permission_set', 'pk', 'pr
epare_database_save', 'refresh_from_db', 'save', 'save_base', 'serializable_value', 'unique_error_message', 'vali
date_unique']
```

To get these attributes printed one per line, you can use the following code:

```
● ● ●  ⌂ kronikaj — python manage.py...
[>>> pprint(dir(ContentType))
['DoesNotExist',
 'MultipleObjectsReturned',
 '__class__',
 '__delattr__',
 '__dict__',
 '__dir__',
 '__doc__',
 '__eq__',
 '__format__',
 '__ge__',
 '__getattribute__',
 '__getstate__',
 '__gt__',
 '__hash__',
```

7. The Django shell is useful for experimenting with QuerySets or regular expressions, before putting them into your model methods, views, or management commands. For example, to check the email validation regular expression, you can type the following into the Django shell:

```
>>> import re
>>> email_pattern = re.compile(r"[^@]+@[^@]+.[^@]+")
>>> email_pattern.match("aidas@bendoraitis.lt")
<_sre.SRE_Match object at 0x1075681d0>
```

8. If you want to try out different QuerySets, you need to execute the setup of the models and apps in your project, shown as follows:

```
>>> import django
>>> django.setup()
>>> from django.contrib.auth.models import User
>>> User.objects.filter(groups__name="Editors")
[<User: admin>]
```

9. To exit the Django shell, press *Ctrl + D,* or type the following command:

```
>>> exit()
```

How it works...

The difference between a normal Python shell and the Django shell is that when you run the Django shell, `manage.py` sets the `DJANGO_SETTINGS_MODULE` environment variable so that it points to the project's `settings.py` path, and then all of the code in the Django shell is handled in the context of your project. With the use of the third-party `IPython` or `bpython` interfaces, we can enhance the default Python shell further, with syntax highlighting, autocompletion, and more.

See also

- The *Using database query expressions* recipe
- The *Monkey patching the slugify() function for better internationalization support* recipe

Using database query expressions

Django **object-relational mapping (ORM)** comes with special abstraction constructs that can be used to build complex database queries. They are called **query expressions**, and they allow you to filter data, order it, annotate new columns, and aggregate relations. In this recipe, you will see how that can be used in practice. We will create an app that shows viral videos and counts how many times each video has been seen by anonymous (versus logged-in) users.

Getting ready

To start, let's create the `viral_videos` app and add it under `INSTALLED_APPS`:

```
# settings.py or conf/base.py
INSTALLED_APPS = (
    # ...
    # local apps
    "utils",
    "viral_videos",
)
```

Next, create a model for viral videos, with creation and modification timestamps, a title, embedded code, impressions by anonymous users, and impressions by authenticated users, as follows:

```python
# viral_videos/models.py
from django.db import models
from django.utils.translation import ugettext_lazy as _
from utils.models import CreationModificationDateMixin, UrlMixin


class ViralVideo(CreationModificationDateMixin, UrlMixin):
    class Meta:
        verbose_name = _("Viral video")
        verbose_name_plural = _("Viral videos")

    title = models.CharField(
        _("Title"),
        max_length=200,
        blank=True)
    embed_code = models.TextField(
        _("YouTube embed code"),
        blank=True)
    anonymous_views = models.PositiveIntegerField(
        _("Anonymous impressions"),
        default=0)
    authenticated_views = models.PositiveIntegerField(
        _("Authenticated impressions"),
        default=0)

    def get_url_path(self):
        from django.urls import reverse
        return reverse("viral-video-detail",
                       kwargs={"id": str(self.id)})

    def __str__(self):
        return self.title
```

Be sure to make and run migrations for the new app, so that your database will be ready to go:

```
(myproject_env)$ python3 manage.py makemigrations viral_videos
(myproject_env)$ python3 manage.py migrate viral_videos
```

How to do it...

To illustrate the query expressions, let's create the viral video detail view and plug it into the URL configuration, as follows:

1. Create the `viral_video_detail` view in `views.py`, as follows:

```python
# viral_videos/views.py
import datetime, logging

from django.conf import settings
from django.db import models
from django.shortcuts import render, get_object_or_404

from .models import ViralVideo

POPULAR_FROM = getattr(
    settings, "VIRAL_VIDEOS_POPULAR_FROM", 500
)

logger = logging.getLogger(__name__)


def viral_video_detail(request, pk):
    yesterday = datetime.date.today() - datetime.timedelta(days=1)

    qs = ViralVideo.objects.annotate(
        total_views=models.F("authenticated_views") +
                        models.F("anonymous_views"),
        label=models.Case(
            models.When(total_views__gt=POPULAR_FROM,
                    then=models.Value("popular")),
            models.When(created__gt=yesterday,
                    then=models.Value("new")),
            default=models.Value("cool"),
            output_field=models.CharField()))

    # DEBUG: check the SQL query that Django ORM generates
    logger.debug(qs.query)

    qs = qs.filter(pk=pk)
    if request.user.is_authenticated:
        qs.update(authenticated_views=models.F(
            "authenticated_views") + 1)
    else:
        qs.update(anonymous_views=models.F(
            "anonymous_views") + 1)
```

```
            video = get_object_or_404(qs)

            return render(request,
                          "viral_videos/viral_video_detail.html",
                          {'video': video})
```

2. Define the URL configuration for the app, shown as follows:

```
# viral_videos/urls.py
from django.urls import path

from .views import viral_video_detail

urlpatterns = [
    path('<int:pk>/', viral_video_detail,
        name='viral-video-detail'),
]
```

3. Include the URL configuration of the app in the project's root URL configuration, as follows:

```
# project/urls.py
from django.urls import include, path

urlpatterns = [
    # ...
    path('videos/', include('viral_videos.urls')),
]
```

4. Create a template for the `viral_video_detail` view, as follows:

```
{# templates/viral_videos/viral_video_detail.html #}
{% extends "base.html" %}
{% load i18n %}

{% block content %}
    <h1>{{ video.title }}
        <span class="badge">{{ video.label }}</span>
    </h1>
    <div>{{ video.embed_code|safe }}</div>
    <div>
        <h2>{% trans "Impressions" %}</h2>
        <ul>
            <li>{% trans "Authenticated views" %}:
                {{ video.authenticated_views }}</li>
            <li>{% trans "Anonymous views" %}:
                {{ video.anonymous_views }}</li>
            <li>{% trans "Total views" %}:
```

```
                                    {{ video.total_views }}</li>
            </ul>
        </div>
    {% endblock %}
```

5. Set up administration for the `viral_videos` app, as follows, and add some videos to the database when you are finished:

```python
# viral_videos/admin.py
from django.contrib import admin

from .models import ViralVideo

admin.site.register(ViralVideo)
```

How it works...

You might have noticed the `logger.debug()` statement in the view. If you run the server in `DEBUG` mode and access a video in the browser (for example, `http://127.0.0.1:8000/videos/1/`, in local development), you will see a SQL query like the following printed in the logs (formatted for readability), depending on your `LOGGING` settings:

```sql
SELECT `viral_videos_viralvideo`.`id`,
       `viral_videos_viralvideo`.`created`,
       `viral_videos_viralvideo`.`updated`,
       `viral_videos_viralvideo`.`title`,
       `viral_videos_viralvideo`.`embed_code`,
       `viral_videos_viralvideo`.`anonymous_views`,
       `viral_videos_viralvideo`.`authenticated_views`,
      (`viral_videos_viralvideo`.`authenticated_views` +
       `viral_videos_viralvideo`.`anonymous_views`) AS `total_views`,
      CASE WHEN (`viral_videos_viralvideo`.`authenticated_views` +
                 `viral_videos_viralvideo`.`anonymous_views`) > 500
            THEN popular
          WHEN `viral_videos_viralvideo`.`created` > 2018-10-06
          00:00:00
            THEN new
          ELSE cool
      END AS `label`
FROM `viral_videos_viralvideo`
WHERE `viral_videos_viralvideo`.`id` = 1
```

Then in the browser, you will see a simple page showing:

- The title of the video
- The label of the video
- The embedded video
- Impressions by authenticated users, anonymous users, and in total

This will be similar to the following image:

The `annotate()` method in Django QuerySets allows you to add extra columns to the `SELECT` SQL statement, as well as properties that were created on the fly, for the objects retrieved from QuerySets. With `models.F()`, we can reference different field values from the selected database table. In this example, we will create the `total_views` property, which is the sum of the impressions by authenticated and anonymous users.

With `models.Case()` and `models.When()`, we can return the values according to different conditions. To mark the values, we are using `models.Value()`. In our example, we will create the `label` column for the SQL query and the property for the objects returned by QuerySet. It will be set to `popular` if it has more than 500 impressions, `new` if it was created today, and `cool` otherwise.

At the end of the view, we have called the `qs.update()` methods. They increment `authenticated_views` or `anonymous_views` of the current video, depending on whether the user looking at the video was logged in. The incrementation happens at the SQL level. This solves issues with so-called race conditions, when two or more visitors are accessing the view at the same time, trying to increase the impression count simultaneously.

See also

- The *Using the Django shell* recipe
- The *Creating a model mixin with URL-related methods* recipe in `Chapter 2`, *Database Structure and Modeling*
- The *Creating a model mixin to handle creation and modification dates* recipe in `Chapter 2`, *Database Structure and Modeling*

Monkey patching the slugify() function for better internationalization support

A monkey patch (or guerrilla patch) is a piece of code that extends or modifies another piece of code at runtime. It is not recommended to use monkey patches often; however, sometimes, they are the only possible way to fix a bug in third-party modules, without creating a separate branch of the module. Also, monkey patching can be used to prepare functional or unit tests, without using complex database or file manipulations.

In this recipe, you will learn how to exchange the default `slugify()` function with the one from the third-party `transliterate` module, which handles the conversion of Unicode characters to ASCII equivalents more intelligently, and includes a number of language packs that provide even more specific transformations, as needed. As a quick reminder, we use the `slugify()` utility to create a URL-friendly version of an object's title or uploaded filename. In its processing, the function strips any leading and trailing whitespace, converts the text to lowercase, removes non-word characters, and converts spaces to hyphens.

Getting ready

1. Install `transliterate` in your virtual environment (as follows), or update your requirements file and rebuild the containers for Docker projects:

   ```
   (myproject_env)$ pip3 install transliterate~=1.10.2
   ```

2. Then, create a `guerrilla_patches` app in your project and put it under `INSTALLED_APPS` in the settings.

How to do it...

In the `models.py` file of the `guerrilla_patches` app, add the following content:

```
# guerrilla_patches/models.py
from django.utils import text
from transliterate import slugify

text.slugify = slugify
```

How it works...

The default Django `slugify()` function handles German diacritical symbols incorrectly. To see this for yourself, run the following code in the Django shell, without the monkey patch:

```
(myproject_env)$ python3 manage.py shell
>>> from django.utils.text import slugify
>>> slugify("Heizölrückstoßabdämpfung")
'heizolruckstoabdampfung'
```

This is incorrect in German, as the letter ß is totally stripped out, instead of substituting it with `ss`; the letters ä, ö, and ü are changed to a, o, and u, whereas they should be substituted with `ae`, `oe`, and `ue`.

The monkey patch that we created loads the `django.utils.text` module at initialization and reassigns `transliteration.slugify` in place of the core `slugify()` function. Now, if you run the same code in the Django shell, you will get different (but correct) results, as follows:

```
(myproject_env)$ python manage.py shell
>>> from django.utils.text import slugify
```

```
>>> slugify("Heizölrückstoßabdämpfung")
'heizoelrueckstossabdaempfung'
```

To read more about how to utilize the `transliterate` module, refer to `https://pypi.org/project/transliterate`.

There's more...

Before creating a monkey patch, we need to completely understand how the code that we want to modify works. This can be done by analyzing the existing code and inspecting the values of different variables. To do this, there is a useful, built-in Python debugger `pdb` module that can temporarily be added to the Django code (or any third-party module) to stop the execution of a development server at any breakpoint. Use the following code to debug an unclear part of a Python module:

```
import pdb

pdb.set_trace()
```

This launches the interactive shell, where you can type in the variables, in order to see their values. If you type `c` or `continue`, the code execution will continue until the next breakpoint. If you type `q` or `quit`, the management command will be aborted. You can learn more commands of the Python debugger and how to inspect the traceback of the code at `https://docs.python.org/3/library/pdb.html`.

Another quick way to see the value of a variable in the development server is to raise a warning with the variable as a message, as follows:

```
raise Warning, some_variable
```

When you are in the `DEBUG` mode, the Django logger will provide you with the traceback and other local variables.

 Don't forget to remove debugging code before committing your work to a repository.

See also

- The *Using the Django shell* recipe

Toggling the Debug Toolbar

While developing with Django, you may want to inspect request headers and parameters, check the current template context, or measure the performance of SQL queries. All of this and more is possible with the Django Debug Toolbar. It is a configurable set of panels that displays various debug information about the current request and response. In this recipe, we will guide you through how to toggle the visibility of the Debug Toolbar, depending on a cookie, whose value can be set by a bookmarklet. A bookmarklet is a bookmark containing a small piece of JavaScript code that you can run on any page in a browser.

Getting ready

To get started with toggling the visibility of the Debug Toolbar, take a look at the following steps:

1. Install the Django Debug Toolbar in your virtual environment, or add it to your requirements and rebuild your containers in a Docker project:

   ```
   (myproject_env)$ pip3 install django-debug-toolbar~=1.10.1
   ```

2. Add `debug_toolbar` under `INSTALLED_APPS` in the settings.

How to do it...

Follow these steps to set up the Django Debug Toolbar, which can be switched on or off using a bookmarklet in the browser:

1. Add the following project settings:

   ```python
   # settings.py or conf/base.py
   MIDDLEWARE = (
       # ...
       "debug_toolbar.middleware.DebugToolbarMiddleware",
   )

   DEBUG_TOOLBAR_CONFIG = {
       "DISABLE_PANELS": [],
       "SHOW_TOOLBAR_CALLBACK": "utils.misc.custom_show_toolbar",
       "SHOW_TEMPLATE_CONTEXT": True,
   }

   DEBUG_TOOLBAR_PANELS = [
       "debug_toolbar.panels.versions.VersionsPanel",
   ```

```
        "debug_toolbar.panels.timer.TimerPanel",
        "debug_toolbar.panels.settings.SettingsPanel",
        "debug_toolbar.panels.headers.HeadersPanel",
        "debug_toolbar.panels.request.RequestPanel",
        "debug_toolbar.panels.sql.SQLPanel",
        "debug_toolbar.panels.templates.TemplatesPanel",
        "debug_toolbar.panels.staticfiles.StaticFilesPanel",
        "debug_toolbar.panels.cache.CachePanel",
        "debug_toolbar.panels.signals.SignalsPanel",
        "debug_toolbar.panels.logging.LoggingPanel",
        "debug_toolbar.panels.redirects.RedirectsPanel",
    ]
```

2. In the `utils` module, create a `misc.py` file with the `custom_show_toolbar()` function, as follows:

```
# utils/misc.py
def custom_show_toolbar(request):
    return "1" == request.COOKIES.get("DebugToolbar", False)
```

3. Open the Chrome or Firefox browser and go to the bookmark manager. Then, create two new bookmarks that contain JavaScript. The first link will show the toolbar, and will look similar to the following:

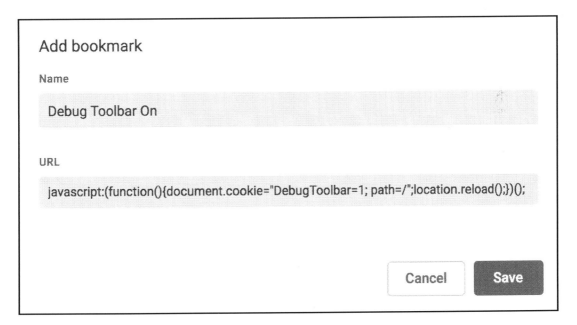

Add bookmark

Name

Debug Toolbar On

URL

javascript:(function(){document.cookie="DebugToolbar=1; path=/";location.reload();})();

Cancel   Save

4. The second JavaScript link will hide the toolbar, and will look similar to the following:

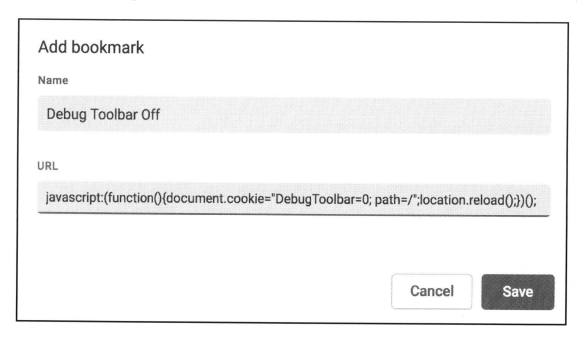

Add bookmark

Name

Debug Toolbar Off

URL

javascript:(function(){document.cookie="DebugToolbar=0; path=/";location.reload();})();

Cancel   Save

If you wish to copy and paste the preceding scripts, they are as follows, with the major difference highlighted in bold:

- On:
  ```
  javascript:(function(){document.cookie="DebugTool
  bar=1; path=/";location.reload();})();
  ```
- Off:
  ```
  javascript:(function(){document.cookie="DebugTool
  bar=0; path=/";location.reload();})();
  ```

How it works...

The `DEBUG_TOOLBAR_PANELS` setting defines the panels to show in the toolbar. The `DEBUG_TOOLBAR_CONFIG` dictionary defines the configuration for the toolbar, including a path to the function that is used to check whether or not to show the toolbar.

By default, when you browse through your project, the Django Debug Toolbar will not be shown. However, as you click on your bookmarklet, **Debug Toolbar On**, the **DebugToolbar** cookie will be set to **1**, the page will be refreshed, and you will see the toolbar with debugging panels. For example, you will be able to inspect the performance of SQL statements for optimization, as shown in the following screenshot:

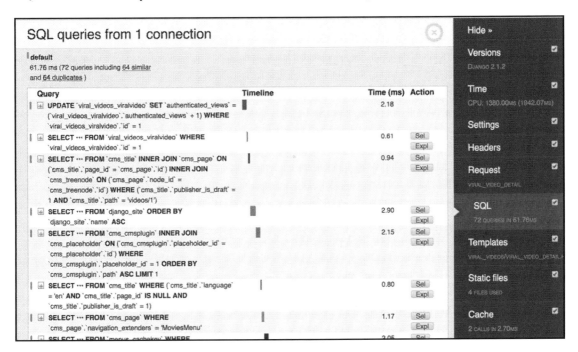

You will also be able to check the template context variables for the current view, as shown in the following screenshot:

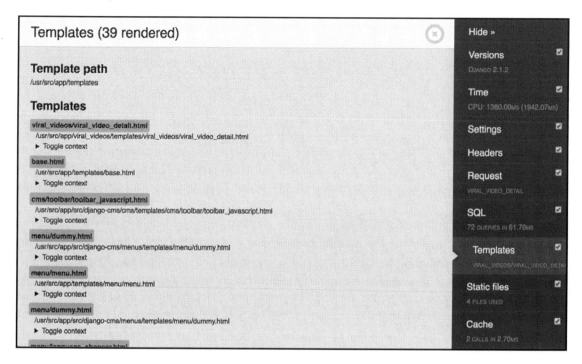

Clicking on the second bookmarklet, **Debug Toolbar Off**, will similarly set the **DebugToolbar** cookie to **0** and refresh the page, hiding the toolbar again.

See also

- The *Getting detailed error reporting via email* recipe in `Chapter 12`, *Testing and Deployment*

Using ThreadLocalMiddleware

The HttpRequest object contains useful information about the current user, language, server variables, cookies, session, and so on. As a matter of fact, HttpRequest is provided in the views and middleware, and you can pass it (or its attribute values) to forms, model methods, model managers, templates, and so on. To make life easier, you can use a so-called ThreadLocalMiddleware that stores the current HttpRequest object in the globally accessible Python thread. Therefore, you can access it from model methods, forms, signal handlers, and any other places that didn't have direct access to the HttpRequest object previously. In this recipe, we will define such a middleware.

Getting ready

Create the utils app and put it under INSTALLED_APPS in the settings, if you have not done so already.

How to do it...

Execute the following two steps:

1. Add a middleware.py file to the utils app, with the following content:

```python
# utils/middleware.py
from threading import local

_thread_locals = local()


def get_current_request():
    """
    :returns the HttpRequest object for this thread
    """
    return getattr(_thread_locals, "request", None)


def get_current_user():
    """
    :returns the current user if it exists or None otherwise
    """
    request = get_current_request()
    if request:
        return getattr(request, "user", None)
```

```
class ThreadLocalMiddleware(object):
    """
    Middleware to add the HttpRequest to thread local storage
    """
    def __init__(self, get_response):
        self.get_response = get_response

    def __call__(self, request):
        _thread_locals.request = request
        return self.get_response(request)
```

2. Add this middleware to MIDDLEWARE in the settings:

```
# settings.py or conf/base.py
# ...
MIDDLEWARE = (
    # ...
    "utils.middleware.ThreadLocalMiddleware",
)
# ...
```

How it works...

ThreadLocalMiddleware processes each request and stores the current HttpRequest object in the current thread. Each request-response cycle in Django is single-threaded. There are two functions: get_current_request() and get_current_user(). These functions can be used from anywhere to grab the current HttpRequest object or the current user.

For example, you can use this middleware to create and use CreatorMixin, which will save the current user as the creator of a new model object, as follows:

```
# utils/models.py
from django.db import models
from django.utils.translation import ugettext_lazy as _


class CreatorMixin(models.Model):
    """
    Abstract base class with a creator
    """
    class Meta:
        abstract = True

    creator = models.ForeignKey(
        "auth.User",
        verbose_name=_("creator"),
```

```
        editable=False,
        blank=True,
        null=True,
        on_delete=models.SET_NULL)

    def save(self, *args, **kwargs):
        from .middleware import get_current_user
        if not self.creator:
            self.creator = get_current_user()
        super(CreatorMixin, self).save(*args, **kwargs)
    save.alters_data = True
```

See also

- The *Creating a model mixin with URL-related methods recipe* in `Chapter 2`, *Database Structure and Modeling*
- The *Creating a model mixin to handle creation and modification dates* recipe in `Chapter 2`, *Database Structure and Modeling*
- The *Creating a model mixin to take care of meta tags* recipe in `Chapter 2`, *Database Structure and Modeling*
- The *Creating a model mixin to handle generic relations* recipe in `Chapter 2`, *Database Structure and Modeling*

Using signals to notify administrators about new entries

The Django framework includes the concept of signals, which are similar to events in JavaScript. There is a handful of built-in signals that you can use to trigger actions before and after the initialization of a model, saving or deleting an instance, migrating the database schema, handling a request, and so on. Moreover, you can create your own signals in your reusable apps and handle them in other apps. In this recipe, you will learn how to use signals to send emails to administrators whenever a specific model is saved.

Getting ready

Let's start with the `viral_videos` app that we created in the *Using database query expressions* recipe.

How to do it...

Follow these steps to create notifications for administrators:

1. Create the `signals.py` file, with the following content:

```python
# viral_videos/signals.py
from django.db.models.signals import post_save
from django.dispatch import receiver
from django.template.loader import render_to_string

from .models import ViralVideo


@receiver(post_save, sender=ViralVideo)
def inform_administrators(sender, **kwargs):
    from django.core.mail import mail_admins

    instance = kwargs["instance"]
    created = kwargs["created"]

    if created:
        context = {
            "title": instance.title,
            "link": instance.get_url(),
        }
        plain_text_message = render_to_string(
            'viral_videos/email/administrator/message.txt',
            context)
        html_message = render_to_string(
            'viral_videos/email/administrator/message.html',
            context)
        subject = render_to_string(
            'viral_videos/email/administrator/subject.txt',
            context)

        mail_admins(
            subject=subject.strip(),
            message=plain_text_message,
            html_message=html_message,
            fail_silently=True)
```

2. Next, we will need a template for the plain text message—something like the following:

```
{# templates/viral_videos/email/administrator/message.txt #}
A new viral video called "{{ title }}" has been created.
You can preview it at {{ link }}.
```

3. We will also need a template for the HTML message, as follows:

```
{# templates/viral_videos/email/administrator/message.html #}
<p>A new viral video called "{{ title }}" has been created.</p>
<p>You can <a href="{{ link }}">preview it here</a>.</p>
```

4. Then, we will need a template for the email subject, as follows:

```
{# templates/viral_videos/email/administrator/subject.txt #}
New Viral Video Added
```

5. Create the `apps.py` file, with the following content:

```
# viral_videos/apps.py
from django.apps import AppConfig
from django.utils.translation import ugettext_lazy as _


class ViralVideosAppConfig(AppConfig):
    name = "viral_videos"
    verbose_name = _("Viral Videos")

    def ready(self):
        from .signals import inform_administrators
```

6. Update the __init__.py file, with the following content:

```
# viral_videos/__init__.py
default_app_config = "viral_videos.apps.ViralVideosAppConfig"
```

7. Make sure that you have ADMINS set in the project settings, similar to the following:

```
# settings.py or config/base.py
ADMINS = (
    ("Admin User", "administrator@example.com"),
)
```

How it works...

The `ViralVideosAppConfig` app configuration class has the `ready()` method, which will be called when all of the models of the project are loaded into the memory. According to the Django documentation, signals allow for certain senders to notify a set of receivers that some action has taken place. In the `ready()` method, therefore, we import the `inform_administrators()` function.

Through the `@receiver` decorator, `inform_administrators()` is registered for the `post_save` signal, and we have limited it to handle only the signals where the `ViralVideo` model is `sender`. Therefore, whenever we save a `ViralVideo` object, the `receiver` function will be called. The `inform_administrators()` function checks whether a video is newly created. In that case, it sends an email to the system administrators that are listed in `ADMINS` in the settings.

We use templates to generate the content of the `plain_text_message`, the `html_message`, and the `subject`, so that we can define default templates for each of these within our app. If we make our `viral_videos` app publicly available, those who pull it into their own projects can then customize the templates as desired, perhaps to wrap them in a company email template wrapper.

Learn more the Django signals in the official documentation at https://docs.djangoproject.com/en/2.1/topics/signals/.

See also

- The *Creating app configuration* recipe in `Chapter 1`, *Getting Started with Django 2.1*
- The *Using database query expressions* recipe
- The *Checking for missing settings* recipe

Checking for missing settings

From Django 1.7 onward, you can use an extensible system-check framework, which replaces the old `validate management` command. In this recipe, you will learn how to create a check if the `ADMINS` setting is set. Similarly, you will be able to check whether different secret keys or access tokens are set for the APIs that you are using.

Getting ready

Let's start with the `viral_videos` app that was created in the *Using database query expressions* recipe and was extended in the previous recipe.

How to do it...

To use the system-check framework, follow these simple steps:

1. Create the checks.py file, with the following content:

```
# viral_videos/checks.py
from django.core.checks import Warning, register, Tags


@register(Tags.compatibility)
def settings_check(app_configs, **kwargs):
    from django.conf import settings

    errors = []

    if not settings.ADMINS:
        errors.append(Warning(
            """
            The system admins are not set in the project settings
            """,
            obj=settings,
            hint="""
            In order to receive notifications when new videos are
            created, define system admins in your settings, like:

            ADMINS = (
                ("Admin", "administrator@example.com"),
            )
            """,
            id="viral_videos.W001"))

    return errors
```

2. Import the checks in the ready() method of the app configuration, as follows:

```
# viral_videos/apps.py
# ...
class ViralVideosAppConfig(AppConfig):
    # ...
    def ready(self):
        from .signals import inform_administrators
        from .checks import settings_check
```

3. To try the check that you just created, remove or comment out the ADMINS setting, and then run the check management command in your virtual environment or Docker app container, as follows:

```
(myproject_env)$ python3 manage.py check
System check identified some issues:

WARNINGS:
<Settings "myproject.settings">: (viral_videos.W001)
The system admins are not set in the project settings

    HINT:
        In order to receive notifications when new videos are
        created, define system admins in your settings, like:

        ADMINS = (
            ("Admin", "administrator@example.com"),
        )


System check identified 1 issue (0 silenced).
```

How it works...

The system-check framework has a bunch of checks in the models, fields, database, administration, authentication, content types, and security, where it raises errors or warnings if something in the project is not set correctly. Additionally, you can create your own checks, similar to what we did in this recipe.

We have registered the settings_check() function, which returns a list with Warning if there is no ADMINS setting defined for the project.

Aside from the Warning instances from the django.core.checks module, the returned list can also contain instances of the Debug, Info, Error, and Critical built-in classes, or any other class inheriting from django.core.checks.CheckMessage. Logging at the debug, info, and warning levels would fail silently, whereas error and critical levels would prevent the project from running.

In this example, the check is tagged as a compatibility check via the Tags.compatibility argument passed to the @register decorator. Other options provided in Tags include: admin, caches, database, models, security, signals, templates, and url.

Learn more about the system check framework in the official documentation at `https://docs.djangoproject.com/en/2.1/topics/checks/`.

See also

- The *Creating app configurations recipe* in `Chapter 1`, *Getting Started with Django 2.1*
- The *Using database query expressions* recipe
- The *Using signals to notify administrators about new entries* recipe

12
Testing and Deployment

In this chapter, we will cover the following recipes:

- Testing views with mock
- Testing APIs created using the Django REST framework
- Releasing a reusable Django app
- Getting detailed error reporting via email
- Deploying on Apache with mod_wsgi
- Setting up cron jobs for regular tasks

Introduction

At this point, you should have one or more Django project or reusable app developed and ready to show to the public. For the final steps of the development cycle, we will take a look at how to test your project, distribute reusable apps to others, and publish your website on a remote server. Stay tuned for the final bits and pieces!

Testing views with mock

Django provides tools for you to write test suites for your website. Test suites automatically check your website and its components, to ensure that everything is working correctly. When you modify your code, you can run the tests to check whether your changes affected the application's behavior in a negative way.

The world of automated software testing has a wide range of divisions and terminologies. For the sake of this book, we will divide testing into the following categories:

- **Unit testing** refers to tests that are strictly targeted at individual pieces, or units, of code. Most commonly, a unit corresponds to a single file or module, and unit tests do their best to validate that the logic and behaviors are as expected.

- **Integration testing** goes one step further, dealing with the way that two or more units work with one another. Such tests do not get as granular as unit tests, and they are generally written under the assumption that all unit tests have passed by the time an integration is validated. Thus, integration tests only cover the set of behaviors that must be true for the units to work properly with one another.
- **Component interface testing** is a higher-order form of integration testing, in which a single component is verified from end to end. Such tests are written in a way that is ignorant of the underlying logic used to provide the behaviors of the component, so that logic can change without modifying the behavior, and the tests will still pass.
- **System testing** verifies the end-to-end integration of all components that make up a system, often corresponding to complete user flows.
- **Operational acceptance testing** checks that all of the non-functional aspects of a system operate correctly. Acceptance tests check the business logic, to find out whether the project works the way it is supposed to, from an end user's point of view.

In this recipe, we will take a look at how to write unit tests. Unit tests are those that check whether individual functions or methods return the correct results. We will look at the `likes` app and write tests that check whether posting to the `json_set_like()` view returns a failure response for unauthenticated users, and a successful result for authenticated users. We will use `Mock` objects to simulate the `HttpRequest` and `AnonymousUser` objects.

Getting ready

Let's start with the `locations` and `likes` apps from the *Implementing the Like widget* recipe in `Chapter 4`, *Templates and JavaScript*.

Since Python 3.3, the built-in `unittest.mock` library has been available for mocking. For earlier versions, install the `mock` module in your virtual environment (as follows), or add it to your Docker project's requirements, and rebuild:

```
(myproject_env)$ pip3 install mock~=2.0.0
```

 We will use the built-in `unittest.mock` library for all code samples in this recipe. If you are using the backwards compatibility `mock` module instead, your imports will be `import mock`, as opposed to `from unittest import mock`.

How to do it...

We will test the liking action with mock, by performing the following steps:

1. Create the `tests.py` file in your `likes` app, with the following content:

```python
# likes/tests.py
import json
from unittest import mock

from django.contrib.auth.models import User
from django.contrib.contenttypes.models import ContentType
from django.test import TestCase
from django.test.client import RequestFactory

from locations.models import Location


class JSSetLikeViewTest(TestCase):
    @classmethod
    def setUpClass(cls):
        super(JSSetLikeViewTest, cls).setUpClass()

        cls.location = Location.objects.create(
            title="Haus der Kulturen der Welt",
            slug="hkw",
            image="locations/2018/10/20181024012345.jpg")

        cls.content_type = ContentType.objects.get_for_model(
            Location)

        cls.superuser = User.objects.create_superuser(
            username="test-admin",
            password="test-admin",
            email="")

    @classmethod
    def tearDownClass(cls):
        super(JSSetLikeViewTest, cls).tearDownClass()
        cls.location.delete()
        cls.superuser.delete()

    def test_authenticated_json_set_like(self):
        from .views import json_set_like
        mock_request = mock.Mock()
        mock_request.user = self.superuser
        mock_request.method = "POST"
```

```
        response = json_set_like(
            mock_request,
            self.content_type.pk,
            self.location.pk)

        expected_result = json.dumps({
                "success": True,
                "action": "add",
                "count": Location.objects.count(),
            })

        self.assertJSONEqual(
            response.content,
            expected_result)

    @mock.patch("django.contrib.auth.models.User")
    def test_anonymous_json_set_like(self, MockUser):
        from .views import json_set_like

        anonymous_user = MockUser()
        anonymous_user.is_authenticated = False

        mock_request = mock.Mock()
        mock_request.user = anonymous_user
        mock_request.method = "POST"

        response = json_set_like(
            mock_request,
            self.content_type.pk,
            self.location.pk)

        expected_result = json.dumps({
            "success": False,
        })

        self.assertJSONEqual(
            response.content,
            expected_result)
```

2. Run the tests for the `likes` app, as follows:

```
(myproject_env)$ python3 manage.py test likes
Creating test database for alias 'default'...
System check identified no issues (0 silenced).
..
----------------------------------------------------------------
---
Ran 2 tests in 0.186s
```

```
OK
Destroying test database for alias 'default'...
```

How it works...

Just like in the previous recipe, when you run tests for the `likes` app, at first, a temporary test database is created. Then, the `setUpClass()` method is called. Later, the methods whose names start with `test` are executed, and, finally, the `tearDownClass()` method is called.

Unit tests inherit from the `SimpleTestCase` class, but, here, we are using `TestCase`, which is a specialization that adds safeguards around test isolation when database queries are involved. In `setUpClass()`, we create a `location` and a `superuser`. Also, we find out the `ContentType` object for the `Location` model; we will need it for the view that sets or removes likes for different objects. As a reminder, the view looks similar to the following, and returns the JSON string as a result:

```
def json_set_like(request, content_type_id, object_id):
    # ...all the view logic goes here...
    return JsonResponse(result)
```

In the `test_authenticated_json_set_like()` and `test_anonymous_json_set_like()` methods, we use the `Mock` objects. These are objects that can have any attributes or methods. Each undefined attribute or method of a `Mock` object is another `Mock` object. Therefore, in the shell, you can try to chain attributes, as follows:

```
>>> import mock
>>> m = mock.Mock()
>>> m.whatever.anything().whatsoever
<Mock name='mock.whatever.anything().whatsoever' id='4464778896'>
```

In our tests, we use the `Mock` objects to simulate the `HttpRequest` object. For the anonymous user, a `MockUser` is generated as a patch of the standard Django `User` object, via the `@mock.patch()` decorator. For the authenticated user, we still need the real `User` object, as the view needs the user's ID to save in the database for the `Like` object.

Therefore, we call the `json_set_like()` function, and check that the returned JSON response is correct:

- It returns `{"success": false}` in the response, if the visitor is unauthenticated.

- It returns something like `{"action": "add", "count": 1, "success": true}` for authenticated users.

In the end, the `tearDownClass()` class method is called, deleting the `location` and `superuser` from the test database.

See also

- The *Implementing the Like widget* recipe in `Chapter 4`, *Templates and JavaScript*
- The *Testing APIs created using the Django REST framework* recipe

Testing APIs created using the Django REST framework

You should already have an understanding of how to write unit tests. In this recipe, we will go through component interface testing for the REST API that we created earlier in the book.

 If you are not familiar with what a REST API is and how APIs are used, you can learn more at `http://www.restapitutorial.com/`.

Getting ready

Let's start with the `bulletin_board` app from the *Using the Django REST framework to create APIs* recipe in `Chapter 10`, *Importing and Exporting Data*.

How to do it...

To test REST APIs, perform the following steps:

1. Create a `tests.py` file in your `bulletin_board` app, with just the setup and teardown methods, as follows:

   ```
   # bulletin_board/tests.py
   from django.contrib.auth.models import User
   ```

```python
from django.core.urlresolvers import reverse
from rest_framework import status
from rest_framework.test import APITestCase

from .models import Category, Bulletin


class BulletinTests(APITestCase):
    @classmethod
    def setUpClass(cls):
        super(BulletinTests, cls).setUpClass()

        cls.superuser = User.objects.create_superuser(
            username="test-admin",
            password="test-admin",
            email="")

        cls.category = Category.objects.create(title="Movies")

        cls.bulletin = Bulletin.objects.create(
            bulletin_type="searching",
            category=cls.category,
            title="The Matrix",
            description="There is no spoon.",
            contact_person="Thomas A. Anderson")

        cls.bulletin_to_delete = Bulletin.objects.create(
            bulletin_type="searching",
            category=cls.category,
            title="Neo",
            description="You take the blue pill - the story ends, "
                        "you wake up in your bed and believe "
                        "whatever you want to believe. You take "
                        "the red pill - you stay in Wonderland, "
                        "and I show you how deep the rabbit hole "
                        "goes.",
            contact_person="Morpheus")

    @classmethod
    def tearDownClass(cls):
        super(BulletinTests, cls).tearDownClass()

        cls.category.delete()
        cls.bulletin.delete()
        cls.superuser.delete()
```

2. Add a method to test the API call listing the bulletins, as shown in the following code:

```
def test_list_bulletins(self):
    url = reverse("rest_bulletin_list")
    data = {}
    response = self.client.get(url, data, format="json")
    self.assertEqual(response.status_code,
                     status.HTTP_200_OK)
    self.assertEqual(response.data["count"],
                     Bulletin.objects.count())
```

3. Add a method to test the API call showing a single bulletin, as follows:

```
def test_get_bulletin(self):
    url = reverse("rest_bulletin_detail",
                  kwargs={
                      "pk": self.bulletin.pk
                  })
    data = {}
    response = self.client.get(url, data, format="json")

    self.assertEqual(response.status_code,
                     status.HTTP_200_OK)
    self.assertEqual(response.data["id"],
                     self.bulletin.pk)
    self.assertEqual(response.data["bulletin_type"],
                     self.bulletin.bulletin_type)
    self.assertEqual(response.data["category"]["id"],
                     self.category.pk)
    self.assertEqual(response.data["title"],
                     self.bulletin.title)
    self.assertEqual(response.data["description"],
                     self.bulletin.description)
    self.assertEqual(response.data["contact_person"],
                     self.bulletin.contact_person)
```

4. Add a method to test the API call creating a bulletin if the current user is authenticated, as follows:

```
def test_create_bulletin_allowed(self):
    # login
    self.client.force_authenticate(user=self.superuser)

    url = reverse("rest_bulletin_list")
    data = {
        "bulletin_type": "offering",
        "category": {"title": self.category.title},
```

```
        "title": "Back to the Future",
        "description": "Roads? Where we're going, "
                        "we don't need roads.",
        "contact_person": "Doc Brown",
    }
    response = self.client.post(url, data, format="json")

    self.assertEqual(response.status_code,
                    status.HTTP_201_CREATED)

    bulletin = Bulletin.objects.filter(pk=response.data["id"])
    self.assertEqual(bulletin.count(), 1)

    # logout
    self.client.force_authenticate(user=None)
```

5. Add a method to test the API call trying to create a bulletin, but failing (as the current visitor is anonymous), as shown in the following code:

```
def test_create_bulletin_restricted(self):
    # make sure the user is logged out
    self.client.force_authenticate(user=None)

    url = reverse("rest_bulletin_list")
    data = {
        "bulletin_type": "offering",
        "category": {"title": self.category.title},
        "title": "Godfather",
        "description": "I'm gonna make him an offer he can't "
                        "refuse",
        "contact_person": "Don Corleone",
    }
    response = self.client.post(url, data, format="json")

    self.assertEqual(response.status_code,
                    status.HTTP_403_FORBIDDEN)
```

6. Add a method to test the API call changing a bulletin if the current user is authenticated, as follows:

```
def test_change_bulletin_allowed(self):
    # login
    self.client.force_authenticate(user=self.superuser)

    url = reverse("rest_bulletin_detail",
                    kwargs={
                        "pk": self.bulletin.pk
                    })
```

```
# change only title
data = {
    "bulletin_type": self.bulletin.bulletin_type,
    "category": {
        "title": self.bulletin.category.title
    },
    "title": "Matrix Resurrection",
    "description": self.bulletin.description,
    "contact_person": self.bulletin.contact_person,
}
response = self.client.put(url, data, format="json")

self.assertEqual(response.status_code,
                 status.HTTP_200_OK)
self.assertEqual(response.data["id"],
                 self.bulletin.pk)
self.assertEqual(response.data["bulletin_type"],
                 "searching")

# logout
self.client.force_authenticate(user=None)
```

7. Add a method to test the API call trying to change a bulletin, but failing (as the current visitor is anonymous), as follows:

```
def test_change_bulletin_restricted(self):
    # make sure the user is logged out
    self.client.force_authenticate(user=None)

    url = reverse("rest_bulletin_detail",
                  kwargs={
                      "pk": self.bulletin.pk
                  })

    # change only title
    data = {
        "bulletin_type": self.bulletin.bulletin_type,
        "category": {
            "title": self.bulletin.category.title
        },
        "title": "Matrix Resurrection",
        "description": self.bulletin.description,
        "contact_person": self.bulletin.contact_person,
    }
    response = self.client.put(url, data, format="json")

    self.assertEqual(response.status_code,
                     status.HTTP_403_FORBIDDEN)
```

8. Add a method to test the API call trying to delete a bulletin, but failing (as the current visitor is anonymous), as follows:

```
def test_delete_bulletin_restricted(self):
    # make sure the user is logged out
    self.client.force_authenticate(user=None)

    url = reverse("rest_bulletin_detail",
                  kwargs={
                      "pk": self.bulletin_to_delete.pk
                  })

    data = {}
    response = self.client.delete(url, data, format="json")

    self.assertEqual(response.status_code,
                     status.HTTP_403_FORBIDDEN)
```

9. Add a method to test the API call deleting a bulletin if the current user is authenticated, as shown in the following code:

```
def test_delete_bulletin_allowed(self):
    # login
    self.client.force_authenticate(user=self.superuser)

    url = reverse("rest_bulletin_detail",
                  kwargs={
                      "pk": self.bulletin_to_delete.pk
                  })

    data = {}
    response = self.client.delete(url, data, format="json")

    self.assertEqual(response.status_code,
                     status.HTTP_204_NO_CONTENT)

    # logout
    self.client.force_authenticate(user=None)
```

10. Run the tests for the `bulletin_board` app, as follows:

```
(myproject_env)$ python manage.py test bulletin_board
Creating test database for alias 'default'...
System check identified no issues (0 silenced).
........
-------------------------------------------------------------
---
Ran 8 tests in 0.774s
```

```
OK
Destroying test database for alias 'default'...
```

How it works...

This REST API test suite extends the `APITestCase` class. Once again, we have the `setUpClass()` and `tearDownClass()` class methods that will be executed before and after the different tests. Also, the test suite has a client attribute of the `APIClient` type, which can be used to simulate API calls. The client provides methods for all standard HTTP calls: `get()`, `post()`, `put()`, `patch()`, `delete()`, `head()`, and `options()`; in our tests, we are using the `GET`, `POST`, and `DELETE` requests. Also, the client has methods to force the authentication of a user based on login credentials, a token, or a `User` object. In our tests, we are authenticating the third way: passing a user directly to the `force_authenticate()` method.

The rest of the code is self-explanatory.

See also

- The *Using the Django REST framework to create APIs* recipe in `Chapter 10`, *Importing and Exporting Data*
- The *Testing views with mock* recipe

Releasing a reusable Django app

The Django documentation has a tutorial on how to package your reusable apps so that they can be installed later, with `pip`, in any virtual environment; this can be viewed at `https://docs.djangoproject.com/en/2.1/intro/reusable-apps/`.

However, there is another (and arguably better) way to package and release a reusable Django app, using the Cookiecutter tool, which creates templates for different coding projects, such as the new Django CMS website, the Flask website, or the jQuery plugin. One of the available project templates is `cookiecutter-djangopackage`. In this recipe, you will learn how to use it to distribute the reusable `likes` app.

Getting ready

Install `cookiecutter` in your virtual environment (as follows), or add it to your requirements file and rebuild Docker containers:

```
(myproject_env)$ pip3 install cookiecutter~=1.6.0
```

How to do it...

To release your `likes` app, follow these steps:

1. Start a new Django app project, as follows:

```
(myapp_env)$ cookiecutter \
> https://github.com/pydanny/cookiecutter-djangopackage.git
```

Or, since this is a GitHub-hosted `cookiecutter` template, we can use a shorthand syntax, as follows:

```
(myapp_env)$ cookiecutter gh:pydanny/cookiecutter-djangopackage
```

2. Answer the questions to create the app template, as follows:

```
full_name [Your full name here]: Your Name
email [you@example.com]: user@example.com
github_username [yourname]: githubuser
project_name [Django Package]: Django Likes
repo_name [dj-package]: django-likes
app_name [django_likes]: likes
app_config_name [LikesConfig]:
project_short_description [Your project description goes here]:
Django-likes allows your website users to like any object.
models [Comma-separated list of models]: Like
django_versions [1.11,2.0]: 2.0
version [0.1.0]:
create_example_project [N]:
Select open_source_license:
1 - MIT
2 - BSD
3 - ISCL
4 - Apache Software License 2.0
5 - Not open source
Choose from 1, 2, 3, 4, 5 (1, 2, 3, 4, 5) [1]: 2
```

This will create a basic file structure for the releasable Django package, similar to the following screenshot:

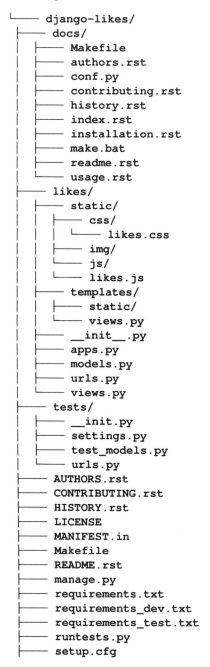

```
└──── django-likes/
├──── docs/
│    ├──── Makefile
│    ├──── authors.rst
│    ├──── conf.py
│    ├──── contributing.rst
│    ├──── history.rst
│    ├──── index.rst
│    ├──── installation.rst
│    ├──── make.bat
│    ├──── readme.rst
│    └──── usage.rst
├──── likes/
│    ├──── static/
│    │    ├──── css/
│    │    │    └──── likes.css
│    │    ├──── img/
│    │    └──── js/
│    │         └──── likes.js
│    ├──── templates/
│    │    ├──── static/
│    │    └──── views.py
│    ├──── __init__.py
│    ├──── apps.py
│    ├──── models.py
│    ├──── urls.py
│    └──── views.py
├──── tests/
│    ├──── __init.py
│    ├──── settings.py
│    ├──── test_models.py
│    └──── urls.py
├──── AUTHORS.rst
├──── CONTRIBUTING.rst
├──── HISTORY.rst
├──── LICENSE
├──── MANIFEST.in
├──── Makefile
├──── README.rst
├──── manage.py
├──── requirements.txt
├──── requirements_dev.txt
├──── requirements_test.txt
├──── runtests.py
├──── setup.cfg
```

```
├──── setup.py*
└──── tox.ini
```

3. Copy the files in the `likes` app from the Django project where you are using it to the `django-likes/likes` directory. In cases where the `cookiecutter` created the same files, the content will need to be merged, rather than overwritten. For instance, the `likes/__init__.py` file will need to contain a version string to work properly with `setup.py` in later steps, as follows:

   ```
   __version__ = "0.1.0"
   ```

4. In the `likes` app, we have a dependency upon the `utils` app, so that also needs to be made available. The ideal option would be to release the `utils` app itself (in the same manner as `likes`), and then change the imports in the `likes` app to draw from the new package location instead. We could also simply copy the `utils` code directly into the files in the `likes` app, but then we would have to maintain the code separately, in at least two places. In this case, let's simply add `utils` to the `django-likes/utils` directory, which is something of a compromise between the two approaches.

5. Add the reusable app project to the Git repository in GitHub, using the `repo_name` that was entered previously.

6. Explore the different files and complete the license, README, documentation, configuration, and other files.

7. Make sure that the app passes the `cookiecutter` template tests:

   ```
   (myapp_env)$ pip3 install -r requirements-test.txt
   (myapp_env)$ python3 runtests.py
   Creating test database for alias 'default'...
   System check identified no issues (0 silenced).
   .
   ----------------------------------------------------------------
   ---
   Ran 1 test in 0.001s

   OK
   Destroying test database for alias 'default'...
   ```

8. If your package is closed source, create a shareable release as a ZIP archive, as follows:

   ```
   (myapp_env)$ python3 setup.py sdist
   running sdist
   running egg_info
   # ...intermediary steps here...
   ```

```
creating dist
Creating tar archive
removing 'django-likes-0.1.0' (and everything under it)
```

This will create a `django-likes/dist/django-likes-0.1.0.tar.gz` file that can then be installed or uninstalled with `pip`, as follows:

```
(myproject_env)$ pip3 install django-likes-0.1.0.tar.gz
(myproject_env)$ pip3 uninstall django-likes
```

9. If your package is open source, you can register and publish your app in the **Python Package Index (PyPI)**:

```
(myapp_env)$ python3 setup.py register
(myapp_env)$ python3 setup.py publish
```

10. Also, to spread the word, add your app to the Django packages by submitting a form at `https://www.djangopackages.com/packages/add/`.

How it works...

Cookiecutter fills in the requested data in different parts of the Django app project template, using the defaults given in `[square brackets]` if you simply press *Enter* without entering anything. As a result, you get the `setup.py` file ready for distribution to the Python Package Index, Sphinx documentation, MIT as the default license, universal text editor configuration for the project, static files and templates included in your app, and other goodies.

See also

- The *Creating a virtual environment project file structure* recipe in `Chapter 1`, *Getting Started with Django 2.1*
- The *Creating a Docker project file structure* recipe in `Chapter 1`, *Getting Started with Django 2.1*
- The *Handling project dependencies with pip* recipe in `Chapter 1`, *Getting Started with Django 2.1*
- The *Implementing the Like widget* recipe in `Chapter 4`, *Templates and JavaScript*

Getting detailed error reporting via email

To perform system logging, Django uses Python's built-in logging module. The default Django configuration seems to be quite complex. In this recipe, you will learn how to tweak it to send error emails with complete HTML, similar to what is provided by Django in the DEBUG mode when an error happens.

Getting ready

Locate the Django project in your virtual environment or Docker project structure.

How to do it...

The following procedure will help you to send detailed emails about errors:

1. If you do not already have LOGGING settings set up for your project, set those up first. Find the Django logging utilities file, available at lib/python3.6/site-packages/django/utils/log.py. This lib/ directory will be in either your virtual environment myproject_env/ or /usr/local/ in a Docker project's app container. You can open the file in a text editor (or via the more command in a terminal) and copy the DEFAULT_LOGGING dictionary to your project's settings.py as the LOGGING dictionary.

2. Add the include_html setting to the mail_admins handler. The result of the first two steps should be something like the following:

```python
# settings.py or conf/base.py
DEFAULT_LOGGING = {
    'version': 1,
    'disable_existing_loggers': False,
    'filters': {
        'require_debug_false': {
            '()': 'django.utils.log.RequireDebugFalse',
        },
        'require_debug_true': {
            '()': 'django.utils.log.RequireDebugTrue',
        },
    },
    'formatters': {
        'django.server': {
            '()': 'django.utils.log.ServerFormatter',
            'format': '[{server_time}] {message}',
```

```
                    'style': '{',
                }
            },
            'handlers': {
                'console': {
                    'level': 'INFO',
                    'filters': ['require_debug_true'],
                    'class': 'logging.StreamHandler',
                },
                'django.server': {
                    'level': 'INFO',
                    'class': 'logging.StreamHandler',
                    'formatter': 'django.server',
                },
                'mail_admins': {
                    'level': 'ERROR',
                    'filters': ['require_debug_false'],
                    'class': 'django.utils.log.AdminEmailHandler',
                    'include_html': True,
                }
            },
            'loggers': {
                'django': {
                    'handlers': ['console', 'mail_admins'],
                    'level': 'INFO',
                },
                'django.server': {
                    'handlers': ['django.server'],
                    'level': 'INFO',
                    'propagate': False,
                },
            }
        }
```

How it works...

The logging configuration consists of four parts: loggers, handlers, filters, and formatters. The following list describes them:

- **Loggers** are entry points into the logging system. Each logger can have a log level: DEBUG, INFO, WARNING, ERROR, or CRITICAL. When a message is written to the logger, the log level of the message is compared with the logger's level. If it meets or exceeds the log level of the logger, it will be further processed by a handler. Otherwise, the message will be ignored.

- **Handlers** are engines that define what happens to each message in the logger. They can be written to a console, sent by email to the administrator, saved to a log file, sent to the Sentry error-logging service, and so on. In our case, we set the `include_html` parameter for the `mail_admins` handler, as we want the full HTML with traceback and local variables for the error messages that happen in our Django project.
- **Filters** provide additional control over the messages that are passed from the loggers to handlers. For example, in our case, the emails will only be sent when the `DEBUG` mode is set to `false`.
- **Formatters** are used to define how to render a log message as a string. They are not used in this example; however, for more information about logging, you can refer to the official documentation at `https://docs.djangoproject.com/en/2.1/topics/logging/`.

See also

- The *Deploying on Apache with mod_wsgi* recipe

Deploying on Apache with mod_wsgi

There are many options for deploying your Django project. In this recipe, I will guide you through the deployment of a Django project on a dedicated Linux server, with Virtualmin.

A dedicated server is a type of internet hosting where you lease an entire server machine that is not shared with anyone else. Virtualmin is a web-hosting control panel that allows you to manage virtual domains, mailboxes, databases, and entire servers, without having deep knowledge of the command-line routines of the server administration.

To run the Django project, we will be using the Apache web server with the `mod_wsgi` module and a MySQL database.

Getting ready

Make sure that you have Virtualmin installed on your dedicated Linux server. For instructions, refer to `http://www.virtualmin.com/download.html`.

How to do it...

Follow these steps to deploy a Django project on a Linux server with Virtualmin:

1. Log into Virtualmin as the root user and set bash (instead of sh) as the default shell for the server's users. This can be done by navigating to **Virtualmin | System Customization | Custom Shells**, as shown in the following screenshot:

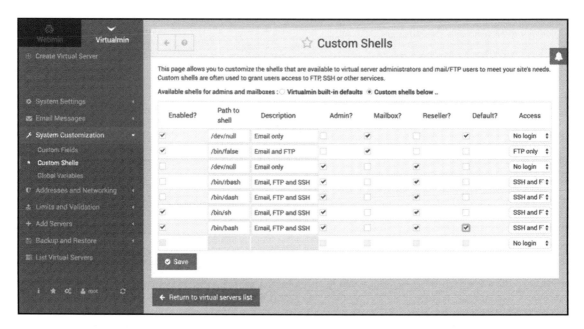

2. Create a virtual server for your project by navigating to **Virtualmin | Create Virtual Server**. Enable the following features: **Setup website for domain?** and **Create MySQL database?**. The **Custom username** and **Administration password** that you set for the domain will also be used for the SSH connections, FTP, and MySQL database access, as follows:

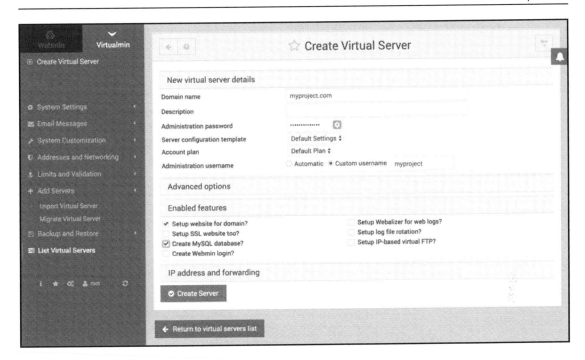

3. Log into your domain administration panel and set the A record for your domain to the IP address of your dedicated server.

 Due to the delays related to DNS propagation, it can be several hours before a new domain mapping takes effect in all parts of the globe. In the interim, it may only be accessible via the IP address, directly.

4. Connect to the dedicated server via **Secure Shell (SSH)** as the root user, and install the Python libraries, `pip`, `virtualenv`, `MySQLdb`, and `Pillow`, system wide.

5. Ensure that the default MySQL database encoding is UTF-8. First, we must edit the MySQL configuration file on the remote server. For example, we can connect via SSH and open the configuration file using the nano editor, as follows:

```
$ ssh root@myproject.com
root@myproject.com's password:

<root@myproject.com>$ nano /etc/mysql/my.cnf
```

Once it has opened, we have to add (or edit) the following configurations:

```
# /etc/mysql/my.cnf
[client]
default-character-set=utf8

[mysql]
default-character-set=utf8

[mysqld]
collation-server=utf8_unicode_ci
init-connect='SET NAMES utf8'
character-set-server=utf8
```

Press *Ctrl + O* to save the changes, and *Ctrl + X* to exit the nano editor. Once the configuration is saved, restart the MySQL server, as follows:

```
<root@myproject.com>$ /etc/init.d/mysql restart
```

Finally, press *Ctrl + D* to exit the SSH connection, or type the `exit` command, as follows:

```
<root@myproject.com>$ exit
$
```

6. When you create a domain with Virtualmin, the user for that domain is created automatically. Connect to the dedicated server via SSH as a user of your Django project and create a virtual environment for your project, as follows:

```
$ ssh myproject@myproject.com
myproject@myproject.com's password:

<myproject@myproject.com>$ virtualenv . --system-site-packages
<myproject@myproject.com>$ echo source ~/bin/activate >> .bashrc
<myproject@myproject.com>$ source ~/bin/activate
(myproject)myproject@server$
```

The `.bashrc` script will be called each time you connect to your Django project via SSH as a user related to the domain. The `.bashrc` script will automatically activate the virtual environment for this project.

7. If you host your project code on Bitbucket, you will have to set up SSH keys, in order to avoid password prompts when pulling from or pushing to the Git repository. To do so, execute the following commands, one by one:

```
(myproject)myproject@server$ ssh-keygen
```

```
(myproject)myproject@server$ ssh-agent /bin/bash
(myproject)myproject@server$ ssh-add ~/.ssh/id_rsa
(myproject)myproject@server$ cat ~/.ssh/id_rsa.pub
```

The last command prints your SSH public key, which you need to copy and paste into the form, under **Settings | General | Access Keys | Add Key**, for your repository on the Bitbucket website, as shown in the following screenshot:

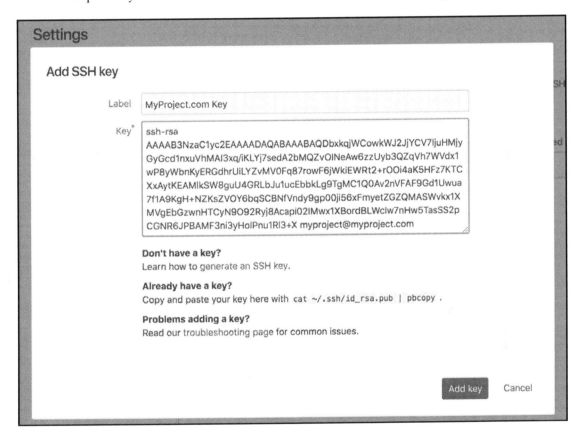

8. Create a project directory, go to it, and clone your project's code, as follows:

```
(myproject)myproject@server$ git clone \
> git@bitbucket.org:somebitbucketuser/myproject.git myproject
```

Now, your project path should be something similar to the following: `/home/myproject/project/myproject`.

9. Install the Python requirements for your project, including a specified version of Django 2.1 (or newer), as follows:

```
(myproject)myproject@server$ pip install -r requirements.txt
```

10. Create the `media`, `tmp`, and `static` directories, under your project's directory.

11. Also, create `local_settings.py`, with settings similar to the following, or use one of the other approaches to environment-specific settings that were mentioned in `Chapter 1`, *Getting Started with Django 2.1*:

```
# /home/myproject/project/myproject/myproject/local_settings.py
DATABASES = {
    "default": {
        "ENGINE": "django.db.backends.mysql",
        "NAME": "myproject",
        "USER": "myproject",
        "PASSWORD": "mypassword",
    }
}
PREPEND_WWW = True
DEBUG = False
ALLOWED_HOSTS = ["myproject.com"]
```

12. Import the database dump that you created locally. If you are using a macOS, you can do that with an app such as Sequel Pro (http://www.sequelpro.com/), using an SSH connection. You can also upload the database dump to the server by FTP, and then run the following in SSH:

```
(myproject)myproject@server$ python manage.py \
> dbshell < ~/db_backups/db.sql
```

13. Collect static files, as follows:

```
(myproject)myproject@server$ python manage.py collectstatic --
noinput
```

14. Go to the `~/public_html` directory and create a `wsgi` file, using the nano editor (or an editor of your choice):

```
# /home/myproject/public_html/my.wsgi
#!/home/myproject/bin/python

import os, sys, site

django_path = os.path.abspath(
    os.path.join(os.path.dirname(__file__),
    "../lib/python2.6/site-packages/"),
```

```
)
site.addsitedir(django_path)

project_path = os.path.abspath(
    os.path.join(os.path.dirname(__file__),
    "../project/myproject"),
)
sys.path += [project_path]

os.environ["DJANGO_SETTINGS_MODULE"] = "myproject.settings"
from django.core.wsgi import get_wsgi_application
application = get_wsgi_application()
```

15. Then, create the `.htaccess` file in the same directory. The `.htaccess` file will redirect all of the requests to your Django project set in the `wsgi` file, as follows:

```
# /home/myproject/public_html/.htaccess
AddHandler wsgi-script .wsgi
DirectoryIndex index.html
RewriteEngine On
RewriteBase /
RewriteCond %{REQUEST_FILENAME} !-f
RewriteCond %{REQUEST_FILENAME}/index.html !-f
RewriteCond %{REQUEST_URI} !^/media/
RewriteCond %{REQUEST_URI} !^/static/
RewriteRule ^(.*)$ /my.wsgi/$1 [QSA,L]
```

16. Copy `.htaccess` as `.htaccess_live`.

17. Then, create `.htaccess_maintenace` for maintenance cases. This new Apache configuration file will show `temporarily-offline.html` for all of the users (except for you, recognized by the IP address of your LAN or computer). The following code snippet shows how the `.htaccess_maintenance` will look:

```
# /home/myproject/public_html/.htaccess_maintenance
AddHandler wsgi-script .wsgi
DirectoryIndex index.html

RewriteEngine On
RewriteBase /
RewriteCond %{REMOTE_HOST} !^1.2.3.4$
RewriteCond %{REQUEST_URI} !/temporarily-offline.html
RewriteCond %{REQUEST_URI} !^/media/
RewriteCond %{REQUEST_URI} !^/static/
RewriteRule .* /temporarily-offline.html [R=302,L]

RewriteCond %{REQUEST_FILENAME} !-f
RewriteCond %{REQUEST_FILENAME}/index.html !-f
```

```
RewriteCond %{REQUEST_URI} !^/media/
RewriteCond %{REQUEST_URI} !^/static/
RewriteRule ^(.*)$ /my.wsgi/$1 [QSA,L]
```

Replace the IP digits in this file, `1.2.3.4`, with your own IP. You can check your IP address by googling *"what's my IP,"* as in `https://www.google.com/search?q=whats+my+ip`.

18. Then, create an HTML file that will be shown when your website is down. The following is a very simple version:

```
<!-- /home/myproject/public_html/temporarily-offline.html -->
The site is being updated... Please come back later.
```

19. Log into the server as the root user via SSH, and edit the Apache configuration. To do so, open the domain configuration file, as follows:

```
<root@myproject.com>$ nano \
> /etc/apache2/sites-available/myproject.mydomain.conf
```

Add the following lines before `</VirtualHost>`:

```
Options -Indexes
AliasMatch ^/static/d+/(.*)
"/home/myproject/project/myproject/static/$1"
AliasMatch ^/media/(.*)
"/home/myproject/project/myproject/media/$1"
<FilesMatch ".(ico|pdf|flv|jpe?g|png|gif|js|css|swf)$">
    ExpiresActive On
    ExpiresDefault "access plus 1 year"
</FilesMatch>
```

Restart Apache for the changes to take effect:

```
<root@myproject.com>$ /etc/init.d/apache2 restart
```

20. Set the default scheduled cron jobs. For more information on how to do this, refer to the *Setting up cron jobs for regular tasks* recipe.

How it works...

With this configuration, files in the `media` and `static` directories are served directly from Apache, whereas all of the other URLs are handled by the Django project, through the `my.wsgi` file.

Using the `<FilesMatch>` directive in the Apache site configuration, all media files are set to be cached for one year. Static URL paths have a numbered prefix that changes whenever you update the code from the Git repository.

When you need to update the website and want to set it down for maintenance, you'll have to copy `.htaccess_maintenance` to `.htaccess`. When you want to set the website up again, you'll have to copy `.htaccess_live` to `.htaccess`.

There's more...

To find other options for hosting your Django project, refer to `http://djangofriendly.com/hosts/`.

See also

- The *Creating a virtual environment project file structure* recipe in `Chapter 1`, *Getting Started with Django 2.1*
- The *Handling project dependencies with pip* recipe in `Chapter 1`, *Getting Started with Django 2.1*
- The *Setting up STATIC_URL dynamically for Git users* recipe in `Chapter 1`, *Getting Started with Django 2.1*
- The *Setting UTF-8 as the default encoding for MySQL configuration* recipe in `Chapter 1`, *Getting Started with Django 2.1*
- The *Setting up cron jobs for regular tasks* recipe

Setting up cron jobs for regular tasks

Usually, websites have some management tasks to perform in the background on a regular interval, such as once a week, once a day, or every hour. This can be achieved by using scheduled tasks, commonly known as **cron jobs**. These are scripts that run on the server after the specified period of time. In this recipe, we will create two cron jobs: one to clear sessions from the database, and another to back up the database data. Both will be run every night.

Getting ready

To start, deploy your Django project to a remote server. Then, connect to the server by SSH.

 These steps are written with the assumption that you are using a `virtualenv`, but a similar cron job can be created for a Docker project, and it can even run directly within the app container. Code files are provided with the alternate syntax, and the steps are otherwise largely the same. A connection can be made to the app container from your Docker project root, with the following command:

```
myproject_docker/$ docker-compose exec app /bin/bash
```

How to do it...

Let's create the two scripts and make them run regularly, via the following steps:

1. Navigate to the project root, where your `bin` and `lib` directories are located.
2. Create the `commands`, `db_backups`, and `logs` folders alongside the `bin` directory, as follows:

```
(myproject)myproject@server$ mkdir commands
(myproject)myproject@server$ mkdir db_backups
(myproject)myproject@server$ mkdir logs
```

3. In the `commands` directory, create a `cleanup.sh` file. You can edit it with a terminal editor, such as vim or nano, adding the following content:

```
# myproject/commands/cleanup.sh
#! /usr/bin/env bash

PROJECT_PATH=/home/myproject
CRON_LOG_FILE=${PROJECT_PATH}/logs/cleanup.log

echo "Cleaning up the database" > ${CRON_LOG_FILE}

date >> ${CRON_LOG_FILE}

cd ${PROJECT_PATH}

# activate if in a virtual environment project
if [[ -f "bin/activate" ]]; then
    . bin/activate
fi
```

```
cd project/myproject

python3 manage.py cleanup --traceback >> ${CRON_LOG_FILE} 2>&1
```

4. Make the `cleanup.sh` file executable, as follows:

   (myproject)myproject@server$ chmod +x cleanup.sh

5. Then, in the same directory, create a `backup_db.sh` file, with the following content:

   # myproject/commands/backup_db.sh
```
#! /usr/bin/env bash

PROJECT_PATH=/home/myproject
mkdir -p "${PROJECT_PATH}/db_backups"
mkdir -p "${PROJECT_PATH}/logs"

CRON_LOG_FILE=${PROJECT_PATH}/logs/backup_db.log

WEEK_DATE=$(LC_ALL=en_US.UTF-8 date +"%w-%A")
BACKUP_PATH=${PROJECT_PATH}/db_backups/${WEEK_DATE}.sql

DATABASE=myproject
HOST=localhost
USER=my_db_user
PASS=my_db_password

EXCLUDED_TABLES=(
django_session
)

IGNORED_TABLES_STRING=''

for TABLE in "${EXCLUDED_TABLES[@]}"; do
    IGNORED_TABLES_STRING+=" --ignore-table=${DATABASE}.${TABLE}"
done

echo "Creating DB Backup" > ${CRON_LOG_FILE}
date >> ${CRON_LOG_FILE}

echo "Dump structure" >> ${CRON_LOG_FILE}
mysqldump -h ${HOST} -u ${USER} -p${PASS} \
        --single-transaction --no-data \
    ${DATABASE} > ${BACKUP_PATH} \
    2>> ${CRON_LOG_FILE}

echo "Dump content" >> ${CRON_LOG_FILE}
```

```
mysqldump -h ${HOST} -u ${USER} -p${PASS} \
    ${DATABASE} ${IGNORED_TABLES_STRING} >> ${BACKUP_PATH} \
    2>> ${CRON_LOG_FILE}
```

6. Make this file executable, too, as follows:

   ```
   (myproject)myproject@server$ chmod +x backup_db.sh
   ```

7. Test the scripts to see whether they are executed correctly, by running the scripts and then checking the `*.log` files in the `logs` directory, as follows:

   ```
   (myproject)myproject@server$ ./cleanup.sh
   (myproject)myproject@server$ ./backup_db.sh
   ```

8. In your project's home directory, create a `crontab.txt` file, with the following tasks:

   ```
   00 01 * * * /home/myproject/commands/cleanup.sh
   00 02 * * * /home/myproject/commands/backup_db.sh
   ```

9. Install the `crontab` tasks, as follows:

   ```
   (myproject)myproject@server$ crontab -e crontab.txt
   ```

How it works...

With the current setup, every night, `cleanup.sh` will be executed at 1:00 A.M., and `backup_db.sh` will be executed at 2:00 A.M. The execution logs will be saved in `cleanup.log` and `backup_db.log`. If you get any errors, you should check these files for the traceback.

The cleanup script is fairly straightforward. Every day, it executes the `clearsessions` management command, which, as its name alludes to, clears expired sessions from the database, using the default database settings.

The database backup script is a little more complex. Every day of the week, it creates a backup file for that day, using a naming scheme of `0-Sunday.sql`, `1-Monday.sql`, and so on. Therefore, you will be able to restore data that was backed up seven days ago or later. First, the backup script dumps the database schema for all of the tables, and then, it dumps the content data for all of the tables, except for any that are given in the `EXCLUDED_TABLES` list (here only including `django_session`).

The `crontab` file follows a specific syntax. Each line contains a specific time of day, indicated as a series of numbers, and then a task to run at that given moment. The time is defined in five parts, separated by spaces, as shown in the following list:

- Minutes, from 0 to 59.
- Hours, from 0 to 23.
- Days of the month, from 1 to 31.
- Months, from 1 to 12.
- Days of the week, from 0 to 7, where 0 is Sunday, 1 is Monday, and so on. 7 is Sunday again.

An asterisk (*) means that every time frame will be used. Therefore, the following task defines that `cleanup.sh` is to be executed at 1:00 AM every day of each month, every month, and every day of the week:

```
00 01 * * * /home/myproject/commands/cleanup.sh
```

You can learn more about the specifics of the `crontab` at `https://en.wikipedia.org/wiki/Cron`.

See also

- The *Deploying on Apache with mod_wsgi* recipe

Other Books You May Enjoy

If you enjoyed this book, you may be interested in these other books by Packt:

Django Design Patterns and Best Practices - Second Edition
Arun Ravindran

ISBN: 9781788831345

- Make use of common design patterns to help you write better code
- Implement best practices and idioms in this rapidly evolving framework
- Deal with legacy code and debugging
- Use asynchronous tools such as Celery, Channels, and asyncio
- Use patterns while designing API interfaces with the Django REST Framework
- Reduce the maintenance burden with well-tested, cleaner code
- Host, deploy, and secure your Django projects

Django 2 by Example
Antonio Melé

ISBN: 9781788472487

- Build practical, real-world web applications with Django
- Use Django with other technologies, such as Redis and Celery
- Develop pluggable Django applications
- Create advanced features, optimize your code, and use the cache framework
- Add internationalization to your Django projects
- Enhance your user experience using JavaScript and AJAX
- Add social features to your projects
- Build RESTful APIs for your applications

Leave a review - let other readers know what you think

Please share your thoughts on this book with others by leaving a review on the site that you bought it from. If you purchased the book from Amazon, please leave us an honest review on this book's Amazon page. This is vital so that other potential readers can see and use your unbiased opinion to make purchasing decisions, we can understand what our customers think about our products, and our authors can see your feedback on the title that they have worked with Packt to create. It will only take a few minutes of your time, but is valuable to other potential customers, our authors, and Packt. Thank you!

Index

Made in the USA
Columbia, SC
19 August 2019